WORK WITH ENGLISH

New Edition

Lehrwerk für berufliche Schulen

David Alexander
Barbara Hammond

Work With English – *New Edition* wurde geplant und entwickelt von der Verlagsredaktion
der Cornelsen & Oxford University Press GmbH, Berlin

Das Lehrwerk wurde im Auftrag des Verlages von de Henseler Books, Oxford erarbeitet.
Verfasser: David Alexander, Oxford
Barbara Hammond, Cheltenham
Design: Oxprint Design, Oxford

Als Mitarbeiter/innen waren beteiligt:
Carolyn Parsons, Cheltenham
Steve Williams, Oxford

Als Berater/innen waren bei der Entwicklung beteiligt:
Marilyn Clifford-Grein, Stuttgart
Heiner Günster, Höhr-Grenzhausen
Gabriele Holtermann, Ludwigsburg
Thomas Pache, Euskirchen
Elke Uthoff, Osnabrück

Verlagsredaktion: James Austin
Außenredaktion: Christine House, Berlin; Vera Olbricht, Berlin

Erhältlich sind auch:
Cassetten (Best.-Nr. 61426)
Workbook (Best.-Nr. 61434)
Workbook mit Lösungsschlüssel (Best.-Nr. 61442)
Lehrerhandbuch (Best.-Nr. 61418)

1. Auflage ✓
02 01 00 99   Die letzten Ziffern bezeichnen
5. 4.   Zahl und Jahr des Druckes.

Alle Drucke dieser Auflage können, weil untereinander
unverändert, im Unterricht nebeneinander verwendet werden.

Bestellnummer 61400

© 1998 Cornelsen & Oxford University Press GmbH, Berlin

Das Werk und seine Teile sind urheberrechtlich geschützt.
Jede Verwertung in anderen als den gesetzlich zugelassenen
Fällen bedarf deshalb der vorherigen schriftlichen
Einwilligung des Verlages.

ISBN 3-8109-61400

Tech. Herstellung: Freiburger Graphische Betriebe, Freiburg
Vertrieb: Cornelsen Verlag, Berlin

Gedruckt auf chlorfrei gebleichtem Papier ohne Dioxinbelastung der Gewässer.

VORWORT

Work With English *New Edition* ist ein Lehrwerk für das Fach Englisch, das in zwei Lernjahren zum mittleren Bildungsabschluss führt. Die neue Ausgabe setzt einen Grundwortschatz von 600 Wörtern voraus.

Work With English *New Edition* besteht aus 18 Units, die nach dem übersichtlichen Doppelseitenprinzip aufgebaut sind. Die neun Units für das erste Lernjahr umfassen jeweils acht Seiten, die neun Units für das zweite Lernjahr zehn Seiten. Letztere beinhalten je eine Doppelseite *Language Workout* mit Wiederholungsübungen zur Prüfungsvorbereitung.

Alle Units sind deutlich strukturiert, die einzelnen Abschnitte hervorgehoben und die Übungen auf einen Blick zu erkennen. Die attraktiven Aufmacherseiten, das moderne Layout und die durchgängig abwechslungsreiche farbige Gestaltung motivieren zum Lernen.

Work With English *New Edition* enthält für Jugendliche interessante Themen wie *fashion*, *advertising*, *driving*, *consumerism*, *multi-media*, *energy resources*, *conservation*, *food*, *transport* usw. In praxisnahen Texten wie Dialogen, *newspaper/magazine articles*, *problem page letters*, *postcards* und verschiedenartigen Sachtexten wird den Lernenden facettenreich modernes, gängiges Englisch dargeboten.

Work With English *New Edition* vermittelt den Lernenden Bezüge zu ihrem beruflichen Leben:

- Der erste Teil (Unit 1–9) enthält auf den *World of Work*-Seiten jeweils eine Doppelseite mit allgemeinen Themen aus dem beruflichen Alltag.
- Im zweiten Teil (Unit 10–18) sind die *World of Work*-Seiten gezielt drei beruflichen Schwerpunkten gewidmet: kaufmännisch, gewerblich-technisch und hauswirtschaftlich-sozialpädagogisch.
- Zwölf *Further Reading*-Texte im Anschluss an die Units bieten darüber hinaus besonders Interessantes: aktuelle Themen sowie landeskundliche Informationen.
- Eine Doppelseite mit elementaren Begriffen der englischen Handelskorrespondenz vervollständigt den berufsspezifischen Lernteil.
- Die *Language Workout*-Seiten wie auch die *Further Reading*-Seiten enthalten Übungen, die auf den mittleren Bildungsabschluss vorbereiten.
- Ein Grundwortschatz, chronologische und alphabetische Wörterlisten, eine Liste der Eigennamen und der unregelmäßigen Verben runden das Lehrwerk ab.

Work With English *New Edition* enthält systematische Übungen zum Textverständnis, abwechslungsreiche Übungen zum Wortschatz und interessante Hörverständnisübungen. Die Kommunikation der Lernenden wird mit speziellen Übungen angeregt. Die Grammatik, die für den mittleren Bildungsabschluss nötig ist, wird Schritt für Schritt wiederholt. Kurze Regelerklärungen auf Deutsch erleichtern das Verständnis derselben.

Work With English *New Edition* ist ein praxisnahes, inhaltlich und gestalterisch modernes Lehrwerk, das einen handlungsorientierten Unterricht ermöglicht und die Lernenden zur Arbeit mit dem Englischen motiviert.

Wir, die Autoren und der Verlag, wünschen viel Freude und Erfolg!

INHALTSVERZEICHNIS

UNIT	TITLE	GRAMMAR	WORLD OF WORK	PAGE
1	Young people in Britain	To be Simple present Possessive adjectives	Jobs, places of work and responsibilities 1	6
2	Free time	Subject and object pronouns Demonstrative pronouns Adverbs of frequency Verbs that express feelings *Have got*	Socialising at work	14
3	What are you studying?	Present continuous Present continuous and simple present Plurals	Jobs, places of work and responsibilities 2	22
4	Time for a holiday	Simple past Comparatives and superlatives of adjectives	Travel enquiries and reservations	30
5	His job or hers?	*Much, many, (a) little, (a) few, more than, less than, fewer than* Possessive pronouns	Advertising	38
6	Food and diet	*Some/any* and compounds Relative clauses Using verbs as nouns	Food and catering	46
7	Problems and anxieties	*Make/let* *Should/shouldn't* Question tags	Problems at work	54
8	On the road!	*Have to/must* Reflexive pronouns Adverbs of manner	Motoring	62
9	The USA and the Big Apple	Present perfect *For* and *since*	Getting around	70

UNIT	TITLE	GRAMMAR	WORLD OF WORK	PAGE
10	Europe and the Europeans	The future	Working in a car factory	78
11	It's not a bad place to live	Prepositions of place Conditional I	Working with people	88
12	The best way to travel	Conditional II	The travel business	98
13	Technology old and new	Past continuous Past perfect *Used to*	Everyday tools and appliances	108

14	Uses and abuses	Must/can't (have)
		   could/should have
		   might have
		Conditional III
			Helping young people: drug rehabilitation	118

15	Do you shop till you drop?	The passive	Banking	128
16	Reduce, repair, reuse, recycle	Present perfect continuous	Green agriculture	138
17	Virtual lives!	*-ing* forms	Helping people by phone	148
18	Choosing a job	Prefixes and suffixes *So/neither* Indirect speech	Getting a job	158

Commercial Correspondence *page 170*

Further Reading texts *page 172*

Tapescripts *page 190*

Grundwortschatz *page 196*

Chronologisches Wörterverzeichnis *page 199*

Alphabetisches Wörterverzeichnis *page 245*

Eigennamen *page 260*

Liste der unregelmäßigen Verben *page 261*

Grammatische Grundbegriffe *page 263*

1 YOUNG PEOPLE IN BRITAIN

1 Hi! I'm Nick. I'm seventeen. I live at home with my family and our dog. Our home is a terraced house in the centre of Aylesbury. I go to school in Aylesbury. It is a town in southern England. I have two brothers and a sister. Our dog's name is Sandy. My brothers are at school, but my sister isn't. She is at college. She lives with her fiancé in London.

2 My name's Anita Jamieson. I live here in Leeds but I am not from Leeds. I'm from Winchester. I'm single. I rent a flat with my friend Karen. We are students. My parents are separated, but they aren't divorced and my two brothers live with our mother, in a cottage in Winchester. I don't have a boyfriend at the moment, but Karen goes out with a guy from Birmingham.

3 I'm Pat. I go to a College of Further Education and I live at home, with my mother, stepfather and grandparents. I get on well with my stepfather. He's very nice. My boyfriend's name is Ron. He is eighteen and he doesn't live with his parents. He has a flat in town and he lives on his own. He doesn't have a job right now.

4
GRAHAM	Hi, Sarah!
SARAH	Oh, hello, Graham ... Er, this is my friend Paolo.
GRAHAM	Hi, Paolo. Are you from Italy?
PAOLO	Yes, I am.
GRAHAM	Do you live there or in England?
PAOLO	I live in England, but my parents live in Italy. Their home town is Naples.
GRAHAM	Where do you live?
PAOLO	I live with my brother.
GRAHAM	Where does he live?
PAOLO	In London. Do you know Shepherd's Bush?
GRAHAM	No, I don't.

Before you start ...

Where do you live? Look at the words in the box and complete the sentence.

➡ *Hi, my name is ... and my home is a ... in the town of ... .*

| terraced house | detached house | cottage | flat |

Working with the texts

1 **True or false? Correct the false statements.**

1. Nick lives in a terraced house.
2. Nick's sister lives with their parents.
3. His sister's name is Sandy.
4. Anita is a student.
5. Anita's parents are divorced.
6. Pat's boyfriend lives on his own.
7. Pat likes her stepfather.
8. Pat's boyfriend goes to college.
9. Sarah is Paolo's friend.
10. Paolo's brother lives in Genoa.

2 **Answer the questions. Use a short answer.**

1. Does Nick's sister go to college?
2. Do Anita's brothers live with their father?
3. Does Anita have a boyfriend?
4. Does Pat like her stepfather?
5. Do Paolo's parents come from England?
6. Does Paolo's brother live in London?

3 **Answer the questions.**

1. Where does Nick live?
2. What do his brothers and his sister do?
3. What do Anita and Karen do?
4. Where is Karen's boyfriend from?
5. Who is Ron?
6. What is Ron's job?
7. Where does Paolo's brother live?
8. Where do Paolo's parents live?

4 **Here are some answers to questions about the texts. What are the questions?**

1. He goes to school in Aylesbury. (Where ... ?)
2. Sandy. (What ... ?)
3. With her fiancé. (Who ... ?)
4. He comes from Birmingham. (Where ... ?)
5. His name is Ron. (What ... ?)
6. He doesn't have a job. (What ... ?)
7. He is Sarah's friend. (Who ... ?)
8. Naples. (Where ... ?)

5 **Work with a partner. Make some questions and answers of your own on the texts.**

Language Review

1 TO BE *(sein)*

Aussagen und Verneinungen			
I	am		
He She It	is	(not)	from Leeds.
We You They	are		

- I'm = I am, he's = he is, she's = she is, it's = it is,
  we're = we are, you're = you are, they're = they are
- I'm not = I am not, he's not/he isn't = he is not, she's not/she isn't = she is not,
  it's not/it isn't = it is not, we're not/we aren't = we are not,
  you're not/you aren't = you are not, they're not/they
  aren't = they are not

Ja/Nein-Fragen	Kurzantworten
Are you ... ?	Yes, I am./No, I'm not.
Is he ... ?	Yes, he is./No, he isn't.
Are we ... ?	Yes, we are./No, we aren't.
Are they ... ?	Yes, they are./No, they aren't.

2 SIMPLE PRESENT *(Einfache Gegenwart)*

Aussagen		
I You We They	live	at home.
He She It	lives	

Verneinungen		
I You We They	don't	live in Leeds.
He She It	doesn't	

Ja/Nein-Fragen		Kurzantworten
Do	you/we/they ... ?	Yes, I do./No, I don't.
Does	he/she ... ?	Yes, he does./No, he doesn't.

UNIT 1 • YOUNG PEOPLE IN BRITAIN

INFORMATIONSFRAGEN				
Fragewort	Hilfsverb	Subjekt	Verb	Satzergänzung
Where	do	you	go	to school?
What	does	Nick	do	at weekends?
Who	does	she	live	with?

- Das *simple present* drückt aus, dass etwas allgemein gültig ist oder regelmäßig geschieht.
- Das *simple present* ist identisch mit der Grundform des Verbs – außer in der dritten Person Singular (*he/she/it*). Hier wird *-s* oder *-es* angehängt.
- Wenn das Verb auf *-y* endet, wird das *-y* zu *-ies* in der dritten Person Singular, z.B. *I carry* → *he carries*.
- Fragen werden mit *do* bzw. in der dritten Person mit *does* gebildet; verneinte Sätze mit *don't* bzw. mit *doesn't*.
- Sind *who* oder *what* Subjekt eines Satzes, ist die *do*-Umschreibung nicht möglich.

Where ... ?	Wo ... ?	How much ... ?	Wie viel ... ?
Who ... ?	Wer ... ?	How many ... ?	Wie viele ... ?
What ... ?	Was ... ?	Why ... ?	Warum ... ?
Which ... ?	Welche ... ?	When ... ?	Wann ... ?
How ... ?	Wie ... ?		

3 POSSESSIVE ADJECTIVES
(Possessivpronomen – besitzanzeigende Fürwörter)

Singular			Plural		
I	**my**	*mein*	we	**our**	*unser*
you	**your**	*dein/Ihr*	you	**your**	*euer/Ihr*
he	**his**	*sein*	they	**their**	*ihr*
she	**her**	*ihr*			
it	**its**	*sein/ihr*			

- Besitz oder Zugehörigkeit wird bei Personen und Tieren mit *-'s* (Singular) bzw. *-s'* (Plural) ausgedrückt. z.B. *The dog's name is Sandy. My parents' house is in Leeds.*
- Bei Sachen wird *of* verwendet, um die Zugehörigkeit auszudrücken, z.B. *Our house is in the centre of town.*

Practice

1 Complete the sentences with the simple present.

1 I ... in Germany. (live)
   → *I live in Germany.*

2 Her boyfriend ... from Italy. (come)
3 Their parents ... in the centre of town. (work)
4 He ... his stepmother. (get on with)
5 She ... to college in London. (go)
6 He ... a dog. (have)
7 He ... my brother. (know)
8 My sister and I ... a flat. (rent)

2 Complete the questions with the simple present.

1 ... she ... with her fiancé? (live)
   → *Does she live with her fiancé?*

2 Who ... she ... out with? (go)
3 ... they ... a flat? (rent)
4 ... she ... her parents? (get on well with)
5 Where ... John ... ? (work)
6 ... she ... a sister? (have)
7 ... you ... my brother? (know)
8 Where ... you ... ? (live)

3 Complete the negative statements with the simple present.

1 He ... his stepmother. (not get on with)
   → *He doesn't get on with his stepmother.*

2 I ... in Birmingham. (not live)
3 She ... to college. (not go)
4 They ... a dog. (not have)
5 She ... in town. (not work)
6 I ... her name. (not know)
7 I ... from Italy. (not come)
8 They ... their flat. (not rent)
9 He ... school. (not like)

4 Look at the cards and say five things about each person.

→ *Ruth is seventeen.*

FAMILY NAME Hopkins
FIRST NAME(S) Ruth
AGE 17
ADDRESS Church Cottage, Lee Road, Swanage, BH19 1HN, UK
FAMILY STATUS single

NAME Reynaldo Carlos ADAME
DATE OF BIRTH 14 April 1968
ADDRESS Apt 630, Antigua Way, Sarasota, Florida 34231 USA

☐ married   ☐ single
☒ divorced   ☐ widowed

5 Put the words in one of the three groups. Can you think of any more?

PLACES TO LIVE	PEOPLE IN THE FAMILY	FAMILY SITUATION

flat   mother   aunt   uncle
divorced   cottage   single
stepfather   married   terraced house
cousin   mother-in-law

6 Match the questions on the left with the answers on the right.

1 Is he divorced?
2 What's your girlfriend's name?
3 Does he have a job?
4 Does he have a sister?
5 Who does she live with?
6 What does he do?

a Her fiancé.
b Yes. Her name is Alice.
c He's a student.
d No. He's single.
e No. He's out of work.
f Her name is Lucy.

7 Give the short answers.

1 Do you come from Germany? (Yes)
   ➡ *Yes, I do.*

2 Do you live in Italy? (No)
3 Does she get on with her father. (Yes)
4 Do you have a dog? (No)
5 Is she from Birmingham? (No)
6 Do you speak English? (Yes)

8 Complete the sentences.

1

4

2

5

3

6

9 Rewrite the sentences.

1 Gregory lives with his parents. (on his own)
   ➡ *Gregory doesn't live with his parents. He lives on his own.*

2 Anna lives in Frankfurt. (Stuttgart)
3 They rent a cottage in town. (flat)
4 She has a boyfriend. (dog)
5 She gets on with her stepmother. (lives)
6 His parents know Italy. (France)

UNIT 1 • YOUNG PEOPLE IN BRITAIN **11**

Jobs, places of work and responsibilities 1
Berufe, Arbeitsstellen und Verantwortungen 1

1 Say what their jobs are and where they work.

➡ Jo's a receptionist. She works in a hotel.

 ◀ Jo

 ◀ Amy

 ◀ Katie

◀ David

hotel	Jo	nurse
hospital	David	receptionist
office	Amy	secretary
workshop	Katie	carpenter

2 Make sentences.

A vet	helps people on holiday.
A shop assistant	repairs cars.
A tour guide	serves people in a shop.
A mechanic	works with animals.

3 Look at the pictures and the texts and say who does what.

| nursery nurse | accounts clerk | tour guide | mechanic |

Mark likes people. He speaks three languages.

Peter likes cars.

12 UNIT 1 • YOUNG PEOPLE IN BRITAIN

THE WORLD OF WORK

Anna is good at numbers and she works with computers.

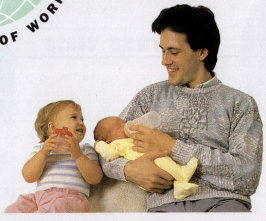

John likes children.

4 Listen to five people talking about their jobs. Match the names with the pictures. Say something about each person.

Bob Hunter   Rita   Alice   Michel   Jutta

5 Read the dialogue. Practise with your partner. Some words are underlined. Replace them.

MIKE   Hi there. My name's <u>Mike</u> and this is my <u>girlfriend</u>, <u>Renate</u>.
CATHY   Hello, <u>Mike</u>. Hi, <u>Renate</u>. I'm <u>Cathy</u>, pleased to meet you.
RENATE   Nice to meet you, too. What do you do, <u>Cathy</u>?
CATHY   I'm a <u>student</u>. What about you?
RENATE   I'm a <u>flight attendant</u>. I work for <u>Lufthansa</u>.
CATHY   Really? What's it like?
RENATE   It's OK. I like <u>travelling</u>.
CATHY   What about you, <u>Mike</u>?
MIKE   I'm a <u>taxi driver</u>, but I'm out of work at the moment. I hope to find another job soon.

UNIT 1 • YOUNG PEOPLE IN BRITAIN

2 FREE TIME

1

NORMAN	Who's this?
VANDA	Where? Oh, that's me.
NORMAN	Really? It doesn't look like you. And who's this guy with you?
VANDA	Er ... oh, that's Geoff. When people see us, they think it is funny, because he's big and I'm small.
NORMAN	He looks fit. Look at those muscles!
VANDA	Yes ... ! He often does weightlifting and he sometimes plays squash.
NORMAN	He's got muscles in places where I haven't got places!
VANDA	Mmmmm ... He's wonderful. I'm really keen on him.
NORMAN	Er ... Does he like you?
VANDA	Yes. I think he likes me a lot. What do you do in your free time, Norman? Do you like sport?
NORMAN	It's OK ... I don't mind it.
VANDA	What do you do to keep fit? Do you exercise?
NORMAN	Er ... yes ... I sometimes go to the gym ... with my girlfriend.
VANDA	Really? What's her name?
NORMAN	Oh, er ... Christine. You don't know her.
VANDA	How often do you go to the gym?
NORMAN	Oh, about two or three times.
VANDA	A week?
NORMAN	No ... two or three times a year.

Before you start ...

What do you do with your free time? Here are some examples of what English teenagers like doing.

watching the television   listening to pop music   reading fashion magazines
going out with friends   keeping fit   going to the cinema

2

JAKE is always very fit. In the summer he goes jogging every morning and plays squash twice a week. He is rarely ill. In winter he is sometimes lazy. He's keen on rock music.

PENELOPE never takes exercise. She can't stand it and she's not keen on sport. She usually goes to the cinema once a week, she often plays the piano and reads books. She always reads them in bed and on the train when she goes to college.

PETE is overweight. He likes eating, he smokes and he drinks a lot of beer. He is crazy about football, too but he usually watches it on TV. His wife worries about these things but Pete doesn't care. He's always happy.

Working with the texts

1 Answer the questions (texts 1 and 2).

| Norman | Vanda | Christine | Geoff | Jake | Penelope | Pete | Pete's wife |

1 Who thinks Geoff is wonderful?
2 Who does weightlifting?
3 Who doesn't mind sport?
4 Who is always happy?
5 Who is rarely ill?
6 Who worries?
7 Who is Norman's girlfriend?
8 Who goes to the cinema once a week?

UNIT 2 • FREE TIME 15

2 Say who it is (texts 1 and 2).

1 Vanda doesn't know her.
2 She often plays the piano.
3 He goes jogging every morning.
4 He plays squash twice a week.
5 He is crazy about football.
6 He is keen on rock music.
7 She is small.
8 She can't stand exercise.

3 Which is the best answer? (text 1).

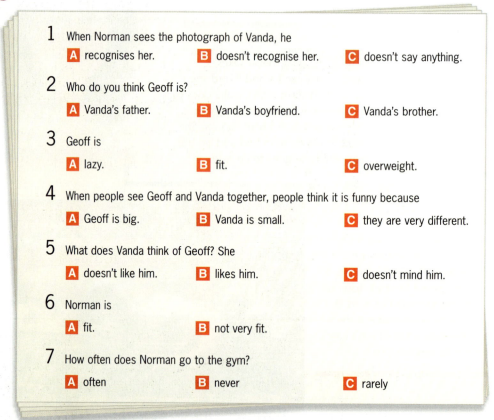

1 When Norman sees the photograph of Vanda, he
 A recognises her.   B doesn't recognise her.   C doesn't say anything.

2 Who do you think Geoff is?
 A Vanda's father.   B Vanda's boyfriend.   C Vanda's brother.

3 Geoff is
 A lazy.   B fit.   C overweight.

4 When people see Geoff and Vanda together, people think it is funny because
 A Geoff is big.   B Vanda is small.   C they are very different.

5 What does Vanda think of Geoff? She
 A doesn't like him.   B likes him.   C doesn't mind him.

6 Norman is
 A fit.   B not very fit.

7 How often does Norman go to the gym?
 A often   B never   C rarely

4 Here are some answers to questions about text 2. What are the questions?

1 In the summer. (When ... ?)
2 Every morning. (How often ... ?)
3 Rarely. (How often ... ?)
4 Rock music. (What ... ?)
5 To the cinema. (Where ... ?)
6 In bed and on the train. (Where ... ?)
7 Football. (What ... ?)
8 A lot. (How much ... ?)

5 Complete the statements with words from the texts.

1 Vanda likes Geoff's ... .
2 Geoff does ... .
3 Vanda thinks Geoff is ... .
4 Norman says he doesn't ... sport.
5 Jake frequently goes jogging to keep ... .
6 Jake is ... rock music.
7 Penelope likes going to ... .
8 Penelope can't stand ... .
9 Pete eats a lot, so he is ... .
10 Pete ... football on TV.

Language Review

1 SUBJECT AND OBJECT PRONOUNS *(Subjekt- und Objektpronomen)*

Subjekt	Objekt	
I	me	mich/mir
you	you	dich/dir
he	him	ihn/ihm
she	her	sie/ihr
it	it	es/ihm
we	us	uns
you	you	euch; Sie/Ihnen
they	them	sie/ihnen

- Pronomen stehen für das Substantiv (Hauptwort).
- Im Englischen gibt es für das Akkusativobjekt (Wen-Fall) und das Dativobjekt (Wem-Fall) nur eine Form. *You can see **me** in the photo. My boyfriend is with **me** in this photo.*

2 DEMONSTRATIVE PRONOUNS *(Demonstrativpronomen – hinweisende Fürwörter)*

	Singular		Plural	
	this	dieses/das hier	these	diese/die hier
	that	jenes/das dort	those	jene/die dort

- *This* (Einzahl) und *these* (Mehrzahl) weisen auf eine Person oder Sache in unmittelbarer Nähe. *Who is **this** guy? That* (Einzahl) und *those* (Mehrzahl) weisen auf eine Person oder Sache, die weiter entfernt ist. *Look at **those** muscles!*

3 ADVERBS OF FREQUENCY *(Häufigkeitsadverbien)*

100% — always (*immer*) — usually (*meistens*) — often/frequently (*oft/häufig*) — sometimes (*manchmal*) — rarely (*selten*) — never (*nie*) — 0%

- Häufigkeitsadverbien beschreiben, wie oft etwas geschieht. Sie werden meist in Verbindung mit dem *simple present* benutzt.
- Sie stehen vor dem Hauptverb. *When do you **usually** go to the gym?*
- Bei dem Verb *be* stehen diese Adverbien nach dem Verb. *Jake is **always** very fit.*

4 VERBS THAT EXPRESS FEELINGS *(Verben, die Gefühle ausdrücken)*

- Verben, die Gefühle ausdrücken, werden entweder mit einem Substantiv oder mit der *-ing*-Form des Verbs verwendet. *He is crazy about **football**. She likes **reading**.*

5 THE VERB HAVE GOT *(das Verb: haben)*

- *Have* und *have got* haben die gleiche Bedeutung – haben.
- *Have got* bildet Fragen und Verneinungen ohne *do*. *Have you got a car? Yes, I have./No, I haven't.*

Practice

1 Rewrite the text. Replace the words in brackets with pronouns.

> My girlfriend is great. I love *her* [1] (my girlfriend) very much. We have got two horses. We usually ride ... [2] (the horses) to college and people often look at ... [3] (my girlfriend and me). We don't care because it is a very nice journey! The horses like ... [4] (the journey), too. It's good for ... [5] (the horses) and it's good for ... [6] (my girlfriend and me). There is a wood between where we live and the college, and we always ride through ... [7] (the wood) instead of along the road.

2 Answer the questions.

1 Do you like jazz? (Yes/I/love)

→ *Yes, I love it.*

2 Is he keen on children? (Yes/he/crazy about)
3 Is she keen on you? (No/she/not crazy about)
4 Do you love me? (Yes/I/love/very much)
5 What do you think of his girlfriend? (I/can't stand)
6 What about Alex? (I/like)
7 Does he like football? (He/not mind)
8 Do they like horses? (Yes/they/crazy about)
9 Do you like sport? (No/I/not keen on)

3 Rewrite the sentences.

1 He goes to the gym at 6.30 in the morning. (always)

→ *He always goes to the gym at 6.30 in the morning.*

2 He plays tennis. (rarely)
3 She watches TV in bed. (always)
4 We go to the cinema every week. (usually)
5 I see her in town. (sometimes)
6 He is late for college. (never)
7 She doesn't go jogging. (often)
8 Do you go to the gym after work? (usually)
9 She is early for school. (always)
10 Do you do weightlifting? (often)

4 Work with a partner. Ask and answer questions.

→ **A** *Do you sometimes go jogging?*
B *No, I don't, but I often go swimming.*

go	football	swimming	television
play	the piano	the guitar	tennis
do	weightlifting	music	jogging
watch	aerobics	the radio	for a walk
listen to			

5 Listen to the statements and match them with the pictures.

6 Complete the sentences with *this*, *that*, *these* or *those* and the words in the box.

| girl's | man | photograph |
| clothes | muscles | books |

1   Come over here and see ... of your parents.

2   Who's ... ?

4   What do you think of ... ?

5   ... name is Jill.

3   Look at ... !

6   ... are for you.

Socialising at work
Gespräche unter Kollegen

1 Match the words with the pictures. Has your partner got the same answers?

1 Pleased to meet you.
2 I'd like you to meet Jane Rolland.
3 Will you excuse me?
4 How about some lunch?, Mary
5 Thank you for inviting me.
6 Take care. Bye.

2 Match the statements and questions with the best answers.

1 How often do you exercise?
2 Hi. I'm Jethro. I'm new here.
3 How do you like your new job?
4 I'm sorry, I must go now. Bye.
5 I am off for the weekend.
6 Why don't you join us for dinner?
7 Do you like rock music?
8 I start work on Monday.

A That would be nice. Thanks.
B Have a nice time.
C It's not bad.
D Bye. Nice meeting you.
E Good luck!
F Pleased to meet you.
G About two or three times a week.
H Yes, I love it!

THE WORLD OF WORK

3 🎧 **Listen to the conversation and match the objects with the people.**

Lucie   Julio   Melissa

1   2   3   4

5   6   7   8

4 Write down three sports with **+** or **–**, as below. Show your partner. Your partner describes what you like or don't like.

++ = love/crazy about   +– = don't mind
–– = can't stand   + = like/be keen on
– = not like/not be keen on

++ *squash*
–– *aerobics*

➡ Claudia is crazy about squash. She can't stand aerobics.

UNIT 2 • FREE TIME   21

3 WHAT ARE YOU STUDYING?

Carla and Tony are at a College of Further Education. They are talking about their courses.

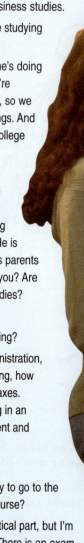

CARLA What are you doing at the moment?

TONY I am revising for my exams.

CARLA What are you studying?

TONY I am doing a one-year GNVQ* course in construction. What about you?

5 CARLA I am doing a GNVQ in business studies.

TONY What about Sarah? Is she studying here in Gloucester?

CARLA No, she's in Bristol, but she's doing business studies, too. We're
10 studying the same course, so we are learning the same things. And Paul? I think he goes to college here. Is he still doing the engineering course?

15 TONY No, he's doing a GNVQ in catering now. He wants to be a chef, so he is learning about food and cooking. He is finding it easy because his parents
20 are caterers. What about you? Are you enjoying business studies?

CARLA Yes, I am.

TONY What things are you learning?

CARLA Oh, things like office administration,
25 computer studies, marketing, how to write letters and send faxes. That's OK, but I'm working in an office in town at the moment and that's very hard.

30 TONY Why?

CARLA It's not easy to get up early to go to the office! What about your course?

TONY It's not bad. I like the practical part, but I'm not enjoying it this week. There is an exam
35 next week and I'm very worried.

* General National Vocational Qualification

Before you start ...

What course are you studying? Is it like these courses in England?

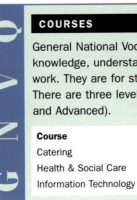

GNVQ

COURSES

General National Vocational Qualifications develop knowledge, understanding and skills needed for work. They are for students of 16 and over. There are three levels (Foundation, Intermediate and Advanced).

Course	Learn about
Catering	cooking and food
Health & Social Care	an occupational therapist
Information Technology	computers, information systems

Working with the text

1 True or false? Correct the false statements.

1. Carla and Tony are at school.
2. Tony is not revising for his exams.
3. Tony is doing a two-year course.
4. Carla is learning about business.
5. Sarah and Carla are studying together.
6. Paul goes to college in Gloucester.
7. Carla likes her course.
8. Carla is not enjoying her work at the moment.
9. Carla is not working in an office at the moment.
10. Tony is not enjoying his course this week.

2 Answer the questions.

1. Who is doing a GNVQ in construction?
2. What is Tony doing at the moment?
3. Who is learning about food?
4. Which two students are learning the same things?
5. Is Paul studying construction?
6. What does Paul want to be?
7. Is he finding his course easy?
8. Why is Tony worried?

3 Complete the sentences with these words from Tony and Carla's conversation.

> GNVQ   catering   week   exam   course   office
> business studies   fax   college   moment

1. I am revising for an ... .
2. I can send you a ... .
3. She is taking a ... in business studies.
4. In ... you learn about marketing and computer studies.
5. In ... you learn about food and cooking.
6. Tony is studying for a one-year ... in construction.
7. Jane is revising for her exam next ... .
8. I am working in town at the ... .
9. She is studying at a ... in London.
10. You learn ... administration in business studies.

Language Review

1 PRESENT CONTINUOUS (Verlaufsform der Gegenwart)

Aussagen und Verneinungen			
I	am	(not)	studying business.
He She	is		revising for exams.
We You They	are		learning about computers.

Ja/Nein-Fragen			Kurzantworten
Are	you we they	studying English?	Yes, I am./No, I'm not. Yes, we are./No, we aren't. Yes, they are./No, they aren't.
Is	he she		Yes, he is./No, he isn't. Yes, she is./No, she isn't.

- Das *present continuous* drückt aus, dass eine Handlung jetzt, d.h. zum Zeitpunkt des Sprechens, passiert. Die Verlaufsform wird oft mit Zeitbestimmungen wie *at the moment* oder *now* benutzt. *I am revising for my exams at the moment.*
- Mit dem *present continuous* wird auch ausgedrückt, dass eine Situation vorübergehend und noch nicht abgeschlossen ist. *I am doing a one-year course in construction.*
- Das *present continuous* wird mit einer Form von *be* und der *-ing*-Form des Verbs gebildet. Die meisten Verben hängen nur *-ing* an: *do → doing*. Wenn die Grundform mit *-e* endet, fällt das *-e* weg: *revise → revising*. Bei einigen Verben wird der Endkonsonant verdoppelt: *sit → sitting*.
- Verneinte Sätze werden gebildet, indem die Form von *be* mit *not* oder *n't* verneint wird.
- Um Fragen zu bilden, wird *am/is/are* mit dem Subjekt getauscht.
- Informationsfragen können mit *what* oder *where* gebildet werden. *What are they studying?*

2 PRESENT CONTINUOUS AND SIMPLE PRESENT
(Verlaufsform der Gegenwart und einfache Gegenwart)

- Bei der Gegenwart im Englischen wird unterschieden, ob eine Handlung regelmäßig stattfindet (*simple present*) oder ob sie gerade jetzt bzw. nur für eine begrenzte Zeit durchgeführt wird (*present continuous*).
  *I am working in an office **at the moment**.* Zur Zeit arbeite ich in einem Büro. (eine begrenzte Handlung)
  *I **always** work eight hours a day.* Ich arbeite immer acht Stunden am Tag. (eine regelmäßige Handlung)

3 PLURAL *(Mehrzahl)*

- Bei den meisten Substantiven wird in der Mehrzahl ein *-s* angefügt: *exam* → *exams*.
- Wenn das Substantiv auf *-s*, *-sh*, *-ch* oder *-x* endet, wird *-es* angefügt: *fax* → *faxes*.
- Wenn das Substantiv auf einem Konsonanten mit *-y* endet, wird das *-y* zu *-ies*: *study* → *studies*.
- Manche Substantive haben unregelmäßige Pluralformen: *child* → *children*, *person* → *people*, *man* → *men*, *woman* → *women*.

Practice

1 What is missing in each picture? What do you think each person is doing?

1

3

2

4

2 Answer the questions. Use short answers.

1 Are you enjoying your course? (Yes)

➡ *Yes, I am.*

2 Is she enjoying her job? (No)
3 Is he revising? (No)
4 Is she studying here at the moment? (Yes)
5 Are they doing business studies? (No)
6 Are we finding it easy? (Yes)
7 Are you learning how to send a fax? (No)
8 Are you working in town? (Yes)
9 Are they doing a GNVQ? (Yes)

3 Look at the pictures and make sentences. Use the words in the box.

➡ *Jane is a police officer. She usually wears a ... , but today she is wearing ... .*

| white coat | dress | raincoat | uniform | old jeans and a sweatshirt |
| suit | overalls | helmet | cap | trousers and a jacket | blouse | jeans |

4 Look back at the text. What are the questions?

1 They are all studying in Gloucester. (Where ... ?)
2 He is revising for his exams. (What ... ?)
3 Yes, they are. But Carla is in Gloucester and Sarah is in Bristol. (Are ... same course?)
4 No, he's doing a GNVQ in catering. (Is Paul ... ?)
5 Because his parents are caterers. (Why ... Paul ... ?)
6 Because there is an exam next week and he is very worried. (Why ... Tony not ... ?)
7 In an office in town. (Where ... at the moment?)

5 🔊 **Listen to the conversations, match them with the pictures and say what each person is doing.**

6 **Complete the text with the correct form of the present continuous or simple present.**

Sally ... ¹(take) a GNVQ in business studies. It is a two-year course. She ... ²(study) at college but she ... ³(have) work experience in an office every Friday but she ... ⁴(like not) getting up early! She ... ⁵(want not) to get a job there after the course, she ... ⁶(want) to go to London. At the moment, she ... ⁷(learn) how to send faxes and letters by computer and how to use the Internet. She ... ⁸(wear) jeans or trousers when she ... ⁹(go) to college, but at the office she usually ... ¹⁰ (wear) a dress. She normally ... ¹¹(like) her course, but she ... ¹² (enjoy not) it at the moment. She ... ¹³(revise) for an exam next week and she ... ¹⁴ (be) worried.

Jobs, places of work and responsibilities 2
Berufe, Arbeitsstellen und Verantwortungen 2

1 Match the words in box 1 with the pictures and say what each person is doing. Then match the jobs in box 2 and say what each job is.

➡ In picture A, he's giving a shampoo. He is a ... .

1
give a shampoo
repair a fridge
booking a ticket
repair a leak

2
plumber
hairstylist
electrician
travel agent

2 Read and practise the dialogue in pairs. Then practise similar dialogues. Replace the highlighted words with words from the boxes.

JAMES What subjects are you taking at college?
JILL   I'm doing a course in catering .
JAMES What are you learning?
JILL   We are learning about food and how to cook .
JAMES What do you want to do after the course?
JILL   I want to be a trainee chef and then I want to run my own restaurant .

business studies	cars	grow corn and other crops
agriculture	animals	repair engines
vehicle maintenance	office administration	shampoo and cut
hairdressing	hairstyles	use computers

mechanic	salon
farm worker	farm
hairstylist	garage
secretary	business

THE WORLD OF WORK

3 🔊 Listen to the conversation. True or false? Correct the false statements.

1 Tom is studying engineering.
2 He is learning typing.
3 He is not doing economics.
4 He is doing a one-year course.
5 He wants to get a job in marketing.

4 Make sentences, as in the example.

➡ *David is learning about horticulture. He's training to be a gardener.*

horticulture	graphic designer
electrical repair	chef
car repair	TV repairer
catering	gardener
art and design	mechanic

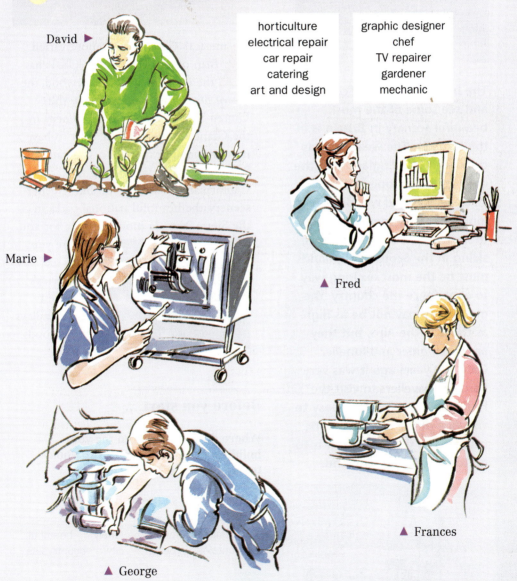

UNIT 3 • WHAT ARE YOU STUDYING?

4 TIME FOR A HOLIDAY

1

Scotland

The best time to visit Scotland and see some of the most beautiful scenery in Britain is in the summer. The weather is as good as it is in England and the days are much longer. The lakes, valleys and woods are lonely but very romantic. For those who like sports holidays, skiing in the Scottish Highlands must be the most exciting way to experience the country; the mountains may not be as high as those in the Alps, but they are much older and lonelier. Only 200 years ago it was very hard for travellers to visit the Highlands. Today it is as easy to visit one of the most romantic countries in the world as it is to go to the south of England.

2

The Great West

America's Great West is more varied than other places in the US. It has the excitement of Hollywood, the fun of Disneyland and probably the United States' most exciting scenery in the Grand Canyon. If you want to have a more romantic experience, you can visit San Francisco or walk along the Californian beaches. If you like greener scenery, the beautiful national parks in the Sierra Nevada mountains are for you.

Here you can see America's prettiest lakes, valleys and woods.

Before you start ...

Where do you like to go for your holidays? Use the words in the box to complete the sentence.

I like ... places, so I go on holiday to the ... .

| exciting | romantic | lonely | beautiful |
| mountains | beach | city | countryside |

3

Hi Karen,
We're having a great time here in Portugal. We went rollerblading in the park yesterday and Dan fell over a million times. Everything is less expensive than at home, believe it or not, and it is far more exciting here. There's so much to see and do. Nobody sleeps here and life goes on around the clock. Sorry you didn't make it this year. How's the leg? I hope it's better, you really must come next time!

Kim

Karen Smith

3 Wellington Road

Cheltenham

GL50 1YD

4

Dear Bob
Everything is going wrong here, so it's good you didn't come. The first week, the weather wasn't nice. It rained every day. Then I got ill because I ate something bad, and I spent three days in bed, so I didn't see much. Everywhere is crowded here and the food is not as good as English food. The scenery is prettier back home! I miss you and can't wait to be back.
Love Jackie

Bob Brodie

21 Park Street

Oxford

OX2 6SN

Working with the texts

1 **True or false (texts 1 and 2)? Correct the false statements.**

1 The Great West is one of the most varied places in the United States.
2 The United States' most exciting scenery is in the Grand Canyon.
3 Californian beaches are romantic.
4 The Sierra Nevada is not very green.
5 America's prettiest lakes, valleys and woods are in the Sierra Nevada.
6 The best time to see the scenery in Scotland is in the summer.
7 In winter the days are longer than in England.
8 The lakes, valleys and woods in Scotland are crowded.
9 The Alps are higher than Scottish mountains.
10 It was easy to visit the Highlands 200 years ago.

2 Read texts 3 and 4. Make sentences which mean the opposite.

1. We're having a terrible time.
2. Dan did not fall over.
3. Everything is more expensive.
4. It is very boring here.
5. There's not much to see and do.
6. Everything is fine here.
7. It's bad you didn't come.
8. I saw a lot.
9. The scenery is prettier here.
10. I don't want to come back.

3 Match these questions and answers about the texts.

1. How long did Jackie spend in bed?
2. What are Scotland's lakes valleys and woods like?
3. What is more varied than other places in the US?
4. Is Kim having a good time?
5. What was the weather like for Jackie?
6. When is the best time to visit Scotland?
7. What does Kim think of Portugal?
8. Where can you go in the US if you like greener scenery?
9. Where can you have a romantic experience in the States?
10. What did Kim do in the park yesterday?

a. America's Great West.
b. San Francisco or the Californian beaches.
c. To the beautiful national parks.
d. In summer.
e. Lonely but very romantic.
f. Yes, she is.
g. She went rollerblading.
h. She finds it exciting.
i. Terrible. It rained every day.
j. Three days.

4 Complete the sentences. Sometimes more than one answer is possible!

excitement
exciting
lakes
lively
mountains
romantic
scenery
wonderful

1. People say that Venice in Italy is the most ... city in the world.
2. For really ... scenery, go to the Victoria Falls in Zimbabwe.
3. Scotland is a very ... place at New Year.
4. New York is one of the most ... cities in the world.
5. The ... in Switzerland is beautiful all through the year.
6. Go to places like St Moritz, Monaco or Beverley Hills and have a holiday with ... .
7. Even in the summer, there is snow on the highest ... in Switzerland.
8. Loch Ness is one of Scotland's biggest ... .

5 Match the sentences.

1. Prices are not as high as in other places.
2. There is always something happening.
3. Everywhere is crowded.
4. Jackie is happy that Bob is not with her.
5. Jackie did not have good weather.
6. Jackie was not well.
7. Jackie wants to be with Bob.
8. She can't wait to be back.

a. she wants to go home
b. she is glad he didn't come
c. she got ill
d. things are less expensive
e. the weather wasn't nice
f. she misses him
g. there are a lot of people
h. life goes on around the clock

Language Review

1 SIMPLE PAST *(Einfache Vergangenheit)*

Aussagen			
I You He/She We They	went	to Portugal to the park	last year. yesterday.

Verneinungen			
I You He/She We They	didn't go	to Portugal to the park	in 1996. two days ago.

Ja/Nein-Fragen				Kurzantworten
Did	you she we they	go on holiday	last summer?	Yes, I did./No, I didn't. Yes, she did./No, she didn't. Yes, we did./No, we didn't. Yes, they did./No, they didn't.

INFORMATIONSFRAGEN				
Fragewort	**Hilfsverb**	**Subjekt**	**Verb**	**Satzergänzung**
When Why	did	you she we they	go	to Portugal?

- Das *simple past* wird gebraucht, um völlig abgeschlossene Handlungen zu schildern. Es wird oft mit Ausdrücken wie *last year, yesterday, two years ago, in 1996* verwendet.
- Bei regelmäßigen Verben wird *-ed* an die Grundform des Verbs angehängt: *start* → *started*.
- Fragen werden mit *did* gebildet, verneinte Sätze mit *didn't*.
- Eine Liste der unregelmäßigen Verben finden Sie auf Seite 261.

2 COMPARATIVES AND SUPERLATIVES OF ADJECTIVES
(Steigerung von Adjektiven)

	Adjektiv	**Komparativ**	**Superlativ**
Einsilbige Adjektive	long	longer	the longest
Adjektive, die auf *-y* enden	pretty	prettier	the prettiest
Adjektive mit zwei und mehr Silben	romantic	more romantic	the most romantic
Unregelmäßige Adjektive	good bad far	better worse further	the best the worst the furthest

- Bei kurzen Adjektiven wird *-er/-est* angehängt. Wenn ein einsilbiges Adjektiv mit einem Konsonanten endet, wird dieser verdoppelt: **big – bigger – the biggest**.
- Zweisilbige Adjektive, die auf *-y* enden (z.B. *happy*, *pretty* etc.), werden auch mit *-er/-est* gesteigert, wobei das *-y* zu *-i* wird.
- Vergleiche können mit *-er/more ... than* oder *(not) as ... as* gebildet werden:
  The mountains in the Alps are **higher than** in Scotland.
  The weather in Scotland in the summer is **as good as** in England.

Practice

1 Look at the pictures and tell the story.

1 go/camping

➡ *Last summer I went camping.*

2 have/a terrible time
3 rain/every day
4 get/wet and ill
5 go/many pubs
6 see/films at the cinema
7 go/home early

2 Listen and match the journey to the transport.

1 England to Calais.   a plane
2 Paris to Marseille.   b bus
3 Marseille to Corsica.   c train
4 Looking at scenery in Corsica. d ferry
5 Corsica to England.   e boat

3 **What do you think?**

➡ *I think German wine is better than French wine.*
I think French wine is more/less expensive than German wine.

| good   bad   enjoyable   attractive   interesting   expensive |

German wine   French wine
the weather in England   the weather in Italy
beach holidays   city holidays
brown eyes   green eyes
Athens   Stuttgart
holiday in a hotel   camping holiday

4 **Now say which things you think are the best. Use the words in the box above and make sentences like this:**

➡ *The best wine comes from California.*
The most expensive city is Tokyo.

5 **What do you think about these photographs? Use the words in the box.**

| lively   quiet   busy   exciting   interesting
attractive   good   bad   romantic   pretty |

➡ *I think Athens is livelier than Stuttgart, but Rio is the liveliest city.*

◀ Rio

▲ Athens

▼ Oxford   Stuttgart ▶

UNIT 4 • TIME FOR A HOLIDAY   **35**

Travel enquiries and reservations
Reiseauskünfte und Reservierungen

1 What are they saying? Match the questions and answers with the situations.

1 I'd like to rent a car.
2 Can I cash some traveller's cheques?
3 I'd like some information about flights to Istanbul, please.
4 Do you have any rooms for the week of June 5 to June 12?

a Yes. For how many nights?
b For how many days?
c Sure. Do you have your passport?
d When do you want to go?

2 Listen to the questions. Match them with the answers.

a Oh, yes. I'm coming back the following Friday.
b By credit card.
c On May 15 in the morning, please.
d No. That's too late.
e Schrandt. Renate Schrandt.
f A single, please. With a bathroom.

THE WORLD OF WORK

3 Choose places for these people.

	Plaza ★★★	OLYMPIA ★★	VISTA BAY APARTMENTS
No. of rooms	100	25	50
Price per night (£)	75–125	54–82	35–48
Beach	15 mins	25 mins	1 min
Shops	3 mins	20 mins	10 mins
Night life	✓	✗	✓
Town centre	3 mins	30 mins	10 mins

comfortable   expensive   near   far   noisy   lively   convenient   quiet

1 My name's Mike Silvester. I'm looking for a cheap, lively place with discos.
2 I'm Josie Lawson. I like peaceful places that are not near the town centre.
3 Hello, I'm Mr Leder and I don't have a lot of money, so I want something clean and simple.
4 This is Jack Thomas. I need a nice hotel, not far from the centre of town and good restaurants.
5 This is Mrs. Jackson speaking. I want a comfortable hotel, convenient for the shops.
6 Hi, I'm Tony Watson. I need a place, not too expensive and right on the beach.

4 Study the pictures and the texts and decide what each person's job is.

a travel agent
c tour guide
b hotel receptionist
d tourist information employee

▲ Melanie greets people on their arrival and checks them in.

▲ Robert helps people with their holiday plans and makes their bookings.

◀ Jane looks after people while they are on holiday and goes with them on excursions.

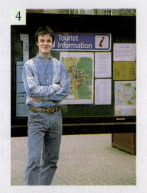

▶ Paul works for the local tourist office. He answers people's enquiries about bus and train timetables.

UNIT 4 • TIME FOR A HOLIDAY

5 HIS JOB OR HERS?

Unequal opportunities

In many areas of work, men often earn more money than women and possibly a few men still
5 believe this is right. However, for models things are different. There are fewer male than female models and the men earn less than the
10 women. There is little opportunity for men: there are only a few men in very good modelling jobs, but female Super Models can earn more than DM10 million a year.

This is not only a case of unequal opportunity, but also
15 of sexism towards men. In the past, businesses usually wanted attractive or sexy women to advertise their products to men, because men often had more money than women. For this reason,
20 there is still not much work for male models. Another reason is that women are often more interested than men in clothes and cosmetics, so there are more females than
25 males to model them.

for models

Peter Symes

However, things are changing a little and there is now some hope for male models. More and more men are now in demand to market clothes and cosmetics. And not just handsome males. Nowadays, plain, ordinary-looking guys are OK, too.

'And about time, too!' says model Gary Jackson. 'At last men are getting good modelling work. The future in this business is ours.'

Why is this? Why are there more men than before on our TVs and in our newspapers and magazines?

One answer is that, thanks to the feminist movement, many people now think that using only women to advertise products is sexist. Women also now have more money to spend and they buy products for their male partners. So, manufacturers are targeting their products at women more than before. As well as the new male models, they are also choosing more educated and intelligent-looking women as models, but still those with good looks, of course.

So, as more men work as models, is this a more equal opportunity? Or is it just another example of sexism, where men are the sex objects instead of women?

Before you start ...

Do you think that looks are important? Can you say why? Describe yourself using the words in the box.

handsome	plain	beautiful
ordinary-looking		sexy
attractive	intelligent-looking	

Working with the text

1 **Answer the questions.**

1. Why is modelling different from other jobs?
2. What do we call models in the best jobs?
3. Why did businesses want women to advertise their products?
4. What are women more interested in than men?
5. Why are male models becoming more popular? Give two reasons.
6. Do all male models have to be handsome?
7. What is different for women now?
8. What sort of women are manufacturers choosing to be models nowadays?

2 **Match the words in the box with the words below.**

| handsome | plain | unequal | earn |
| guys | jobs | cosmetics | sexy |

1. get money
2. good-looking
3. not good-looking
4. men
5. work
6. not equal
7. make-up
8. attractive to the opposite sex

3 **Find words in the text to describe men or women, or both men and women. Use them to describe well-known people.**

➡ *I don't think Michael Schumacher is very attractive.*
I think Pamela Anderson is very sexy.

4 **Look at how we use the following words in the text. Then complete the sentences with these words.**

possibly (line 4)   however (line 6)   nowadays (line 29)   thanks to (line 34)

1. There is now more equal opportunity in jobs ... the feminist movement.
2. There is less sexism in advertising today, ... there is still too much of it.
3. ..., women have more money to spend.
4. It is ... true to say that some men still think it is normal for them to earn more than women.

Language Review

1 QUANTIFIERS *(Mengenangaben)*

zählbar	nichtzählbar
Many people now think … There are only **a few** men … There are **more** female than male models. There are **fewer** male than female models.	There isn't **much** work … Things are changing **a little** … There is **little** opportunity for men … Men earn **more** money than women. Women earn **less** than men.

many	= *viele*	little	= *wenig*
much	= *viel*	more	= *mehr*
a few	= *einige*	fewer	= *weniger*
few	= *wenig*	less	= *weniger*
a little	= *ein wenig*		

- *Many* und *a lot of* werden bei zählbaren Substantiven verwendet; *much* und *a lot of* bei nichtzählbaren.
- *A lot of* wird in positiven Sätzen (bejahten Aussagesätzen), *many* und *much* in negativen Sätzen (verneinten Aussagesätzen) und Fragen benutzt.
- *(A) few* wird bei zählbaren Substantiven verwendet; *(a) little* bei nichtzählbaren.

2 POSSESSIVE PRONOUNS *(Possessivpronomen – besitzanzeigende Fürwörter)*

Besitzanzeigende Adjektive	Besitzanzeigende Pronomen
It's my house.	It's **mine**.
It's your house.	It's **yours**.
It's his house.	It's **his**.
It's her house.	It's **hers**.
It's our house.	It's **ours**.
It's their house.	It's **theirs**.

- *Possessive adjectives* und *possessive pronouns* drücken aus, dass etwas jemandem gehört.
- *Possessive adjectives* stehen zusammen mit einem Substantiv; *possessive pronouns* stehen allein anstelle eines Substantivs.

"This house is no longer mine – I sold it to Mrs Jennings last week, so now it's hers."

Practice

1 With a partner, make questions and answers about the pictures using the words in the box.

| how much | not much/a lot (of) | a little |
| how many | many/a lot (of) | a few |

1

2

3

4

2 Complete the sentences with the words in the box.

| more | less | a few | fewer | a little | little | much | many |

1 Only ... men get the best jobs in modelling, so I am afraid that there is ... hope for you as a Super Model, Tom.
2 ... women than men have the good jobs in modelling.
3 I do the same job as George but I earn ... than him because I am a woman.
4 There still aren't ... opportunities for women in top business positions.
5 You don't earn ... in this business, but things are changing so there is ... hope at last.
6 Only two or three years ago there were ... men in the fashion business.

3 Write the opposite of each statement. Change the words in *italics*.

1 There are *more* women in management now.
2 I've got *a lot of* CDs in my collection.
3 He had *a few* job interviews.
4 She has *more* boyfriends than her sister.
5 You've got *a few* pounds to spend.
6 We have *more* homework this year.
7 I want to lose *a lot of* weight.
8 I have *a lot of* time.

4 Compare the amounts.

1 I earn £20,000. He earns £10,000.

➡ *I earn more than he does. He earns less than I do.*

2 I have two newspapers. She has four newspapers.
3 He has few opportunities. We have many opportunities.
4 They do a lot of marketing. We don't do much marketing.
5 She has little free time. He has much free time.
6 She has a lot of modelling work. I have a little modelling work.
7 We advertise our product in four magazines. They advertise their product in two magazines.
8 There are many female models. There are only a few male models.

5 Rewrite the sentences.

1 These are not my clothes. (These clothes ...)

➡ *These clothes are not mine.*

2 That is not my job! (That job ...)
3 Is this his money or her money? (Is this money ...)
4 This is our great opportunity. (This great opportunity ...)
5 It's their future. (The future ...)
6 This is not your dress. (This dress ...)
7 It's your fault. (The fault ...)
8 This is my product. (This product ...)

6 Answer the questions.

1 Is this your coat? (her)

➡ *No, it's not mine, it's hers.*

2 Is this her magazine? (my)
3 Is this our hotel? (their)
4 Is it their job? (our)
5 Is this his school? (your)
6 Is it her idea? (my)
7 Is this my letter? (his)
8 Is this our taxi? (your)

7 Listen to the model. Correct the following sentences.

1 She had a lot of work when she began in the modelling business.
2 She had a lot of interesting jobs.
3 She now does a lot of modelling for magazines and a little advertising work.
4 She earns less than before.
5 She thinks there are more women than men in other media jobs.
6 She thinks there are fewer male models these days.

THE WORLD OF WORK

Advertising
Werbung

1 Look at the advertisements.
What do you think they are advertising?

What do you like about them?
What don't you like?

2 Match the slogans with the advertisements in exercise 1.

A *The new car for the* **NEW WOMAN**

B ARE YOU ON TIME?

C *Look after yourself in the sun*

D Be a SMOOTH guy

UNIT 5 • HIS JOB OR HERS?

3 Look up the words in the back of the book and put them into groups.

| cosmetics | mail shots | clothes | commercials | free gifts | magazines |
| competitions | discount offers | | sponsorship | snack foods | drinks |

PRODUCTS   GIMMICKS   TYPES OF ADVERTISING

4 Complete the text with the correct form of the words from the box in exercise 3.

We all see advertising, because it is everywhere: in ^{1}... , on TV and radio ^{2}... and through ^{3}... at sports events. And we often get ^{4}... through our letter boxes. Of course, we do not all decide to buy a product just because of advertising, but we all like gimmicks. It is always nice to get ^{5}... , or ^{6}... are good because we can pay less money for things, or we can win a wonderful holiday when we enter ^{7}... . Advertising is used to persuade us to buy what we don't really need, ^{8}... to make make us look younger for example, or ^{9}... and ^{10}... which make us fat. Advertising can make us feel bad as well, especially women looking at the ^{11}... advertised by very beautiful models. But like it or not, advertising is here to stay!

5 Choose a product and advertise it. Say how you are advertising it and what gimmicks you are using. Give your reasons.

➡ I am advertising trainers and I am targeting teenagers through TV commercials because teenagers watch TV a lot. I am offering a discount because price is important.

6 Listen to the conversation and fill in the missing words from the box.

| marketing | magazines | slogans | advertising | design |

1 Brian works in the ... department.
2 He helps with ... .
3 They advertise in ... .
4 The ... is his.
5 Sometimes he thinks of ... .

UNIT 5 • HIS JOB OR HERS?   45

6 FOOD AND DIET

1

A school experiment

All the pupils from a school in England who usually have lunch at school were unhappy when someone decided to change their menu. Ostrich burgers were on the menu for them to try for a week. But many of the pupils were not happy and some decided to go home for lunch instead. The catering manager said the children did not want any ostrich burgers. 'I don't understand,' she said. 'They don't mind eating chicken. Ostrich tastes very similar, but there aren't any pupils who even want to try the ostrich burgers.'

Many caterers think that, although it is more expensive, ostrich meat may replace beef, which a lot of people stopped eating after the BSE scare, but eating ostriches may be too much for the British, many of whom are animal lovers. 'Ostriches are really nice animals,' said one pupil. 'How can anybody eat them?'

Before you start ...

FOOD FACT

People love to eat Fu-gu fish in Japan, but it is a fish which is also very poisonous. Cooking it is a very difficult job and it is only qualified chefs who can do this. Every year, about 200 people die there because they don't cook it correctly. If you are not sure, don't eat any!

2 In a restaurant

Jutta and Ralf are ordering some food in a restaurant.

WAITER Hi. What can I get you?
JUTTA   What's the dish of the day today?
WAITER It's shepherd's pie.
JUTTA   What's that?
WAITER It's a hot pie that the chef cooks with beef and potatoes.
JUTTA   Er ... no, thanks. I'm not too keen on beef at the moment. Do you have any fish?
WAITER Sure. We have some salmon, with potatoes and green beans.
JUTTA   Fine.
WAITER Anything to start with?
JUTTA   No, thanks.
WAITER And for you?
RALF   I'm not very hungry and I'm on a diet. What have you got?
WAITER Well, how about one of the low-calorie dishes?
RALF   What are they?
WAITER They are dishes which the chef cooks with no fat and which we serve with a choice of salads.
RALF   Er ... no, thank you.
JUTTA   There's a pasta dish here. You like pasta.
RALF   Yes, I know, but ... er ... The hamburger, please.
WAITER With some french fries or salad?
RALF   French fries, please.
WAITER And anything to follow?
JUTTA   Nothing for me, thanks.
RALF   Er ... can I have some grilled tomatoes?
WAITER As a dessert?
RALF   No, as a starter. I didn't order a starter. Let's order the dessert later.

Menu

Shepherd's Pie
Salmon
with potatoes and green beans

Hamburger
Lasagne
with french fries or salad

✳ LOW-CALORIE DISHES ✳
Pasta
Choice of salads

Would you like to eat Fu-gu fish? We think that Japanese people are very strange because they eat things like Fu-gu fish. What food do you think is strange?

Working with the texts

1 Choose the correct answers, A, B or C (text 1).

1. The school served ostrich meat because
   - **A** the children did not eat beef.
   - **B** it was an experiment.
   - **C** the children didn't like beef.

2. The children
   - **A** didn't like the ostrich burgers.
   - **B** didn't try the ostrich burgers.
   - **C** loved the ostrich burgers.

3. The children
   - **A** ate chicken.
   - **B** didn't like chicken.
   - **C** didn't want to try chicken.

4. Ostrich meat ... on the menu instead of beef.
   - **A** was
   - **B** may be
   - **C** was not

5. A lot of people stopped
   - **A** eating ostrich meat.
   - **B** eating beef.
   - **C** eating ostrich meat after the BSE scare.

6. The catering manager didn't understand the children because
   - **A** she liked ostrich meat.
   - **B** ostriches are like chickens.
   - **C** they didn't like chicken.

7. The reason why the children didn't try the ostrich burgers is probably that
   - **A** ostrich meat is not good.
   - **B** ostrich meat is expensive.
   - **C** they think that ostriches are nice animals.

2 Correct the wrong sentences (text 2).

1. Jutta likes beef.
2. Jutta didn't want a starter.
3. Ralf wasn't hungry.
4. Ralf wanted the low-calorie dish because he was on a diet.
5. Ralf doesn't like pasta.
6. Ralf wanted tomatoes for his dessert.

3 Can you replace the sentences with words from texts 1 and 2?

1. Someone who decides what will go on the school menu.
2. An animal which tastes like an ostrich.
3. Someone who likes animals very much.
4. Someone who cooks food in a restaurant.
5. Someone who serves food in a restaurant.
6. A dish which is good for someone who is on a diet.
7. The part of the meal which we eat before the main course.
8. The part of the meal which we eat after the main course.

Language Review

1 SOME AND ANY *(some und any)*

Aussagen	Verneinungen	Fragen	Angebote/Bitten
Some children went home for lunch.	They didn't want **any** ostrich meat.	Do you have **any** fish?	Would you like **some** french fries?
Somebody decided to change the menu.	They didn't know **any**body at the party.	How can **any**body eat them?	Would you like **some**body to help you?
The children bought **some**thing for lunch.	She hasn't got **any**thing to do.	Have you got **any**thing to drink?	Would you like **some**thing to eat?

- *Some* und *any* werden mit Pluralformen und nichtzählbaren Begriffen wie *fish* und *meat* gebraucht.
- *Some* wird in Aussagen, Angeboten und Bitten verwendet; *any* in Verneinungen und Fragen.
- *Some* und *any* können mit *body* und *thing* verbunden werden.

2 RELATIVE CLAUSES *(Relativsätze)*

Personen	Tiere/Dinge
There aren't any pupils **who** even want to try it.	An ostrich is a bird **that** tastes very similar to chicken.

- Relativsätze sind Nebensätze, die ein Substantiv näher definieren.
- Relativsätze werden mit Relativpronomen eingeleitet: *who* oder *that* beziehen sich auf Personen und *which* oder *that* beziehen sich auf Tiere und Dinge.
- *Who*, *which* und *that* können entfallen, wenn sie die Stelle des Objekts im Relativsatz einnehmen. *The meat (**which/that**) you eat is bad for you.*

3 USING VERBS AS NOUNS (GERUNDS) *(Gerundium)*

-ing-Form als Subjekt	*-ing*-Form als Objekt
Eating ostrich meat is too much for some pupils.	They don't like **eating** ostrich meat.

- Die *-ing*-Form eines Verbs kann als Substantiv benutzt werden. Es kann sowohl als Subjekt wie auch als Objekt in einem Satz verwendet werden.
- Für Ausnahmen bei der Bildung der *-ing*-Form, siehe Unit 3.

Practice

1 Look at the pictures and make sentences with *some* and *any*.

➡ There aren't any potatoes but there are some apples.

2 Work with a partner. Ask and answer questions about this picture.

➡ Is there any wine?
No, there isn't.

Are there any apples?
Yes, there are.

3 Complete the sentences. Use the correct word from the box.

| any | some | anything | something | anybody | somebody |

1 Have you got ... free time?
2 I haven't got ... to wear!
3 Is there ... there? said the traveller.
4 Well, ... has got to do it!
5 I knew ... would go wrong.
6 Yes, I've got ... money, but not as much as that.
7 Isn't there ... here who can speak German?
8 ... said that she's not coming.
9 Is there ... I can do to make it better?
10 I'm sorry, there aren't ... apples left, but there are ... tomatoes.

4 **Complete the following sentences using *who* or *which*.**

1. The chef ... cooked the meal is really great!
2. The food ... you eat on a diet is low calorie.
3. The children ... go to school there don't like the school lunches.
4. The restaurant ... we went to last night was very crowded.
5. The office ... he works in is not very busy just now.
6. The man ... told me the time was very handsome.
7. The city ... we went to on holiday is very beautiful.
8. My friend ... is a doctor lives in Paris.

5 **Make each of these pairs of sentences into one sentence, using *who*, *which*, *that* or nothing.**

1. I had some beef last night. It was really nice.

   ➡ *The beef (which/that) I had last night was really nice.*

2. It's a meat pie. They cook it in wine.
3. The man serves meals in a restaurant. He is a waiter.
4. The farmer killed the cows. They had BSE.
5. Ostriches are birds. They don't fly.
6. Some people eat well-balanced diets. They are usually healthier.
7. Low-calorie food has little fat in it. It is good for people who are on a diet.
8. You eat fast food. It is not good for you.
9. Why not try our pies? We serve them with french fries and salad.
10. That person is the chef. The chef cooks the food.

6 **Listen to Gary and Julie talking about getting ready for a party. Make three lists: the things they are going to buy, those that they don't need and those that you are not sure about.**

7 **Change the sentences. Use a gerund.**

1. It is not always easy to go on a diet.

   ➡ *Going on a diet is not always easy.*

2. It is not good for you to eat a lot of meat.
3. It is usually expensive to eat out in restaurants.
4. I think it is healthier to eat fish rather than meat.
5. It is not good for you to eat only fast food.
6. It may be good for you to try low-calorie dishes.
7. I don't think it is easy to save money.
8. It is often good for you to drink a lot of water.
9. Some people think it is wrong to kill animals for us to eat.
10. He said that it is best to be a vegetarian.

THE WORLD OF WORK

Food and catering
Nahrungsmittel und Ernährung

1 Match the jobs and places of work with the pictures.

➡ Picture 1 is of a chef. A chef is a person who usually works in a hotel or restaurant kitchen and who cooks the meals.

a catering manager orders food	health centre
a dietician advises on good diet	laboratory
a shop assistant helps to sell the food	hotel/restaurant kitchen
a chef cooks meals	hotel/restaurant
a food scientist studies food products	school or company kitchen
a waiter takes orders and serves meals	supermarket/shop

52   UNIT 6 • FOOD AND DIET

THE WORLD OF WORK

2 The texts below are about balanced diets, but some things are missing. Complete the information with the words from the box.

avoid	food	healthy	diseases
low	weight	smoking	good
	fruit	balance	

Having a ¹ ... diet does not mean going without ² .... It is more a question of balance. Getting the right balance helps keep your ³ ... down and stops you getting some ⁴ .... Also, of course, taking exercise and not ⁵ ... are things which help.

Eating less fat is important. Try to ⁶ ... food with a lot of fat and sugar, like cake and ice cream. The protein in dairy food is ⁷ ... for you, but choose products with ⁸ ... fat.

A good balance means eating bread, cereals, pasta and rice, a lot of ⁹... and vegetables, which have vitamins and fibre, some meat or fish and a little dairy food.

To help you get the right ¹⁰..., look for the information on products, which give their calories and fat content.

3 🎧 Listen to two people talking about food and their jobs. Match the photos with the right speakers. Do they have the same opinions about food? What do they think a good diet is?

4 Below are some words from this unit. Work with a partner to put the words into the right lists.

JOBS	WAYS OF COOKING	TYPES OF FOOD	MEALS

dietician   ostrich meat   fry   lunch   breakfast   rice   ice cream
chef   tomatoes   catering manager   grill   pasta   salmon   cereals
dinner   beef   boil   vegetables   bread   chicken   cheese

5 Work with your partner again and decide together which of the types of food in the list above have one or more of the following:

1 protein   2 fibre   3 carbohydrates   4 fat

UNIT 6 • FOOD AND DIET

7 PROBLEMS AND ANXIETIES

1 Teenagers write to Pamela's Mailbag about their problems.

'I'm so depressed that I don't know what to do. I feel awkward and I don't know what to say when I am with people. When I say something, I sound stupid and I am sure people laugh at me behind my back. I know they try to avoid me and they don't let me join in. Everyone seems to be against me. Even one of my teachers picked on me the other day. She gave me bad marks, but I'm so afraid of making things worse that I don't want to complain. I can't stand it! People shouldn't treat me like this, should they?'

Tony (age 17)

'My family and I argue all the time. They don't let me do what I want to do, like wear the things I want, even though I am sixteen, and they try to make me do stupid things, like tell them where I am going. They say I should get home by eleven o'clock and that I should tell them where I was and who I was with. I mean, I'm not a baby, am I? I'm so frustrated that I want to leave home. They are driving me crazy. I think I am right to complain, aren't I? Eleven o'clock isn't very late.'

Shona (age 16)

Before you start ...

Are you a happy person or do you think one of the words in the box describes you better?

| worried | depressed |
| frustrated | bored | shy |

Do any of these words describe how you feel when you are learning English? Can you say why?

2 Pamela replies.

REPLIES

Dear Tony

You are feeling pretty low, aren't you? But your feelings are quite normal for someone of your age. I can tell from your letter that you are not stupid. I think you are shy and lonely, that's all. You should look around you and find a friend to talk to. If you really think your teacher picks on you, you should talk to her first and then to your parents. You should look in the mirror tomorrow morning and decide you are as good as anyone and even better than many others!

Dear Shona

Maybe you are right to complain, but you shouldn't see things from your own point of view all the time, which is just what your parents are doing! I cannot say who is to blame and perhaps you should at least try to see why they are worried and do what they want for a while. Then if you are reasonable with them, they may change their opinions! Next time you go out, you should change what you do and tell them everything, before they ask. There's no harm in trying, is there? It may work!

PAMELA'S MAILBAG

UNIT 7 • PROBLEMS AND ANXIETIES

Working with the texts

1 Answer the questions on the teenagers' letters (text 1).

1. How does Tony feel?
2. Give two examples of how Tony thinks other people treat him.
3. Why is Tony unhappy about one of his teachers?
4. Why doesn't Tony complain about this teacher?
5. Which of these words, in your opinion, describes Shona: *worried*, *depressed*, *crazy* or *lonely*? Say why.
6. Give three examples of things Shona is not happy about with her parents.
7. Does Shona think that eleven o'clock is late?
8. What does Shona think she should do about her problem?

2 Find words in the teenagers' letters (text 1) to complete the sentences.

1. Tony is ... .
2. Tony thinks that people try to ... him.
3. Tony thinks his teacher ... him.
4. Tony doesn't want to ... .
5. Shona and her family ... a lot.
6. Shona thinks she is not a ... .
7. Shona is very ... with her family and wants to leave home.
8. Shona's family are driving her ... .

3 Answer the questions about Pamela's replies (text 2).

1. What is Pamela's opinion of Tony?
2. Give two examples of Pamela's advice to Tony.
3. Does Pamela think that Tony's problem is unusual?
4. In what way does Pamela suggest that Shona and her parents are the same?
5. What should Shona do to change her parents' opinions?
6. What should she do next time she goes out?

4 Correct the sentences that are wrong from Pamela's replies (text 2).

1. Pamela thinks that Tony's situation is unusual.
2. Pamela thinks that one of Tony's problems is that he hasn't got a good friend.
3. Pamela advises Tony to decide that he is as good as anyone.
4. Pamela thinks Shona is to blame for the situation.
5. Pamela says that Shona should give in to her parents.
6. Pamela thinks that Shona should make the first move.

5 Look at the texts. Find words that mean the opposite to the ones underlined below.

1. She's really clever, so she's bored in the lesson.
2. He goes to lots of parties because he is very confident.
3. I got home early last night.
4. He wants to stay at home.
5. We're a little worried about our exams.
6. My teacher gives me bad marks, it drives me crazy.
7. The situation may get better.
8. He is wrong to think that.

Language Review

1 MAKE/LET *(zwingen/lassen)*

zwingen	lassen
They **make me** tell them where I am going.	They **don't let me** join in.

- Jemanden zwingen, etwas zu tun wird ins Englische mit *to make somebody do something* übersetzt.
- Jemanden etwas tun lassen wird mit *to let somebody do something* übersetzt.

2 SHOULD/SHOULDN'T *(sollen/nicht sollen)*

- *Should/shouldn't* werden benutzt, um Ratschläge zu erteilen bzw. um auf eine Pflicht hinzuweisen.

Positiv	Negativ
They say I **should** be home by eleven o'clock.	You **shouldn't** only see things from your own point of view.
You **should** change what you do.	People **shouldn't** treat me like this.

3 QUESTION TAGS *(Frageanhängsel)*

Aussage	Anhängsel
You are feeling pretty low,	**aren't you**?
It isn't right,	**is it**?
People shouldn't treat me like this,	**should they**?
You don't know what to do,	**do you**?
You feel unhappy,	**don't you**?
The teacher gave him bad marks,	**didn't she**?
He didn't know what to do,	**did he**?

- Ein Frageanhängsel ist eine Kurzfrage, die an eine Aussage angehängt wird, um die angesprochene Person zu einer Reaktion aufzufordern.
- Ist die Aussage positiv, folgt ein verneintes Anhängsel.
- Ist die Aussage negativ, folgt ein bejahtes Anhängsel.
- Das Frageanhängsel wird mit dem in der Aussage verwendeten Hilfsverb gebildet.
- Wenn die Aussage kein Hilfsverb enthält, wird das Frageanhängsel im *simple present* mit *do/does* und im *simple past* mit *did* gebildet.

"You realise you only have to say 'yes' or 'no', don't you?"

Practice

1 Rewrite these sentences with the correct form of *make* or *let*.

1 When he was young, his parents … him do what he wanted all the time.
2 Please don't … me go to school today. I feel too ill.
3 I am a very nice parent. I … my children go to bed when they want.
4 She doesn't … her children read when they are in bed.
5 She didn't … her son marry the woman of his choice.
6 Please … me go home early today. I'm tired.
7 Don't … me eat it! I don't like cheese.
8 You … me do it – I didn't want to.

2 Study the pictures and give advice using the phrases below. Decide with a partner when to use *should* or *shouldn't*.

1

argue so much
try to understand each other

2

pick on each other
treat everyone the same

3

tell the police
let them get away with it

4

find a friend
be shy and lonely

5

treat her like that
tell her why it's wrong

6

complain
accept bad service

3 Complete the sentences with *should* or *shouldn't*.

1 I don't get on with my stepfather. What do you think I … (do)?
2 We argue all the time. … (I/try) to see his point of view?
3 You … (worry) about the situation. It is not too bad.
4 I think she … (get home) before eleven o'clock. She's only fifteen.
5 … (he/talk) to his best friend or not?
6 It is a very interesting film, so you … (watch) it.
7 I'm on a diet, so I … (have) another chocolate.
8 Do you think I … (tell) her? No, you … (tell) her because it's a secret.

4 Turn these statements into questions using question tags.

1 He's right.
   → He's right, isn't he?

2 I remembered to phone him.
3 You like sugar in your coffee.
4 We are going to the zoo today.
5 I didn't do my homework very well.
6 He shouldn't argue with me.
7 She doesn't eat breakfast.
8 You aren't worried about them.

5 Complete these sentences using the words from the box.

| reasonable | shy | bored | avoid | depressed |
| frustrated | awkward | worry | picks on | crazy |

1 She is unhappy. She feels very … .
2 When you are shy, you often feel … with other people.
3 If you don't like someone, you usually try to … them.
4 Tony says his teacher … him.
5 When people are not happy about something, they usually … about it.
6 When two people start to argue, this sometimes means they are … about something.
7 You are so … with your life that you are depressed about it.
8 When people don't want to meet other people, it is often because they are … .
9 If parents are at least … with their children, the children shouldn't complain too much.
10 When we are frustrated about something, we often say it drives us … .

6 Complete these statements with the right question tags.

1 It isn't right, … ?
2 They shouldn't complain so much, … ?
3 I'm not to blame, … ?
4 I brought my passport, … ?
5 He was very frustrated, … ?
6 They don't have the right to be happy, … ?
7 She laughed behind his back, … ?
8 You think you are always right, … ?

7 Match the words in the box to the pictures. Then listen to the speakers. Which of the words in the box describes how they feel?

| happy | stupid | lonely |
| bored | afraid | depressed |

UNIT 7 • PROBLEMS AND ANXIETIES

THE WORLD OF WORK

Problems at work
Probleme am Arbeitsplatz

1 Read what the people say about themselves and work in pairs to decide what they are worried about.

unemployment   health and safety   stress
racial discrimination   pension
redundancy   sexual harassment

1. My name is Matt. I am 17 and left school with no 'A' levels. I live in a town where the factory closed last year. I am worried about ... .

2. Hi. I'm Ravi. I'm having a really frustrating time at work at the moment because of the way my employer treats me. I don't think he likes Pakistanis. I am worried about ... .

3. Hello. My name is Edith Potts. I am nearly 65 years old and I started work as a secretary when I was 20 but I only work part-time because I have to look after my parents. Now I'm getting old, I'm very worried about my ... .

4. I am Martin Evers. I love my work as a teacher but things are changing fast. The classes keep getting bigger and there is less and less money for education. I am really worried about the amount of ... in my job.

5. I'm Alison Hardy and I work in a food factory. It's so noisy in there that I can't hear myself think! And I think I saw a rat the other day. I'm worried about ... .

6. Hello. I'm Patrick Selman. I'm the chairperson of a big company and I earn lots of money but I am still worried about ... .

7. I'm Derek Peters. I've got a very unusual problem for a man. My manager is a woman and she keeps touching my bottom. I think what she does is called ... .

2 Listen to the conversation. Which of the following sentences agree with what Pete says. Correct the ones which are wrong.

1. It's easy to explain what it's like being on the dole.
2. He does not have a degree.
3. It's more stressful being on the dole than having a job.
4. You need to be positive when you're unemployed.
5. Unemployment is unusual nowadays.
6. He is not doing a training course in marketing.
7. He has a degree in German.
8. He thinks his new qualification will make him more attractive to an employer.

THE WORLD OF WORK

3 What's the problem and what should I do about it? Work with your group to decide which problem goes with which reply.

1. I'm on the dole and I'm really bored.
2. This really terrible guy at work is sexually harassing me.
3. I'm really stressed by the amount of work I've got to do. I can't stand it any more.
4. It's so difficult to get a job because of my colour. I'm really frustrated.
5. I think my office is pretty good about Health and Safety, but my house is not!
6. I'm worried, depressed, frustrated, bored and I'd love to lose my job!

a. You should look at your work and see where you can leave things out or do things more quickly. Make time to take exercise.
b. You should tell him to stop doing it. If he keeps on doing it, then you should tell your manager.
c. You should do a training course and with your new qualifications you may get a job!
d. You should talk to a careers adviser. No one should want to lose their job!
e. You're right to be worried. You should treat your home in the same way as your place of work. Make it safe!
f. I can understand how you feel, but are you really sure that your problem is racial discrimination? You should ask employers to say why you didn't get the job and then you can decide if you want to complain.

4 Read the letters of application. Can you find 12 mistakes in Melanie's letter? Use Janet's letter as a model for rewriting Melanie's.

Dear Sir,

I left skool over a year ago and I still don't have a job. I wants to work in an ofice like yours becos I have a friend called Mary who work for you and she is very hapy. I don't want study becos I think it's boring. I don't have any sekretarial exams but I think I can learn quick on the job. Please anser this letter and let me come see you. I now that I can be of use in your company.
See you soon, I hope!

Melanie Brooks

January 19th 19..

Dear Mr Edwards

I would like to apply for the secretarial job advertised in the 'Evening Gazette' on 16 January.

I left school last July and, while looking for employment, I took a part-time secretarial course which I finished a month ago. The course covered all the qualifications you ask for in your advertisement, so I enclose my full CV for your consideration.

I look forward to hearing from you.

Yours sincerely

Janet Andrews

UNIT 7 • PROBLEMS AND ANXIETIES

8 ON THE ROAD!

1 🔊 Klaus and Jenny are talking about driving in Britain and in Europe.

KLAUS I don't understand the British. Why do you have to drive on the left in Britain?

JENNY Because everyone does. If you don't drive on the left, you are likely to have an accident pretty quickly!

5 KLAUS Very funny. No, what I mean is, why does everyone have to drive on the left? Why do the British have to drive differently?

JENNY That's easy. In Roman times when people drove chariots or rode horses, they had to ride on the left.

KLAUS Why did they have to?

10 JENNY Most people were right-handed and they had to protect themselves against people who came in the opposite direction. They had to keep to the left so that they could fight each other more easily.

KLAUS Er ... wait a minute. In that case, why didn't people in Europe ride on the left as well?

15 JENNY All the left-handed people had to leave Britain because they couldn't defend themselves very well. They all went back to Europe where they drove on the right and fought with their left hands. And then when we stopped fighting like this, we still kept driving on the left.

KLAUS Jenny ... Are you pulling my leg?

Before you start ...

In Britain, most road accidents are the fault of young drivers between the ages of 17 and 25. For this reason, some people say that you shouldn't learn to drive until you are 25. Do you agree? At what age can you learn to drive in Germany? Do you think this is the right age?

Working with the texts

1 Answer the questions on the dialogue between Klaus and Jenny.

1 What doesn't Klaus understand about driving in Britain?
2 In what way does Jenny first pull Klaus' leg?
3 When does Jenny say the practice of driving on the left began in Britain?
4 Why, says Jenny, did people start driving on the left in Britain?
5 At what point does Klaus understand that Jenny is pulling his leg?

2 ROAD SIGNS in Britain

The Romans were the first people in Britain who used traffic signs. They marked their roads with 'milliaries', stones placed every 1000 paces. This is where the word 'mile' comes
5   from. When the bicycle became popular in the last century, they decided that those who rode them should have signs to warn them about things like hills and bends and by 1900 there were about 4000 of them. Then came the car and in 1903 they introduced a red triangle for signs telling drivers what they must or should do and a red circle for signs telling them
10   what they mustn't do.

In the 1920s, white lines appeared on the roads and ten years later drivers had to stop before the lines at road junctions. 'Cat's eyes' appeared in 1934 and there are now about seven million of them in Britain. People say that the person who invented 'cat's eyes' became a millionaire!
15   In 1944, they introduced white lines for traffic lanes and in 1959 double white lines to stop overtaking became the law.

Britain finally had to change its traffic signs in line with Europe in 1965. These come in three classes: circles which give orders, triangles which give warnings and rectangles which give information.

2 Which of the pictures show Jenny's story? Which don't, and why not?

a   b   c

3 Answer the questions on text 2.

1. When did traffic signs begin in Britain?
2. What was the first sort of sign?
3. Why did more signs appear in the late 19th century?
4. How did things change when the motor car arrived?
5. What three things happened in the 1920s and 1930s?
6. What happened in 1965?
7. Which signs give orders in Europe?
8. Which signs give warnings in Europe?

4 Here are some examples of the things which you read about in text 2. What do they mean?

5 Find words in texts 1 and 2 which mean the following.

1. something is probable (text 1, lines 2–5)
2. very soon (text 1, lines 2–5)
3. protect (text 1, lines 15–20)
4. fashionable (text 2, lines 1–5)
5. where two or more roads meet (text 2, lines 12–15)
6. when one vehicle goes past another (text 2, lines 15–18)
7. at last (text 2, lines 16–20)
8. categories (text 2, lines 16–20)

Language Review

1 HAVE TO/MUST *(müssen)*

- *Must* drückt eine Verpflichtung aus, die vom Sprecher ausgeht. *You **must** visit Oxford when you go to England – it's a beautiful city.*
- *Have to* drückt eine Verpflichtung aus, die von einer Person/Institution auferlegt wird. *You **have to** drive on the left in England.*
- *Must* wird nur in der Gegenwart benutzt und hat für alle Personen die gleiche Form.
- *Have to* kann für alle Zeiten verwendet werden. Bei Fragen wird die Umschreibung mit *do* gebildet. *Why **did** they **have to** ride on the left in Roman times?*
- *Mustn't* drückt aus, dass etwas nicht erlaubt ist. *You **mustn't** park here.* (Sie dürfen hier nicht parken.)
- *Don't have to* drückt aus, dass etwas nicht notwendig ist. *You **don't have to** come.* (Sie brauchen nicht zu kommen.)

2 REFLEXIVE PRONOUNS *(Reflexivpronomen)*

I	**myself**	we	**ourselves**
you	**yourself**	you	**yourselves**
he	**himself**	they	**themselves**
she	**herself**		
it	**itself**		

- Reflexivpronomen werden benutzt, um auf das Subjekt des Satzes zurückzuverweisen. *He killed **himself**.*
- Reflexivpronomen werden im Englischen weniger häufig als im Deutschen verwendet. Manchmal ist ein Verb sowohl im Englischen wie auch im Deutschen reflexiv, z.B.: *enjoy yourself* (sich amüsieren) und *introduce yourself* (sich vorstellen).
- Reflexivpronomen können auch zur Betonung verwendet werden. *She repaired the car **herself**.*

3 ADVERBS OF MANNER *(Adverbien der Art und Weise)*

- Mit Adverbien beschreibt man, wie etwas geschieht.
  *Why do the British have to drive **differently**?*
- In der Regel werden Adverbien gebildet, indem man *-ly* an Adjektive anhängt.
  *He is a **quick** driver. He drives **quickly**.*
- Beachten Sie die Rechtschreibung nach *-y*: *easy* → *easily*.
  *They could fight each other more **easily**.*
- Das zu *good* gehörende Adverb ist *well*.
  *They couldn't defend themselves very **well**.*
- Die Adverbien *hard* und *fast* sind identisch mit dem Adjektiv.
  *She is a **fast** driver. She drives **fast**.*
- Nach *be*, *feel*, *look* und *seem* folgt kein Adverb, sondern ein Adjektiv.
  *It is **easy** to drive on the left. It seems **difficult** at the beginning.*

Practice

1 Make statements about the pictures using *have to* or *must not*.

1 drive on the left in the UK
2 go faster than 40 mph
3 wear seatbelts
4 go round roundabouts clockwise

5 overtake on the left in the UK
6 wear a helmet in the UK
7 turn right
8 turn left
9 give way

2 Express the following using a form of *must* or *have to*.

1 It is wrong to drink and drive.
2 It is not necessary to park with your lights on.
3 It is the law that you stop when the lights are red.
4 It was necessary for me to drive with care when I first passed my driving test.
5 Many years ago it wasn't necessary to wear seatbelts.
6 It is against the law to drive at more than 70 miles per hour.
7 You do not need to make hand signals when you turn nowadays.
8 It is necessary to stop when a policeman tells you to.

3 Complete these sentences using the reflexive form of the verb in brackets, if necessary.

1 When he had the accident, he ... (hurt).
2 I don't need help to repair the car. I can ... it (do).
3 You can't go out in those clothes. You must ... (change).
4 The first day I drove by myself in my car, I really ... (enjoy).
5 He is usually so late for work that he ... (dress) on the way in the car.
6 When I was seventeen, I ... to drive (teach).
7 The food is on the table through there. Go and ... (help).
8 I don't think it was an accident. I think she ... (kill).

4 There is a mistake in each of the following sentences. Find and correct the mistakes.

1. You mustn't to drive so fast.
2. I hurt me in a car accident.
3. The children are too young to drive themselves.
4. Learner drivers have show special plates.
5. Does she has to have a driving licence?
6. We didn't had to wear seatbelts in 1980.
7. Let's meet us at 11 o'clock.
8. You don't have to tell him the secret.

5 Rewrite the sentences using adverbs.

1. She is a quick learner.
   ➡ *She learns quickly.*
2. They eat a healthy diet.
3. He is a slow driver.
4. I am a bad tennis player.
5. I am a hard worker.
6. We are safe skiers.
7. I am happy to go to school.
8. He is a good cook.

6 🎧 Listen to the people talking. Work with a partner and write about driving in the 1930s and the 1990s using the pictures and questions.

How did people drive in the 1930s?
How do people drive in the 1990s?
Did they have to have a driving licence?
How old do you have to be to take your driving test?
Did people like driving then?
Why did people like driving then?

What things are difficult to learn?
Was it easy to park?
Is it easy to park?
How many people were there on the roads?
How many people are there on the roads?

THE WORLD OF WORK

Motoring
Autofahren

1 Can you match the driver and car with what they say about themselves?

1. My name's Ron Mead. I'm a driving instructor and I drive a normal family saloon. I think safe driving is very important, but I'm not sure that my 17-year-old pupils agree!

2. I'm a racing driver. I love driving fast but I train very hard, so that I can do it safely. Accidents happen when people get frustrated and bored.

3. I'm PC Graves and I'm a traffic police officer. I have to drive a high-speed car because I need to drive after all the speed freaks who go too fast and very dangerously. I don't think that it is safe to drive faster than 70 miles per hour.

a

b

c

2 Practise the dialogue using the words in the box.

In a car showroom ...

SALESPERSON   Hello, what sort of car are you interested in?

CUSTOMER   Hello, I'm a ... , so I'm looking for something ... .

SALESPERSON   I see. Well, I think you should have a look at our ... . What price do you have in mind?

CUSTOMER   Mmm, well I'd love to try something really expensive but I shouldn't really spend more than ... .

SALESPERSON   OK, fine. How about test-driving this model? I think it's just what you're looking for!

family man	safe	family saloons	£10,000
business woman	expensive-looking	executive models	£35,000
house husband	small as a second car	hatchbacks	£6,000
farmer	big	4-wheel drive, off-road vehicles	£25,000
speed freak	fast	sports car	£100,000

THE WORLD OF WORK

③ 🎧 **Listen to the sounds and say what you think is happening. Form sentences from the words in the box.**

> *It sounds like someone is starting a car.*

open the car door
put on the seatbelt
start a car
accelerate
change gear
slow down
brake hard
crash into something!

④ **Changing a tyre: put the pictures in the correct order.**

a Take off the old wheel.

b Make sure the brake is on.

c Use the jack and lift the car up.

d Lower the car and do up the nuts.

e Put on the new wheel.

f Take off the hubcap.

g Take off the nuts.

h Put back the hubcap.

⑤ **Look at the form below and work with a partner to describe what Tom did well and what he did badly/didn't do in his driving test. Did he pass or fail?**

Name: Tom Watkins   Date: 12 March

Passed ✓   Failed ✗

1. Good eyesight ✓	7. Look in the mirror before
2. Know the Highway Code ✓	signalling ✓
3. Start the car ✓	changing direction ✓
4. Stop the vehicle in an	changing speed ✗
emergency ✗	8. Keep to the correct speed limit ✓
5. Reverse ✗	9. Follow behind other vehicles
6. Turn round in the road ✓	at a correct distance ✗
	10. Act properly at road junctions ✓

UNIT 8 • ON THE ROAD!

9 THE USA AND THE BIG APPLE

1 🔊 **Two European visitors are talking in New York.**

BOB How long have you been over here?

LEILA I've been here for three days. And you?

BOB I have just arrived. What have you done since you've been here?

LEILA Oh, quite a lot. I've done all the tourist things ... You know, I went up the World Trade Center. There's a great view from the 110th floor. I saw the Statue of Liberty, I walked round Chinatown, ... all that sort of thing. I have never seen a livelier city. It's true when they say it never sleeps. Have you been here before?

BOB Yes, but I haven't been here since I was a child, when I came with my parents, so this is like my first time, really. Have you seen Central Park yet?

LEILA No, I haven't. Not yet.

BOB They say it's really great. You forget you are in the city. You know, it's bigger than the country of Monaco!

LEILA Really? I've heard they do some great concerts and plays there, but I spoke to a police officer this morning and he told me that it is too dangerous to go there at night. I'd still like to go though – but not when it's dark.

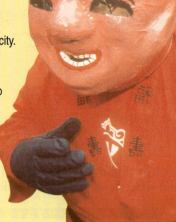

Before you start ...

People say that in America everything is bigger than in the UK. The cars are bigger, the buildings are bigger and the people are bigger. Some British people also think that Americans are too loud and that they have no sense of humour. Do you agree with them? What do you think about America and the Americans?

2 Here is an interview with Sergeant Moreno of the New York Police Department, who gives some advice about the Big Apple.

INTERVIEWER Is your job a stressful one?
MORENO Yeah. I guess it is pretty stressful. I mean, New York City is probably the most exciting city in the world and working the streets here in a patrol car is no joke, I can tell you.
INTERVIEWER Can you give me any examples of stressful things you have seen or done recently?
MORENO Well, take last night, for example. In a couple of hours or so, I filled out three accident reports, I picked up two guys for drug dealing, and I arrested a pickpocket. I haven't been home since the night before last.
INTERVIEWER Have you ever seen anything violent?
MORENO You kidding? Practically every week there's something. It's gotten a lot better over the last few years but, for example, last week there was an armed robbery and er ... I helped a guy with a bad knife wound.
INTERVIEWER What advice can you give to tourists?
MORENO Well, for a start, walking the streets of New York at night is not advisable. You should stay away from places like Harlem, Times Square and even parts of Upper West Side. And I warn you, don't go into Central Park at night. That's where a lot of the murders take place! But that doesn't mean you've got to miss the night life. I mean, that's what New York is all about.
INTERVIEWER So what's the best way to get around?
MORENO My advice: if you want to see the night life, take a cab. During the day, the subway is cheap and fast and you should take a ride just to see the grafitti, but don't choose empty cars.
INTERVIEWER It all sounds a bit frightening.
MORENO No, don't get me wrong. New York's a great place. I mean, we have the best hot dogs in America. You just got to be careful when you're walking around on the streets.

Working with the texts

1 Answer these questions about text 1.

1 Who has been in New York City longer, Bob or Leila?
2 List three places that Leila has visited so far.
3 How does Leila describe New York City?
4 Has Bob visited New York City before?
5 Has Bob visited Central Park before?
6 What does Bob think of Central Park?
7 What happens in Central Park?
8 Does Leila want to visit Central Park?

UNIT 9 • THE USA AND THE BIG APPLE

2 Which sentences in text 1 tell us the following?

1 Bob has not been in New York very long.
2 New York is a very busy city.
3 This is the first time Bob has been to New York for many years.
4 Bob has heard good reports about Central Park.
5 Central Park is big.
6 There are interesting things to do in Central Park.

3 Which of the following pictures are described in text 2? Use the examples to make your answers.

➡ *Sergeant Moreno has recently … .*
Sergeant Moreno has not recently … .

arrested a young pickpocket

had a quiet life

rescued a dog

chased a speed freak

arrested people for drug-dealing

filled out a road accident report

looked after a wounded man

shot a murderer

4 Look at text 2 and correct the statements. Say why they are wrong.

1 The American name for the USA is 'Big Apple'.
2 Sergeant Moreno walks around the streets of New York in his job as a police officer.
3 His job is an easy one and he doesn't work very hard.
4 Violence in New York City is worse than it was.
5 Central Park is peaceful at night.
6 Sergeant Moreno doesn't think that tourists should go out in New York at night.
7 Sergeant Moreno says that tourists shouldn't use the subway.
8 Sergeant Moreno says that other cities in America have better hot dogs.

Language Review

PRESENT PERFECT *(Das Perfekt)*

Aussagen und Verneinungen			
I / You / We / They	have	(not)	seen Central Park.
He / She / It	has		

Informationsfragen			
Where	have	I / you / we / they	been?
	has	she / he / it	

Ja/Nein-Fragen		
Have	I / you / we / they	walked round Chinatown yet?
Has	he / she	

Kurzantworten
Yes, I have./No, I haven't.
Yes, we have./No, we haven't.
Yes, they have./No, they haven't.
Yes, he has./No, he hasn't.
Yes, she has./No, she hasn't.

- Das *present perfect* wird mit *have(n't)/has(n't)* und dem Partizip Perfekt gebildet. Bei regelmäßigen Verben hat das Partizip dieselbe Form wie die des *simple past* (Infinitiv + *-ed*). Unregelmäßige Verben haben eine besondere Form, die man lernen muss (Liste s. S. 261.)
- Das *present perfect* verbindet die Vergangenheit mit der Gegenwart. Es bezeichnet Handlungen oder Zustände, die in der Vergangenheit begannen und in der Gegenwart noch andauern. Es wird häufig ohne Zeitangabe benutzt. Dabei ist nicht der Zeitpunkt, sondern die Handlung wichtig.
  I've heard that they do some great concerts in Central Park.
- Es wird oft mit folgenden Signalwörtern benutzt: *already, ever, just, never, yet, today, this week, so far.*
- *For* und *since* sind wichtige Signalwörter für das *present perfect. Since* bezeichnet einen Zeitpunkt, während *for* auf einen Zeitraum hinweist. *I've been here* **since Tuesday/for three days**.
- *Been to/gone to*: Mit *been to* wird über eine Erfahrung berichtet: *I've been to* Chinatown. *Gone to* wird verwendet, wenn die Person noch nicht zurück ist: *Bob isn't here, he* **has gone to** *America*.

"I've never seen anybody drive through New York so fast."

"Yes, you have – you arrested me last month for the same thing!"

Practice

1 Look at these verbs and say what the infinitives are.

> lived   been   seen   drunk   felt   stayed
> visited   begun   written   driven   had

2 Make sentences with the same verbs.

1. she/never/to the USA
2. you/the Statue of Liberty/many times
3. I/ten postcards since breakfast
4. her children/already/to enjoy life in the USA
5. he/fast/all his life but he/not/an accident
6. he/in the USA/for eight years but/Coke/yet
7. she/excited/about going back to New York since her first visit
8. I/in the USA a few times, but I/never/the Grand Canyon

3 Complete the sentences with *for* or *since*.

1. She has lived in the USA ... seven years.
2. He hasn't seen his family ... 1982.
3. They haven't taken a holiday ... a long time.
4. I have been in love with New York ... the day I first saw it.
5. They haven't seen each other ... ages!
6. There have been 41 US presidents ... George Washington.
7. She hasn't driven a car ... she had an accident.
8. I haven't been home ... quite a while.

4 Louisa still has a day left in San Francisco. Look at her plans for the trip. Say what she has and hasn't done yet.

UNIT 9 • THE USA AND THE BIG APPLE

5 In pairs, ask and answer questions.

1   she/see/Statue of Liberty?   not yet
    ➡ **A** *Has she seen the Statue of Liberty yet?*   **B** *No, she hasn't seen it yet.*
2   he/be/to New York?   5   he/visit/USA?
    yes/twice   yes/already/several times
3   she/write/to her parents?   6   they/be/to Central Park?
    not since/arrive   yes/see/concert
4   how long/he live/USA?
    since 1986

6 Listen to Leila phoning home from New York and answer the questions.

1   Has she been to see the Statue of Liberty?
2   When did she go to the World Trade Center?
3   Has she been to the Bronx?
4   Why hasn't she been to Central Park at night?
5   When did she go to meet Paddy and where?
6   Why didn't Paddy arrive?
7   How did she find out that Paddy wasn't coming?
8   Do you think she is having a good time? Why?

7 Rewrite the sentences using the words in brackets.

1   I have lived in America for over fifteen years. (1982)
2   Do you know San Francisco? (ever/be)
3   America has been independent since 1788. (for)
4   I do not know New York. (never/visit)
5   She looks very worried. Is this her first flight? (fly/before)
6   He left for the airport. (already/go)
7   He wants to go to Disneyworld, but he still hasn't been. (he/always/want)
8   I'm sorry. I can't remember the way there. (forget/how/get there)

8 Complete the text with the correct form (simple past or present perfect) of the words in the box.

arrive	become	like	decide	go	use	miss	have
plan	spend	be	work	develop		make	

BORIS STELZL [1]... in the US a year ago. He [2]... there on holiday, but he [3]... it so much that he [4]... to stay. For the last four months, Boris [5]... a student at USC. He says he [6]... not ... very hard and [7]... a lot of lectures so far but he [8]... a great time! He [9]... nearly all of his time on the beach and he [10]... a pretty good surfer. Maybe he [11]... not ... his brain very much but he [12]... certainly ... his body and his English. He [13]... lots of friends and has a girlfriend Patti, who looks like the girls from Baywatch. Boris expects to go back to Europe this month, but he [14]... already ... to come back to the States next year.

THE WORLD OF WORK

Getting around
Bummeltipps

The Tourists' New York

★ Coming in to JFK Airport in the borough of Queens.

★ Go to 5th Avenue for the best window-shopping in the world.

★ Is baseball your game? See the NY Mets at the Shea Stadium in Queens or the New York Yankees at the Yankee Stadium in the Bronx.

★ Ride the elevator to the top floor of the World Trade Center in Manhattan.

★ Come to Brooklyn for the best delicatessens and the real New York accent.

★ The world-famous Statue of Liberty in the harbor of NYC.

★ The Manhattan skyline from the Staten Island Ferry.

THE WORLD OF WORK

1 Look at the photos of New York and answer the tourists' questions.

1 Can you tell me where the airport is, please?
2 Where can I find the Statue of Liberty?
3 I'd like to see a baseball game. Where do I go for that?
4 I've heard a lot about the World Trade Center, but where is it, please?
5 I've seen everything but a real New York delicatessen. Where can I find one?
6 I want to see that famous Manhattan skyline! What's the best way to do it?
7 I've come to New York for the shops. Where are the most famous ones?

2 Imagine you are on holiday in New York. Work with a partner to write a postcard home about your stay.

How long have you been in New York?
Which parts of the city have you visited?
Have you had a good time?
Which is the best part of the city?
What has the weather been like?

3 Match the questions and answers.

1 Where can I get a cab downtown?
2 Can you take me to the airport, please?
3 How much is a round trip ticket to the station?
4 How far is it to the next gas station, please?
5 Where is the nearest subway station?
6 Where can I find a mailbox?
7 Is there a drugstore near here?
8 Is there a restaurant in this hotel?

a About two miles.
b Certainly, madam, take the elevator to the top floor.
c You have to get two one way tickets, one there and one back. A one way ticket is $3.50.
d Yes, get in.
e There's one just round that corner. You can't miss it.
f Yes, there is. It's along here on the right.
g Over there, by the departure gate.
h There's one on the sidewalk over there.

4 Say the questions and answers again, putting in the British words from the box in place of the American words.

| chemist's | tube | taxi | into town | return ticket |
| lift | petrol | pavement | postbox | single ticket |

5 🎧 Listen to two girls talking about themselves. Which is English and which American? If you can, make a list of the things which are different in American English and British English.

UNIT 9 • THE USA AND THE BIG APPLE   77

10 EUROPE AND THE EUROPEANS

🔊 Some British teenagers are talking about their future and their opinions about Europe.

LEO I hate learning French and German. I really don't see the point. I mean, I'll never work anywhere but here and when you go on holiday everyone speaks English anyway.

JACK You don't know where you'll end up working. I'll go wherever there's a job. But I know what you mean about the languages ... other people in Europe really have to learn English but at least it's easy for them to know that it will be useful.

HANNAH Yeah, ... but we never know which one to learn ... French, Spanish, Italian, Dutch ... it just goes on and on. We can't see which one we'll need in the future.

MELANIE Well, I think it's great to learn a language, so that you can go to other countries and really find out how they live. I'm going to get my NNEB * and then I'm going to work as a nanny in lots of different countries. I'll be able to learn the language while I'm there ... it'll be much better than doing it in the classroom!

LEO But teenagers in other countries live mostly like us anyway, don't they? I mean they eat hamburgers and drink Coke. They see the same films and listen to the same music.

Before you start ...

People say that you shouldn't think in stereotypes but sometimes it's very difficult not to! Do you think the adjectives in the box describe these nationalities?

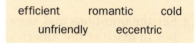

efficient   romantic   cold
unfriendly   eccentric

British

German

French

Italian

Swedish

What words would you use to describe a typical German person? Are you like that?

78 UNIT 10 • EUROPE AND THE EUROPEANS

MELANIE I know lots of things are the same for everyone nowadays but national differences are still very strong. I mean we all know about the efficient Germans, the snobby French and the passionate Italians, don't we?

JACK Oh, Melanie ... those are just stereotypes. There are millions of people in those countries. I wonder what other countries think British people are like?

JACK They probably think we all speak like the Queen and live in little cottages and drink tea all day.

MELANIE In other words, they think all British people are English. I know some Scottish people who get really cross about that.

HANNAH And the Welsh and the Irish. I wonder if other countries have such different sorts of people in them?

LEO Of course they do! What about the Basques in Spain and I've heard the Bavarians in Germany are very different from other Germans.

Jack I bet Europe in the future will be just like the UK then. Loads of people all speaking the same language but all making sure that they stay different from each other.

*The NNEB is the qualification necessary to work as a nursery nurse in the UK.

Working with the text

1 **Correct the statements about the text.**

1 The teenagers agree that all British people are English.
2 Jack says that people in Europe don't have to learn English.
3 Melanie doesn't want to learn a language.
4 Leo likes learning French and German.
5 Leo says that the Bavarians are the same as all other Germans.
6 Hannah knows which language to learn.
7 Melanie is going to work as a receptionist.
8 Leo says that the Basques come from France.
9 Jack only wants to work in Britain.
10 Leo thinks that teenagers in other countries don't eat fast food.

2 Look at this map which shows the countries in the European Union and complete the sentences below.

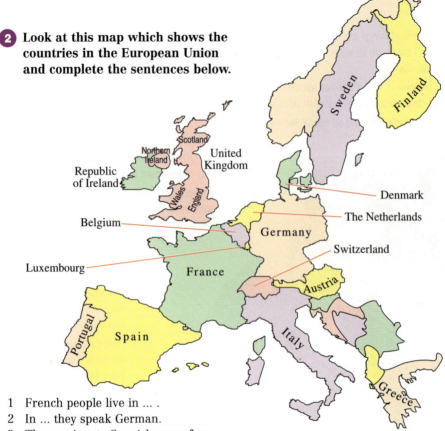

1. French people live in ... .
2. In ... they speak German.
3. The passionate Spanish come from ... .
4. Italian cheese is made in ... .
5. In ... the Dutch grow lots of tulips.
6. People speak English all over the world but the English live in ... .
7. Three countries make up Britain. They are ... .
8. Southern Irish people are not British. They live in ... .

3 Work in pairs. Which nationalities of the European Union were in the text and which were not? Use the map to help you.

4 Look at the statements below. Which of the teenagers would agree with each one?

1. French people are rather snobbish.
2. The Bavarians are different from other German people.
3. English people find it hard to know which foreign languages to learn.
4. When English people go on holiday abroad, they find that most people speak English well.
5. It's better to learn another language in that country rather than in the classroom.
6. Teenagers all over the world listen to the same music and see the same films.
7. People in the UK all speak the same language but there are still strong national differences.
8. National differences in Europe are very strong.

80 UNIT 10 • EUROPE AND THE EUROPEANS

Language Review

1 WILL-FUTURE (Will-*Zukunft*)

Europe in the future **will be** just like the UK.
I **won't** ever **work** anywhere but here.
I**'ll phone** you later – **will** you **be** at home?

- *Will* wird verwendet, um über zukünftige Ereignisse zu sprechen, die nicht beeinflusst werden können, aber auch um subjektive Vorhersagen zu machen.
- Diese Form wird auch benutzt, um Versprechungen und spontane Entscheidungen auszudrücken.
- *Will* + Infinitiv wird für alle Personen verwendet. Die Verneinung von *will* heißt *won't*.
  Um Fragen zu bilden, wird *will* mit dem Subjekt vertauscht.

2 PRESENT CONTINUOUS WITH FUTURE MEANING
(Verlaufsform der Gegenwart mit zukünftiger Bedeutung)

We **are flying** to France next week.
He **isn't coming** with us.
What **are** you **doing** tomorrow?

- Das *present continuous* mit Zeitbestimmungen wird gebraucht, um feste Abmachungen und Pläne für die Zukunft auszudrücken.

3 GOING TO-FUTURE (Going to-*Zukunft*)

I**'m going to get** my NNEB.
She **isn't going to have** a holiday this year.
What **are** you **going to do** after school?

- *Going to* wird verwendet, um über zukünftige Pläne und Absichten zu sprechen.
- Die *going to*-Zukunft wird mit *am/is/are* + Infinitiv gebildet.

4 SIMPLE PRESENT-FUTURE *(Einfache Gegenwart für die Zukunft)*

The next performance of the film **starts** at 6 o'clock.
This train **doesn't run** next Sunday.
What time **does** your plane **land**?
Now look at your schedule: at 6.00 pm the plane **arrives**, then you **go** to your hotel and **check in** and at 8.00 pm we all **meet** for dinner.

- Das *simple present* wird verwendet, um über Stunden-/Fahrpläne, Kino-/Theaterveranstaltungen usw. zu sprechen.

Practice

1 Put the verbs in brackets into the correct form, using *will/won't*.

1 I ... (meet) you at the airport on Friday.
2 I ... (not see) you tonight because I ... (be) late.
3 They ... (return) from their holiday with a suntan.
4 You ... (not like) Switzerland if you don't like walking.
5 I think the play at the New Theatre ... (finish) late tonight.
6 I dón't like French food, so I don't think I ... (go) to France.
7 I ... (not go) to the disco tonight if you don't want me to.
8 I know he's late but he ... (be) here. I know he ... (come).

2 Answer these questions using *going to*.

1 What are you going to do this evening?
2 When are you going to revise for your exams?
3 Where are you going to spend your holiday this year?
4 When are you going to finish school and start work?
5 When are you going to do your English homework?
6 Are you going to see a film soon?
7 When are you going to take your driving test?
8 Are you going to have a maths lesson this week?

3 Make statements about the Europe of the future.

1 be/one European currency

➡ *It is possible that, by the year 2050, there will be one European currency.*

2 German people/not speak German
3 Russia/be in the European Union
4 being European/normal
5 people/not stereotype other nationalities
6 be/president of Europe
7 England/not be in Europe
8 the British/drive on the right
9 be/one European police force

4 🔊 Listen to the people talking and answer the questions.

1 Which of the speakers is English?
2 Which speakers use English in their jobs?
3 Which speakers are going to work abroad?
4 Which speakers are going to learn a new language next year? Which one?
5 Who just uses English for leisure activities?
6 Who works in London?
7 Who speaks English on the telephone?
8 Who doesn't want to learn a language?

5 🔊 Make a list of the countries and nationalities of the people speaking.

Which is the most difficult speaker to understand? Can you tell that they have different accents? Can you understand Mike's accent?

UNIT 10 • EUROPE AND THE EUROPEANS

6 Imagine you are telling a friend what he/she will see when he/she visits the different European countries shown in the brochures below. Look at the words in each of the boxes to help you. Use your own words as well.

➡ When you go to Italy, you'll see some beautiful clothes.
In Italy you'll have some delicious food.

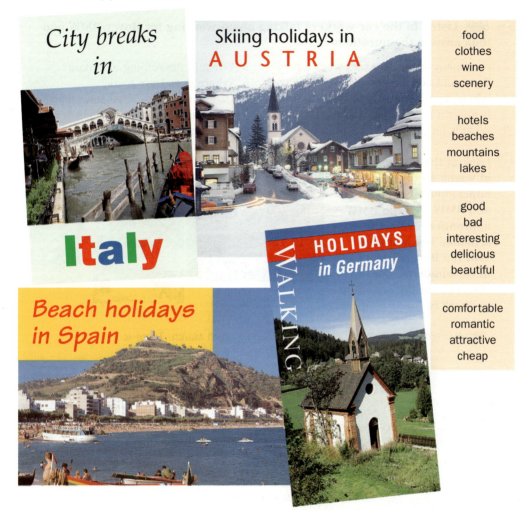

food
clothes
wine
scenery

hotels
beaches
mountains
lakes

good
bad
interesting
delicious
beautiful

comfortable
romantic
attractive
cheap

7 Complete the sentences using one of the future forms.

1 We ... (camp) in the south of France this year.
2 I ... (learn) German next year, so that I can go and work there.
3 He doesn't like his new jeans, so he ... (change) them.
4 The disco ... (go on) until 1.00 am tonight.
5 We're really excited because we ... (get) a new car.
6 They ... (go) to the travel agent's to buy their plane tickets on Thursday.
7 ... (your girlfriend/come) with us on holiday to Turkey?
8 ... (you/do) your homework before you go out?

THE WORLD OF WORK

Working in a car factory
Arbeiten im Automobilwerk

1 🔊 Listen to the car workers talking about working for Rover/BMW and then answer the questions below.

1. How many of the speakers work for Rover and how many for BMW?
2. Where does Lynn work in the factory?
3. Is Rover a popular place to work? Why?
4. What is Birgit's job?
5. When is she coming to Britain?
6. Where does Dave work?
7. Can you describe what Dave does?
8. Which of the British workers is going to Germany?

2 Look at the photographs of young engineering apprentices from Rover and BMW. Tell the BMW apprentices what the schedule is when they visit the Rover factory in Birmingham. Use the verbs in the schedule or *there is*.

➡ You arrive at Heathrow at 10.30 on Tuesday 18th March. There is …

TUESDAY 18th MARCH

10.30	*Arrive Heathrow.*
12.30	*Lunch in the factory canteen.*
1.30	*Welcome from the Rover Managing Director.*
2.00	*English and German apprentices meet.*
2.30	*Tour of the factory.*
4.00	*Introduction to project work.*
5.30	*Leave the factory to meet the host families.*

WEDNESDAY 19th MARCH – FRIDAY 21st MARCH

9.00 to 5.00	*English and German apprentices work in teams to design and build a radio-controlled car.*	5.30	*Demonstration of radio-controlled cars.*
		6.00	*Prize-giving for best design.*
		7.00	*Farewell meal and disco.*

SATURDAY 22nd MARCH

9.00	*Leave Birmingham for Heathrow.*

UNIT 10 • EUROPE AND THE EUROPEANS

THE WORLD OF WORK

3 Look at the curriculum vitae (CV) below and write your own.

CURRICULUM VITAE

NAME Ruth Jackson

DATE OF BIRTH 18.9.1980

NATIONALITY British

HOME ADDRESS 19 Park Avenue, Solihull, Birmingham B21 8UJ

EDUCATIONAL QUALIFICATIONS
1992–97 Banner Park Comprehensive, Solihull

GCSE	English	C
	Maths	B
	Science	C
	Art	A
	History	D
	Geography	D

1997– Perry Barr College, Birmingham

GNVQ Engineering (June 1999)

REFEREES

Ms Helen Wells Personal Tutor, Perry Barr College, Frith Road, Perry Barr, Birmingham B34 7BN

Mr Martin Stubbs Manager, British Supermarkets, Avonlea Trading Estate, Birmingham B42 2SG

4 When you apply for a job, employers like you to tell them about your hobbies. Below is what Ruth Jackson put on her CV. What would you write?

HOBBIES AND LEISURE ACTIVITIES

I am a very active person and enjoy outdoor pursuits very much. I belong to a climbing club and I am learning how to do water-skiing. At school I was the captain of the tennis team and I took part in hockey and athletics as well. At college I am in the tennis team and have also had the chance to join the girls' football team. In my leisure time, I like going to concerts with my friends. My favourite bands are Blur and Oasis.

UNIT 10 • EUROPE AND THE EUROPEANS

LANGUAGE WORKOUT

HOLIDAY COTTAGE

This lovely holiday cottage has beautiful views from all its windows across the romantic scenery of the lakes and mountains of North Wales. It is only five minutes' walk
5 from the nearest shops but it is very peaceful. There are two bedrooms with beds for five people, the kitchen has a cooker, a fridge, a table and six chairs and the living room has a colour TV and video. An ideal
10 cottage for the perfect family holiday!

Revision

1 Correct the statements. Start each sentence with *No, it isn't* or *No, there isn't/aren't*.

1 The cottage is in England.

➡ *No, it isn't. It is in Wales.*

2 There are horrible views from the cottage.
3 It is twenty minutes' walk from the nearest shops.
4 The cottage is near a beach.
5 There are three bedrooms in the cottage.
6 There are five chairs in the kitchen.
7 There is a hi-fi in the living room.
8 The cottage is big enough for eight people.
9 The cottage is ideal for single people.

2 Work with a partner to find the opposites of three of the adjectives in the text.

3 Change all the sentences to the third person singular of the simple present (*he* or *she*).

1 They go to a holiday cottage every Christmas.
2 You have a nice time in the mountains.
3 We like going to the cinema.
4 I prefer lively cities to peaceful lakes.
5 You choose to ski in April rather than December.
6 I like going to the beach when I am on holiday.
7 When we are on holiday, we often eat out in restaurants.
8 You often fly to America.

4 Find the odd ones out and say why.

1 Dutch   Spanish   Irish   England
2 house   flat   car   cottage
3 England   German   Wales   Scotland
4 town   shop   city   village
5 New York   London   Oxford   Birmingham
6 nice   awful   great   badly
7 go   come   was   see
8 banana   dinner   breakfast lunch

Revision exercises and exam practice

Exam practice

a Find a noun.

beautiful (line 1)
romantic (line 3)
peaceful (line 6)

b Find a verb.

shops (line 5)
cooker (line 7)

c Explain in a complete sentence.

cottage (line 1)
living room (lines 8–9)

d Give the principal parts of the verbs.

has (line 1)
is (line 4)

Writing: A letter to a penfriend

Look at the letter written by a penfriend. Write an answer using the example as a model.

> Jenny Grove
> 1 Hendon Road
> London NW10 9ZF
>
> 10 August 19..
>
> Hello!
>
> I am looking for a German penfriend. I hope you will like my letter and write back. I already have penfriends in America and Japan and I really enjoy reading all about life in different countries in their letters.
>
> My name is Jenny and I am 16. I live with my mother, father and two brothers in Hendon, which is in London, England. I have just finished at school and I am waiting for my GCSE exam results. I hope I pass because I want to go on to college and do a GNVQ in catering. I think catering is a good qualification to get because you can go anywhere in the world afterwards and get a good job.
>
> In my spare time, when I'm not writing to penfriends, I listen to music and go to discos. I won't tell you what sort of music I like until you write back and tell me what you like!
>
> Bye for now!
> Jenny

11 IT'S NOT A BAD PLACE TO LIVE

1 🔊 **A visitor asks the way.**

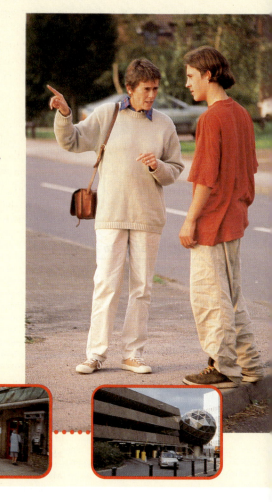

VISITOR Excuse me. Is there a place round here where I can get a passport photo?

WOMAN Yes. Let me see ... Do you know where the newsagent's is? There's a post office just opposite and there's a photo booth inside, at the back.

VISITOR No. I'm afraid I don't know my way round here.

WOMAN Oh, well ... er ... Go along here till you get to the optician's on the corner of the crossroads. If you turn left down the High Street, you'll find the post office half way down, on the right. Just next to a launderette. There's a post box in front of it, so you can't miss it.

VISITOR Great! Thank you ... Er, if I go in my car, will I be able to park round there?

WOMAN Not really. There are double yellow lines all along there, but there's a multi-storey car park in the town centre, behind the supermarket.

Before you start ...

What sort of place is it where you live?

| lively | quiet | boring | exciting |

Is there a lot to do? What sort of facilities are there?

| pub | library | leisure centre | hospital | cinema |

88 UNIT 11 • IT'S NOT A BAD PLACE TO LIVE

2 🔊 Some young people describe where they live.

Ken

If you like a lively atmosphere, this village won't appeal to you. It has a church, a farm and a few cottages and that's it! There aren't any shops and there isn't even a pub. The nearest town is about ten miles away and the village isn't on a bus route, so if you haven't got your own transport, it's a bit of a problem. For me, it's just perfect.

Tracy

I live in the suburbs. I don't like it because there's nothing to do and it is not easy to get in and out of town. If I get the chance, I will move somewhere more central in another town. The last bus here is at ten, so you can't do very much. I don't think this town has got a lot to offer young people and the shops are pretty boring. If you like going out a lot, you won't like living here.

Carole

I live right in the centre of town. It's great because everything's so handy. It's a little noisy sometimes, but you get used to it. We've got more or less everything here. There's a leisure centre with a cinema, a swimming pool and squash courts, there are good bus and rail services, all the main types of shops, a hospital and some good restaurants. Parking can be a pain at times, but on the whole, it's OK.

Working with the texts

1 Are the following statements right or wrong? Correct the wrong ones.

1 The visitor wants to know where the post office is.
2 The visitor knows the town well.
3 The post office is next to the newsagent's.
4 The post office is not in the High Street.
5 The woman thinks it will be easy for the visitor to find the post office.
6 The visitor is travelling on foot.
7 The visitor probably won't be able to park.
8 There is a multi-storey car park in front of the supermarket.

2 Which of these maps matches the directions in text 1 correctly?

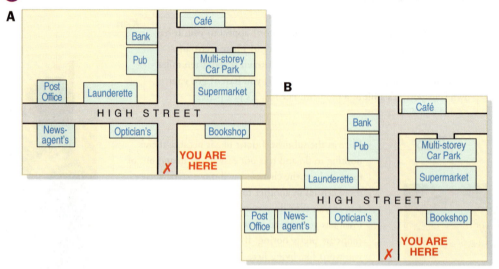

3 Answer the questions on text 2.

1 How does Ken feel about where he lives?
2 What disadvantages does Ken's village have?
3 Carole mentions two possible disadvantages of her town. What are they?
4 Why does Carole like where she lives?
5 How does Tracy feel about where she lives? Why?
6 What is the main disadvantage of where Tracy lives?
7 Which of the three speakers is the most satisfied with where he/she lives?
8 Who is the least satisfied?

4 Find the place in text 2 where ...

1 ... you grow food.
2 ... you can get a beer.
3 ... you can go for sport and entertainment.
4 ... you can see a film.
5 ... you go when you are ill.
6 ... you can eat out.
7 ... there are lots of houses and not much else.
8 ... you can buy things.

5 Complete the statements with words from texts 1 and 2.

1 If you don't like something, you can say it doesn't ... to you.
2 In Britain, you can usually buy magazines, sweets and cigarettes at a ... .
3 They test your eyes at an ... .
4 If a place is easy to find, we say you can't ... it.
5 In Britain, you can't park your car where you see ... .
6 ... can be above ground or below ground and there is usually room for lots of cars.
7 ... are small houses, usually in the country.
8 Many things are difficult at first but then you get ... to them.
9 If you do not have your own transport, it is useful to live ... .
10 ... are areas where people live, a few miles outside the town centres.

Language Review

1 PREPOSITIONS OF PLACE *(Präpositionen des Ortes)*

behind
hinter

in front of
vor

on the corner of
an der Ecke von

on the left/right
*auf der linken/
rechten Seite*

opposite
gegenüber

2 CONDITIONAL I *(Bedingungssätze 1)*

If I **get** the chance, I **will move**.
If you **don't like** a quiet atmosphere, this village **won't appeal** to you.

- Ein Bedingungssatz besteht aus zwei Teilen: einem Nebensatz mit *if (if-clause)* und einem Hauptsatz *(main clause)*.
- Bei *if*-Sätzen des Typs 1 werden reale Bedingungen genannt. Diese Bedingungen werden im *if-clause* mit dem *simple present* ausgedrückt. Die Folge dieser Bedingung wird im *main clause* mit der *will*-Zukunft ausgedrückt.
- Vorangestellte *if-clauses* werden vom Hauptsatz durch ein Komma getrennt.

Practice

1 Look at the map and describe the place.

2 **Look at the map again and complete the sentences using the words in the box.**

> on the right of   on the left of
> next to   behind   in front (of)
> on the corner (of)   opposite

1 The supermarket is ... the launderette.
2 The newsagent's is ... the car park.
3 If you go along Marton Road, from Ship Street, you'll see the cinema ... you.
4 The chemist's is ... the newsagent's.
5 There is a pub ... the railway station.
6 The petrol station is ... the library.
7 The bookshop is ... Ship Street and Park Street.
8 There is a café ... Market Place.

3 **Listen, follow the directions on this map and say where you are.**

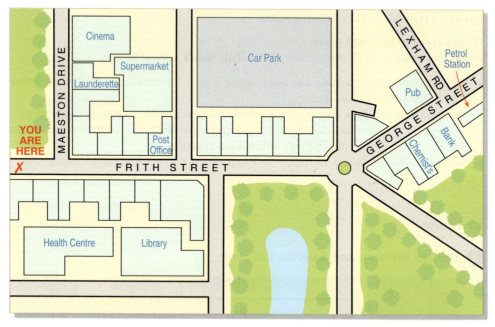

4 **With a partner, study the different ways of asking directions and practise asking the way to the places in the box. Use the map above.**

Can you	tell me	the way to	... ?
		how to get to	... ?
		if there is a	... round here?
	direct me to		... ?
Is there a			... round here?
Where can I find the nearest			... ?

| Go along ... |
| Turn left/right at ... |
| Take the first/second left/right. |
It's	next to ...
	opposite ...
	on the corner of ...
	on the left/right.

chemist's   bank   library   petrol station   pub

5 Complete the sentences using conditional I.

1. What ... (happen) if they ... (build) a new supermarket?
2. You ... (not be able) to park anywhere near the town centre if you ... (take) your car.
3. If she ... (not choose) a house near a bus route, it ... (not be) easy to get to school.
4. Parking ... (be) a bit difficult if you ... (not get) there early.
5. If we ... (take) the third turning at the roundabout, we ... (see) the college on the left.
6. If he ... (wait) until nine o'clock, he ... (have to) use the multi-storey car park.
7. He ... (find) it great living here if he ... (like) peace and quiet.
8. I ... (not go) to college if I ... (not pass) my exams.

6 Rewrite the following sentences using *if* and the other words in brackets.

1. Join the library. You are able to borrow books. (If/join/be able)

   ➡ *If you join the library, you will be able to borrow books.*

2. Turn left at the crossroads. The pub is on the left. (If/turn/see)
3. Hurry up! The last bus is at ten. (If/not hurry/miss)
4. I am bringing a street map. Is your house easy to find? (If/bring/be able)
5. I want to come by car. Can I park there? (If/come/be able)
6. Go along here. There is a chemist's at the crossroads. (If/go along/find)
7. Become a member of the leisure centre! Get fit! (If/become/get fit)
8. Move to the town. Make more friends. (If/move/make)
9. Move to the country. Have a quiet life. (If/move/have)

7 Look at the estate agent's details and make sentences about each house.

➡ *If you like/want ..., ... will appeal to you / will be ideal / will be just right for you.*

E S T A T E   A G E N T S

Rose Cottage
- £220,000
- built in 1821
- 2 bedrooms, bathroom, kitchen, living room
- beautiful garden
- in a quiet country village
- 10 miles from the shops and town centre

Blackwell Flats
- £75,000
- built in 1991
- 1 bedroom, bathroom, small kitchen, living room
- balcony
- in the town centre
- 5 minutes from the shops

Park View
- £198,000
- built in 1960
- 4 bedrooms, bathroom, kitchen, dining room, large living room
- garage + large garden
- near the park
- 1 mile from the town centre

THE WORLD OF WORK

Working with people
Mit Menschen arbeiten

1 Which of the jobs do you think these people are best suited to?

▲ care assistant

nursery nurse ▶

▲ social worker

district nurse ▶

1 Gina is very practical and she is good with people. At college, her favourite subject was biology. She loves talking to old people as well as children. She has already done a first aid course.
2 Tom is strong but very gentle. He is unusual for someone of his age because he likes talking to old people and thinks what they say is interesting.
3 Elizabeth wants to help others and is very patient. She is concerned about people worse off than herself. When she lived at home, she often visited an elderly man next door and helped him with his shopping and cleaning.
4 Jonathan loves children. He has a lot of experience in looking after them because he has six brothers and sisters, all younger than himself! He is a bit worried about being the only male on his course at college.

2 Here are some responsibilities and qualities for the same jobs. Make some sentences, following the examples.

➡ If I become a nursery nurse, I will look after children.
You won't become a district nurse if you can't stand the sight of blood.

1 If I become a nursery nurse/social worker/district nurse/care assistant, I will ...
... help families with problems.
... make old people comfortable.
... know about child development.
... care for sick people in their own homes.
2 You won't become a nursery nurse/social worker/district nurse/care assistant if you ...
... are very impatient.
... are nervous of children.
... don't know what to say to old people.
... faint at the sight of a needle.

3 Can you make sentences like these about other jobs?

UNIT 11 • IT'S NOT A BAD PLACE TO LIVE

THE WORLD OF WORK

4 🔊 Listen to four people talking about their needs. Listen again and look at these leaflets from a community centre in Britain. Which leaflet does each speaker need?

1
People with special needs
How we can help.

2

Providing HIV Education
How to avoid getting it, where to go for a test if you are worried.

3
Job Seekers Allowance

What you can claim and how to claim it.

4
Home Security
HOW TO crack crime

5
Caring for someone?

You could claim money and get other kinds of help.

6
BE A CARING MOTORIST
Save energy, save the environment.

7
Part-time work
Your rights as a part-time worker.

8
YOUNG PEOPLE AND DRUGS
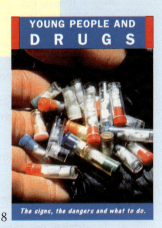
The signs, the dangers and what to do.

5 Look at the leaflets which the people on the cassette do not talk about. Who are they for, do you think?

6 The following are also connected with working for the community. Describe two of them.

dental nurse	traffic warden
fire officer	police officer
	prison officer

UNIT 11 • IT'S NOT A BAD PLACE TO LIVE

LANGUAGE WORKOUT

Revision

roundabout	salesperson	model
sports car	fast	car showroom
crashed	brake	speed limit
car	signs	drive

1 Look at the pictures and fill in the missing words.

Jed is in a ...¹. He wants to buy a new ...². He loves driving ...³, so he wants to buy a ...⁴. He wants to be able to ...⁵ from 0–60 miles per hour in 20 seconds! The ...⁶ shows him the latest ...⁷ and asks him if he would like a test drive. Jed is very happy and drives carefully away. In town he does not drive faster than the 30 mph ...⁸, but soon he is away and ignores the ...⁹. Suddenly he comes up to a ...¹⁰ and cannot ...¹¹ quickly enough. He has ...¹² the car: what is he going to do about it?

2 Finish the statements below with a question tag.

1. Jed loves driving fast, ...?
2. He wants a test drive, ...?
3. Jed is very happy, ...?
4. He drives carefully away, ...?
5. In town he does not drive faster than 30 mph, ...?

Make three questions of your own by putting question tags onto statements in the text.

3 Fill in the correct form of the simple present or present continuous.

1. I ... (drive) my parents' car at the moment.
2. What ... (you/do) this weekend?
3. He usually ... (go) faster than the speed limit.
4. We always ... (put) the car in the garage at night.
5. Sally is out at the moment because she ... (take) her driving test.
6. When I ... (come) to a roundabout, I ... (brake) gently.
7. Look at him. He ... (drive) too fast. There is a speed limit on this road.
8. She normally ... (like) driving, but she ... (not enjoy) her test.

Revision exercises and exam practice

Exam practice

a Find the infinitive form.

wants (line 1)
would like (line 3)

b Find the missing forms.

positive	comparative	superlative
happy (line 3)		
		latest (line 3)

c Find a modal verb in the text, then make a list of three other modal verbs you know.

d Find an opposite.

new (line 1)
loves (line 1)
happy (line 3)

e Find the adjectives.

fast (line 1)
carefully (line 4)
quickly (line 5)

Writing: The driving test

Look at the drawing of Sarah's driving test and write a description of the route she took and how she did, using some of the expressions given. Did she pass or fail?

| start the engine | brake | drive faster than the speed limit | reverse the car |
| go round the roundabout | turn left | turn right | road signs | crash |

➡ Last week Sarah took her driving test and …

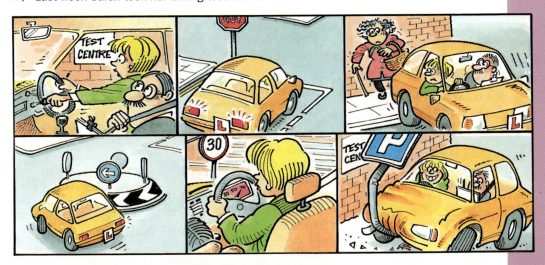

UNIT 11 • IT'S NOT A BAD PLACE TO LIVE

12 THE BEST WAY TO TRAVEL

1

Around the world on a moped

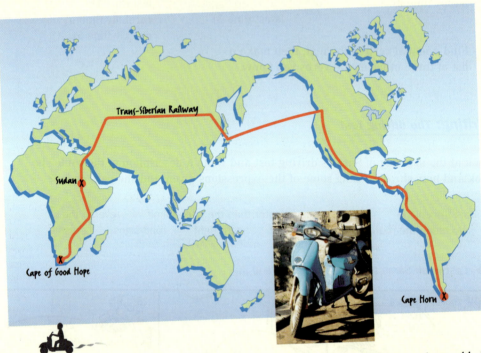

ADAM PAUL will soon start a trip around the world which will last for two years. There is nothing unusual about that except that he is going on an 85cc moped which has a top speed of 64 kph. He is going from Cape Horn to the Cape of Good Hope, through over thirty countries, over a total distance of 72,000 kilometres. Following the Trans-Siberian railway and crossing the Sudan desert will be the most difficult parts of the journey. This would be difficult even if he had a big 4-wheel drive vehicle, but Adam is confident. "If I had a car or a bigger bike, it would be more difficult and more expensive," he said. "Mopeds are more reliable and economical. Mine is a design from the fifties and people use it all over the world. I chose it, so if anything went wrong, it would be easy to repair it." The trip will cost about £15,000. Adam has saved up some of the money over the last two years and the manufacturer of his moped has given him the rest. After all, if Adam finishes the trip, the company will get some very good advertising out of it!

2
Travel now and in the future

There are approximately 125 million cars in the European Union, on about 2.5 million kilometres of roads. Apart from the problems of pollution, we will face serious problems of congestion if we do not do something soon. If we built more roads and governments charged higher taxes, this would help, but it wouldn't solve the problem. For example, people would use their cars less if we decided to improve public transport and employees would commute less if employers let them work from home. For those who hate the idea of public transport, the ideal form of transport would surely be some sort of micro-light machine which would transport us to our destination just a few feet above the ground. There would be no traffic jams, no pollution and imagine what fun this would be!

Before you start ...

| on foot | by plane | on horseback | by rail | by car | by bus |

Which is your favourite form of transport? Look at the words in the box and say how you travel to school. For what sort of journey would you use each form of transport?

Working with the texts

1 Answer the questions on text 1.

1. Where is Adam Paul going?
2. How is he travelling?
3. How long will his journey be?
4. How many countries will he visit?
5. Why does he want to go by moped rather than by a bigger bike? Give three reasons.
6. How does Adam feel about his journey?
7. How old is the design model of Adam's moped?
8. Why has the manufacturer of Adam's moped given him some money for his trip?

2 Which definition fits which word from text 1?

> unusual   top speed   confident   reliable   economical

1. This means that Adam was sure everything would be OK.
2. Not expensive to use.
3. Not normal or common.
4. This means you can always depend on it.
5. The fastest something will go.

3 Read text 2 and find ...

1. ... two problems with transport.
2. ... two things which might help the problem.
3. ... two real solutions to the problem.
4. ... an example of possible transport in the future.

4 Say what these words from text 2 mean.

1. pollution (line 3)
2. public transport (line 9)
3. commute (line 10)
4. destination (line 14)
5. traffic jams (line 15)

5 Work with a partner. Look at the way the writer uses the following words in texts 1 and 2. Complete the sentences with these words.

> except that (line 5)   even if (line 18)
> after all (line 36)   apart from (text 2, line 3)

1. ... more people worked from home, this would not solve the problems of traffic congestion and pollution totally.
2. ... the fact that many people don't want to work from home, many of them don't have a room where they could work.
3. A lot of drivers don't realise how big the problem is and that they can help. ... what difference does one car make?
4. Motorways in Europe are more or less the same everywhere, ... some countries now charge drivers for using them.

UNIT 12 • THE BEST WAY TO TRAVEL

Language Review

CONDITIONAL II *(Bedingungssätze 2)*

If I **had** a bigger bike, it **would be** more difficult.
If I **didn't have** such a small bike, it **wouldn't be** so easy.

- Das *conditional II* wird benutzt, um über unwahrscheinliche Bedingungen zu sprechen.
- Das Verb im *if-clause* ist im *simple past*; im *main clause* steht *would (could)* + Infinitiv.
- Es ist nicht möglich, *if* mit *would* im Nebensatz zu verbinden.
- *if* = falls; *when* = wenn immer

Practice

1 Choose the best sentences (a–f) to complete the statements (1–6).

1. If we used our cars less, ...
2. If public transport was more efficient and convenient, ...
3. There would be far less pollution ...
4. If I could choose how to travel, ...
5. If I lived nearer my work, ...
6. I wouldn't go there ...

a ... even if you paid me.
b ... if people didn't commute by car.
c ... I wouldn't commute.
d ... I'd go everywhere on horseback.
e ... I'd use it all the time.
f ... there would be less congestion.

2 Complete these conditional II sentences with the correct forms of the verbs.

1. If I ... (have) a car, I ... (drive) everywhere.
2. She ... (fly) round the world if she ... (can) save enough money.
3. If they ... (go) on holiday with me, they ... (have) a good time.
4. He ... (walk) to work if he ... (not be) so lazy.
5. If there ... (be) a railway station there, we ... (travel) by train, but there isn't.
6. You ... (not take) the bus even if someone ... (pay) you to do it.
7. ... (you/come) to see me if I ... (buy) you your plane ticket?
8. If your Mum ... (say) yes, ... (you/like) to come on holiday with us?

3 Complete the sentences with your own examples.

1. If I had a free ticket to go anywhere in the world, ...
2. If he went by train instead of flying, ...
3. I wouldn't be happy if ...
4. Public transport would be more popular if ...
5. If I really felt like having an adventurous holiday, ...
6. She would definitely drive more carefully if ...
7. If I could work in another country, ...
8. If I had the chance to work from home, ...

4 Conditional I or conditional II? Complete the sentences in the best way.

1 If something is not done soon, we ... (destroy) many of our cities by pollution.
2 Hurry up! You will not arrive in time if you ... (miss) the 9.15 bus.
3 Travelling to work would be much more pleasant if we ... (can) fly over the traffic jams.
4 I am sorry there's not much room. If I had a bigger car, you ... (be) more comfortable.
5 Even if she gets up early, she ... (not arrive) on time.
6 Even if we travelled by spaceship, we still ... (not reach) the stars.
7 I would go round the world by moped if I ... (have) the money.
8 She will be very angry if they ... (stay out) late.

5 Listen to the instructions given to a secret agent about his mission. Study his notes and then correct them.

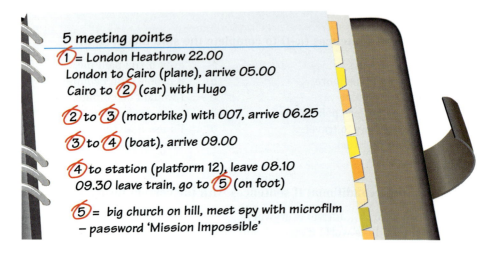

6 Work in pairs. Look at the following situations and first decide if they are (a) possible or (b) not very possible. Then ask and answer questions about what you *will do* or *would do*.

1 There's a good film on TV tonight.

➡ possible

   A *What will you do if there is a good film on TV tonight?*
   B *I'll watch it.*

2 You can speak perfect English!
3 You don't have any homework tonight.
4 A good friend invites you out this evening.
5 You win £100,000 in the lottery.
6 You can't do this exercise.
7 You are the president of the United States.
8 You have the chance to go to the moon.
9 The weather is good this weekend.
10 Your parents offer to buy you a car.

7 Look at the pictures and the statements which describe the situation as it is and use conditional II sentences to describe what would or could happen.

1 He isn't working on his motorbike, so it will never be ready for his next trip.

 If he worked on his motorbike, it would be ready for his next trip.

2 She can't go on holiday because she hasn't got any money.

3 She is stuck in a traffic jam. Going by train is so much quicker.

4 He always has problems finding a parking space for his big car.

5 I have an old bike and my friends always laugh at me when we go out together.

8 You are going to spend a long time on a very small island. You can take the following things with you: 3 CDs, 1 form of transport, 1 luxury item, 1 useful item and 2 items of your choice. What would you take and why? Complete the table in your exercise books.

ITEMS	DETAILS	WHY?
3 CDs		

Now write 80 words starting like this:

If I went to a very small island, I …

UNIT 12 • THE BEST WAY TO TRAVEL

The Travel Business
Tourismus-Branche

1 Match the texts, the jobs and the pictures.

> taxi driver   tourist office clerk
> driving instructor   cabin attendant

MARTIN I'm with a school at the moment but, in two weeks' time, I'm going to work independently. The hours are irregular because most people want lessons at lunchtime, evenings or weekends. I have eight pupils on average a day. You have to get on with people and remain calm!

JUDY It's not a very exciting job as, most of the time, you have to tell people train and bus arrival and departure times. And their connections of course. But you get the satisfaction of helping them. Sometimes you get someone with a really interesting journey. If I had the choice, I think I would like to move to an agency where the work is more to do with international travel.

CLAIRE It's a good job for young, single people. The hours are crazy of course, and it's very tiring because sometimes you work all night. But I wouldn't change it even if I could. I enjoy seeing a bit of the places we go to and the great thing is the discount travel!

TERRY People think it's boring sitting down all day, seeing the same old things, but it's quite interesting actually. There's always something going on and every fare is different. I get some real characters who tell me their life stories. And sometimes you get the rich and famous, though you can't be sure they'll tip well.

2 Answer the questions.

1. Which person do you think works the most regular hours?
2. Which job is the least interesting?
3. Which job is the most interesting, in your opinion, and why?
4. Which of the four people doesn't travel with the job?
5. Can you explain what people's 'connections' are in Judy's text?
6. Would you like any of these jobs? Why?

UNIT 12 • THE BEST WAY TO TRAVEL

THE WORLD OF WORK

3 Which of the jobs opposite would use the following expressions?

1 "Would you put your seat in an upright position, please?"
2 "The fare into town will be about £4.00."
3 "Reverse round the corner and park."
4 "The 8.25 gets in at 10.55. If you missed that, you wouldn't get another connection until the one that leaves at 9.10."

4 Listen to a conversation between a travel agent and a client wanting to fly to Berlin. Take notes of the flight details. Listen again and say what the problem is with the first two flights mentioned.

5 With a partner look at the dialogue below and then use the words given to make new dialogues.

CUSTOMER   Excuse me, could you tell me the best way to travel to ... ?
TRAVEL CLERK Let's see. I think the best way is to go by ... because it's the ... way to get there.
CUSTOMER   Thank you. Could you tell me when the next ... goes?
TRAVEL CLERK I'll just have a look for you. Ah, yes, you need the ... from ... .

Birmingham	rail	quickest	train	11.55	Euston
Edinburgh	air	most convenient	plane	18.20	Heathrow
Brighton	road	cheapest	coach	09.05	Victoria
Isle of Wight	sea	only	boat	04.30	Southampton

6 Look at the photographs of three holiday destinations. Imagine you are writing a description of one of them to go in a travel brochure. What are the attractions of the place you have chosen and what sort of client would it appeal to?

➡ *If you are an outdoor person, a camping holiday will appeal to you. You can ...*

UNIT 12 • THE BEST WAY TO TRAVEL

LANGUAGE WORKOUT

Revision

1 Translate the postcard into German.

Dear Mum

New York is a wonderful place to be. It is exciting to see all the enormous buildings and to know that you are in the best city in the world. At the moment I am sitting in
5 Central Park where all the New Yorkers go jogging every day. Tomorrow I am going to see the Statue of Liberty and I'll send you another postcard from there. My plane leaves for home on Friday next week – I'll ring
10 you from the airport when I arrive.

Love Sharon

Mrs. Hawkins
7 Hazel Avenue
Bristol BS9 6TR
England

2 Find examples of the following tenses in the text and explain their use.

simple present   the future using the simple present
present continuous   the future using *will*
the future with *going to*

3 Complete the following sentences with *will* or *going to*.

1 Sharon ... (see) Statue of Liberty tomorrow.
2 She hopes the weather ... (be) nice.
3 Sharon and her friend Lesley ... (buy) some tickets for the Oasis concert.
4 The tickets ... (cost) a lot of money but it's Sharon's birthday on Wednesday.
5 Sharon ... (be) 18 and she ... (have) a party when she gets back to England.
6 'I ... (invite) all my friends to the party,' she tells Lesley, 'I hope everyone ... (come).'

Exam practice

a Find an adverb.

wonderful (line 1)   enormous (line 2)

b Ask for the underlined parts of the sentences.

I am sitting <u>in Central Park</u>.
Tomorrow I am going to see <u>the Statue of Liberty</u>.
My plane leaves <u>next Friday</u>.

Revision exercises and exam practice

c Find the plurals.

place (line 1)   city (line 3)

d Find a synonym.

wonderful (line 1)   enormous (line 2)   ring (line 9)

e Fill in the missing forms.

positive	comparative	superlative
wonderful (line 1)	. . .	. . .
. . .	. . .	best (line 3)

Writing: Going on holiday

Write a description of Jenny's journey next week from her home in Bristol to New York. Use the expressions given.

At 8 o'clock Jenny will …
The bus for the airport leaves at …
She will arrive at the airport at …
At 2 o'clock …
The flight lasts …
The plane will land at …
Finally, at 10 o'clock …

13 TECHNOLOGY OLD AND NEW

1 🔊 **A technology quiz is in progress.**

BART OK, your question Julia. Which came first? Coke, radio, the telephone or the zip fastener?

JULIA Er ... the zip fastener was first, then the telephone, radio and then Coke?

BART Sorry! The correct order is the telephone in 1876, then Coke in 1886, the zip fastener in 1892, and radio in 1895. Over to you now, Alex. Ready?

ALEX Yes.

BART While the Americans were fighting their Civil War, between 1861 and 1865, which invention did they use in the fighting?

ALEX The machine gun?

BART Yes! Well done. So here's another one for you. Which well-known construction were they building at the same time as the first man went into space?

ALEX Er ... that was Yuri Gagarin in 1961 I guess ... just a moment ... I used to know this but now I've forgotten ... Er, was it the Sears Tower in Chicago?

BART No. It was the Berlin Wall! Back to you Julia. Which important world event was taking place when they invented the following things? Nylon, the aerosol spray, instant coffee and the artificial heart?

JULIA Er ... Sorry, I haven't got a clue.

BART Well ... it was World War II! And your turn again, Alex. Two of these three things appeared within three years of each other. Which is the odd one out? The match, the sewing machine and ice cream?

ALEX Ice cream? I guess that was much later on.

BART No!

Julia I know! The sewing machine!

Before you start ...

One of the major innovations in recent times has been the silicon chip. It has allowed all sorts of appliances to be 'smart' in the home, the office and in shops. Which of these things do you think contains a silicon chip nowadays?

| cooker | fridge | credit card | microwave | iron | video | television |

BART   Yes. Ice cream and the match had appeared much earlier, the sewing machine came along about 150 years later, in 1830. Well done, Julia. And your question is: What inventions had made Alfred Nobel's fortune before he awarded his first Nobel prizes in 1901?

JULIA   Er ... I think he had made his money from inventions of explosives like dynamite, before he became famous when he set up the Nobel Prizes and one of these prizes was the Nobel Peace Prize. Rather funny when you think about it!

BART   Yes. Absolutely right! and your next question. André Citroën became famous for making inexpensive cars but before that he used to make a lot of money from something else. What was it?

JULIA   That's a difficult one. Maybe he was making bicycles?

BART   No. He was making weapons for the First World War!

Working with the text

1 **Answer the questions.**

1   How many inventions appear in the text?
2   What invention did they use during the American Civil War?
3   What were they building while Yuri Gagarin was in space?
4   What did Alfred Nobel become really famous for?
5   What had André Citroën done before he started to manufacture cars?
6   Name three things which they invented during World War II.
7   If Alex and Julia got one point for each correct answer, what were their scores?
8   Which two things had come along before the sewing machine?

2 What came first? Work with a partner, look at the text and put these in chronological order.

a

b

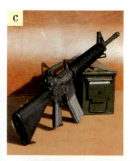
c

d

e

f

g

h

i

j

k

l

3 Say if these statements are right or wrong. Correct the wrong ones.

1 Coke was an eighteenth century invention.
2 At the beginning of the American Civil War, they had not invented the machine gun.
3 They invented very few things between 1939 and 1945 because of World War II.
4 Ice cream is about two hundred years old.
5 The sewing machine came after the match.
6 André Citroën was manufacturing cars at about the same time that Nobel invented dynamite.

4 Which information about these inventions surprises you? Did you think that some were earlier or later?

UNIT 13 • TECHNOLOGY OLD AND NEW

Language Review

1 PAST CONTINUOUS (*Verlaufsform der Vergangenheit*)

Aussagen und Verneinungen		
I He She	was wasn't	working when the phone rang.
We You They	were weren't	reading at 9 o'clock.

Ja/Nein Fragen	Kurzantworten
Was she reading at 9 o'clock? Were they working when the phone rang?	Yes, she was./No, she wasn't. Yes, they were./No, they weren't.

- Das *past continuous* drückt aus, dass eine Handlung zu einem bestimmten Zeitpunkt stattgefunden hat.
- Mit dem *past continuous* wird oft eine Handlung beschrieben, die im Gange war, als sich eine zweite Handlung ereignete.
- Das *past continuous* wird mit *was(n't)/were(n't)* und der *-ing*-Form des Verbs gebildet.
- Um Fragen zu bilden, vertauscht man *was/were* mit dem Subjekt.
- Das *past continuous* wird oft nach *while* (= während) benutzt. *While* + Verb betont die Handlung: *While I was having breakfast ...*
- *During* (= auch während) wird mit einem Substantiv benutzt und betont den Vorgang: *During breakfast ...*

2 PAST PERFECT (*Vollendete Vergangenheit*)

- Das *past perfect* wird oft nach *when* und *after* benutzt, wenn eine Handlung bereits abgeschlossen war, bevor eine zweite begann. *After Alfred Nobel **had made** his money from the invention of explosives, he set up the Nobel Prizes.*
- Das *past perfect* wird mit *had(n't)* + Partizip Perfekt gebildet.
- Um Fragen zu bilden, vertauscht man *had* mit dem Subjekt.

3 USED TO

- *Used to* + Infinitiv wird verwendet, um Gewohnheiten zu beschreiben, die nur in der Vergangenheit, d.h. früher stattgefunden haben. ***I used to know** this but now I've forgotten.*
- *Used to* + Infinitiv ist für alle Personen gleich.
- Fragen werden mit *did* gebildet. *What **did** he **use** to **make**?*

Practice

1 Look at the pictures and say what each person was doing when the earthquake started.

> watch TV   listen to music
> play on the computer   cook   do the ironing
> repair the car   speak on the phone
> send an e-mail message   sleep

2 Put the verbs in brackets into the past perfect.

1 I ... (finish) my shopping before I met Dan and went for lunch with him.
2 She went out before she ... (finish) her homework.
3 Before she realised what was happening, the car ... (crash) into the wall.
4 They said they didn't want a drink because they ... (have) one earlier.
5 He ... (want) to go to the football match, but then he was not sure about it.
6 No one ... (tell) me about the meeting, so I missed it.
7 We ... (be not) to Germany until our holiday last year.
8 You ... (already leave) when I arrived.

3 Rewrite the sentences with *used to*.

1. I wrote all my assignments by hand before I got a computer.
2. What did people do in the evening before there was radio and television?
3. My father kept lots of cash in his wallet, now he just has his credit card.
4. We microwave most of our food now because it takes less time. It took us ages before!
5. When I was little, we missed lots of good things on the television because we didn't have a video.
6. Coke was my favourite drink, until I discovered beer!
7. My mother did all the ironing until she got fed up and made my father share it.
8. I wonder how they kept things fresh before fridges were around.

4 Listen to the sound effects and match them with the sentences.

1. He was having a shower when the phone rang.
2. He had already finished talking when the storm broke.
3. She was working on the computer when it crashed.
4. She was waiting to catch her plane when someone called her.
5. She had finished working on the computer when someone came to the door.
6. He was driving his car when the accident happened.
7. They had already left the house by the time the explosion took place.
8. They were enjoying themselves when the alarm went off.

5 Complete the sentences using *while* or *during*.

1. ... I was having a bath, he was getting my breakfast.
2. She didn't pay attention ... the lesson.
3. My grandmother was born ... the war.
4. I ate my dinner ... I was watching the television.
5. They went on holiday ... the summer.
6. ... she was away, her children had parties in her house every night!
7. ... the interview I was very nervous.
8. They interrupted me three times ... I was talking.

6 Work with a partner. These are answers to questions. What do you think the questions are?

1. At 8 o'clock I was cleaning my teeth.
2. Yes, I had been to see Mary before I came home.
3. She used to live in London.
4. We were going to a football match when you saw us this afternoon.
5. Yes, we were still having lunch when Jane arrived.
6. Yes, we had finished breakfast when you phoned.
7. I couldn't go out last night because I was washing my hair.
8. Yes, I used to be good at English when I was at school.

7 What did you use to do as a child?

Work in a group. Everyone writes down something about what they used to do as a child. Put the pieces of paper into the middle, then pick them out one by one. Guess who wrote the paper!

THE WORLD OF WORK

Everyday tools and appliances
Werkzeuge und Geräte für den Alltag

1 Look at these pictures. Put them into pairs and say which one people used to use and which one we use today.

➡ *People used to use a screwdriver for putting in screws.
Today we use an electric screwdriver.*

working out calculations
washing clothes
copying documents
making holes
blowing cool air
cleaning carpets

▲ drill

▲ calculator
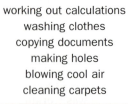
▼ washer women

▲ paper fans

▲ abacus

▲ electric fans

▲ hoover

◀ electric drill
▼ washing machine

▲ scribe

▲ carpet beater

◀ photocopier

2 Look at the pictures again and work with a partner. One person says what he/she was doing, the other asks which appliance the person needed.

➡ **A** *I was working out some prices.*
B *Did you have a calculator?*

UNIT 13 • TECHNOLOGY OLD AND NEW

THE WORLD OF WORK

3 🔊 **What appliances are they talking about? Match what you hear with the pictures. Do you know the names of them?**

a   b   c   d

4 **Look at the picture of the parts of a computer. Put the sentences below in the right order to explain how to set up the computer.**

1
◆ Next plug in the monitor.

2
◆ Then put the monitor on top of the computer or CPU.

3
◆ You are finally ready to turn your computer on. First the monitor and then the computer.

4
◆ Now attach the monitor cable to the back of the computer.

5
◆ Then plug the mouse cable into the keyboard.

6
◆ Next plug the keyboard into the back of the computer.

7
◆ Of course, before you can do any work, you have to install the software.
Turn to Chapter 2 for instructions on this.

8
◆ First plug in the computer before you connect anything to it.

5 **Is your computer like the one above? What are the differences? What computing words do you know which are the same in German and English?**

UNIT 13 • TECHNOLOGY OLD AND NEW

LANGUAGE WORKOUT

Starters

tomato soup
grilled tomatoes
salmon salad

Main Course

fish pie
beefburgers
tomato and cheese pasta
all served with french fries and salad

Dessert

ice cream
apple pie
chocolate cake
all served with cream

Revision

1 Look at the menu. Can you guess which dishes your partner will choose? Work with your partner and write a menu for your favourite dinner.

2 Fill in the correct form of the verb using either the simple past or the present perfect.

1. We … (go) out for a meal yesterday.
2. She … (not be) to this restaurant before.
3. He … (have) this dish before and he … (not like) it.
4. … (you/wash) your hands before you … (start) to eat?
5. … (you/order) your meal yet?
6. They can't leave yet because they … (not pay) their bill.
7. The food … (not arrive) so we … (leave) without paying.
8. Waiter! We … (finish) and we would like the bill, please.

3 Find the questions for these sentences.

1. Yes, I have ordered my main course.
2. Yes, I went to the new Italian restaurant last night.
3. No, I haven't been to the new Indian restaurant yet.
4. He has been a waiter for five years.
5. He was a waiter before he went to college.
6. No, she didn't like her starter.
7. Yes, he had a dessert even though he is on a diet.
8. Yes, I have eaten ostrich meat, but never again!

4 Fill in the correct form of the verb using either the simple past or the present perfect.

CUSTOMER Have you got any fish pie?
WAITER We …[1] (have) some but I'm afraid it's all gone.
CUSTOMER That's a pity, I …[2] (not forget) the fish pie from last time I …[3] (be) here, it …[4] (be) so delicious.
WAITER We've got a lovely beef pie instead.
CUSTOMER No, thanks, I don't like beef. I think I'll have some pasta with tomatoes.
WAITER Thank you, sir/madam. It'll be with you in a moment.

Now practise the dialogue with a partner and put your own favourite foods into it.

Revision exercises and exam practice

Exam practice

It is much easier and quicker to make a cake since the inventions of soft margarine, the electric food mixer and the microwave. Now you can put all the ingredients into a mixing bowl together, then you mix them with the electric mixer and finally you cook the cake in the microwave for five minutes. You have a cake in ten minutes with no work rather than a cake in an hour with lots of work!

(line 5) ingredients *Zutaten*   (line 5) mixing bowl *Rührschüssel*

a Find an opposite.

easier (line 1)   quicker (line 1)   soft (line 3)

b Find a verb.

invention (line 2)   work (line 9)

c Give the principal parts of the verbs.

make (line 2)   put (line 4)   mix (line 6)   cook (line 7)

Writing: Food old and new

Look at the pictures and compare the food and kitchens in Britain today and in the 1950s. What does your kitchen look like?

The food is different because …
I think … is better because …
The food has changed because …
The kitchens are different because …

The 1990s kitchen has … which the 1950s one does not.
My kitchen at home is …

14 USES AND ABUSES

1

DRUGS

Are we terrified for no reason?

Half a million people in the UK take ecstasy every weekend, some people estimate, but it is against the law to study the long-term effects of the drug on people because the use of it is illegal. Politicians will not discuss ecstasy, or the other drugs which are such a part of youth culture nowadays, except to repeat that they are very dangerous and should be illegal. Yet there are more deaths per dose recorded for paracetamol than for ecstasy. Think about the views that these people have on drugs.

■ GARY GOES TO RAVES AND TAKES ECSTASY MOST WEEKENDS

"It's like everyone over 21 thinks we're a threat to society because we like to enjoy ourselves. But the politicians were young once, they must have tried all sorts of different things in the 60s."

2

Suspected Suicide

Alan Bradfield, 20, of Solihull died at his home last night. We understand that Mr Bradfield, a footballer for Aston Villa, part of last season's cup-winning team, was depressed because he had not played well all season. Police suspect that he took an overdose of sleeping tablets.

"If he had lived, he would have had a brilliant career ahead of him," said his mother yesterday. "I think the pressure to succeed was just too great."

■ ANNA IS A VERY UNUSUAL MOTHER

"I know Mark takes soft drugs. They all do these days and it worries me to death! I haven't tried to stop him taking them because I don't think he's addicted to them. At least he doesn't drink or smoke, so he's not addicted to alcohol or tobacco. I just hope I'm right and that, in the future, I don't regret being liberal with him. I don't want to think, 'If I had been stricter with him, he wouldn't have got into trouble.' I don't discuss it with my family or other mothers because I know they would think that I'm completely crazy, an unfit mother."

■ WINIFRED IS 65 YEARS OLD AND HAS SMOKED 60 CIGARETTES A DAY SINCE SHE WAS 25

"I've had a really bad cough for years and now they tell me I've got cancer. I might have had an easier old age if I hadn't smoked but we didn't know about the dangers when I was young. If the government had banned tobacco, lots of people would not have died of cancer. I should have stopped when they first started saying how dangerous it is. I think I could have done it when I was younger, but not now. My advice is – don't start in the first place."

As a society we find it difficult to think straight about the drugs we use. It is not that we should make all drugs legal but at least we should not have a hysterical reaction to them. It's very sad that drugs are part of the leisure life of a whole generation.

Before you start ...

| ecstasy | caffeine | tobacco | alcohol | paracetamol |

**Do you use any of these drugs? What about your parents?
Which of these drugs do you think we should ban?**

Working with the text

1 Correct these statements about text 1.

1. Very few people in the UK take ecstasy.
2. Politicians are very keen to discuss drugs.
3. Gary thinks that politicians were never young.
4. Anna is a normal mother.
5. Anna is quite happy for her son to take soft drugs.
6. Winifred has never smoked.
7. Winifred is very healthy.
8. The text says that all drugs should be made legal.

2 Say whether each statement about text 2 is true, false, or the text does not say.

1. Mr Bradfield came from an unhappy, broken home.
2. He was a successful footballer.
3. He killed himself with an overdose.
4. Mr Bradfield was happy.
5. His future had looked promising.
6. His mother didn't really care about what happened to him.

3 Find words in both texts which mean the same as the following.

1. A drug which young people sometimes take at parties.
2. A drug which people use to relieve pain.
3. An all-night party with very loud, fast music.
4. Drugs which are not very addictive.
5. The drug which is part of beer, wine, etc.
6. An illness which kills people who have smoked a lot.
7. When someone kills himself/herself.
8. When someone is feeling very low and unhappy.

4 We use the words on the left from the texts when we talk about drugs. Match them with the meanings on the right.

1. youth culture   a something which is against the law
2. addict   b when someone takes too much of a drug
3. dose   c the things which young people do
4. tobacco   d a drug which helps people to sleep
5. illegal   e someone who is dependent on drugs
6. overdose   f the amount taken of a drug
7. sleeping tablets   g the drug which is in cigarettes

Language Review

1 MUST/CAN'T + INFINITIVE *(Must/Can't + Infinitiv)*

- *Must/Can't* + Infinitiv wird benutzt, um eine sichere Annahme auszudrücken. *He looks terrible – he **must be** ill.*

2 MUST/CAN'T + HAVE + PAST PARTICIPLE
(Must/Can't + have + Partizip Perfekt)

- *Must/Can't* + *have* + Partizip Perfekt drückt aus, was möglicherweise geschehen ist. *They **must have tried** all sorts of different things in the 60s.*

3 COULD/SHOULD + HAVE + PAST PARTICIPLE
(Could/Should + have + Partizip Perfekt)

- *Could/Should* + *have* + Partizip Perfekt drückt aus, was hätte geschehen können/sollen. *I **should have stopped** smoking earlier.*

4 MIGHT + HAVE + PAST PARTICIPLE *(Might + have + Partizip Perfekt)*

- *Might* + *have* + Partizip Perfekt wird verwendet, um über frühere Möglichkeiten zu sprechen. *If he hadn't taken drugs, he **might have lived**.*

5 CONDITIONAL III *(Bedingungssätze 3)*

*If I **had been** stricter with him, he **wouldn't have got** into trouble.*
*If he **hadn't taken** an overdose, he **would have had** a brilliant career.*

- Das *conditional III* wird verwendet, um eine Situation in der Vergangenheit zu erläutern, die nicht passiert ist, aber hätte passieren können.
- Das Verb im *if-clause* ist im *past perfect*, im *main clause* steht *would have* + Partizip Perfekt.

Practice

1 Complete the sentences using a form of *must have* or *can't have* and the words in brackets.

1. He killed himself. He ... (be depressed).
2. The lights are off and it's very late. They ... (go to bed).
3. She feels awful after last night's party. She ... (drink too much).
4. My daughter didn't finish her lunch yesterday. She ... (be hungry).
5. He ran away from home when he was thirteen. He ... (have a happy childhood).
6. Her parents died when she was a child. It ... (be easy).
7. He wasn't very clever but he passed all his exams. He ... (work hard).
8. She lived alone on the streets when she was a teenager. She ... (enjoy it).

2 Make statements about the photographs, using *must/must have, can't/can't have, might have/mightn't have*.

3 🎧 Listen to the speakers. What can you guess about them from what they say? Use *must/can't (have)* for things you are sure about and *might (have)/mightn't (have)* for possibilities.

can't have had an easy childhood
must have been spoilt at home
must be between thirty and forty years old
can't be optimistic about the future
might have been a drug addict

must be very brave
must be very satisfied
must feel pretty miserable
might have had a breakdown
might be about fifteen or sixteen

4 Complete the sentences using a form of *should have* or *could have*.

1 He died of cancer last week. He ... stopped smoking.
2 I found some drugs in my daughter's bedroom. She ... got them from school.
3 I ... gone to college, but I dropped out.
4 Her mother really misses her. She ... gone to visit her.
5 You ... known what would happen if you took drugs.
6 That accident ... killed you.
7 I know you didn't get the shopping, but you ... done.
8 You ... told me, then I ... helped you.

5 Match the two halves of the sentences.

1 If I had gone by train, ...
2 If you had known the dangers, ...
3 If we hadn't missed the plane, ...
4 If she hadn't gone to the doctor about her cough, ...
5 If her mother had been stricter with her, ...
6 If they had been wiser, ...
7 If he hadn't been unhappy, ...
8 If I had known how difficult it was to give up, ...

a ... she wouldn't have known she had cancer.
b ... she would not have started taking drugs.
c ... he would not have taken the overdose.
d ... we would have been in the crash.
e ... I would have arrived too late.
f ... you would not have taken the new drug.
g ... I would never have started smoking.
h ... they would not have had a drink before they drove home.

"If I hadn't started reading this, I wouldn't have smoked so much today."

6 Put the verb in brackets into the correct form of conditional III.

1 If he ... (not take) drugs when he was a teenager, he ... (not die) young.
2 We ... (start) smoking if we ... (not know) about the danger of cancer.
3 If I ... (not come) home yesterday, I ... (be involved) in that awful train crash today.
4 If she ... (take) her friend's advice, she ... (be) a lot happier by now.
5 ... (you/go) to that rave if you ... (know) that there would be drugs there?
6 If he ... (not have) that last drink, he ... (not lose) his driving licence.
7 I ... (not finish) my homework if I ... (not drink) lots of coffee to keep me awake.
8 If you ... (know) about the dangers of drugs, ... (you/start) taking them?

7 What is the most dangerous thing that has happened to you? Write about it using some of the sentences below.

I might have killed myself. I might not be alive today, if I hadn't ...
I should have done something differently.
I shouldn't have done it.
I could have killed someone.
I couldn't have done anything else.
If I had been unlucky, I would have been in the accident.

Helping young people
Jungen Menschen helfen

1 🎧 **Listen to Matty talking about her work with young people then complete the sentences below using these words.**

down and out	habit	drying out
homelessness	counsellor
alcoholics	poverty

1 Drug addicts have a ... which they have to satisfy by taking more drugs.
2 ... are people who have the problem of drinking too much.
3 People with problems can be helped by a qualified ... .
4 People who are giving up drink or drugs are ... .
5 ... is the problem of people who have nowhere to live.
6 Poor people suffer from ... .
7 Someone who has dropped out of society and who lives on the streets is often called a ... .

2 Counselling can help people with the following problems. Look at the list and answer the questions.

Counsellors can help people:

- with psychiatric or psychological problems
- who have got into problems with debt
- who have a problem with drug or alcohol abuse
- who are suffering stress after a disaster
- who are suffering stress at work
- who are depressed and not coping with their life
- with problematic children
- who are married but the relationship is not working
- who are depressed because they have lost their job

1 Which types of counselling would you *most* like to do? Why?
2 Which types of counselling would you *least* like to do? Why?
3 Take one of the problems outlined above and explain in more detail what the problem is. What do you think the solutions might be?

UNIT 14 • USES AND ABUSES

THE WORLD OF WORK

3 🔊 **Listen to Gemma and Tom talking about working for a charity and answer the questions below.**

1. What sort of organisation is Comic Relief?
2. What types of people does it help? And where?
3. What is the day called when they raise most of their money?
4. What do people in Britain wear to help Comic Relief?
5. How much money did they raise this year?
6. What two problems are mentioned by Tom?
7. What two bad situations are mentioned by Gemma?
8. What work do Gemma and Tom do?

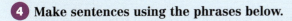

4 **Make sentences using the phrases below.**

Overseas aid …	… schools.
Organisations like Comic Relief …	… are charities.
They give out …	… help families.
They help rebuild …	… easy work at times.
It can't be …	… food and clothing.
It must be very satisfying to …	… helps poor people in other countries.

5 **Would you like to work to help young people? Choose two of the jobs below and say why you would or would not like to do that job.**

1 SPORTS DEVELOPMENT WORKERS
These people work with young people in the community to introduce them to sports which they might not be able to do otherwise. They organise holiday schemes where children can try out different sports and they work to raise money for new sports facilities.

2 STREET WORKERS
These people work with people who are poor and deprived and who don't go to the authorities for help. They often help young people, especially ethnic minorities, who have problems with drugs, crime and homelessness. They try to meet and advise young people on the street and then they get them into schemes which can offer housing, work or other help.

3 CAREERS ADVISERS
Careers advisers work with young people at school and college, helping them to choose the right job for their particular skills and abilities. The job market is much more changeable than it used to be, so they have to make sure they keep up to date.

> I would/would not like … because …
> I might/might not like … because …
> It must/can't be easy to …
> It must/can't be satisfying to …

UNIT 14 • USES AND ABUSES   125

LANGUAGE WORKOUT

Revision

CATHY

Cathy left school when she was 16. She wanted to leave because she and her boyfriend, Mike, decided to live together and start a family. Mike got a new job with a transport company and
5   they moved to Scotland. Mike was very busy and was often away from home. A year later when the baby was two months old, Mike met Michelle, fell in love and left Cathy. Cathy had no job, no boyfriend, very little money and was all alone
10 with her baby miles from all her friends and family.

1 What would have happened if …

1   … Cathy and Mike had not started a family? (Cathy/stay at school for longer)

➡ *Cathy would have stayed at school for longer.*

2   … Cathy had stayed at school? (she/better qualifications)
3   … Mike had not got a new job? (Mike and Cathy/not move to Scotland)
4   … they had not moved to Scotland? (Cathy/not leave all her friends and family)
5   … Cathy had not lived so far away from her friends and family? (she/feel happier)
6   … Mike had not met Michelle? (Mike and Cathy/stay together)

2 Rewrite the sentences to make the adjectives into the comparative and superlative forms.

Cathy has got the …¹ (big) problems of anyone I know. Her flat is …² (bad) than anyone else's because it is a lot …³ (small), it is …⁴ (far) from the shops and it is in the …⁵ (bad) part of town. The only …⁶ (good) thing that can be said about it is that it is …⁷ (good) than living on the street. Her situation is …⁸ (difficult) now than it was two years ago because she has no friends and no family near her to help her.

3 These sentences are wrong. Correct the underlined words using, *a few*, *a lot (of)*, *many*, *little*, *fewer*.

1   Cathy has a lot of money.
2   Cathy has more opportunities than most people.
3   There are a lot of trees where Cathy lives.
4   Most young women have more problems than Cathy.
5   There are a few problems with drugs where Cathy lives.
6   There are a lot of jobs in the area.
7   Cathy can do little to make her situation better.

Revision exercises and exam practice

4 Complete these questions with *how much* or *how many*.

1 friends/Cathy/have
   ➡ How many friends does Cathy have?

2 money/Cathy/have
3 qualifications/Cathy/get at school
4 time/Cathy and Mike/spend together
5 friends/Cathy and Mike/have in Scotland
6 help/Cathy/get from her family

5 Look at the text and put in apostrophes (') where they are necessary.

> Cathys problem is that she didnt plan her future before she had a baby. Its easy to be critical when you havent got any problems of your own, but the future will not be hers until shes been to college and got some qualifications.

Exam practice

a Give the principal parts of the verbs.

left (line 1)   met (line 7)   fell (line 8)

b Fill in *some* or *any*.

Has Cathy got … friends in Scotland?
Cathy didn't get … qualifications at school.
Mike and Cathy had … good times together before Mike met Michelle.

c Ask for the underlined parts of the sentences.

She left school <u>because she wanted to live with Mike</u>.
Mike got a new job <u>in Scotland</u>.

Writing: Help!

Cathy has decided to write a letter to a problem page asking for help. Write the letter for her using the words below.

Dear …
I feel … because …
The place where I live is …
I haven't got …
I don't know what to do …

bad place to live   no job   no partner
no money   worried   depressed
unhappy   alone with a young child

15 DO YOU SHOP TILL YOU DROP?

❇ There has been a shopping revolution in Britain over the last ten years. The beginning of the revolution was when shops started opening late on Thursdays for people who go to work during the day. At about this time shops stopped closing early on Wednesdays too. Then the law against Sunday shopping was changed because the big stores all started to open on Sundays. Now most High Street shops are open on Bank Holidays too. People are even beginning to talk about the advantages of all-night shopping! The only day now with no shopping, except window shopping, is Christmas Day.

❇ As well as the new shopping hours, pub opening hours have also changed dramatically in recent times. Pubs are now allowed to stay open all day, even on Sunday, although they must still shut at 11.00 pm every night. The police would like even this to change. They say that if pubs were open all night, people would not drink more than they do now. Then, in the evening, there would not be the problems with violence on the streets when the pubs close and all the drunken youths are put out onto the streets together.

❄ Both shopping time and drinking time have been increased in our consumerist society and now we are starting to spend our money at home as well. Shopping channels on the television were once seen as a joke but now they are becoming more popular because they are more sophisticated. You look at the goods on the screen, ring the telephone number and then the goods are delivered to your door.

❄ Another new development is 'virtual shopping', where you can 'walk around' a 'virtual supermarket', key in the items you want and then your weekly order is delivered and you don't even have to get off the sofa! This is all very different from mail order catalogues which are beginning to seem old-fashioned. The big question, though, is whether all these new methods and new shopping times will encourage us to spend more money!

Before you start …

Shopping is one of our main leisure activities today. Do you shop till you drop? What sort of shopping do you do and how often?

> going to the supermarket
> home shopping
> using small, specialist shops
> using mail order catalogues
> virtual shopping by computer
> home delivery   window shopping

Working with the text

1 Answer the questions.

1. Do shops open on Sundays in Britain?
2. When is late night shopping in Britain?
3. What do you understand by 'window shopping' (line 7)?
4. When do pubs shut in Britain?
5. What would the police like to happen to pub opening times?
6. What new methods of shopping does the text mention?
7. What older method of home shopping does the text mention?
8. What is the difference between virtual shopping and ordering from a mail order catalogue?

2 Correct the statements.

1. Britain is going to have a shopping revolution.
2. Shops do not open on Bank Holidays.
3. The shops are open in Britain on Christmas Day.
4. Pub opening hours have stayed the same.
5. Pubs are now open all night.
6. The police would like pubs to shut at 6.00 pm.
7. People do not like shopping channels on television.
8. Mail order catalogues are a new way of shopping.

3 Put the events in the correct order using the words in the box.

> first   then   finally   next

Shopping channels on television became more popular.
Shopping on Bank Holidays started.
Shopping on Sundays was allowed.
Virtual shopping will become popular and we won't have to go shopping at all.
Late shopping on Thursdays was introduced.

4 These are the answers to questions on the text. What are the questions?

1. Over the last ten years.
2. Christmas Day.
3. At 11.00 pm each night.
4. The police.
5. Virtual shopping.
6. Mail order catalogues.

Language Review

1 PRESENT PASSIVE *(Passiv der Gegenwart)*

- Das Passiv wird oft verwendet, wenn man auf eine unpersönliche Art und Weise über Fakten, Vorgänge usw. berichten will. Es wird auch benutzt, wenn man die Ursache / den Verursacher nicht kennt oder nicht nennen will.
- Das *present passive* wird mit *is/are* + Partizip Perfekt gebildet. *Your weekly order **is delivered**. The goods **are delivered** to your door.*
- ‚Von' wird in Passivsätzen durch das Wort *by* ausgedrückt.

2 PAST PASSIVE *(Passiv der Vergangenheit)*

- Das *past passive* wird mit *was/were* + Partizip Perfekt gebildet. *Then the law against Sunday shopping **was changed**.*

3 PRESENT PERFECT PASSIVE *(Passiv des Perfekts)*

- Das *present perfect passive* wird mit *has/have been* + Partizip Perfekt gebildet. *Both shopping time and drinking time **have been increased**.*

Practice

1 Look at the pictures and make sentences about each one.

➡ *Cigarettes are sold in a packet.*

jar	packet
carton	bag
bottle	tin
box	tube

2 🔊 Listen to the cassette. Each person needs several things. Say where one of the things each person needs is normally bought or sold.

> baker's   toy shop   hi-fi shop   do-it-yourself shop
> florist's   chemist's   supermarket   bookshop

➡ *Beer is normally sold at a supermarket.*

3 Make sentences with the words below. Use the simple past passive.

1 TV/invent/John Baird

➡ *Television was invented by John Baird.*

2 Penicillin/discover/Alexander Fleming
3 ice cream/first/make/1677
4 aspirin/first/use/1899
5 CDs/invent/1979
6 soap powder/first/use/1920s
7 the fax/invent/1907
8 the electric guitar/first play/1931
9 the telephone/invent/Alexander Bell

4 In pairs, make mini-dialogues as in the example.

1 when/first/make ice cream (17th century)

➡ **A** *Do you know when they first made ice cream?*
B *Yes. It was first made in the 17th century.*

2 when/invent the telephone (1876)
3 where and when/first eat breakfast cereal (USA, 1893)
4 where/make the first tea bags (San Francisco)
5 where/sell the first petrol-driven cars (Germany)
6 where and when/make the first hamburger (Connecticut, 1895)
7 when/invent the biro (1938)

5 Look at the signs below which all have 'hidden' passives in them. Make them into complete sentences. Where might you find these signs?

1 Service not included
2 Same day delivery GUARANTEED
3 Under 18s not served
4 Breakfast served at 8.00
5 PHOTOGRAPHY FORBIDDEN
6 No PETS ALLOWED
7 No credit allowed
8 SHOP CLOSED ON SUNDAYS

6 Change the sentences from active to passive, beginning with the words in brackets.

1   They opened that big supermarket last year. (That big supermarket ...)
2   You don't buy food from mail order catalogues. (Food ...)
3   I do my weekly shopping on Saturdays. (My weekly shopping ...)
4   She buys her clothes from mail order catalogues. (Her clothes ...)
5   She has paid for her new dress. (Her new dress ...)
6   They deliver your shopping on the day of your choice. (Your shopping ...)
7   They haven't delivered my shopping yet. (My shopping ...)
8   We now allow shops to open on Sundays. (Shops ...)
9   They close their shop at 1.00 pm on Wednesdays. (Their shop ...)
10 The milkman delivered the milk at 6.00 am yesterday. (The milk ...)

7 Writing exercise

Here is a letter from an American pen-friend who works in an all-night shop. You are a shop assistant, too and you often have to work until 8 pm. Write back to Annie and tell her about your job.

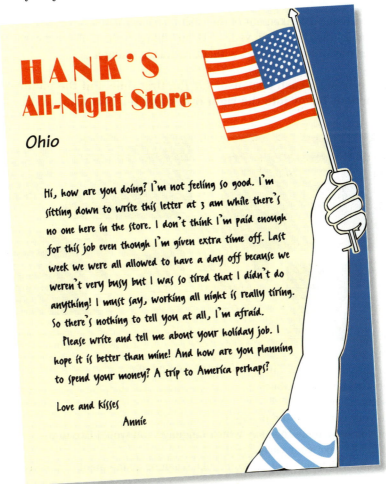

HANK'S
All-Night Store

Ohio

Hi, how are you doing? I'm not feeling so good. I'm sitting down to write this letter at 3 am while there's no one here in the store. I don't think I'm paid enough for this job even though I'm given extra time off. Last week we were all allowed to have a day off because we weren't very busy but I was so tired that I didn't do anything! I must say, working all night is really tiring. So there's nothing to tell you at all, I'm afraid.

Please write and tell me about your holiday job. I hope it is better than mine! And how are you planning to spend your money? A trip to America perhaps?

Love and kisses
    Annie

Banking
Bankgeschäfte

1 🔊 **Listen to Terry talking about opening a bank account with his first pay packet. Use the words in the box to complete the sentences.**

| overdraft | bank manager | bank clerk | cheque book |
| banker's card | cash dispenser | credit card | loan |

1 You are given a ... by the bank if you need to buy something big, like a car.
2 The person who runs the bank is called the ... .
3 The ... is where you can get cash 24 hours a day.
4 The person that customers normally see in the bank is called a ... .
5 You have an ... if you take more money out of the bank than you have in your account.
6 Money can only be taken out of the cash dispenser if you have got a ... .
7 You can use the cheques in your ... to buy things instead of using cash.
8 Another way of buying things without cash is by using a ... .

2 **Terry is using a cash dispenser for the first time. Put the pictures and the instructions below into the right order and tell him what to do.**

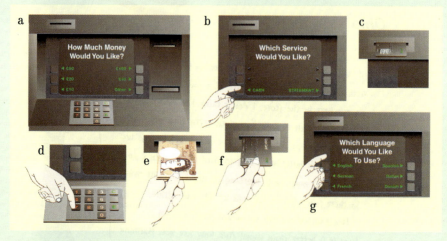

1 After that decide how much money you would like.
2 Then key in your number.
3 First insert your card.
4 Take your card from the machine.
5 After you have done this, say which language you would like to use.
6 And finally, take your cash.
7 Next, say which service you would like (cash or a statement of account).

THE WORLD OF WORK

3 Work with a partner to practise the dialogue below. Take turns at being the bank clerk and the customer.

BANK CLERK Good morning. How may I help you?
CUSTOMER Hello, I'd like … .
BANK CLERK Certainly sir/madam, … .
CUSTOMER Thank you.

to pay some money into my account.
to see the manager about my overdraft.
a new cheque book, please.
to find out about a loan for a car.
to withdraw £50 from my account.

pass me the money and your cheque book.
I'll make an appointment for you.
we'll put one in the post for you.
here is the form you need. Please fill it in.
write a cheque to self and I'll give you the money.

4 Look at the bank statement below and answer the questions.

DATE		PAID OUT (DEBIT)	PAID IN (CREDIT)	BALANCE
10 SEP 97	BALANCE BROUGHT FORWARD			640.30 C
13 SEP 97	EBLEY GARAGE, OXFORD	40.00		600.30 C
14 SEP 97	THOMAS COOK TRAVEL, CHELTENHAM	150.00		450.30 C
15 SEP 97	HMV CD STORE, CHELTENHAM	23.00		427.30 C
17 SEP 97	BOOTS THE CHEMIST	25.00		402.30 C
18 SEP 97	SAINSBURY'S SUPERMARKET	98.00		304.30 C
19 SEP 97	TOMORROW'S WORLD BOUTIQUE	75.00		229.30 C
27 SEP 97	AVANT GARDE ADVERTISING AGENCY SALARY SEP 97		1262.70	
30 SEP 97	BALANCE CARRIED FORWARD			

1 Was the bank account 'in the black' or 'in the red' at the beginning of September?
2 What type of person do you think has this bank account?
3 How much does this person earn a month?
4 Did this person spend a lot of money on clothes in September?
5 How much has been spent on luxuries and how much on necessities?
6 What was the balance carried forward?

UNIT 15 • DO YOU SHOP TILL YOU DROP?

LANGUAGE WORKOUT

Revision

1 Sandy has been on a huge shopping trip! Look at the items she has bought and answer the questions.

1 Make a list of the shops that you think Sandy has just been to.
2 Do you think Sandy has been influenced by advertising? Why?
3 What marketing gimmicks can you see? Look at the list below to help you.

| mail shots | discount offer | free gift | sponsorship |

4 Does Sandy really need all the things she has bought?
5 Which things would you buy and which things wouldn't you buy?

2 Make conditional II sentences using the information from the two sentences.

1 Sandy is going to pay £50 for her trainers. They are £5 cheaper at the other sports shop.

➡ *If Sandy went to the other sports shop, her trainers would be £5 cheaper.*

2 Ben is buying his washing powder at the shop on the corner. There is a discount offer at the supermarket.
3 I am going to buy some peaches at the supermarket. They are bigger at the grocer's.
4 She is paying £2.50 for parking in the multi-storey car park. It is free at the little car park round the corner.
5 They are going to buy their table from the mail order catalogue. There are better quality tables for the same price at the new showroom in town.
6 The travel agent is offering us a holiday in Tenerife. The one over the road is offering a 25% discount.
7 This car showroom does not let you test drive their Ferraris. The other one does.

3 Complete the sentences with the correct form of the conditional (II or III).

1 If you had gone to the discount shop, you … (save) a lot of money.
2 What would you have bought if you … (go) shopping yesterday?
3 If I … (buy) that type of washing powder, I would get 50 pence off.

Revision exercises and exam practice

4 If I chose that holiday, I ... (get) a free ferry ticket as well.
5 She ... (not buy) it if there was no discount offer to go with it.
6 What ... (we/get) if we won that competition?
7 People would not have bought that product if there ... (not be) a marketing gimmick.
8 They would be very happy if they ... (get) a free gift.

Exam practice

Look at the text on page 128.

a Find an opposite.

beginning (line 1)   started (line 2)   advantages (line 6)

b Explain the following in complete sentences.

revolution (line 1)   Bank Holidays (line 5)

c Add question tags to the following.

The police would like things to change, ...?
Shops started opening late a few years ago, ...?

Writing: *If you were rich ...*

Sandy is dreaming that she has just won £50,000. She is imagining what she would spend the money on. Write about her dream.

Would she spend all the money on herself?
What would she buy – a house, a Ferrari, lots of designer clothes?
Would she save the money and keep it in the bank?
Would she buy anything for her family? What would it be?
Does she think £50,000 is a lot of money?

16 REDUCE, REPAIR, REUSE, RECYCLE

1

We have been producing far too much waste in developed countries. If we want to protect our environment, it is clear that we must reduce the amount of waste. Some people think that we can reduce household waste by 50% if we do the following:

- reduce the amount of things we buy
- repair things and not throw them away
- reuse things for some other purpose and not throw them away
- recycle things which we cannot repair or reuse

People have been trying to reduce the amount of packaging we use. In Germany, for example, customers have been taking the packaging off food at the supermarket before they take it home. This means that a greater percentage has been reused or recycled. Britain has not gone that far yet but, since the important Earth Summit in Rio in 1992, the big stores have been taking the problem more seriously. Shop assistants now ask people if they want a bag for their shopping or not and big stores have been using recycled paper and plastic for these bags.

2 The 'cooling can'

In California a company has produced a soft drink can which cools itself! Unfortunately, the cooling gases in the product are very bad for global warming. They are CFCs which are worse than methane or CO_2, the other greenhouse gases. Britain wants to forbid this product. Do you agree, or would you like your can to cool itself?

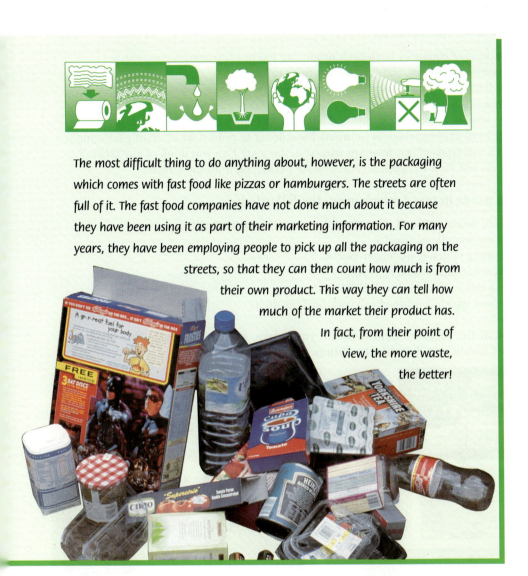

The most difficult thing to do anything about, however, is the packaging which comes with fast food like pizzas or hamburgers. The streets are often full of it. The fast food companies have not done much about it because they have been using it as part of their marketing information. For many years, they have been employing people to pick up all the packaging on the streets, so that they can then count how much is from their own product. This way they can tell how much of the market their product has. In fact, from their point of view, the more waste, the better!

Before you start ...

Imagine you had £100. Which of the things below would you spend this money on to save the environment? Explain why.

saving the tiger   improving public transport   reducing air pollution in cities
saving the rainforest   reducing third world poverty

Working with the text

1 Answer the questions on text 1.

1. What kind of countries have been producing too much waste?
2. What does the figure '50%' in the text refer to?
3. Recycling is one of the answers to our problem with waste, according to the text. What are the others?
4. What should we do with things that are broken before we throw them away?
5. What have supermarkets in Germany been doing to reduce waste from packaging?
6. Which two types of fast food are named in the text? Can you think of any others?
7. Why do fast food companies collect waste packaging from the streets?

2 Find words in text 1 which mean the following:

1. The air, water and land where people, animals and plants live.
2. To make something smaller.
3. Something which is no longer useful.
4. To fix something which is broken.
5. To use things like glass and metal again.
6. Fast food which is a bread roll with beef inside it.

3 Look at the pictures below. Would you reuse, repair or recycle this waste? What would you do with the things which you can reuse?

4 The 'cooling can' adds to global warming. What other things from the list below also produce greenhouse gases?

> cars   trees   washing powder   human waste
> hamburgers   refrigerators

140   UNIT 16 • REDUCE, REPAIR, REUSE, RECYCLE

Language Review

PRESENT PERFECT CONTINUOUS *(Verlaufsform des Perfekts)*

| I/You/We/They | have(n't) | been | producing too much waste. |
| He/She | has(n't) | | using recycled paper. |

- Das *present perfect continuous* wird für Handlungen benutzt, die in der Vergangenheit anfingen und bis in die Gegenwart hineinreichen oder gerade abgeschlossen sind. Es wird oft in Fragen mit *How long ...?* benutzt.
- Das *present perfect continuous* wird mit *have(n't)/has(n't)* + *been* + *-ing*-Form des Verbs gebildet.
- *Since* wird für einen Zeitpunkt verwendet; *for* für einen Zeitraum. *She's been learning English **since 1994/for several years**.*
- Mit dem *present perfect continuous* betont man das Andauern der Handlung. *We **have been producing** too much waste.* = *We are still producing too much waste.*
- Mit dem *present perfect* wird Nachdruck auf das Ergebnis der Handlung gelegt. *A company **has produced** a soft drink can which cools itself.* = *This can is now on the market.*

Practice

1 Complete the sentences with the present perfect continuous form of the words in brackets.

1 People ... (worry) about the environment for many years.
→ *People have been worrying about the environment for many years.*
2 Over the last few years, the Earth ... (get warmer).
3 Scientists ... (try) for many years to understand global warming.
4 For the last two years they ... (eat) only organic beef.
5 She ... (protest) about new roads since 1985.
6 How long ... (we/pollute) our planet with harmful chemicals?
7 I ... (work) on waste reduction for five years.
8 How long ... (you/worry) about air pollution?
9 What ... (this supermarket/do) to reduce waste from packaging?
10 How long ... (your firm/use) recycled paper?

UNIT 16 • REDUCE, REPAIR, REUSE, RECYCLE

2 **Make statements about the pictures, as in the example.**

1   use/solar energy/1987

> They have been using solar energy since 1987.

2   study/air quality/1980

3   pollute/environment thousands of years

4   lie/in the sun/too long

5   get hot/recent years

6   waste energy/a long time

3 **Make sentences using the present perfect continuous and *for* or *since*.**

1   I recycle my glass bottles. (five years)

> I have been recycling my glass bottles for five years.

2   We worry about the amount of waste we produce. (20 years)
3   He reuses all his plastic bags. (1990)
4   They grow their own food. (1975)
5   You worry about global warming. (a long time)
6   She works here. (January)
7   I try to reduce my waste. (six months)
8   I smoke (the age of 15), but now I am going to give up.
9   He uses public transport. (he sold his car)
10 We use recycled paper. (several years)

4 🔊 **Listen to the statements and then say which of the pictures below illustrate them.**

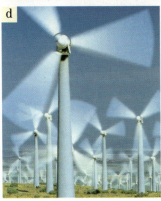

5 **Complete the sentences using either the present perfect or the present perfect continuous and then translate your answers into German.**

1. She … (collect) fast food packaging all morning.
2. You … (make) the situation much worse.
3. We … (reuse) our plastic bags since March.
4. Big companies … (not do) much about waste yet.
5. He … (not visit) Germany since he was made redundant.
6. They … (go) to Germany on holiday for as long as I can remember.
7. How long … (you/come) here?
8. … (you/be) here before?

6 **Do you live in an environmentally friendly way? What do you do 'wrong' and what changes do you think you could make? Write about 100 words.**

Here are some ideas:

Use the car (motor bike, moped, scooter) less / cycle more / use public transport more / only buy drinks in bottles with a deposit / recycle more (plastic, paper, metal, etc) / don't leave lights on / turn down the heating / take a shower rather than a bath / persuade your friends (family) that … etc.

THE WORLD OF WORK

Green Agriculture
Ökologische Landwirtschaft

1 🔊 **Listen to the person talking about his life on a big farm. Find the words in the box which fit the descriptions below.**

| factory | crops | pesticides | fertilizers |
| tractor | BSE | profit | cows |

1 Chemicals used by farmers to kill diseases.
2 The machine farmers use to drive across fields and pull machinery.
3 The things which farmers grow in fields.
4 Chemicals used by farmers to help things grow.
5 The money which you make from a business.
6 A disease which cows get and which makes them go mad.
7 A place where things are manufactured.
8 Animals which produce milk.

2 **Matt Brown is a farmer who is changing from traditional methods of agriculture. Look at what he says and answer the questions.**

Hi, I'm Matt Brown. I'm changing my farm to a new method of agriculture called permaculture. Permaculture is a word which means 'permanent agriculture' and it is all about farming without causing environmental problems. We grow a mixture of things. The things which need most care, like the kitchen herbs and the animals, are nearest the house and the things which need least care, like the fruit trees and woodland, are furthest away. All of the organic waste produced on the farm is recycled and we catch all the rain, so that we don't need to use drinking water for the crops. This sort of farming is hard work, but I love it, it's a whole way of life!

1 What is the new method of agriculture called?
2 What does the name of the new method mean?
3 What are the aims of the new method?
4 List four things which Matt has on his farm.
5 What does Matt do with the organic waste?
6 Why does Matt catch the rainfall?

UNIT 16 • REDUCE, REPAIR, REUSE, RECYCLE

THE WORLD OF WORK

3 **Work with a partner. Compare the two methods of farming on page 144.**

1 Which method is best for the environment? Why?
2 Which method do you think makes most profit? Why?
3 If you were a farmer, which method would you choose to follow?

4 **Look at the two meals and say which one is probably made with organic food.**

Describe the meals and say which one you would prefer to eat. Which of your favourite foods do you think you should give up to save the environment?

5 **Study the pictures and the texts below and decide what each person's job is from the words in the box.**

gardener
landscape contractor
tree surgeon
nursery worker

1 This person looks after trees. S/he cuts down trees when they are dead, dying or dangerous and cuts off branches when necessary. You have to be strong and fit to do this job because you need to climb trees and use big saws.
2 This person helps to grow plants for sale. S/he knows how to grow plants from seed. S/he spends a lot of time working in greenhouses.
3 This person builds landscapes designed by others. S/he works on big projects like office developments, golf courses and new housing.
4 This person looks after private gardens and public parks. In the summer, s/he spends most of the time looking after the flowers. In the winter, s/he mostly plants new things, looks after older plants and repairs fences and paths.

6 **Which of the jobs described in this World of Work would you most like to do? If you wouldn't like to do any of them, say why!**

LANGUAGE WORKOUT

Revision

1 Complete the sentences using the correct form of *must (not)* and *(not) have to* and the verbs in brackets.

1 You ... (come) and try out the new gym, it's fantastic!
2 I ... (take) any exercise if I don't want to!
3 We will soon ... (recycle) all our household waste, the government says so.
4 I ... (do) my aerobics today, do I?
5 ... (you/show) your passport when you go to France?
6 You ... (forget) your passport when you travel in the EU but you ... (not/always/show) it.
7 It ... (be) good news if we are all going to have more leisure time!
8 ... (the people in the EU/work) as much today as they did ten years ago?

2 Complete the text, using *must (have)*, *can't (have)*, or *might (have)*.

> Gazza ...¹ been a really great footballer but he has never quite made it, even though he has played for England. He shows that it is not enough to have great talent and fitness, you ...² also learn how to control yourself. It ...³ been easy for him because the press kept saying how wonderful he was from a very early age. It ...⁴ been very difficult living up to the image and being afraid that you ...⁵ not be as good as they said. His career playing for England is not yet over, so we ...⁶ say that he is finished but it is unlikely that he will ever be as great a player as he ...⁷ been.

3 Look at these words and put them into three groups. Give each group a title.

squash	football	nightclub	TV
aerobics	cinema	disco	radio
tennis	theatre	hi-fi	leisure centre
pub	walkman	swimming	skiing

Exam practice

LIFESTYLE 2000

What might our lifestyle be like in the next century? That of the 80s was about health, fitness and consumerism. You had to be young, good-looking and successful. In the 90s people were more caring about others and about the environment. What will life be like in the 2000s? In the UK some people are worried that the EU will tell us more and more about what we have to do and what we must not do. On the other hand, perhaps we will all be able to work and live where we want and actually have more leisure time and that the family will become more important again. Or, as we will not have to show our passports all the time, perhaps some of us will choose to become travellers with no permanent home. The only certainty is that predictions like these are often wrong!

Revision exercises and exam practice

a Find a verb.

consumerism (line 3)   travellers (line 16)

b Find a synonym.

good-looking (line 4)   wrong (line 18)

c Find an opposite.

young (line 3)   life (line 6)

d Explain in a complete sentence.

lifestyle (line 1)   fitness (lines 2–3)

e Give the principal parts of the verbs.

tell (line 8)   choose (line 15)   become (line 15)

f Put the following sentences into the passive.

You do not need a visa to visit this country.
In the 90s people told us to be more caring about the environment.

Writing: Look to the future

What would you like your lifestyle in the future to be like? Write a description of your dreams of the future using the pictures and sentences below to help.

I'm going to be really green and not damage the environment.
I might drop out and become a traveller.
I want to earn a lot of money and spend it all on keep fit and holidays.
I must have a Rolls Royce.
I'm going to live in a tent and never earn any money.
I want to live in a palace.
I want to get married and have six children.

UNIT 16 • REDUCE, REPAIR, REUSE, RECYCLE

17 VIRTUAL LIVES!

1

A GROWING TREND in employment is working from home. More and more people are choosing to use their spare rooms as their office. Many jobs these days involve data-handling which can all be done using new technology. If you have a computer, a modem, e-mail and a fax machine, it is possible to do anything from graphic design to marketing from your home and your employer could be anywhere from Birmingham to Brazil.

There are many attractions of this way of working. You can avoid commuting, you can work in the comfort of your own home and you can keep away from all the boring office politics. A further advantage, especially for working women, is that it means you can be more flexible with your hours of work. Childcare and running the home become easier to manage because you are not tied so strictly to the 'nine-to-five' working day.

For many people, the attraction of being more in control of your working hours and office environment is very great and we envy those who have changed to working at home. There are some serious disadvantages, however, and some big implications for future working practices.

Trade Unions in Britain are very worried about the trend because they think that employers could start expecting their employees to work from home. After all, it saves employers money if they can avoid having offices big enough for all their employees! This could put the poor and the young at a further disadvantage because they may not have anywhere at home where they can put an office. They may not even have a home from which to work! The message from the unions is: think about it very carefully before doing it.

2
Romance
ON THE INTERNET

♥♥♥♥♥♥♥♥♥♥♥

Surfing the Internet is one of the fastest growing leisure activities. Some people go online every evening and surf until bedtime. But what about meeting your future partner on the Internet? That's exactly what happened to Robert Jones, who kept up a virtual
5 romance with his fiancée, Eva, for eighteen months before they actually met. But what will they do for entertainment once they live under the same roof? 'We'll carry on surfing of course,' says Robert, 'but we'll put the computers very close together!'

♥♥♥♥♥♥♥♥♥♥♥

Before you start ...

Which methods of communication do you use? Which of these things do you find the most useful? Explain why.

> mobile phone   fax machine
> answering machine   e-mail   letter

Working with the text

1 Answer the questions on text 1.

1. Which two jobs are mentioned in paragraph 1?
2. Name three machines which help us to communicate which are mentioned in the text.
3. Name three attractions of working from home.
4. Why is childcare easier if you work from home?
5. What things can you control if you work at home?
6. More and more people are working at home. Who is worried by this growing trend?
7. Why would employers be pleased for their employees to work at home?
8. What does 'it' in line 23 refer to?

2 Look at the picture on page 148 of a self-employed accounts clerk's office at home. Describe what you can see.

3 Find words or expressions in the text which mean the same as these.

1. A fashion or general direction.
2. A room in someone's house not used for anything particular.
3. A piece of office equipment which connects a computer to a telephone line.
4. A job which is to do with layout and illustration of books, advertisements, etc.
5. Looking after children.
6. An association of employees.
7. Someone who works for someone.
8. A bad aspect of something.

4 Correct the statements about text 2.

1. Robert does not like surfing the Internet.
2. What he does is the slowest growing leisure activity.
3. Some people surf the Internet every morning.
4. Robert met his wife on the Internet.
5. His fiancée is called Elaine.
6. It was two years before they met.
7. They'll give up surfing the Internet when they live together.
8. They'll have computers in different rooms.

Language Review

1 THE *-ING* FORM AFTER CERTAIN VERBS
(Die -ing-Form nach bestimmten Verben)

- Auf einige Verben folgt immer die *-ing*-Form, z.B. *admit, appreciate, avoid, can't help, dislike, enjoy, feel like, finish, give up, hate, involve, like, mind, miss, start, suggest.*

2 THE INFINITIVE AFTER CERTAIN VERBS
(Der Infinitiv nach bestimmten Verben)

- Auf andere Verben folgt immer der Infinitiv, z.B. *agree, arrange, choose, decide, expect, hope, intend, learn, manage, offer, promise, want, wish, would like.*

3 THE *-ING* FORM AFTER VERBS WITH PREPOSITIONS
(Die -ing-Form nach Verben mit Präpositionen)

- Die *-ing*-Form steht nach einem Verb mit Präposition. *She is thinking **of working** from home.*

4 THE *-ING* FORM AFTER ADJECTIVES AND PREPOSITIONS
(Die -ing-Form nach Adjektiven und Präpositionen)

- Die *-ing*-Form wird verwendet nach Adjektiven und Präpositionen, z.B. *afraid of, bad/good at, fond of, interested in, responsible for, tired of, used to, worried about.*

Practice

1 Put the verb in brackets into the *-ing* form.

1. I am sorry but I don't feel like … (come) into the office today.
2. I suggest … (try) the Internet if you want really up-to-date information.
3. They dislike … (work) in an office where there is so much stress.
4. Could you wait until I have finished … (send) a fax?
5. He would do anything he could to avoid … (commute).
6. My office job involves … (speak) to a lot of people all day on the telephone.
7. I enjoy … (work) from home.
8. Some people hate … (travel) by air.
9. She started … (work) from home three years ago.
10. Working from home is great! I really appreciate … (not have to) go to so many meetings.

2 Can you find any verbs in the texts which take the *-ing* form? What are they?

3 What are they saying? Look at the pictures and use the words in the box.

enjoy   avoid   give up   mind   admit   feel like   miss   can't help

4 Complete the sentences with a verb from the box.

| checking | getting | hearing | sending | spending |
| surfing | | typing | using | working |

1 I hate the idea of ... my leisure time ... the Internet.
2 The thought of ... at home is horrible.
3 We're tired of ... about the Internet.
4 She's very good at ... new technology.
5 A typewriter was used for ... letters before everyone had a computer.
6 Have you got anything for ... spelling on your computer?
7 They have a good chance of ... a job in computing.
8 A fax is a machine for ... messages more quickly than by post.

5 Complete the sentences using the correct prepositions from the box.

| without | by | to | of | about |

1 I always look forward ... coming home after a hard day's work.
2 It is not easy running a business from home ... having computer equipment.
3 For some time I have been thinking ... becoming self-employed.
4 He is not happy ... working on his own.
5 She is really not sure ... working from home.
6 We finished the project on time ... working at the weekend.
7 I want to work ... having to commute.
8 They are not going to get on at work ... being late all the time.

6 Put the verbs into the correct form: the *-ing* form or the infinitive.

1 I enjoy ... (use) computers.
2 She wants ... (work) at home.
3 We all hate ... (do) the photocopying.
4 He missed ... (chat) with his colleagues when he gave up work to look after the children.
5 I was really surprised when you decided ... (stop) work.
6 She has agreed ... (come) into the office for a meeting today.
7 The children love ... (surf) the Internet.
8 I would like ... (get) a mobile phone.

7 What are your likes and dislikes? Use the verbs in the box and tell a partner about them.

| like | appreciate | feel like | enjoy | avoid | dislike | not mind |

➡ *I like surfing the Internet.*
I don't mind working at the weekend.

Helping people by phone
Hilfe per Telefon

1 Listen to the telephone calls and match them with the description of the telephone helplines below.

Childline is a service which children can ring for help, especially if they have been abused by an adult. It is very important that this helpline is available because children find it very difficult to tell adults they know about problems of abuse.

The Samaritans is a helpline which is run for anyone who is very depressed and needs someone to talk to. It is there to help those who are thinking of killing themselves. The people who work on the helpline have to do a thorough training before they can do the job. One of the most important things they learn is not to give advice; they are there to listen.

999 is the telephone number which you ring if you need one of the emergency services. There are three emergency services, the police, the fire brigade and the ambulance service. The people who answer the calls on this number have to be very good at finding out information quickly from people who are probably very upset. They haven't got time to discuss the problem, they just need to know where it is!

Dial-a-taxi is a service which is there for old and disabled people who don't have a car and who cannot use public transport very easily. They can use the service to go shopping or to see friends, things which, otherwise, they would not be able to do.

2 Complete the chart with expressions from the list.

May I know who's calling?
Sorry to keep you waiting.
I have John Moss in reception for you.
What is it to do with?
Sorry the line's engaged/busy.
Can you spell that, please?
I'm sorry but he's not in.
Can I help you?

Can I get someone to call you back?
Go ahead. You're through.
Hold the line, please.
Can I put you through to someone else?
Will you hold or do you want to call back?
I'll see if I can get her for you.
Can I take a message?

Apologising	Offering to help	Enquiring/Requesting	Giving information/instructions

THE WORLD OF WORK

3 Make a response to these requests using some of the expressions on page 154.

1 Is that the dentist's surgery?
2 Can you put me through to someone in Social Services, please?
3 This one of Nurse Montgomery's patients. Is she there?
4 I wanted to speak to Doctor Frost, but her line's busy. Can you help?
5 Is that the right number for the hospital?

4 What would you say to callers in these situations?

1 The number the caller wants is busy.
2 The number the caller wants doesn't reply.
3 The person the caller wants is busy, but you will try the secretary.
4 You want to know the caller's business.
5 You are going to find the person the caller wants. Ask the caller to wait.
6 You suggest that the person the caller wants can return the call.

5 Change the sentences to make more polite ways of saying the same thing.

1 I didn't understand a word. (Would/mind/repeat/that?)
2 Who are you? (May/have/name?)
3 He's busy. (Sorry/he/not available/right now.)
4 Try again. (Can/call back/later?)
5 What do you want? (What/do/with?)
6 I've never heard of her. (Sorry/but/not think/anyone/that name/here.)
7 This isn't 675543. (I think/have/wrong number.)

6 Listen to the telephone calls. What answers would you give?

7 Work with a partner. Write down the conversation in this story. The expressions in the box may help you.

Hello, how may I help you?
I'm worried because …
I'm afraid he's not here …
Can I try another doctor …
May I have your name?
Doctor … will call at …

UNIT 17 • VIRTUAL LIVES!

LANGUAGE WORKOUT

Revision

1 Put the missing verbs into the text.

are misunderstood	are talking
is telephoned	lives	need
spending	using	

♥ Long distance love ♥

Barbara and Andy are a very modern couple. She …¹ in Los Angeles and he lives in Glasgow. They have kept their relationship going at long distance for three years by …² all the new methods of communication and by …³ a lot of money on air tickets. But it can be difficult to make it work. Barbara is driven crazy when she …⁴ by Andy in the middle of the night and Andy gets worried when he is not e-mailed by Barbara for more than a day. They long for the day when videophones are widely available, so that their faces are shown on screen while they …⁵ to each other. Barbara says, 'Using e-mail and the Internet is great but you still …⁶ to see the other person. You need the body language, otherwise the words on their own …⁷ so easily.'

(line 5) long for *sehnen nach*   (line 6) available *verfügbar*

2 Put the following sentences into the passive.

1 Barbara wrote the letter yesterday.
2 Andy and his friend set up the computer.
3 We told him about the meeting.
4 You sent the fax on Monday.
5 They taught me how to use the e-mail.
6 The secretary sent a parcel to him.
7 You gave her the disk.

3 Complete these sentences using *for* or *since*.

1 Barbara and Andy have been living in different towns … three years.
2 They have known each other … 1994.
3 Barbara has been using e-mails … she moved to Los Angeles.
4 They have been talking about buying a videophone … a long time.
5 They have not seen each other … last year.
6 Andy has been looking for a job in LA … the last three months.

4 Find four adjectives in the text and give the opposites.

5 Find the odd ones out and say why.

1 telephone   fax   videophone   answering machine
2 e-mail   fax   body language   letter
3 screen   keyboard   mouse   fax machine
4 couple   relationship   modern   distance
5 modern   easily   crazy   great

Revision exercises and exam practice

Exam practice

a Find a noun.

difficult (line 3)   worried (line 5)

c Find a synonym.

methods (line 3)   great (line 7)

b Find an adjective.

widely (line 6)   easily (line 8)

d Explain in a complete sentence.

relationship (line 2)   videophone (line 6)

e Ask for the underlined part of the sentences.

They have known each other for three years.
Barbara e-mailed Andy in the middle of the night.
They want a videophone because body language is so important.
They are meeting again next month in New York.

Writing: Meeting in New York

Here is an e-mail which Andy sent to Barbara. Write a reply using the information below.

MEMO

From .....Al Greenwood, Head Office.............

To .....Barbara...

Dear Barbara

Thanks for your memo which arrived yesterday. Yes, I think we should meet when you are in NY. Can you come to the office on Friday for a meeting at 12.00?

MANHATTAN rise

F A X

Dear Ms Hamlock,

We have booked you a double room with bathroom for 4 nights from Thursday 9.10. The room rate is $155. This is a weekend special

Incoming Message   Page 1 of 1

Hi Barbara

Good news! I have just booked my flight to NY. I leave on Friday and arrive at JFK at 3.10 in the afternoon. Can you tell me when you arrive? Do you have to go to head office again this time? And what about the hotel? Have you booked one yet? If so, can you tell me which one we are staying at? I hope it is the Manhattan Rise with the swimming pool and sauna. Let's meet at the hotel, OK?

Do you want me to bring anything from Scotland except for myself, of course!

Really looking forward to seeing you again!

All my love

Andy

Ask Andy to bring 2 packets of tea and photos of Jack and Carol's wedding.

dep. LA 13.10 Thurs. 3.10
arr. JFK 21.50

18 CHOOSING A JOB

1

Anne Chatwell, Careers Adviser

CAREERS

● Choosing the sort of job you would like to do is one of the most important things you will ever have to do. At the moment you probably think that it is an impossible choice to make. So do most other students of your age, I can assure you. It can be especially difficult if your parents are ambitious and are trying to push you in a certain direction when you are unambitious or you don't know where you want to go!

● If you don't know yet what you want to do and feel unable to make the choice yourself, there is help available. Careers advisers can give you an independent opinion of your strengths and weaknesses. They are trained to help you to sort out which jobs are suitable for you and which are definitely unsuitable. It is no good being a veterinary nurse if you are allergic to animals and it isn't a good thing being an office worker if you are an outdoor person. You certainly don't have to take their advice but it might help to talk your ideas over with someone.

Before you start ...

Discrimination against others is often because of:

| ability | age | colour | race | religion | sex |

Have you or your friends ever experienced discrimination? Can you describe what happened?

● Something which careers officers find useful are computer-based multiple choice questionnaires called 'psychometric tests'. When you have finished the questions, the computer is able to match your answers with a very wide range of jobs. It gives you a list of possible, suitable jobs arranged from the one which is most compatible down to ones which it thinks are less compatible. Some of the jobs it lists will almost certainly be ones which you have completely overlooked before. And the job of your dreams may be totally incompatible with your abilities.

● Perhaps it seems very mechanical to think about your future in this way but at least these tests might help you to see where your abilities lie and where you will probably be most successful in the world of work.

● The computer can never make that difficult, final decision for you. Neither can careers advisers, but they might help to make it a little easier for you!

2

Equal and unequal language

Something which might influence your choice of job is whether it is a traditionally 'male' or 'female' one. These stereotypes are very strong and are difficult to break. One way of dealing with the problem is to be careful about not using sexist language. For example, words such as 'mankind', 'chairman', 'policeman', 'headmaster' should not be used because they exclude women. They should be rephrased as 'humankind', 'chairperson', 'police officer' and 'headteacher'.

Working with the text

1 Answer the questions about text 1.

1. Why is it is useful to talk to a careers adviser about your future.
2. Explain what a psychometric test is.
3. What is the point Mrs Chatwell is making when she talks about people being 'allergic to animals'?
4. What sort of job shouldn't you do if you are an outdoor person?
5. According to the text, the computer can never make the final, difficult decision for you. Why not?

2 **Find words in text 1 which mean the following:**

1 When you select something.
2 Something is very serious.
3 Something cannot be done.
4 Something is there to be used.
5 When someone is sensitive to something.
6 An opinion which you give to help someone.

3 **How ambitious are you?**

1 In ten years do you want to
   a be married and have children?
   b have an interesting but not very well-paid job?
   c have a well-paid job that is not very interesting?

2 Which of these jobs would you like to do? Choose one only.
   teacher   engineer   police officer   nurse
   journalist   pop star   politician

3 Do you think people who have money should help people with no money?
   a Yes   b No

4 How old do you want to be when you have children?
   a 18–21   b 22–26   c 27–30   d over 30

5 Do you work hard to be successful?
   a Yes   b No

6 Do you want to have more money than your parents?
   a Yes   b No

7 If you have a job to do, do you do it immediately or wait until the last moment?
   a immediately   b last moment

8 Which of these is most important to you? Choose one only.
   happiness   love   money   health

You will find the points on page 163

4 **Read text 2 and use the advice in it to help you correct the sexist language.**

1 The chairman of the company is very well paid.
2 If you want to know the time, ask a policeman.
3 Environmental problems are the fault of mankind.
4 I do a lot of overtime so I haven't got time for housework. I need a cleaning lady.
5 Businessmen have very stressful lives these days.
6 Being headmistress of a school is a very responsible job.
7 I'm thinking of becoming a fireman.

Language Review

1 PREFIXES AND SUFFIXES *(Vor- und Nachsilben)*

Verneinende Vorsilben	Adjektive	Verben
dis-	dissatisfied	disagree disappear dislike
im-	impolite impossible	–
in-	incompatible independent inexpensive	–
un-	unambitious unimportant unsuccessful	–

- Die häufigste Verneinungsform für Adjektive ist *un-*.
- Bei vielen Wörtern wird die Negativform mit *in-* gebildet.
- Bei manchen Wörtern, die mit *p* anfangen, wird *im-* benutzt.

Verb + Nachsilbe	Adjektive
-able	drinkable enjoyable likeable
-ful	helpful useful

- *-able* zeigt an, dass es möglich ist, dieses zu tun.

2 SO/NEITHER

- Mit *so* kann man Zustimmung zu einer positiven Aussage ausdrücken.
  *She is a careers adviser. **So is he**.*
- Für Verneinung der Aussage wird *neither* benutzt. *The computer can't make that difficult decision for you. **Neither** can careers advisers.*
- Um Zustimmung in der einfachen Gegenwart auszudrücken, wird das Hauptverb durch *do/does* ersetzt. *You probably think it is an impossible choice to make. **So do** most other students of your age.*
- Wenn das Verb im Aussagesatz in der einfachen Vergangenheit steht, wird es mit *did* ersetzt. *She talked to a careers adviser. **So did** he.*

Practice

1 Complete the sentences with the words from the box.

independent	unemployed	unpleasant	unfair	unpopular
unusual	impossible	impolite	unfriendly	unambitious

1. In many countries, it is still ... for women to get senior jobs.
2. It is ... to speak with your mouth full.
3. Our boss is very ... with his employees because he always wants us to work late.
4. He has been ... ever since she became his boss.
5. It's not that I want to divorce you, it's just that I want to be more ... .
6. The ... treatment of women in the past caused the rise of feminism.
7. It is ... to satisfy the demands of some employees.
8. Just because I'm a secretary, it doesn't mean that I'm ... .
9. My colleague is very ... . He never says hello.
10. Although he is very well qualified, John has been ... since he left school.

2 Match the words below with the lists of prefixes and suffixes. How many new words can you make?

un- in- im- dis-	compatible fair able like agree help use	-able -ful

3 Complete the boxes.

adjective	opposite
helpful	
	impossible
expected	
	inexpensive
	unfriendly
satisfied	
	unemployed

verb	adjective
enjoy	
	useful
drink	
help	
like	
	laughable
wash	

verb	opposite
	disappear
agree	
	dislike

UNIT 18 • CHOOSING A JOB

4 Respond to these statements using *so* or *neither* and the words in brackets.

1   I like going to the cinema. (I)
   ➡ So do I.
2   I don't like ice cream. (he)
   ➡ Neither does he.
3   He thinks she is crazy. (I)
4   They went to the USA last year. (we)
5   Harry will be very angry. (his wife)
6   He hasn't seen the film yet. (she)
7   They won't read it before the meeting starts. (the others)
8   I have apologised. (the teacher)
9   The scientists wouldn't believe that. (politicians)
10 She always works at the office until 8 pm. (her boss)

5 Practise the dialogue below with a partner. Replace the underlined words with words from the box.

A What shall we do today?
B Whatever we do, I don't want to go shopping.
A Neither do I. Actually, I'd quite like to see a film.
B Oh, yes, so would I! OK, That's settled then.

what	do today	go shopping	see a film
where	go on holiday	go to the beach	go skiing
what	eat	eat pizza	have an Indian take-away
how	travel	go by air	go by sea

6 Write about your view on equal opportunities.

I think they are important because …   As a woman, I find that …
I don't think they are important because … As a man, my view is that …

POINTS

1 a 0   b 5   c 10
2 pop star 0
   teacher, police officer, journalist 2
   engineer, nurse 5
   politician 10
3 Yes 0   No 10
4 a 0   b 2   c 5   d 10
5 Yes 0   No 10
6 Yes 0   No 10
7 immediately 10
   last moment 0
8 love, health 0
   happiness 5
   money 10

0–25 You are not very ambitious.
       You are happy with a quiet life.
26–45 You are quite ambitious. You do
       not want to work too hard.
46–80 You are very ambitious. But
       don't forget your friends!

THE WORLD OF WORK

Getting a job
Auf Jobsuche

1 Job adverts

1

BLEASDALE ELECTRICS

ELECTRICIAN REQUIRED

Permanent position with small, local firm. Driving licence necessary. *Apply in writing to:* Linda Harper, Bleasdale Electrics Ltd., 2 Jubilee Way, Hunter's Way Trading Estate, Oxford, OX9 2BU.

Closing date: 10th September

2

Ryton ❖ College

Office administrator required for educational administration centre. She must be able to work on her own. Salary £15,500 depending on experience. Applicants must be between 20 and 25 years of age.

Write with full details to Mrs J Philips, Ryton College, Church Lane, Framlington, Manchester MU4 9DX.

1. Which job would you apply for?
2. Do you think any of the language in the adverts is sexist?
3. Do you think it is fair, or unfair, that the advert for office administrator asks for applicants to be between 20 and 25 years of age?
4. What do you think of the salary offered for the office administrator?

2 Read these extracts from the letters of application for the job as electrician.

1 I believe I am a very efficient, hardworking and loyal employee. I have worked as an electrician for over fifteen years and two years ago I completed my Higher National Diploma in Electronic Engineering.

2 I have been with my current employer for five years. I joined the company straight from school and am studying for my HND in the evenings. I am deaf but have never had a problem understanding my colleagues or being understood by them.

3 I started at this firm a year ago after college, where I got a very good HND in Electronic Engineering. I am ambitious and imaginative and I am looking for a job which will be interesting.

1. Which applicant is best qualified? Why?
2. Which is the least experienced applicant?
3. Say which applicant you would appoint to the job and why.
4. Say which applicant you think is least suited to the job and why.

THE WORLD OF WORK

3 Choose one of the jobs advertised. Write a letter of application using some of the phrases below.

I am replying to your advertisement ...
I have qualifications in ...
I have experience in ...
I would like to work for you because ...
I look forward to hearing from you ...

4 📼 Listen to the people talking about their experiences in applying for jobs. Write down the particular type of discrimination they believe they have suffered from.

What sort of jobs would be suitable for these people? Can you name two jobs which would not be suitable.

5 These pictures show the people who were interviewed for the job as office administrator. Work in pairs to decide which person you think looks most suitable for the job.

Are you sure you are not being sexist?
How do you choose between the applicants?
How can someone make a good first impression at an interview?

UNIT 18 • CHOOSING A JOB

LANGUAGE WORKOUT

Revision

CONGRATULATIONS! You have made it past the interview and you have got that all-important first job! You are now part of the world of work. So, what happens now and how will your life change? Well, of
5 course, you might have guessed, now comes the really hard part. You have to get up on time every day, you have to be smart all the time and you have to be polite to people even when you don't agree with them. For the first few weeks you will be more tired than you have been for ages. You might think that the money you earn is not worth
10 the effort you have to put in, and the worst part is that people will expect you to be thankful that you have a job and are no longer unemployed. Try to stay with it, it will get better as you get more experience and are given more responsibility. You might even find at the end of your first year that you have been enjoying yourself
15 without even noticing it!

1 Answer these questions.

1 List three changes that might happen to someone when they get their first job.
2 Why might you be depressed about the money you earn?
3 In what two ways will the job get better?
4 What might happen after a year?

2 Translate the following sentences into English.

1 Ich bin deprimiert, seitdem ich meine Prüfungsergebnisse erhalten habe.
2 Letzte Woche hatte ich ein Vorstellungsgespräch für einen Job in einem Hotel.
3 Susan hatte 21 Vorstellungsgespräche, seitdem sie die Schule verlassen hat.
4 Während Paul auf eine Antwort auf seine Bewerbungsschreiben wartete, arbeitete er als Postbote.
5 Während des Vorstellungsgesprächs wurden Cathy viele schwierige Fragen gestellt.
6 Sarah arbeitet bei einer Computerfirma und lernt zur Zeit, wie man die Datenbank nutzt.
7 Wenn ich diesen Job bekommen hätte, wäre ich sehr glücklich gewesen.
8 Ich könnte einen besseren Job bekommen, wenn ich mehr Qualifikationen hätte.

Revision exercises and exam practice

3 This is part of an interview. What questions did the interviewer ask?

A ...¹
B I've been unemployed for exactly two months.
A ...²
B At a small travel agency in Harper Street.
A ...³
B For four and half years.
A And, ...⁴
B Because they had to close. Business was very bad at that time, you see.
A Yes, and that new travel agency in Mount Road can't have helped either.
B Yes, that's true.
A Tell me a bit about your office skills. ...⁵
B Oh yes, I learnt how to use a computer at the travel agency.
A What about e-mail? ...⁶
B Yes, we did.
A One last question: ...⁷
B Oh, I can start immediately because I have no plans to go on holiday.
A ...⁸
B Yes, of course you can. My phone number is 832792.

Exam practice

a Find a verb.

interview (line 2)   life (line 4)

b Find an adverb.

hard (line 5)   polite (line 7)

c Find a synonym.

hard (line 5)   smart (line 6)

d Find an opposite.

first (line 2)   worst (line 10)

Writing: Getting a better job

What can you do to have a better chance of getting a job? Write about 80 words. You may use the following expressions.

training	qualifications	job applications	CV
	experience	voluntary work	

LANGUAGE EXTRA

🔊 In the evening, after her interview for a job at *World of Electronics*, Melanie met her friend Sandra for a coffee.

SANDRA Well? How did it go?
MELANIE OK, I think.
SANDRA What do you mean 'OK'? Did they offer you the job or not?
5 MELANIE Oh, no. Not there and then, but the interviewer, a Mr Evans, said he would phone me.
SANDRA Did he? When?
MELANIE He didn't say. He just asked me if he could have my number and he wanted to know when I could start.
10 SANDRA That must mean he'll offer you the job! Anyway, what did you say?
MELANIE I told him that I didn't have any plans to go on holiday, so I could start immediately.
SANDRA But what about our plans? You promised to come to London with me next week. I phoned my cousin yesterday and told her we were coming.
MELANIE I know, but I have to wait and see. Perhaps we can still go.
15 SANDRA Well I'll have to let Susan know soon. But come on, tell me about the interview. What else did he ask?
MELANIE Of course, one of the first things he wanted to know was how long I'd been unemployed and why I had left the travel agency.
SANDRA You didn't tell him about, you know what, did you?
20 MELANIE Don't be stupid, of course I didn't! Anyway, then he asked me if I knew how to use a computer and e-mail and a few more boring questions which they always ask at interviews and that was it really.
SANDRA But what about clothes if you get the job? You can't always borrow something from your sister and you certainly can't go to work looking like that!
25 MELANIE We'll just have to look for something in London then, won't we?

Working with the text

1 Answer the questions about the text.

1. Why is Sandra so sure that Melanie will get the job?
2. If Mr Evans decides to offer Melanie the job, how will he tell her?
3. Why wasn't Sandra very happy when she heard that Melanie had told Mr Evans she could start immediately?
4. What do you think 'you know what' (line 19) could mean?
5. What do you think the 'boring questions they always ask at interviews' were?
6. What do you think Melanie borrowed from her sister?
7. What would you wear if you had to go to an interview?

UNIT 18 • CHOOSING A JOB

Language Review

INDIRECT SPEECH *(Indirekte Rede)*

Direkte Rede	Indirekte Rede
simple present	*simple past*
I like going to the cinema.	She said she **liked** going to the cinema.
present continuous	*past continuous*
We are coming to London.	Sandra told Susan they **were coming** ...
simple past	*past perfect*
I worked at the travel agency for four years.	Melanie explained that she **had worked** ...
present perfect	*past perfect*
I have been unemployed for two months.	She said she **had been** unemployed for ...
will/can	*could/would*
I'll/I can phone you soon.	Mr Evans said he **would/could** phone ...

- In der indirekten Rede wird einem Dritten berichtet, was jemand gesagt hat.
- Wenn das einleitende Verb in der Vergangenheit steht (*said, told, explained* etc.), verschieben sich die Zeiten der Verben im berichtenden Satzteil (indirekter Rede).
- Die Zeiten der Verben verschieben sich in indirekten Fragesätzen entsprechend, wobei die Wortstellung die gleiche wie in Aussagesätzen ist. *Where do you live* → *He asked me where I **lived***.
- Bei Fragen ohne Fragewort, wird die indirekte Frage mit *if* eingeleitet. *Can you start immediately?* → *He asked me **if (whether)** I **could** start immediately*.

Practice

1 Here are some things Melanie told Mr Evans at the interview. Put them into indirect speech, using *She said (that) ...* or *She told Mr Evans (that) ...* .

1. I want to work for an electronics company because I'm interested in learning something new.
2. I've applied for three other jobs.
3. I enjoy going to the cinema and meeting my friends in my free time.
4. I left school at sixteen.
5. Working on Saturdays was the only thing I didn't like about my last job.
6. I'm not going on holiday.
7. I can use the computer and e-mail.
8. If you offer me the job, I'll be able to start immediately.

2 Look at exercise 1 again. What did Mr Evans ask Melanie?

➡ *He asked Melanie why she wanted to work for ...*

COMMERCIAL CORRESPONDENCE

BETTER VISION Optical Supplies Limited — *letterhead*

Maxwell House
43-45 Regent Street
London SW1Y 4LR
Great Britain
Tel + 44 171 845 0099   Fax + 44 171 845 8967
E-mail: bvos1067,11@world.net

Your ref: — *for the recipient*
Our ref: SW/ep — *for your firm*

27 October 19.. — *date of writing*

The Marketing Manager
Brille-ant GmbH
Kirchstraße 8
10557 Berlin
Germany
— *inside address*

Dear Sir or Madam — *salutation/start*

Catalogue & Sales Presentation — *subject line*

introduction of firm: We are the largest suppliers of optical instruments in Great Britain. Please find enclosed a copy of our company brochure.

reason for writing: At the trade fair in Frankfurt last month some of our representatives took the opportunity of inspecting your range of products and were very impressed with your line of frames for reading glasses.

making a request: We would like to order your firm's catalogue. Could you please send it to us at your earliest convenience? We would be grateful if you could also enclose your current price list.

referring to future contact: We look forward to hearing from you soon.

Yours faithfully — *complimentary close*

Mark Lawrence — *signature*

pp Ms Sandra Wilkinson — *per pro*
Sales Manager — *position in company*

Enc: company brochure — *enclosures*
cc: Dr Jane Parsons, General Manager — *carbon copy*

Letter Layout
Business letters can vary in layout. The letter on page 170 has been written in 'block style'. There is no punctuation in the date, address, salutation, complimentary close and abbreviations.

Letterhead
The letterhead shows the company's name and address, its telephone and fax numbers. It can also contain an e-mail address.

Reference
When you answer a letter from another firm, give the reference letter under Your Ref: and your own reference under Our Ref:. The reference usually gives the initials of the person who wrote the letter (in capitals) and of the person who keyed it in (in small letters): SW/ep.

Date
There are different ways of writing the date. The simplest method is to write it like this:

> *14 May 1998*

Never use just numbers, for example 4.10.98. In Europe this always means 4 October 1998 but in America and many Asian countries it can mean 10 April 1998.

Salutation and complimentary close
You start your letter with a salutation and finish it with a complimentary close.

	Salutation	*Complimentary close*
To a firm	Dear Sir or Madam	Yours faithfully
To a person	Dear Mr (or Mrs) Smith	Yours sincerely
	Dear Mike	Best wishes

If you are nor sure whether the woman you are writing to is married or not, you can use the form *Ms* instead of *Miss* or *Mrs*.

Subject line
The subject line says what the letter is about and helps the firm you are writing to decide who should answer your letter.

Signature block
The firm's name often comes directly above the signature and the sender's name and position directly after it. Sometimes the letter is signed by an assistant and then the letters *pp* (= on behalf of) are used to show this.

Enclosures
If you put something in a letter, you should write Enc or Encs at the end. This shows the reader that there was an enclosure.

Circulation (cc = carbon copy)
This tells you who has been sent a copy of the letter.

FURTHER READING

1 THE WAY WE LOOK TODAY

People often say that the grass is greener on the other side of the fence and this is also true of the way we think about ourselves. Magazine surveys of young women show that they never like the way they look and always want to look more like models in magazines. More and more of them are doing
5 something about it by paying to have plastic surgery. They change the shape of their noses or their lips or they lose weight instantly. The market is especially big for women who want to stop the signs of ageing. Current prices are:

> £1200–1800 for a new nose, £800–1300 for bigger lips, £1200–2500 for bigger breasts, £1500–3000 for a facelift and £1800–3300 for reducing stomach and bottom.
10 So, for £6500 you could have a whole new you!

Increasingly, however, it is not just women who want to make themselves bigger, smaller, younger, more beautiful in this way. In America men are now spending as much as women on plastic surgery. Michael Jackson is probably the extreme example of this. He says that he has not done anything to himself but, if you compare
15 his looks now to the way he looked in the 70s, it is obvious that his skin is much whiter and his nose is a completely different shape.

Michael Jackson is also a good example of the dangers of plastic surgery too. People say that his nose is falling to pieces because of all the work done on it. It is difficult to see whether this is true or not because he never appears in public without
20 a mask now – perhaps this means that the reports are true.

272 words

1 Questions on the text

1. What do magazine surveys show about young women?
2. What sort of things do they change with plastic surgery?
3. Which market is the biggest?
4. Who else is interested in plastic surgery?
5. What is different about Michael Jackson now?
6. Why is it difficult to see Michael Jackson's face now?

2 Vocabulary

a Find an opposite.
   often (line 1)   true (line 2)   never (line 3)

b Find a noun.
   true (line 2)   lose (line 6)   different (line 16)

c Find a synonym.
   instantly (line 6)   completely (line 16)

d Explain in a complete sentence.
   plastic surgery (line 5)   lose weight (line 6)

3 Grammar

a Put the adverb in the correct position.
I think that models in magazines are more beautiful than me. (always)
He is worried about his looks. (never)
We wonder about Michael Jackson's nose. (often)

b Ask for the underlined words.
I have got a big nose.
Michael Jackson always wears a mask when he appears in public.

c Fill in the missing forms.

positive	comparative	superlative
big (line 6)		
beautiful (line 12)		
difficult (line 19)		

4 Writing

Imagine you have decided to have plastic surgery. What sort of plastic surgery would you choose? Explain why. Find out how much you need to pay for it using the prices in the text. Is there anything else you would like to change that is not in the list?

2 THE COST OF TEENAGERS

Many people say that teenagers are rude, lazy and awful to their parents. But it seems that they are also more expensive than we thought. The total cost can be as much as £67,000 to bring up a teenager, according to a recent survey. Even for parents on average incomes, who
5 have to say no to some of their teenagers' demands, the cost is still likely to be around £25,000. This compares with the average cost of £20,000 for the first five years of a child's life.

The survey looked at the costs of keeping someone between the ages of sixteen and twenty-one, including food, transport and education. Food and
10 clothes are probably the most expensive things but transport costs are enormous too, especially if you include the cost of a car when the teenager is old enough to drive. Then there are things like electricity, telephone bills, Christmas and birthday presents and holidays. And it doesn't stop when they leave home to go to college because most parents now have to make a
15 contribution to the living costs of students. Then, when they finally enter the real world of employment (or unemployment), there is one more cheque to sign. The marriage cheque.

All this is good news for those who decide that they don't want children. Those without the expensive type of teenager can save about £36 a day.
20 Think what you could do with that: a small country cottage, a Caribbean holiday once a year, thirty round the world flights, 240 cigarettes a day, a really good meal for two every two days or three bottles of champagne a day. There's no comparison!

279 words

1 Questions on the text

1. What is the main finding of the survey about bringing up teenagers?
2. Explain what these three figures mean: £25,000; £67,000; £20,000.
3. Name five things which are included in the costs.
4. Why doesn't it get cheaper when teenagers go to college?
5. What do you think the meaning of 'the marriage cheque' is?
6. What does the last sentence mean?

2 Vocabulary

a Find a noun
   expensive (line 2)   average (line 4)   real (line 16)

b Find an opposite.
   lazy (line 1)   expensive (line 2)   good (line 18)

c Explain in a complete sentence.
   teenager (line 1)   average income (line 4)

3 Grammar

a Change the simple present to the simple past.
   This compares with the average cost … (line 6)
   All this is good news … (line 18)

b Fill in the missing forms.
   positive   *comparative*   *superlative*
   expensive (line 2)
   good (line 18)

c Give the singular.
   holidays (line 13)   children (line 18)   cigarettes (line 21)

4 Writing

Write a paragraph about the cost of teenagers, from a teenager's point of view.

3 THE RETURN OF THE SCOOTER

Forget rollerblades! Scooters are back in fashion! In the seventies, eighties and most of the nineties, Lambrettas and Vespas were definitely not 'cool'. But now, scooters are OK again. After all the Oasis band have got one each!

Corradino d'Ascanio designed the first scooter in 1946 and the design has remained more or less the same ever since: small wheels, handlebars like those of a bicycle, and a covered engine at the back. He called it a Vespa, which means 'wasp' in Italian, not because of its noise, but because of its shape. Within a year, the rival Lambretta arrived on the scene and in the fifties and early sixties, they were both extremely popular. They were cheap to buy and to run compared with cars and they had advantages over motorbikes. It was easier to ride them than a motorbike and people felt that scooters were cleaner to ride, too. In Britain in particular, their sophisticated image was popular with the 'mods' at the time, who were young people interested in pop music and fashionable clothes. The 'rockers', on the other hand, rode large, noisy motorbikes and dressed in black leather jackets and boots.

15 But, like many new fashions, scooters disappeared almost as quickly as they appeared. By the mid-sixties, young people had more money and small cars like the Mini became the new fashion. By the early seventies, production of scooters more or less ended.

Now, you can get Vespas for about £1800, which compares well with the price of a new car which is at least £7500. Scooters are very attractive in today's cities, where there are 20 too many cars, but the main reason for their comeback has probably more to do with fashion than anything else. There is no question that they are back in fashion, but will they stay there?

307 words

1 Questions on the text

1. What happened to scooters in the seventies, eighties and most of the nineties?
2. Who designed the first scooter?
3. What happened in the fifties and sixties?
4. Why were scooters so popular compared with cars and motorbikes?
5. Who were the young people that liked scooters so much in Britain?
6. Why have scooters become popular again?

2 Vocabulary

a Find an adjective.
fashion (line 1)   noise (line 7)

b Find an adverb.
particular (line 11)   fashionable (line 12)

c Find a verb.
production (line 17)   attractive (line 19)

d Explain in a complete sentence.
definitely not 'cool' (line 2)   comeback (line 20)

3 Grammar

a Find the missing forms.

positive	comparative	superlative
cool (line 2)		
	easier (line 10)	
popular (line 11)		

b Fill in the correct form of the simple present or present continuous.
Today I ... (ride) my scooter.   She always ... (go) to work on her motorbike.

c Give the singular.
people (line 16)   cities (line 19)

d Fill in the correct form of the simple past.
I ... (go) to the rock concert yesterday.
We ... (not/ride) our scooters to school on Monday.
... (they/design) a new scooter last year?

4 Writing

Do you prefer scooters or motorbikes? Write a paragraph of 80 words.

4 THE US IN ALL ITS GLORY

The US is a vast country of many different regions, each with its own attractions. We tend to forget this because we concentrate on the parts we know about, like New York, but we should find out what else there is on offer.

Probably the place which most children want to visit is Florida and
5 Disneyworld, the theme park capital of the US. Their parents are quite happy to let them go to Florida, so that they can enjoy relaxing under the palm trees along the white, sandy beaches and in the clear, warm water. But it is not a perfect paradise. Recently tourists have seen its other side when local criminals have robbed and murdered visitors.

10 The part of the US most familiar from films and television programmes is California. This is where Baywatch is set and is where the world's largest film and TV studios are. It is also home to most of the American wine producers. People are different in California, they make most of us look very ordinary because of their strange lifestyles and religions.

15 Completely different to California, is the Deep South. If you like jazz, country or blues music, you must come here to the cities like New Orleans where they were born. This part of the US has many historic houses and monuments and was on the losing side in the American Civil War.

Different again is the Pacific North West, the land of the Rocky Mountains with
20 their snowy peaks, deep valleys and dark forests. The list is really endless. What should you do when you come to the US on a visit, because you can't possibly see everything on one trip? The best advice is probably that you should make lots of trips, choose one region at a time, hire a car and then see what happens!

306 words

1 Questions on the text

1 Which part of the US is good for warm, family holidays with things that the children want to do?
2 Why isn't Florida a perfect paradise?
3 Where should you go to see lots of film stars?
4 Where was jazz born?
5 This is a beautiful, wild area with mountains and forests. What is it called?
6 Why can't you see everything in the US in one trip?

2 Vocabulary

a Find an opposite.
   happy (line 5)   warm (line 7)

b Find a noun.
   different (line 1)   happy (line 5)   warm (line 7)

c Find a verb.
   attraction (line 2)   offer (line 3)   visitor (line 9)

d Explain in a complete sentence.
   theme park (line 5)   criminal (line 8)

3 Grammar

a Fill in the missing forms:.

positive	comparative	superlative
		most (line 4)
warm (line 7)		

b Fill in the correct form of the simple past or present perfect.
We ... (not/visit) the US before.
Last year I ... (visit) Disneyworld with my family.
... (you/ever/visit) Disneyworld?

c Find the three principal parts of the verbs.
is (line 1)   know (line 3)   like (line 15)

d Give the plural.
country (line 1)   place (line 4)

4 Writing

Where would you like to go in the US? Write a paragraph of 80 words about your ideal American holiday.

5 IT'S ALL IN THE PACKAGING!

When you next go shopping, remember that the manufacturers of the products have carefully designed each box, bottle, can or packet to persuade you to buy that product and only that product.

In the 1930s, Louis Cheskin, a marketing specialist, discovered some
5 interesting things about packaging. He put the same product in two different packets and tested them on several hundred people, asking them which they preferred. More than 80% chose the packet with a particular design and even after trying the product, most said they preferred the same one. He did similar experiments with many different products and his conclusion was that the
10 packaging is very important. People very often form their opinions about products because of the packaging.

In another test, they put one type of deodorant into three different cans. People who tried the deodorant had different opinions about it, ranging from good to awful, according to the image of the can. The power of the packet
15 depends on a combination of elements: some attract your attention immediately and some keep your attention when you look more closely. For example, the use of sharp, angular yellow shapes with attractive slogans and messages like 'improved', '25% off' or 'environmentally friendly' printed on the labels is good. Feminine forms too, like circles and curves, have very positive associations for
20 package design. For example, when a well-known fast food company wondered whether to change their famous logo of the golden arches, they eventually decided to keep them, as they had very positive feminine associations!

255 words

1 Questions on the text

1. Why do manufacturers design packaging so carefully?
2. How long ago did Louis Cheskin do his experiments?
3. What did he find out?
4. What did the people think about the deodorant in the second test?
5. What two elements do packaging designers try to combine in their designs?
6. What sort of shapes have positive associations? Why?

2 Vocabulary

a Find a verb.
   manufacturer (line 1)   product (line 2)   packaging (line 5)

b Find a synonym.
   discover (line 4)   experiment (line 9)   attractive (line 17)

c Explain in a complete sentence.
   marketing specialist (line 4)   logo (line 21)

3 Grammar

a Fill in the correct form of the verbs.
   She always … (study) the packaging before she buys anything.
   The perfume I … (use) at the moment is horrible, but the packaging is nice!
   When … (you/buy) those trainers?

b Fill in the missing forms.

personal pronoun	possessive adjective
	my
he	
	their

c Ask for the underlined words.
   Louis Cheskin did a lot of experiments <u>in the 1930s</u>.
   <u>Feminine forms</u> have very positive associations.

4 Writing

Write about 80 words describing an advertisement which you particularly like.

6 THE TRUTH ABOUT VIOLENCE

Do your parents let you go out by yourself or do they drive you everywhere and never let you have any real freedom? It is very difficult to be a parent today because you want to protect your adolescent against the violent strangers which the newspapers are always talking about. The way that many parents
5 protect their children is to make them stay at home all the time and not to let them go out on their own with their friends. But is this protected life good for young people? Not according to the young people themselves, who say they are driven crazy by their parents. Experts are also becoming increasingly worried

about children who spend hours at home on their own in front of the computer
10 or in front of the television. They don't get enough exercise and can become overweight and unfit. They don't spend enough time with other people so they don't learn how to make friends and they don't learn about protecting themselves in the real world either.

So what should parents do? The papers, the television and the radio are all so
15 full of news about violence against children that parents feel they must keep control over their children to make sure they are safe. But do parents need to worry so much? Is it really true that our society is so much more violent than that of our parents and grandparents? Information about violence against children shows that it is not, we just know more about it now because of the newspapers.
20 The sad truth is that our families and people we know are far, far more likely to hurt us than strangers in the street. In nine cases of violence out of ten, the victims knew the person who attacked them. It is not a comfortable thought at all but it should make parents worry less about their children, shouldn't it? There is a message here for the young people too.

328 words

1 Questions on the text

1. Why are child experts worried about modern children?
2. Why do newspapers make parents worry?
3. What does information about violence show?
4. What is the sad truth about violence?
5. Which type of people should parents worry about?
6. What is the message for young people?

2 Vocabulary

a Find an adjective.
freedom (line 2)   stranger (line 3)   truth (line 20)

b Find a noun.
difficult (line 2)   protect (line 3)   violent (line 3)

c Find an opposite.
never (line 2)   difficult (line 2)

d Explain in a complete sentence.
the real world (line 13)   violence (line 21)

3 Grammar

a Fill in the question tags.
Children should be careful with strangers, … ?
Parents drive their children crazy, … ?
Children don't know about the real world, … ?

b Ask for the underlined words.
He never goes out by himself.
Experts are worried because a lot of children spend too much time in front of the television.

c Fill in *much* or *many*.
   … parents worry too much about their children.
   They don't give their children … freedom.
   A lot of children don't get … exercise because they spend too … hours in front of the TV.

d Fill in the correct form of *make* or *let*.
   We … our children go to bed early.
   They … their parents think they are asleep and then they go out.

4 Writing

What drives you crazy about your parents? Write a paragraph of 80 words.

7 A DAY IN THE LIFE OF A EUROPEAN

A recent survey shows some interesting differences in the everyday habits of Europeans. The survey was based on questions about people's activities over the same twenty-four hour period. It is interesting to look at some of the results to see whether our stereotyped images of different nationalities seem to be correct.

5 Perhaps it is not surprising that the Czechs and Hungarians get up the earliest, with over 40% getting up before 6 am or that the Spanish and Irish tend to get up later. The Czechs and Hungarians also seem to be the cleanest taking the most baths and showers with the Irish and Russians taking the least. It does seem surprising, however, that the French and Italians wash more frequently than the Germans!

10 One stereotyped view of people in Turkey is that they have hot tempers. This is probably supported by the information that nearly 40% of Turks shouted at someone in the last 24 hours. However, they are not the only ones with hot tempers – the survey showed that the British were only just behind Turkey for hot tempers. So, our stereotyped image of the cool, controlled British may not be so accurate!

15 Which nationality would you choose as the happiest? Probably the Italians or the Spanish with their warm, latin characters would be the choice of most people, but in fact it is the Dutch. Over 75% of the people asked in Holland said they felt happy. Another surprise is that it is not the Italians or French who are the sexiest, it is the Danes and the Finns. But, on the other hand, it is another Scandinavian nationality, the

20 Swedes, who are the coolest, most reserved in Europe.

What can we conclude from statistics which come out of a survey like this? We certainly cannot use them to make a new stereotype of a nation, if they seem to show that our existing stereotyped images are incorrect. Perhaps the conclusion should be that it is important to treat people as individuals, and not to think in stereotypes.

342 words

1 Questions on the text

1 What do the Czechs and the Hungarians do differently from other Europeans?
2 How is this different from the Spanish and the Irish?
3 Who appear to be the cleanest? Why?
4 Where do people shout a lot?
5 Why is it surprising that British people have hot tempers?
6 According to the text, what can we learn from a survey like this?

2 Vocabulary

a Find a verb.
   choice (line 16)   conclusion (line 23)

b Find an opposite.
   correct (line 4)   earliest (line 5)   accurate (line 14)

c Find an adverb.
   different (line 4)   happy (line 17)

d Explain in a complete sentence.
   survey (line 1)   stereotyped image (line 4)

3 Grammar

a Put in the reflexive pronoun where necessary.
   He washes … every day.
   The Dutch enjoy … the most.
   They behave … in a very cool, reserved way.

b Ask for the underlined words.
   The survey was based on questions about people's activities over the same twenty-four hour period.
   The Czechs and the Hungarians get up the earliest.

c Fill in the question tags.
   The British are cool and controlled, …?
   The Irish don't get up early, …?
   We should treat people as individuals, …?

d Fill in *some* or *any*.
   This survey shows … interesting differences in people's habits.
   … people think the British are reserved.
   Are … of our stereotyped images correct?

4 Writing

What do you think the British are like? Write a paragraph of 80 words about your view of a typical British teenager.

8 CANDLE IN THE WIND

On 31st August 1997, Diana, Princess of Wales was tragically killed in a car crash. People all over the world were shocked by the news. It seemed impossible that someone so young and glamorous and who appeared on our television screens and in our newspapers so often could be dead. It was not just people in English-speaking
5 countries like the USA, South Africa and Australia, but people from all over the world who sent letters and flowers to her funeral because everyone thought they knew her.

Ever since her death people have been wondering what caused the accident which killed her. Most people believe that if the 'paparazzi' had not been following her, the accident would not have happened. It was a sad fact of her life that we, the public,
10 wanted to see more and more photographs of her and so the photographers intruded on her life more and more to get the photographs which we wanted. One photograph of her could sell around the world for £200,000, so it is not surprising that she was followed by so many people who wanted to make their fortune. This seems to mean that, in some way, we were all responsible for her death and so we all felt very strongly
15 about it.

But if she had lived, would we have felt as strongly about her as she got older and less attractive? It is very probable that we would not. The media image can easily become far more real than the person themselves and we start to think that someone must be good and interesting because they are beautiful and we lose interest in them
20 when they are no longer beautiful. Princess Diana, like Marilyn Monroe, will always be interesting because she will never lose her looks. Is it right that we should concentrate so much more on the image than on the person?

Whatever might have been, could have been or should have been, it is certain that the legend of Princess Diana will live on for far longer than the brief candle of her life.

349 words

1 Questions on the text

1. When did Princess Diana die?
2. How did Princess Diana die?
3. What might have caused her death?
4. Why were we all, in some way, responsible for her death?
5. How much could a photograph of her be worth?
6. Why, according to the text, will Princess Diana always be interesting?

2 Vocabulary

a Find a noun.
  dead (line 4)   interesting (line 19)   beautiful (line 19)

b Find an opposite.
  impossible (line 2)   dead (line 4)   sad (line 9)

c Find a synonym.
  sad (line 9)   strongly (line 14)   beautiful (line 19)

d Explain in a complete sentence.
  car crash (line 1)   media image (line 17)

3 Grammar

a Find the three principal parts of the verbs.
  see (line 10)   sell (line 12)   lose (line 19)

b Put into the active form.
  She was followed by the paparazzi.
  The photograph was sold to the newspapers by the paparazzi.

c Put into the passive form.
   People from all over the world sent flowers to the funeral.
   The driver probably caused the accident.
d Ask for the underlined words.
   Princess Diana died on 31st August 1997.
   People from all over the world sent letters and flowers to her funeral.

4 Writing

Which famous person do you most admire? Write about 80 words.

9 WINNING THE DRUGS WAR

Young drug addicts in Sweden have been learning how to manage their lives again, thanks to a peaceful place in the countryside. At the Hassela Kollektivet, which is in a beautiful part of north-east Sweden, thirty young people are given a second chance at life.

5 Former drug addicts and other difficult teenagers live there and they all look healthy and happy. As it is so far away from the city, the centre obviously keeps them away from drugs, but above all it is the place itself that must be the real reason for success. It gives students a feeling of well-being and it offers them understanding. After a period during which they come off drugs completely, the
10 teenagers are given training in life skills as well as an academic education. They also do a lot of sport, look after animals on the farm and learn to find joy in nature. It must be the education as well as the treatment, that has helped them to find new directions in their lives.

Europe's drug policies are different in each country. For example, in Holland
15 and Spain, cannabis and heroin use is legal, but in France, Greece and Sweden, policies are very tough. The Swedes tried making drugs legal but the experiment did not work. In the 1960s they tried to control the sale of drugs, but this created a huge black market instead and led to a big increase in the number of addicts. After two years they gave up and made drug use illegal again.
20 Since then, Sweden has become one of the strictest countries on drugs in Europe. Most of the drug addicts in Sweden used to be under 30 but in 1992 only 30% were under 30 and just 1% under 20. This shows that the policy is working and that it is just that the main users are getting older. The Hassela community must have contributed to this success rate.

325 words

1 Questions on the text

1 What is the Hassela Kollektivet centre in Sweden?
2 What sort of people live there?
3 What is so special about the centre?
4 Give examples of how Europe's drugs policies are different.
5 What did Sweden try in the 1960s and what happened?
6 What is Sweden's policy on drugs like now?

2 Vocabulary

a   Find an opposite.
    young (line 1)   beautiful (line 3)   healthy (line 6)

b   Find a noun.
    manage (line 1)   peaceful (line 2)   healthy (line 6)

c   Find a synonym.
    healthy (line 6)   tough (line 16)   huge (line 18)

d   Explain in a complete sentence.
    addict (line 1)   illegal (line 19)

3 Grammar

a   Fill in the correct form of the simple past or present perfect.
    Last year she ... (have) treatment for six months and now she seems a lot better.
    You ... (try) to come off drugs twice before and it hasn't worked.

b   Fill in the correct form of the future.
    We ... (start) treatment tomorrow.
    I am sure I ... (never/take) drugs.
    She has made plans and she ... (do) something about her problem soon.

c   Fill in the correct form of the verb.
    If I ... (be) a drug addict, I would like to go to the Hassela community.
    If he is not careful, he ... (become) a drug addict.

d   Ask for the underlined words.
    Cannabis is illegal in the UK.
    Cannabis and heroin are legal in Holland.

4 Writing

Do you think drugs should be legal? Write a paragraph of 80 words giving your point of view.

10 HEALTH CRAZES

We are unfit, we are fat, we are unhealthy and we are worried about it. So it is not surprising that every now and then different health crazes come along which will, we are told, solve our problems quickly and forever. If we eat only bananas or do strange exercises in front of a video every day or if we buy a
5   really expensive exercise machine, we will achieve our ideal shape and look like the latest supermodel. We must believe what we are told because we spend billions of pounds on every new craze and we make a few people very rich by doing so.

Our obsession with eating healthy, organic food has even got to the point
10   where some babies of health-conscious parents have been undernourished because the 'healthy' food they have been given does not have enough fat or carbohydrates in it.

The strange thing is, though, that all this effort and money is making no difference at all! We are getting fatter and more unhealthy, not thinner and
15 healthier. We take fat out of our milk but put it into our fast food, we exercise in the gym for half an hour but we travel everywhere by car.

The really crazy thing is that, for most people, the difference between being overweight or being the right weight is only 50 calories, two biscuits a day or walking up and down the stairs a few times. This is because we eat 750 calories
20 less food than people did in the 1950s but we do 800 calories less exercise. There is nothing difficult about it, the changes we need to make are very small and we certainly don't need to spend lots of money on expensive health crazes!

291 words

1 Questions on the text

1. Give an example of a health craze mentioned in the text.
2. Who gets the most benefit from the health crazes?
3. Why do some babies have health problems?
4. How do we know that the health crazes are not working?
5. What is the difference between being fat and slim for most people?
6. How much more or less do we eat than people in the 1950s?

2 Vocabulary

a Find a noun.
fat (line 1)   healthy (line 9)   difficult (line 21)

b Find an adjective.
craze (line 2)   difference (line 14)

c Find a synonym.
quickly (line 3)   really (line 5)

d Find an opposite.
unfit (line 1)   expensive (line 5)   rich (line 7)

e Explain in a complete sentence.
health craze (line 2)   exercise machine (line 5)

3 Grammar

a Find the three principal parts of the verb.
are (line 1)   buy (line 4)   need (line 21)

b Fill in the missing forms.

positive	comparative	superlative
fat (line 1)		
	thinner (line 14)	

c Fill in the correct form of the verbs.
We would be thinner if we … (do) more exercise.
She … (lose) a lot of weight since she … (start) walking to work.

d   Put into the passive form.
    The doctor told me to go on a diet.
    My girlfriend gave me an exercise machine.
e   Ask for the underlined words.
    We need to walk everywhere to keep fit.
    We spend billions of pounds on every new craze.

4 Writing

What is your favourite way of keeping fit and healthy? Write about 80 words.

11 EQUALITY AND DISCRIMINATION

Everyone in the UK can go to college if they have the right 'A' levels or GNVQs. Some people, however, find it very difficult to attend college because of their personal situation. Tutors need to have training in equal opportunities, so that they can help students with all the different needs they
5   might have. We tend to organise our institutions with the 'normal' person in mind, but at some point in our lives all of us will have problems, for example when we are old or pregnant or injured. So, it is in our own interests to try hard to include all types of people in our society.

Students who are disabled need college buildings with lifts as well as stairs,
10 so do students who come to college with small children or who have an injury such as a broken leg. Students who have learning difficulties do not look disabled, neither do those for whom English is a second language, but both types of student need extra time to complete project work and examinations. The message to tutors is that all of their students are in some way special. Even
15 if they have no disability, they may be unusual in other ways. Students caring for children or for old relatives need help with their time if they are to do their studies and run a home.

Charles Norton is a good example of an unusual student because he is studying photography even though he is blind! He can only see very simple
20 forms in black and white but this seems to help his photography. He needs help in taking lecture notes and he has friends who read textbooks onto tape for him but otherwise he gets around by himself and has even learnt to develop his own photographs.

298 words

1 Questions on the text

1   What does everyone in the UK have a right to?
2   What do tutors need training in?
3   Name three ways in which most normal people will have problems at some point in their lives?
4   Which three sorts of students need lifts?
5   Which sorts of students need more time to complete examinations?
6   Why is Charles Norton special?

2 Vocabulary

a Find an opposite.
everyone (line 1)   include (line 8)   unusual (line 18)

b Find a noun.
organise (line 5)   injured (line 7)   disabled (line 9)

c Find a synonym.
organise (line 5)   types (line 8)   complete (line 13)

d Explain in a complete sentence.
'A' levels (line 1)   disabled (line 9)

3 Grammar

a Fill in the correct form of the verbs.
When I … (be) pregnant last year, I … (find) it difficult to get around.
He … (be) blind since he … (be) a baby.

b Put into the passive form.
The college gave him training in equal opportunities.
A private nurse cares for our disabled mother.

c Put into the active form.
She has been helped a lot by her tutor.
They were given more time for the examination by the college.

d Ask for the underlined words.
He has special needs <u>because he is blind</u>.
She was given <u>15 minutes'</u> extra time for the exam.

4 Writing

Do you think people with disabilities should be given special treatment at college? Write about 80 words giving your point of view.

12 INTERVIEW TECHNIQUES

*I*magine. You have applied for the job of your dreams. You have waited nervously for days wondering whether the employer will be interested in you and then suddenly the letter arrives inviting you to an interview.
What now? How do you make the most of this golden opportunity? The interview might only last for half an hour, how can you prepare yourself to make the best impression possible? This is the advice given by the Careers Service of Anglia College.
Firstly, think about what the interview is for. Why does the employer want to see you, why don't they just offer the job to the person with the best qualifications? Of course, you will be asked questions about how you would do the job to make sure that you really have the knowledge and experience you claim. But to do the job well you need to get on with people at work; there is more to work than just knowing the job. Your future employer wants to see whether your face 'fits', whether you will get on well with your future colleagues and be a 'good' employee.

Secondly, look at yourself through the employer's eyes. What would impress you about a future employee? Remember that first impressions are very important, so dress carefully to make the right impression rather than the wrong one. A short, tight skirt, high heels and lots of make-up is probably not a good idea unless the interview is for a job as a fashion model!

Finally, think about the interview itself. What questions can you prepare for and, just as important, what would you like to know about the job? Think also about how you would answer questions. A short, direct answer which gives the information required is far better than a long, nervous one which never gets to the point. But remember above all that the interviewers want to know about you, about your personality, so don't be afraid to be natural.

In the end, there are no mysterious and difficult interview techniques at all. Just be yourself and make friends with your interviewers!

351 words

1 Questions on the text

1. How long do many job interviews last for?
2. What are interviews for?
3. What do you need as well as good qualifications?
4. How should you dress for an interview?
5. What sort of answers do you need to give?
6. What is the best interview techniques of all?

2 Vocabulary

a Find an opposite.
   best (line 5)   well (line 10)   direct (line 21)

b Find a noun.
   imagine (line 1)   prepare (line 5)   impress (line 14)

c Find a verb.
   qualification (line 8)   knowledge (line 10)   impression (line 15)

d Find an adjective.
   well (line 10)   carefully (line 16)

e Explain in a complete sentence.
   interview (line 3)   qualifications (line 8)

3 Grammar

a Find the three principal parts of the verb.
   think (line 7)   make (line 9)   know (line 20)

b Ask for the underlined words.
   I wanted to know how much I would earn.
   He went for his interview on Friday.

c Fill in *for* or *since*.
   She has been trying to get a job ... almost a year.
   He has been doing the job ... March.

d Put into the active form.
   I was made very nervous by the people interviewing me.
   The job has been offered to me by the person who interviewed me.

e Fill in the correct forms of the verbs.
   I would only work here if I ... (not have) any other job.
   She ... (go) to another interview next Saturday.

4 Writing

What is the job of your dreams? Write about 80 words describing it.

TAPESCRIPT

UNIT 1 Young People in Britain
World of Work, exercise 4
1 I'm Bob Hunter, from Chicago. I work for IBS. That's International Book Shop, by the way. I work in sales. My job is to help customers and ... to sell books!
2 Hello. My name's Rita. I'm a secretary in a big office in London. I work with computers, I answer the phone, make appointments ... that sort of thing.
3 I'm Alice and I'm a shop assistant. I'm out of work at the moment, but I hope to find a new job soon. I have an interview next week.
4 Hi. My name's Michel. I'm from Strasbourg. I am a student but I have a part-time job on a building site. The money's good.
5 I'm Jutta from Stuttgart. I work in a large hotel in the centre of the city.

UNIT 2 Free time
Practice, exercise 5
1 MAN I usually go to the cinema on Saturday evenings.
2 MAN My friend Petra worries me. She never wants to go out. She always stays in.
3 WOMAN My boyfriend is so lazy. He always sits at home and watches football.
4 MAN I'm not fond of sport. I like listening to music in my spare time.
5 WOMAN At the weekends, I usually go window shopping. I rarely buy anything, but I love looking!

World of Work, exercise 3
MARK Hi. I'm Mark. Is this your party?
WOMAN Yes, it is.
MARK Thanks for inviting me. Er ... Who's that person over there, in the jeans?
WOMAN That's Lucie. She's a hotel receptionist.
MARK Aha!
WOMAN She plays tennis like you. She's a great player. And she sings, too. Every Saturday at the Mondeo Club.
MARK And the guy next to her?
WOMAN His name's Julio. He's an engineer. He's keen on ...
MARK It looks like he's keen on Lucie.
WOMAN Yes! But he's also keen on jogging and weightlifting.
MARK Oh, *that* sort ...
WOMAN Yeah ... And over there, the one in the cool black dress ...
MARK Yes?
WOMAN That's Melissa. She loves fast cars ...
MARK And their drivers? Does she love them too?
WOMAN Ha! Maybe. She's a secretary. She gives yoga classes and she's crazy about horse riding.
MARK Mmmnn ... Maybe she's crazy about me. Can you introduce me to her?

UNIT 3 What are you studying?
Practice, exercise 5
1 MAN Can you come to the cinema tonight?
   WOMAN Sorry, I can't. I'm revising for my exam.
2 MAN What are you studying?
   MAN I'm doing a catering course.
3 MAN How is Mary finding her job?
   WOMAN She's really enjoying it.
4 WOMAN What's Jim doing?
   MAN He's working on the computer.
5 MAN Can I speak to Sheila please?
   WOMAN I'm afraid not. She's taking an exam today.

World of Work, exercise 3
WOMAN Where are you studying at the moment, Tom?
MAN At the College of Further Education.
WOMAN What are you studying?
MAN I'm doing a business studies course.
WOMAN That sounds very interesting. What subjects are you taking?
MAN Information technology, typing, economics, English and maths.
WOMAN How long is the course?
MAN Two years.
WOMAN What sort of job do you want?
MAN I want to get into marketing.

UNIT 4 Time for a holiday
Practice, exercise 2
MAN From England, we took the ferry to Calais and then the train to Paris. I think crossing the Channel by ferry is better than going through the tunnel or flying because it is less complicated and you can enjoy looking at the sea. Anyway, we spent one night in Paris and then took the train to Marseille. I love that city. I think it's more exciting than any other town in France, it's lively, romantic and dangerous! We explored Marseille for a couple of days, found a really great restaurant and had drinks at some really lively bars, they seemed to stay open around the clock! Then...er...we took the boat to Corsica. Corsica is incredibly beautiful with lots of mountains and valleys, although the buses we travelled on to look at the beautiful scenery made me travel sick. We stayed on Corsica for about ten days and then we flew home.

World of Work, exercise 2
1 WOMAN When do you want to travel?
2 MAN What name did you book it under?
3 WOMAN Do you want a return?
4 MAN What about a flight leaving at 10.30 in the morning?
5 MAN How do you want to pay?
6 MAN What kind of room do you want?

UNIT 5 His job or hers?

Practice, exercise 7
MAN When you began in the modelling business, did you have much work?
WOMAN No, I didn't. I had a few jobs modelling clothes for catalogues and I did a little work modelling cosmetics. I didn't get many interesting jobs and I didn't have much money.
MAN How did things change?
WOMAN One evening, in a disco, a famous photographer discovered me. Now I only do a little modelling for magazines, the busiest work is advertising various different products. I earn a lot more than before.
MAN How do you feel about using your body to advertise products?
WOMAN Well, I don't think I am a sex object, if that's what you mean. I am attractive and I have a good body and I don't see anything wrong in earning a living from it. The advertisers don't exploit me. The decision to do a job is mine not theirs.
MAN Modelling is very much a woman's career, isn't it? Do you feel that it's a bit unfair on the men?
WOMAN Not at all. There are fewer women than men in other media jobs, and if men like to see adverts with beautiful women, that's OK. Anyway, there are more and more male models around these days to keep the women happy, so things are becoming a bit more equal.

World of Work, exercise 6
GINA What's your new job in the marketing department like, Brian?
BRIAN It's great. I am responsible for helping with new publicity campaigns and advertisements.
GINA Where do you advertise?
BRIAN Mainly in catalogues and brochures, but also in a few magazines.
GINA Is this ad here yours?
BRIAN The design is mine, but not the rest. Sometimes I think of a few good slogans and I decide where to advertise, what to advertise and when.
GINA Well, it's great that you're doing well, Brian. The future's yours!

UNIT 6 Food and diet

Practice, exercise 6
GARY Er, let's see … We need some bottles of wine, some beer … oh, and some vodka.
JULIE Vodka? Why?
GARY Er … For Natasha.
JULIE Who's Natasha?
GARY Oh, she's … she's the one … the one who only drinks vodka at parties … and some soft drinks, of course, for those who don't drink alcohol. Now, what about the food?
JULIE Well, we've got some crisps and nuts and things like that. But is there any bread?
GARY Not enough. Write down, say, six baguettes and two loaves of brown bread.
JULIE Now, we need a main dish. How about some chicken? Nobody's vegetarian, as far as I know.
GARY Er … Natasha is, I think. But she doesn't mind fish. How about some salmon? Put it down, anyway. And two chickens for the rest of us.
JULIE Are there any fresh vegetables?
GARY I think we've got some potatoes.
JULIE OK. I want to buy some green beans, too.
GARY Oh, and a lettuce and some avocado … for …
JULIE For Natasha?
GARY Well, yes … and for the others that like salad.
JULIE Mmm … And some breakfast cereals, some eggs of course.
GARY Breakfast cereals? Why?
JULIE Oh, nothing … I just thought maybe they may be a good idea.

World of Work, exercise 3
WOMAN The food that we eat is very important. I mean, we are what we eat, aren't we? I get very upset when I see the fast food that young people eat nowadays. They think their diets are fine, but they are not well balanced. The trouble is, we get used to things like hamburgers, crisps, chips and cake, and so good food seems boring. That's why I think my job as a dietician is important. I try to educate people to have a healthy, balanced diet.
MAN I work in a supermarket. I help to sell the food and I just don't understand how people live on the rubbish they buy every week. I tell you, it puts me off eating. I have a very basic diet of vegetables, fruit, bread and water. I drink a lot of water. I think that helps to keep my body healthy. Even so, life is never fair, is it? I may get some terrible disease while some of those people that don't worry about what they eat live for ever.

UNIT 7 Problems and anxieties

Practice, exercise 7
1 WOMAN My life is awful at the moment. I can't stand it anymore.
2 MAN I'm not interested in anything.
3 WOMAN Everything's fine … No problems. Life's just great!
4 MAN I never listen to advice from anyone.
5 WOMAN I don't have any friends.
6 WOMAN I cannot tell him the truth. He frightens me too much.

World of Work, exercise 2
WOMAN You are unemployed, Pete. What's it really like?
PETE It's very difficult to explain to people who are earning, who are OK. They think think you're doing it deliberately and that you're stupid. I'm actually a graduate, with a good degree. I never thought I would be living on the dole. It's probably more stressful than having a job.
WOMAN What are you doing about it?
PETE The big thing is to be positive about yourself. You shouldn't blame yourself or complain about it. It's a fact of life now. So you have to keep active and take all the help you can get. I'm on a training course at the moment. I'm doing a

marketing qualification to add to my German degree, so I should be more attractive to an employer when I have finished.

WOMAN I hope it all works out for you, Pete. Good luck!

UNIT 8 On the road!

Practice, exercise 6

1 Hello, my name is Fred Carter and I started driving in the 1930s when I was fourteen years old. My father had an Model T Ford and he taught me. It was wonderful driving in those days! You didn't have to have a licence, you could park where you liked and there weren't many people on the roads. We didn't drive very quickly, well you couldn't because the cars didn't go very fast, but you felt free with the wind whistling in your hair. There was none of this nonsense about seat belts and crash helmets then. And everyone was very polite, not like now!

2 Hi, I'm Jenny Logan. I'm seventeen and I'm learning to drive. I want to get my licence quickly, so I can borrow Mum and Dad's car to go out with my friends in the evening. I don't really like learning to drive though, because the roads are so crowded and everyone does things so quickly. I drive so slowly that they get cross with me. The things I find most difficult are going round roundabouts in the right lane and parking. It's a nightmare finding anywhere which isn't about 6 inches longer than the car! I'm looking forward to going really fast on the motorway though. I'm a bit of a speed freak and 70mph is too slow!

UNIT 9 The USA and the Big Apple

Practice, exercise 6

Leila is phoning home to her mother from New York.

Hi, Mum! It's me, Leila. ... Yep, I'm having a great time ... yes, I'm fine, honestly, I've been everywhere and done everything! ... What have I done exactly? ... Well, yesterday I went to see the Statue of Liberty, Central Park and Brooklyn and the day before that, Tuesday, I went to the World Trade Center and looked at the shops on 5th Avenue ... What? ... No, I haven't been to the Bronx ... no, I know Central Park is dangerous at night ... I haven't been anywhere on my own at night, all right? You know Paddy from college ... yeah? ... well I went to meet him at the airport on Sunday but there was a message there to say he was ill and couldn't come ... Yes, it was a shame, I like Paddy ... well, I think that's all the news. I have been busy, haven't I? Love to Dad ... yes and you ... Bye!

World of Work, exercise 5

1 Hi, I'm fourteen and I live in a flat in the East End of London with my family. I go to secondary school but I don't like it very much, especially maths! At the weekend, I usually hang 'round the shopping arcade with my friends. Sometimes, we go into town on the tube and see a film. My Mum and Dad would like me to be a lawyer but, with my marks at school, shop assistant is more likely! My aunt Jane lives in New York and one day I'd really like to go and see the city and meet my cousins!

2 Hi, I'm fourteen years old and I live in an apartment on the Upper East Side of Manhattan with my folks. I go to high school but I don't like it a whole lot, especially math! On the weekend, I usually hang out at the mall with my friends. Sometimes, we take the subway downtown and see a movie. My Mom and Dad would like for me to be an attorney, but with my grades in school, store clerk is more like it! My Mom comes from London and someday I'd really like to go see the city and meet my cousins!

UNIT 10 Europe and the Europeans

Practice, exercise 4 and 5

1 My name is Petra and I come from Germany. I learnt English because I am a travel courier and I work in London. Next year I'm going to work in Boston, America and then I will need to learn American English.

2 Hello, I'm Françoise and I'm from France. I learnt English because I'm a secretary working in a bank in Paris. I often need to speak English on the phone. Next year I am going to start learning Portuguese because we have a lot of business in Brazil.

3 Hi, I'm Mike and I'm from Newcastle in the north of the country, I have a very strong accent. Other English people tell me that they can't understand me! I've just got a job on a building site in Berlin. I hope I won't need to learn German; I'm terrible at languages.

4 I'm Sven from Sweden. We all speak English here from a very early age. I don't use my English for work but for all my leisure activities. Most of the films I watch and the music I listen to is in English. My English friends say that my accent is very good.

World of Work, exercise 1

1 My name is Dave Travers and I work in Quality Control at Rover. My job is to make sure that the cars which leave the plant drive well and look good. I am going to Germany soon for training in the Quality Control system used by BMW.

2 I'm Lynn Davies and I'm a production-line worker ... shopfloor worker if you like. Everyone round here wants to work for Rover because it's a safe, well-paid job, especially now that BMW has taken over the company. I hope I won't have to learn German, though!

3 My name is Birgit. I work for BMW in Bavaria. I am a design technician working on new models of car. Most of my work involves using a

computer. A group of us is going to Britain next month to do a project with designers at Rover. It will be interesting to see how they work there.

UNIT 11 It's not a bad place to live

Practice, exercise 3
1 WOMAN Turn left into Maeston Drive and it's next to the cinema.
2 MAN It's not far from here – it's behind the library.
3 WOMAN Go along Frith Street until you get to the roundabout, take the second turning into George Street and it's the fifth building on the right.
4 MAN Go along Frith Street and take the first left after the post office on the corner, and you'll find it opposite the car park.
5 WOMAN Go along Frith Street until you get to the roundabout, take the second turning into George Street and it's on the corner of George Street and Lexham Road.

World of Work, exercise 4
1 WOMAN   It's so difficult these days with teenagers. You try to be a good parent but things are so different from when I was their age. You hear such stories on the radio, especially about drugs like crack and ecstasy. I'm so worried that my children will be addicts but I don't know where to turn.
2 MAN I've tried to talk to my family about AIDS, but they just tell me I'll be all right as long as I don't go out with anyone and they didn't say much in the Sex Education lessons at school. I'd like to know about HIV and AIDS, so that I can protect myself.
3 MAN I've just bought my first house and suddenly I've got all sorts of things which might attract a burglar like my TV and CD player. I'm not sure if my house is very secure but I don't think I should bother the police with my questions.
4 WOMAN My father has just died and my mother is quite ill, so she'll have to come and live with me, so I can care for her. It's not that I'm not willing to look after her. I love her very much, but I have to work and I'm just not sure if I can do it myself.

UNIT 12 The best way to travel

Practice, exercise 5
WOMAN Right. Here are your instructions. Listen carefully. There are five meeting points. Point 1 is at London Heathrow at 2300 hours. From there you will go by plane to Cairo. You will arrive at 0500 hours. Hugo will meet you there and take you to meeting point 2 by car. From there agent 006 will take you to meeting point 3 by motorbike. You must arrive at meeting point 3 by 0625 hours. Then you will go by sea to meeting point 4. The boat will arrive there at 8 o'clock in the morning. From there, you must make your way to the railway station and get on the train which you will find at platform 11. The train will leave at 0810 hours. When the train stops for a few moments at 0930, you must jump off and go on foot to meeting point 5. Meeting point 5 is a little church on a hill. Here you should find the spy with the microfilm. To get in the password is 'Mission Impossible'.

World of Work, exercise 4
MAN If you left Gatwick at 9.30, you'd get in at 12.15 local time.
WOMAN Oh dear, that's a bit late. Is there anything earlier?
MAN There is an 8 o'clock flight which gets in at 10.45.
WOMAN That would be OK.
MAN Oh, wait a minute ... when are you travelling?
WOMAN On Sunday 17th.
MAN Oh, I'm sorry. That flight only goes on Monday to Friday.
WOMAN That's annoying. I can't change the day. What do you suggest?
MAN If you went from Heathrow, you could get a flight at 7.55.
WOMAN That would be good. Heathrow is more convenient. What time does it get in?
MAN It arrives in Tegel at 10.40. Is that OK?

UNIT 13 Technology old and new

World of Work, exercise 3
1 MAN With this, you can film things inside or outside. You look through here and you press this button. If you want to see things closer, you press this.
2 WOMAN This enables you to listen to your favourite music wherever you are. You just put the cassette in here and put the earphones on like this. If you want, you can clip the whole thing to your belt and go jogging or cycling.
3 MAN This is very handy. You can call or receive calls from almost anywhere you like.
4 WOMAN You record your messages or the letters you want to write by moving this switch and speaking here. To listen to what you have recorded, you rewind until you get to where you want, then press PLAY. The cassette comes out when you press this – look, it's got the word EJECT on it.

UNIT 14 Uses and abuses

Practice, exercise 3
1 YOUNG GIRL I'm really in a bad way. I'm so depressed, I hate school and I am unhappy at home. On top of that, my boyfriend has left me and I have no money. Life just doesn't seem worth living.

2 WOMAN My parents were divorced and I lived with my mother, but she died when I was twelve. But I faced up to it and worked hard at school. No matter how bad things are, you have to be positive, don't you? Things have worked out OK and I'm happy.
3 MAN I ... I suppose you'd say I'm homeless ... One of life's drop-outs. I live over there ... just under that bridge ... . Winter's the worst. It really gets cold ... Sometimes we get soup and things ... shelter when things get really bad ... You can't really call it a life ... When I look back, I don't really know what went wrong.
4 MAN I'm not sure when I first took drugs. My family were quite well-off and I had everything I needed, but I guess I was bored and I wanted some excitement. Anyway, luckily I stopped before it was too late. It was sport which saved me in the end. That is my drug now! I have to do some sport every day or I am terrible.

World of Work, exercise 1
My name's Matty and I'm on work experience at the Norton Project in Sheffield. It's a place where anyone can walk in off the street and get help with drug-related problems. People who come to us are not just drug addicts with a heroin habit but alcoholics as well.

I'm not a qualified counsellor yet, but I hope to go to college in the autumn to get my Diploma in Social Work.

Most places help people to dry out but here we try to help by counselling, by trying to find out what the real problem is, like homelessness or poverty.

I really like it here and I can't wait to get my training so I can work here full-time.

exercise 3
GEMMA We work for Comic Relief. It's a charity run by a group of British comedians to help the poor in the UK and Africa.
TOM Red Nose Day is when people give us all the money for our projects. Every two years, we have a big national TV show where loads of people do really crazy things to make money. On the day itself most people in Britain buy and wear a red nose.
GEMMA It sounds silly but it's for a serious purpose and this year we raised about 12 million pounds.
TOM We help people who are suffering because they are poor or hungry.
GEMMA We also help those who have a bad situation, like they're disabled or come from broken homes.
TOM We really make a difference, even people like Gemma and me, who just answer the phones.

UNIT 15 Do you shop till you drop?

Practice, exercise 2
1 I need to buy butter, breakfast cereal and some bananas.
2 I need a new book to take on holiday. I'd like a good detective story
3 I need some new video tapes and I'd like a new CD as well.
4 We have got any more shampoo or soap and I need to get my medicine, too
5 I'm going to get some nice cakes for our tea and I think I'll get the bread at the same time.
6 I'd like a nice bouquet of flowers for my mother's birthday. Oh yes, and I'll buy a plant, too.
7 My son, Jamie, would like some new games and a toy car for his birthday.
8 I really must repair this table. When I go shopping I must remember to buy some nails and a hammer.

World of Work, exercise 1
Hi, I'm Terry. I've just been to the bank to open a bank account. I got my first pay cheque on Friday, so I've got to have somewhere to keep the money I earn. It was a bit difficult ... the bank clerk made an appointment with the bank manager and I had to sign papers and show my identification. I think it was all right, though, because she said I would get my cheque book and bank card in a few days. She said I have to be careful when I use the cash dispenser because it is so easy to take out too much and having an overdraft is expensive these days! I'm not allowed to have a credit card yet but if I want, I can have a small loan to buy a car.

UNIT 16 Reduce, repair, reuse, recycle

Practice, exercise 4
1 MAN It's difficult to know which sort of energy we should have. Nuclear power is dangerous, petrol and coal damage the environment and people say that wind farms don't look very pretty.
2 WOMAN I'm very worried about poor air quality in cities. The number of cars we have all been driving around as fast as possible is crazy! I think we should all walk or cycle and then we wouldn't have as much air pollution.
3 MAN I love hamburgers and I'm going to carry on eating them whatever anyone says. Why shouldn't I? I just throw the packaging down on the pavement because I can't be bothered to find a bin for it. Anyway, all the fast food places send people round to pick it up – their marketing people can tell from the waste who's eating what. Great!

World of Work, 1
MAN I work on a farm which has a mix of crops. The farm is owned by a big business which runs it like a factory for producing food. We grow wheat and we have a herd of cows. I spend a lot of my time sitting on a tractor treating the crops with pesticides and fertilizers. We have had trouble with BSE. I know that cheap food for the cows is to blame but I can't see how else the business can make a profit.

UNIT 17 Virtual lives!
World of Work, exercise 1
1 Hello, is that Dial-a-Taxi? Oh, good. Yes, I'd like you to come and pick me up at 2.00 this afternoon. I'd like to go shopping at Price Right. My name and address? Oh, yes. It's Edna Purves, 10 Sunnyside Avenue. Thank you. Goodbye.
2 Hello … I need to speak to someone … my boyfriend and I have just split up … I feel awful … nobody likes me. I feel like ending it all.
3 Hello … hello … ? I need an ambulance quickly. 19 Eldon road. A woman has just collapsed on the street outside … I think she's had a heart attack …
4 Hello … I'm Natalie. I'm six. I don't like the man down the road …

exercise 6
1 MAN Hello? Doctor's surgery? Can you put me through to the health visitor, please?
2 WOMAN Hello, I'm trying to get hold of Nurse Page, is he there?
3 MAN Hello? I'd like to report a car accident. Can you send someone urgently?
4 WOMAN Hello, I'd like to make an appointment for Thursday, please.
5 MAN Hello. I need some help, but I'm not sure who I should speak to.
6 WOMAN Hi. This is Mike Hill's phone. I'm sorry there's no one here to take your call right now, but if you'd like to leave your name and number, or leave a message, I'll get back to you as soon as I can. Please speak after the tone.

UNIT 18 Choosing a job
World of Work, exercise 4
1 WOMAN I couldn't believe it when one of the interviewers started asking about whether I had any children. That's against the law. If I had been a bit quicker, I would have lied. I'm sure that's why I didn't get the job.
2 MAN I am from Vietnam and so English is my second language. I know people sometimes find it difficult to understand what I say but I try very hard. I want to be a computer programmer. I had an interview for a job last week. I wouldn't need to talk a lot for the job but I didn't get it and I think my bad English was the reason.
3 MAN I was made redundant at the age of 55. I have been to lots of interviews since then but I never get the job. I'm sure my age is against me although I know that I could do the job better than any 25-year-old.
4 WOMAN I always find it difficult filling in application forms because I have dyslexia. You know, that means I don't see the letters in the right order, so I find it difficult to read and to spell. I prefer to do a CV on the computer because I know it will be right. But lots of employers these days want to see your handwriting. I try my best, but I'm sure my strange spelling is a problem.

GRUNDWORTSCHATZ

Diese Liste enthält ca. 650 Grundwörter, die in WORK WITH ENGLISH als bekannt vorausgesetzt werden. Nicht aufgeführt, jedoch vorausgesetzt sind internationale Wörter (Taxi, Fax, TV usw.) und einige sehr elementare Wörter, wie Pronomen, Zahlen und Tage.

a lot viel(e); sehr
about über; etwa, circa
above über; oben; obenstehend
address Adresse
after nach
afternoon Nachmittag
again wieder
against gegen, an
age Alter
air Luft
airport Flughafen
all alle
along entlang; weiter, vorwärts
also auch, außerdem
always immer
a.m. vor 12 Uhr
America Amerika
American Amerikaner/in; amerikanisch
animal Tier
answer beantworten; Antwort
any irgendetwas; irgendwelche
anyone jemand, jeder
anything etwas
apple Apfel
arm Arm
arrive ankommen
ask fragen; bitten
at in; an; bei; auf; zu … hin
at home zu Hause
at the moment im Augenblick
aunt Tante
Austria Österreich
Austrian Österreicher/in
autumn Herbst
available erhältlich, verfügbar

baby Baby, Säugling
back Rücken
bacon Schinkenspeck
bad(ly) schlecht, schlimm
baker Bäcker/in
banana Banane
bank Bank; Ufer
bar Bar, Lokal; Theke
barman Barkeeper
bath Bad, Badewanne
be sein
beautiful schön
because weil
bed Bett
bedroom Schlafzimmer
beer Bier
before bevor; zuvor
begin anfangen, beginnen
beginning Anfang
behind hinter; hinten
between zwischen
below unter; unten
bicycle Fahrrad
big groß
bike Fahrrad
bird Vogel
birthday Geburtstag
black schwarz
blood Blut
boat Boot, Schiff
body Körper
book Buch
bottle Flasche
box Kästchen
boy Junge
boyfriend Freund
branch Ast
bread Brot
breakfast Frühstück
bring bringen, mitbringen, holen
Britain Großbritannien
British britisch
brother Bruder
brown braun
build bauen
bus (Linien-)Bus
but aber; sondern; als
butcher Fleischer/in
buy kaufen
by bis; durch, per; von; an … vorbei

cake Kuchen, Torte, Gebäckstück
camera Fotoapparat; Kamera
camping Zelten
can können
cannot = **can not**
canal Kanal
car Auto
cat Katze
central zentral, Zentral-, mittlere/r/s
chair Stuhl
change (sich) (ver)ändern
check Scheck
check (über)prüfen
cheese Käse
child Kind
chips Pommes frites
chocolate Schokolade; Praline
choose wählen, aussuchen
church Kirche
cigarette Zigarette
cinema Kino
circle Kreis
city Stadt
class (Schul-)Klasse; Unterricht
classroom Klassenraum, Klassenzimmer
clean sauber
climb klettern
clock Uhr
close zumachen
closed geschlossen
clothes Kleidung, Kleider
coat Mantel
coffee Kaffee
cold kalt
college (Berufs-)Fachschule; Fachhochschule; Universität
colour Farbe
come kommen
computer Computer
concert Konzert
cook kochen; Koch/Köchin
corner Ecke
cost kosten
country Land
cousin Cousin/e
cow Kuh
cream Sahne; Creme
cross Kreuz
cup Tasse
cupboard Schrank

dad Papa, Vater
dance tanzen
dangerous(ly) gefährlich
date Datum
daughter Tochter
day Tag
dead tot
dear liebe/r
describe beschreiben
die sterben
difficult schwer, schwierig
dinner Abendessen
disco Disko(thek)
do tun, machen
doctor Arzt/Ärztin
dog Hund
door Tür
double Doppel-
down nach unten, hin-/herunter; unten
dress Kleid
drink trinken; Getränk
drive fahren
driver Fahrer/in

each jede(r, s)
ear Ohr
early früh
east Osten; Ost-; nach Osten
easy (easily) einfach, leicht
eat essen; fressen
egg Ei
empty leer
England England
English Englisch
enjoy genießen
Europe Europa
European europäisch; Europäer/in
evening Abend
every jede/r/s
everyone jede/r/s, alle
everything alles
everywhere überall; überallhin
example Beispiel
excuse entschuldigen
exercise Übung
expect erwarten
expensive teuer
eye Auge

family Familie
family name Familienname
far weit
farm Bauernhof
farmer Bauer, Bäuerin
fast schnell
father Vater
film Film
find finden
finger Finger
finish beenden, abschließen
first erste(r, s)
first name Vorname
fish Fisch
fit fit
flat flach
flat Wohnung
floor Etage; Fußboden
fly Fliege

fly fliegen
follow folgen
food Essen; Nahrung; Lebensmittel
foot Fuß
football Fußball
for für
fork Gabel
form Form; Formular; bilden
France Frankreich
free kostenlos; frei
French französisch
friend Freund/in
from von, aus
front Vorderseite, Vorderteil
fruit Obst, Frucht
full voll
funny komisch

game Spiel
garden Garten
GB Großbritannien
German deutsch
Germany Deutschland
get bekommen; werden
girl Mädchen
girlfriend Freundin
give geben; schenken
go gehen; fahren
good gut
goodbye auf Wiedersehen
grandad Opa
granddaughter Enkelin
grandfather Großvater
grandma Großmama
grandmother Großmutter
grandparents Großeltern
great toll
green grün
group Gruppe
grow wachsen
guitar Gitarre

hair Haar
hairdresser Friseur/Friseuse
half Hälfte
hand Hand
happy glücklich, zufrieden
have haben
head Kopf
health Gesundheit
healthy gesund
hear hören
hello Hallo
help Hilfe; helfen
here hier
high hoch
holiday Ferien, Urlaub; Feiertag
home Zuhause
homework Hausaufgaben
hooray hurra

horse Pferd
hospital Hospital, Krankenhaus
hot heiß, warm
hotel Hotel
hour Stunde
house Haus
how wie
how much wie viel
how many wie viele
hungry hungrig
husband (Ehe-)Mann

ice Eis
idea Idee, Gedanke, Vorstellung
if wenn, falls
ill krank
important wichtig
in in; auf; hinein/herein
into in ... hinein
Italy Italien

jacket Jacke, Jackett
jeans Jeans
job Arbeit; Aufgabe
joke Witz, Scherz
just nur; gerade

key Schlüssel
kill töten, umbringen
kilometre Kilometer
king König
kitchen Küche
knife Messer
know kennen; wissen

label Aufkleber; Etikett
lamp Lampe
language Sprache
large groß
last letzte(r, s)
late spät
learn lernen
leave abreisen; weggehen; verlassen
left linke(r, s), links
leg Bein
lesson (Schul-)Stunde
let lassen
letter Buchstabe; Brief
life Leben
lift Aufzug
like wie
like mögen, gern haben
line Linie; Zeile
list Liste; auflisten
listen zuhören
listen to hören, sich anhören
little klein; wenig
live leben; wohnen
long lang
look sehen, schauen
look at sich anschauen
look for suchen (nach)
lose verlieren
lot Menge

love lieben
low niedrig
lucky Glücks-, glücklich
lunch Mittagessen

magazine Zeitschrift, Magazin
make tun, machen; bilden
man Mann
manager Leiter/in
many viele
match Streichholz
may dürfen; können
maybe vielleicht
meat Fleisch
meet (sich) treffen; (sich) begegnen
mile Meile
milk Milch
million Million
minute Minute
miss verpassen
mom (US) Mama
moment Moment
money Geld
month Monat
moped Moped, Mofa
morning Morgen
mother Mutter
mouth Mund
move (sich) bewegen
much viel
mum Mutti
music Musik
must müssen

name Name
nearly beinahe, fast
neck Hals
never nie(mals)
new neu
newspaper Zeitung
next nächste(r, s)
nice schön; nett
night Nacht
no nein; kein/e
nobody niemand
none keine(r, s)
nonsense Unsinn
normal normal, üblich
north Norden, Nord-
nose Nase
not nicht
nothing nichts
notice bemerken
now nun, jetzt
number Nummer, Zahl

o'clock (fünf usw.) Uhr
odd ungerade
of von
offer Angebot; anbieten
office Büro
often oft, häufig
old alt
on auf; an
only nur

open offen; aufmachen
opinion Meinung
or oder
other andere(r, s)
out draußen; hinaus/heraus
over über

page Seite
pair Paar
palace Palast
paper Papier
parent Elternteil
park Park
park parken
part Teil
partner Partner/in
party Party, Fest
pay bezahlen
pea Erbse
pen Füllfederhalter; Kugelschreiber
pence Pence
people Leute, Menschen
perhaps vielleicht
person Mensch, Person
phone Telefon; anrufen
photo Foto
phrase Redewendung
piano Klavier
picture Bild
piece Stück, Teil
place Platz; Ort
plan Plan; planen, vorhaben
plane Flugzeug
plate Teller
play spielen
please gefallen
please bitte
pleased froh, erfreut
p.m. nach 12 Uhr
police Polizei
policeman Polizist
policewoman Polizistin
pop music Popmusik
post Post
poster Plakat
postman Briefträger
postwoman Briefträgerin
potato Kartoffel
pound Pfund (Sterling)
present Geschenk
pretty hübsch
problem Problem
pub Wirtshaus, Kneipe
pullover Pullover
put setzen, stellen, legen

quarter Viertel
queen Königin
question Frage
quick(ly) schnell
quite ziemlich

radio Radio, Rundfunk
rain Regen; regnen
read lesen

real echt, wirklich
reason Grund
red rot
remember sich erinnern, daran denken
rice Reis
ride reiten
right rechts; richtig
be right Recht haben; richtig sein
road Straße
room Zimmer; Raum; Platz
round rund; um (... herum)
run laufen, rennen

sad traurig
safe(ly) sicher
salad Salat
sale Verkauf; Ausverkauf
same gleiche(r, s), der-, die-, dasselbe
sandwich Sandwich
say sagen
school Schule
sea Meer
second zweite(r, s)
second Sekunde
see sehen
sell verkaufen
send senden, schicken
ship Schiff
shop Laden, Geschäft
shopping Einkaufen
short kurz; klein
show zeigen
shower Dusche
side Seite, Rand
sight Anblick; Sehvermögen
sing singen
sister Schwester
sit sitzen
sleep schlafen
slow(ly) langsam
small klein
smoke rauchen
snow Schnee
so also
sofa Sofa
soft leise; weich
some einige; etwas
somebody jemand
someone jemand
something etwas

sometimes manchmal
son Sohn
soon bald
sorry traurig
south Süden, Süd-
speak sprechen, reden
square Quadrat
stand stehen
start beginnen
station Bahnhof
stay bleiben; übernachten
still immer noch
stop (an)halten
story Erzählung, Geschichte
street Straße
strong stark
student Student/in
sugar Zucker
suitcase Koffer
summer Sommer
sun Sonne
supermarket Supermarkt
sure sicher, freilich
surname Nachname
survey Umfrage
sweets Süßigkeiten
swim schwimmen
Switzerland Schweiz

table Tisch; Tabelle
take nehmen; bringen
talk (about) sprechen (über)
tea Tee; (frühes) Abendbrot
teacher Lehrer/in
telephone Telefon
television Fernsehen, Fernseher
tell sagen, erzählen
text Text
than als
thank danken, sich bedanken
thank you, thanks danke
that dies; der, die, das; jene(r, s)
that dass
then dann
there dort; dorthin
there are es gibt
these diese
thing Sache, Ding
think denken, glauben, meinen

this dies, diese(r, s)
those jene
through durch ... hindurch, durch
ticket (Fahr-)Karte; Ticket
time Zeit; Mal; Uhrzeit
timetable Fahrplan; Stundenplan
tired müde
to zu; nach; in; um zu
today heute
toe Zehe
together zusammen
tomorrow morgen
tonight heute Abend
too zu; auch
town Stadt
traffic (Straßen-)Verkehr
train Zug
tram Straßenbahn
transport Verkehrsmittel
travel reisen
tree Baum
triangle Dreieck
trouble Schwierigkeiten, Ärger
trousers Hose
true richtig, wahr
try probieren; versuchen
tube U-Bahn
typical typisch

uncle Onkel
under unter
understand verstehen, begreifen
unhappy unglücklich, unzufrieden
unit Lektion
until bis
unusual(ly) ungewöhnlich
up oben; nach oben
US(A) die Vereinigten Staaten (von Amerika)
use verwenden
usual(ly) gewöhnlich

vegetable Gemüse
very sehr
visit Besuch; besuchen

wait (for) warten (auf)
waiter Kellner

waitress Kellnerin,
walk Spaziergang, (zu Fuß) gehen
wall Wand, Mauer
want wollen
warm warm
wash (sich) waschen
watch Armbanduhr
watch (zu)sehen, beobachten
water Wasser
way Weg; Art und Weise
wear tragen
weather Wetter
week Woche
weekend Wochenende
welcome willkommen heißen
well gesund
west Westen, West-
what was; welche(r, s)
wheel Rad
when wenn; als; wann
where wo; wohin
which welche(r, s)
white weiß
who wer; der, die
whom wen; wem
why warum
wife Ehefrau
will werden
win gewinnen; siegen
wind spulen
window Fenster
wine Wein
winter Winter
with mit
without ohne
woman Frau
wonderful wunderbar, wundervoll
word Wort
work Arbeit; arbeiten; funktionieren; klappen
world Welt
write schreiben
wrong falsch

year Jahr
yellow gelb
yesterday gestern
young jung

zoo Zoo

CHRONOLOGISCHES WÖRTERVERZEICHNIS

Dieses Wörterverzeichnis enthält alle Wörter, die nicht in der Liste des Grundwortschatzes enthalten sind, d.h. die nicht als bekannt vorausgesetzt werden.
Von Unit 10 bis Unit 18 werden die Wörter der **World of Work** Seiten bei den darauffolgenden Units nicht vorausgesetzt. Sie sind durch **ww** gekennzeichnet.

Abkürzungen und Zeichen

s.o.	**someone**
s.th.	**something**
GB	britische Variante
US	amerikanische Variante
⚠	Achtung!

◆▶ Gegenteil
≈ (ungefähr) gleichbedeutend mit
▮ vor einem Stichwort: auf der Cassette
ww **World of Work**; bei den darauffolgenden Units nicht vorausgesetzt

UNIT 1 Young People in Britain

6 terraced house [ˌterəst 'haʊs] — Reihenhaus — **terrace**: *Häuserreihe*
centre ['sentə] — Mitte, Zentrum — ≈ middle
southern ['sʌðən] — Süd- — ~ England
fiancé [fɪ'ɒnseɪ] — Verlobter — weibl. **fiancée** (gleiche Aussprache)
single ['sɪŋgl] — ledig — ◆▶ **married** – *verheiratet*
rent [rent] — mieten — ⚠ auch Nomen: *Miete*
separated ['sepəreɪtɪd] — getrennt — von **separate** – *sich trennen*
divorced [dɪ'vɔːst] — geschieden — von **divorce** – *sich scheiden lassen*
cottage ['kɒtɪdʒ] — kleines Haus — bes. in ländlichen Gegenden
go out with [ˌgəʊ 'aʊt wɪð] — gehen mit — im Sinne: *ein Verhältnis haben mit*
guy [gaɪ] — Kerl — Umgangssprache
further education [ˌfɜːðə edʒu'keɪʃn] — Weiterbildung — nicht an einer Universität
stepfather ['stepfɑːðə] — Stiefvater — ebenso: **stepmother** usw.
get on well with [ˌget ɒn 'wel wɪð] — gut auskommen mit
on his own [ɒn hɪz 'əʊn] — alleine — he lives ~
right now [raɪt 'naʊ] — zur Zeit
home town [ˌhəʊm 'taʊn] — Heimatort

7 complete [kəm'pliːt] — vervollständigen, abschließen — ⚠ auch Adjektiv: *vollständig*
detached house [dɪ'tætʃt haʊs] — Einfamilienhaus — von **detach** – *abtrennen*
work with ['wɜːk wɪð] — arbeiten mit — ~ the text
false [fɔːls] — falsch — ◆▶ **true** – *wahr*
correct [kə'rekt] — berichtigen — ⚠ auch Adjektiv: *richtig, korrekt*
What does ... do? [ˌwɒt dʌz ... 'duː] — Was macht ... (beruflich)?
Where is ... from? [ˌweə ɪz ... 'frɒm] — Woher kommt ...?
come from ['kʌm frəm] — stammen aus
work with ['wɜːk wɪð] — zusammenarbeiten mit — ~ a partner
of your own [əv jɔːr 'əʊn] — eigene(r, s) — immer nach dem Nomen: **make some questions** ~

8 review [rɪ'vjuː] — Wiederholung, Rückblick — auch Verb: wiederholen

9 at weekends [ət wiːk'endz] — am Wochenende — ⚠ nur im Sinne: *an jedem Wochenende*; **at the weekend** – *an einem einzigen Wochenende*

10 practice ['præktɪs] — Übung — ⚠ im Sinne: *das Üben, Geübtsein*; **an exercise** – *eine Übung*
stepmother ['stepmʌðə] — Stiefmutter — ebenso: **stepfather, stepchild** usw.
in town [ɪn 'taʊn] — in der Stadt — ⚠ kein Artikel
card [kɑːd] — Karte
family status [ˌfæməli 'steɪtəs] — Familienstand — ⚠ Aussprache: **status**
date of birth [ˌdeɪt əv 'bɜːθ] — Geburtsdatum — What's your ~? – *Wann sind Sie geboren?*

married ['mærɪd] — verheiratet — von **marry** – *heiraten*
◆▶ **single** – *ledig*

widowed ['wɪdəʊd] — verwitwet — **widow** – *Witwe*

tʃ	dʒ	ʃ	ʒ	θ	ð	ŋ	s	z	v	w
chips	jet	ship	garage	thing	the	ring	ice	as	very	wet

	think of [ˈθɪŋk əv]	denken an		in Fragen: **Can you think of ~?**
	any more [eni ˈmɔː]	weitere(r, s)		
	place to live [pleɪs tə ˈlɪv]	Wohnort		
	situation [ˌsɪtʃuˈeɪʃn]	Situation, Lage	⚠	Aussprache
	mother-in-law [ˈmʌðər ɪn lɔː]	Schwiegermutter		ebenso: **father-in-law** usw.
11	match (with) [ˈmætʃ wɪð]	zusammenfügen		
	on the left [ɒn ðə ˈleft]	auf der linken Seite		
	on the right [ɒn ðə ˈraɪt]	auf der rechten Seite		
	out of work [aʊt əv ˈwɜːk]	arbeitslos	≈	**unemployed**
	rewrite [ˌriːˈraɪt]	umschreiben		
	get on with [ˌget ˈɒn wɪð]	(gut) auskommen mit	≈	**get on well with**
12	place of work [pleɪs əv ˈwɜːk]	Arbeitsstelle		
	responsibility [rɪˌspɒnsəˈbɪləti]	Aufgabe		
	receptionist [rɪˈsepʃənɪst]	Empfangschef, -dame		
	nurse [nɜːs]	Krankenschwester, Krankenpfleger/in		
	secretary [ˈsekrətri]	Sekretär/in		
	workshop [ˈwɜːkʃɒp]	Werkstatt		
	carpenter [ˈkɑːpəntə]	Tischler/in		
	vet [vet]	Tierarzt, -ärztin		
	on holiday [ɒn ˈhɒlədeɪ]	auf Urlaub		
	shop assistant [ˈʃɒp əsɪstənt]	Verkäufer/in		
	repair [rɪˈpeə]	reparieren		
	tour guide [ˈtʊə gaɪd]	Reiseleiter/in		
	serve [sɜːv]	bedienen		
	mechanic [mɪˈkænɪk]	Mechaniker/in		
	nursery nurse [ˈnɜːsəri nɜːs]	Kindergärtnerin		
	accounts clerk [əˈkaʊnts klɑːk]	Buchhalter/in	⚠	Aussprache: **clerk**
13	good at [ˈgʊd ət]	geschickt in		**~ numbers** – *gut im Rechnen*
	international [ˌɪntəˈnæʃnəl]	international	⚠	Aussprache
	book shop [ˈbʊkʃɒp]	Buchhandlung		
	by the way [baɪ ðə ˈweɪ]	übrigens		
	customer [ˈkʌstəmə]	Kunde, Kundin		
	appointment [əˈpɔɪntmənt]	Termin		**make an ~**
	that sort of thing [ðæt ˌsɔːt əv ˈθɪŋ]	derlei		
	sort [sɔːt]	Art, Sorte		
	hope [həʊp]	hoffen		
	interview [ˈɪntəvjuː]	Vorstellungsgespräch		
	part-time [ˌpɑːtˈtaɪm]	Teilzeit-		**a ~ job**
	building site [ˈbɪldɪŋ saɪt]	Baustelle		
	dialogue [ˈdaɪəlɒg]	Dialog	⚠	Aussprache
	practise [ˈpræktɪs]	üben	⚠	Schreibweise Nomen: **practice**
	underlined [ˌʌndəˈlaɪnd]	unterstrichen		
	replace [rɪˈpleɪs]	ersetzen		
	Hi there. [ˈhaɪ ðə]	Grüß dich.		
	Pleased to meet you. [ˌpliːzd tə ˈmiːt ju]	Es freut mich, Sie kennenzulernen.		
	flight attendant [ˌflaɪt əˈtendənt]	Flugbegleiter/in		
	Really? [ˈriːəli]	Tatsächlich?		drückt hier Interesse aus
	What's it like? [ˌwɒts ɪt ˈlaɪk]	Wie ist es?		
	What about you? [ˌwɒt əbaʊt ˈju]	Wie ist es mit dir?		d.h.: *Und was machst du?*
	another [əˈnʌðə]	ein(e) andere(r, s)		**~ job** – *eine neue Stelle*
	UNIT 2 Free time			
14	free time [ˌfriː ˈtaɪm]	Freizeit		**What do you do in your ~?**
	that's me	das bin ich	⚠	nicht: **that's I** ebenso: **that's her, that's him** usw.
	look like [ˈlʊk laɪk]	(jmdm./etw.) ähnlich sehen		
	muscle [ˈmʌsl]	Muskel		
	weightlifting [ˈweɪtlɪftɪŋ]	Gewichtheben		**he does ~**

i:	ɪ	e	æ	ɑ:	ɒ	ɔ:	ʊ	u:	ʌ	ɜ:	ə
see	sit	ten	bad	arm	got	saw	put	too	cut	bird	about

	have got [həv gɒt]	haben	gleichbedeutend mit **have** im Sinne von *besitzen*
	be keen on (s.o.) [bi 'ki:n ɒn]	scharf auf jmdn. sein, jmdn. sehr gern mögen	
	(not) mind [maɪnd]	(nichts) gegen etw. haben	**I don't ~ it** – *ich habe nichts dagegen*
	keep fit [ki:p 'fɪt]	fit bleiben, in Form bleiben	
	exercise ['eksəsaɪz]	sich bewegen	
	gym [dʒɪm]	Turnhalle	
	... times (a week/year) [taɪmz]	... mal (in der Woche/im Jahr)	
	watch (the) television [wɒtʃ 'telɪvɪʒn]	fernsehen	
	fashion ['fæʃn]	Mode	
15	go jogging [gəʊ 'dʒɒgɪŋ]	joggen	auch: **he jogs every morning**
	rarely ['reəli]	selten	Adverb
	in winter [ɪn 'wɪntə]	im Winter	
	lazy ['leɪzi]	faul	
	be keen on (s.th.) [bi 'ki:n ɒn]	etw. sehr gern mögen	**he's keen on rock music**
	... can't stand ... [kɑ:nt 'stænd]	nicht leiden können	**she can't stand it**
	take exercise [teɪk 'eksəsaɪz]	sich bewegen	**exercise**: hier Nomen, gleiche Form wie das Verb
	piano [pi'ænəʊ]	Klavier	
	in bed [ɪn 'bed]	im Bett	⚠ ohne Artikel
	on the train [ɒn ðə 'treɪn]	im Zug	⚠ **on**, nicht **in**
	overweight [,əʊvə'weɪt]	übergewichtig	**he's ~** – *er hat Übergewicht*
	crazy about ['kreɪzi əbaʊt]	verrückt auf	**she's ~ football**
	on TV [ɒn ti:'vi:]	im Fernsehen	⚠ **on**, nicht **in**
	worry (about) ['wʌri əbaʊt]	sich Sorgen machen (um)	**she worries about these things/him**
	care [keə]	sich kümmern	**he doesn't ~** – *es ist ihm egal*
16	photograph ['fəʊtəgrɑ:f]	Foto	⚠ nicht: *Fotograf*
	recognise ['rekəgnaɪz]	erkennen	
	different ['dɪfrənt]	verschieden	
	think of ['θɪŋk əv]	halten von	**what do you ~ her?**
	frequently ['fri:kwəntli]	oft	Adverb
17	express [ɪk'spres]	ausdrücken	im Sinne: *zum Ausdruck bringen*
	feeling ['fi:lɪŋ]	Gefühl	
18	bracket ['brækɪt]	Klammer	
	journey ['dʒɜ:ni]	Reise, Fahrt	
	wood [wʊd]	(kleinerer) Wald	
	instead of [ɪn'sted əv]	anstatt	
	What about ...? [wɒt ə'baʊt]	Wie ist es mit ...?	hier: *was hältst du von ...?*
	in the morning [ɪn ðə 'mɔ:nɪŋ]	morgens	**at 6.30 ~** – *um 6.30 Uhr morgens* ⚠ je nach Zusammenhang auch: *morgen früh*
	after work [,ɑ:ftə 'wɜ:k]	nach der Arbeit	⚠ ohne Artikel
	be early (for) [bi 'ɜ:li fə]	(zu) früh kommen	**he's always early for work** – *er kommt immer früh zur Arbeit*
	ask questions [ɑ:sk 'kwestʃənz]	Fragen stellen	
	go swimming [gəʊ 'swɪmɪŋ]	schwimmen gehen	
	guitar [gɪ'tɑ:]	Gitarre	⚠ Schreibweise
	go for a walk [gəʊ fər ə 'wɔ:k]	spazieren gehen	
19	over here [,əʊvə 'hɪə]	herüber	**come ~** – *komm 'rüber*
	stay in [,steɪ 'ɪn]	zu Hause bleiben	
	be fond of [bi 'fɒnd əv]	gern mögen	**she's fond of sport/him**
	spare time [,speə 'taɪm]	Freizeit, freie Zeit	
	go window shopping [gəʊ 'wɪndəʊ ʃɒpɪŋ]	einen Schaufensterbummel machen	auch: **window shop**; **he likes to ~**
20	socialise ['səʊʃəlaɪz]	sich mit Leuten unterhalten	**do you ~ much?** – *kommen Sie viel unter Leute?*
	at work [ət 'wɜ:k]	bei der Arbeit	⚠ ohne Artikel
	Pleased to meet you. [,pli:zd tə 'mi:t ju]	Es freut mich, Sie kennen zu lernen.	

tʃ	dʒ	ʃ	ʒ	θ	ð	ŋ	s	z	v	w
chips	jet	ship	garage	thing	the	ring	ice	as	very	wet

I'd like you to meet … . [aɪd laɪk ju tə 'miːt] — Ich möchte dich/Sie bekannt machen mit … .
Will you excuse me? [wɪl ju ɪk'skjuːz mi] — Entschuldigen Sie, bitte.
How about …? [haʊ ə'baʊt] — Wie wär's mit …?
invite [ɪn'vaɪt] — einladen
Take care. [teɪk 'keə] — Pass gut auf dich auf. — Abschiedsformel
Bye. [baɪ] — Tschüs. — Verkürzung von **good bye**
Have a nice time. [hæv ə ˌnaɪs 'taɪm] — Viel Spaß.
How do you like …? [ˌhaʊ də ju 'laɪk] — Wie gefällt dir/Ihnen …?
I'm sorry. [aɪm sɒri] — Es tut mir leid.
Nice meeting you. [ˌnaɪs 'miːtɪŋ ju] — Nett, Sie kennenzulernen.
be off [ˌbiː 'ɒf] — wegfahren — **I'm off for the weekend** – *ich fahre übers Wochenende weg*
I must be off – *ich muss jetzt gehen*

Good luck! [ˌgʊd 'lʌk] — Viel Glück!
join [dʒɔɪn] — sich anschließen, mitgehen — ~ **us for lunch** – *iss/essen Sie mit uns zu Mittag*

21 conversation [ˌkɒnvə'seɪʃn] — Gespräch — ⚠ Aussprache
over there [ˌəʊvə 'ðeə] — dort drüben
player ['pleɪə] — Spieler/in
engineer [ˌendʒɪ'nɪə] — Ingenieur/in, Techniker/in

it looks like [ɪt 'lʊks laɪk] — es sieht aus, als ob — ~ **he's keen on her**
weightlifting ['weɪtlɪftɪŋ] — Gewichtheben
the one [ðə 'wʌn] — der/die/dasjenige — hier: *die Frau/das Mädchen*
horse riding ['hɔːsraɪdɪŋ] — Reiten
introduce [ˌɪntrə'djuːs] — vorstellen
write down [raɪt 'daʊn] — aufschreiben — ~ **the answers**

UNIT 3 What are you studying?

22 study ['stʌdi] — studieren, lernen — **what are you ~ing?**
be at college [biː æt 'kɒlɪdʒ] — studieren — **she's at the College of Further Education**

course [kɔːs] — Kurs, Lehrgang — **I'm doing a ~ in construction**
revise [rɪ'vaɪz] — wiederholen — **they're revising for their exams**
exam [ɪg'zæm] — Prüfung, Examen
one-year ['wʌnjɪə] — einjährig — **a ~ course**
construction [kən'strʌkʃn] — Bau (als Fach)
business studies ['bɪznəs stʌdiz] — Betriebswirtschaftslehre (BWL)

engineering [ˌendʒɪ'nɪərɪŋ] — Ingenieurwesen, Technik (als Fach)

catering ['keɪtərɪŋ] — Gastronomie (als Fach)
chef [ʃef] — Chefkoch/köchin,
cooking ['kʊkɪŋ] — Kochen — **we're learning about ~**
caterer ['keɪtərə] — Lieferant/in von Fertiggerichten

office administration [ˌɒfɪs ədmɪnɪ'streɪʃn] — Büroorganisation
computer studies [kəm'pjuːtə stʌdiz] — Informatik
hard [hɑːd] — schwierig — ⬌ **easy** – *leicht*
practical ['præktɪkl] — praktisch — **it's a ~ course**
⬌ **theoretical** – *theoretisch*

worried ['wʌrid] — besorgt, beunruhigt — **I'm very ~ about the exam**
general ['dʒenrəl] — allgemein
national ['næʃnəl] — National-, Staats- — ⚠ Aussprache
vocational [vəʊ'keɪʃənl] — beruflich
qualification [ˌkwɒlɪfɪ'keɪʃn] — Qualifikation — ⚠ Aussprache

23 develop [dɪ'veləp] — entwickeln
knowledge ['nɒlɪdʒ] — Wissen, Kenntnis(se)
understanding [ˌʌndə'stændɪŋ] — Verständnis
skill [skɪl] — Fertigkeit, Fähigkeit

iː	ɪ	e	æ	ɑː	ɒ	ɔː	ʊ	uː	ʌ	ɜː	ə
see	sit	ten	bad	arm	got	saw	put	too	cut	bird	about

	need [niːd]	brauchen, benötigen	
	level [ˈlevl]	Stufe	
	of 16 and over [əv ˈsɪkstiːn ənd ˈəʊvə]	ab 16 Jahren	students ~
	foundation [faʊnˈdeɪʃn]	Grund-	~ level
	intermediate [ˌɪntəˈmiːdjət]	Mittel-	~ level
	advanced [ədˈvɑːnst]	fortgeschritten	~ level
	health and social care [ˌhelθ ənd ˈsəʊʃl keə]	Gesundheits- und Sozialfürsorge (als Fach)	
	occupational therapist [ˌɒkjuˌpeɪʃənl ˈθerəpi]	Beschäftigungstherapeut/in	
	information technology [ɪnfəˈmeɪʃn tekˈnɒlədʒi]	Informatik (als Fach)	
	information system [ɪnfəˈmeɪʃn sɪstəm]	Informationssystem	
	two-year [ˈtuːjɪə]	zweijährig	ebenso: one-year usw.
24	a day [ə ˈdeɪ]	am Tag	eight hours ~
25	study [ˈstʌdi]	Studium	bes. Plural: studies
26	police officer [pəˈliːs ɒfɪsə]	Polizeibeamte/r	
	raincoat [ˈreɪnkəʊt]	Regenmantel	
	uniform [ˈjuːnɪfɔːm]	Uniform	⚠ Aussprache
	suit [suːt]	Anzug (für Männer), Kostüm (für Frauen)	
	overalls [ˈəʊvərɔːlz]	Overall	⚠ Plural: a pair of ~ – ein Overall
	helmet [ˈhelmɪt]	Schutzhelm	
	cap [kæp]	Mütze	
	fire officer [ˈfaɪər ɒfɪsə]	Feuerwehrmann/frau	
27	really [ˈrɪəli]	sehr	she's ~ enjoying it
	I'm afraid not [aɪm əˌfreɪd ˈnɒt]	leider nicht	als Antwort auf eine Frage
	take an exam [teɪk ən ɪgˈzæm]	eine Prüfung ablegen	
	work experience [ˈwɜːk ɪkspɪəriəns]	Praktikum	
	get up [ˌget ˈʌp]	aufstehen	
	normally [ˈnɔːməli]	normalerweise	
28	give a shampoo [ʃæmˈpuː]	(jmdm.) die Haare waschen	
	fridge [frɪdʒ]	Kühlschrank	Verkürzung von refrigerator
	book a ticket [bʊk ə ˈtɪkɪt]	eine Fahrkarte bestellen	
	leak [liːk]	undichte Stelle, Leck	
	plumber [ˈplʌmə]	Installateur/in, Klempner/in	
	hairstylist [ˈheəstaɪlɪst]	Coiffeur/Coiffeuse	
	electrician [ɪˌlekˈtrɪʃn]	Elektriker/in,	
	travel agent [ˈtrævl eɪdʒənt]	Reiseverkehrskaufmann/ -frau	
	in pairs [ɪn ˈpeəz]	paarweise	practise ~
	similar [ˈsɪmələ]	ähnlich	⬌ different – verschieden, anders
	dialogue [ˈdaɪəlɒg]	Dialog	⚠ Aussprache
	highlighted [ˈhaɪlaɪtɪd]	hervorgehoben	von highlight – hervorheben
	subject [ˈsʌbdʒɪkt]	(Schul-)Fach	
	trainee chef [ˌtreɪˈniː ʃef]	Küchenlehrling	ebenso: trainee mechanic usw.
	run [rʌn]	leiten, führen	
	agriculture [ˈægrɪkʌltʃə]	Landwirtschaft	
	vehicle maintenance [ˌviːəkl ˈmeɪntənəns]	Fahrzeugwartung	
	hairdressing [ˈheədresɪŋ]	Friseurhandwerk	
	hairstyle [ˈheəstaɪl]	Frisur	
	use [juːz]	bedienen	Can you ~ a computer?
	grow [grəʊ]	anbauen	
	corn [kɔːn]	Getreide	
	crop [krɒp]	Feldfrucht	corn and other ~s
	engine [ˈendʒɪn]	Motor	
	shampoo and cut [ʃæmˌpuː ənd ˈkʌt]	waschen und schneiden	
	salon [ˈsælɒn]	Friseursalon	
	garage [ˈgærɑːʒ]	Autowerkstatt	sonst auch: Garage
	business [ˈbɪznəs]	Unternehmen	
	farm worker [ˈfɑːmˌwɜːkə]	Landarbeiter/in	gleiche Form für beide Geschlechter

| tʃ chips | dʒ jet | ʃ ship | ʒ garage | θ thing | ð the | ŋ ring | s ice | z as | v very | w wet |

29

correct [kə'rekt]	berichtigen	sonst auch Adjektiv: *richtig*
sound [saʊnd]	sich anhören	that ~s interesting
interesting ['ɪntrəstɪŋ]	interessant	◆ **boring** – *langweilig*
typing ['taɪpɪŋ]	Maschineschreiben	
economics [ˌiːkə'nɒmɪks]	Volkswirtschaftslehre (VWL)	als Singular behandelt: ~ **is interesting**
maths [mæθs]	Mathe(matik)	als Singular behandelt: ~ **is difficult**
what sort of ...? [ˌwɒt 'sɔːt əv]	was für ein(e)	~ **job do you want?**
get into [get ɪntʊ]	einsteigen in	we want to ~ **marketing**
train ['treɪnɪŋ]	ausgebildet werden	he's ~ **to be a chef**
horticulture ['hɔːtɪkʌltʃə]	Gartenbau	
electrical repair [ɪ'lektrɪkl]	Reparieren von Elektrogeräten	
art and design [ˌɑːt ən dɪ'zaɪn]	Kunst und Design (Fach)	
graphic designer [ˌgræfɪk dɪ'zaɪnə]	Grafiker/in	
TV repairer [tiːˌviː rɪ'peərə]	Fernsehmonteur/in	
gardener ['gɑːdnə]	Gärtner/in	

UNIT 4 Time for a holiday

30

Scotland ['skɒtlənd]	Schottland	⚠ Aussprache und Schreibung
scenery ['siːnəri]	Landschaft	
lake [leɪk]	(Binnen-)See	**sea** – *Meer*
valley ['væli]	Tal	
lonely ['ləʊnli]	einsam	◆ **busy** – *belebt*
romantic [rəʊ'mæntɪk]	romantisch	
sports holiday ['spɔːts hɒlədeɪ]	Sporturlaub	ebenso: **beach holiday** usw.
ski [skiː]	Ski laufen	⚠ Aussprache
exciting [ɪk'saɪtɪŋ]	aufregend	◆ **boring** – *langweilig*
experience [ɪk'spɪərɪəns]	erleben	sonst auch Nomen: *Erlebnis*
mountain ['maʊntɪn]	Berg	**hill** – *Hügel*
may not be [meɪ nɒt 'biː]	sind zwar nicht	sonst auch: *mag wohl nicht ... sein*
... ago [ə'gəʊ]	vor	**five years** ~ – *vor fünf Jahren*
traveller ['trævlə]	Reisende/r	
varied ['veərɪd]	vielfältig	~ **scenery**
than [ðən]	als	mit Komparativ: **more varied** ~ –*abwechslungsreicher als*
excitement [ɪk'saɪtmənt]	Aufregung	◆ **boredom** – *Langeweile*
fun [fʌn]	Spaß	
probably ['prɒbəbli]	wahrscheinlich	Adverb
if [ɪf]	falls	
Californian [ˌkælə'fɔːnɪən]	kalifornisch	
beach [biːtʃ]	Strand	
national park [ˌnæʃnəl 'pɑːk]	Nationalpark	⚠ Aussprache
for your holidays [fə jɔː 'hɒlədeɪz]	in Urlaub	**where are you going** ~?
countryside ['kʌntrɪsaɪd]	Landschaft, Land	**in the** ~ – *auf dem Lande*

31

have a great time [hæv ə ˌgreɪt 'taɪm]	sich großartig amüsieren	
rollerblade ['rəʊləˌbleɪd]	Inline-Skates fahren	
fall over [ˌfɔːl 'əʊvə]	hinfallen, umkippen	⚠ unregelmäßig
fell [fel]	simple past: **fall**	⚠ unregelmäßig
believe it or not [bɪ'liːv ɪt ɔː nɒt]	ob Sie es glauben oder nicht	
far more [fɑː 'mɔː]	weit mehr	~ **interesting** – *weit interessanter*
nobody ['nəʊbədi]	niemand	
go on [ˌgəʊ 'ɒn]	weitergehen	**life goes on around the clock**
around the clock [əˌraʊnd ðə 'klɒk]	rund um die Uhr	
make it ['meɪk ɪt]	es schaffen	
really ['rɪəli]	unbedingt	bes. mit **must**: **you** ~ **must** – *du musst unbedingt*
go wrong [ˌgəʊ 'rɒŋ]	schief gehen	
nice [naɪs]	schön	~ **weather**
ate [et]	simple past: **eat**	⚠ unregelmäßig
spend [spend]	verbringen	⚠ unregelmäßig

iː	ɪ	e	æ	ɑː	ɒ	ɔː	ʊ	uː	ʌ	ɜː	ə
see	sit	ten	bad	arm	got	saw	put	too	cut	bird	about

	spent [spend]	simple past: spend	⚠	unregelmäßig
	crowded ['kraʊdɪd]	überfüllt		bes. mit Menschen
	miss [mɪs]	vermissen		I miss you – du fehlst mir
	I can't wait [aɪ kɑːnt 'weɪt]	ich kann es kaum erwarten		~ to be back
32	mean [miːn]	bedeuten		
	opposite ['ɒpəzɪt]	Gegenteil		
	terrible ['terəbl]	schrecklich	◆▶	wonderful – wunderbar
	fine [faɪn]	in Ordnung		everything's ~
	boring ['bɔːrɪŋ]	langweilig	◆▶	interesting – interessant
	possible ['pɒsəbl]	möglich, denkbar	◆▶	impossible
	at New Year [ət ˌnjuː 'jɪə]	zu Neujahr		
	all through the year [ɔːl θruː ðə 'jɪə]	das ganze Jahr über		
	even ['iːvn]	selbst, sogar		~ in the summer
	price [praɪs]	(Kauf-)Preis		
	happen ['hæpən]	passieren, geschehen		
	glad [glæd]	froh	◆▶	sorry
	lively ['laɪvli]	lebendig, rege, lebhaft		
34	worse [wɜːs]	schlechter		
	worst [wɜːst]	am schlechtesten		
	further ['fɜːðə]	weiter		
	furthest ['fɜːðɪst]	am weitesten		
	wet [wet]	nass, feucht	◆▶	dry – trocken
	transport ['trænspɔːt]	Verkehrsmittel		
	ferry ['feri]	Fähre		
	cross [krɒs]	überqueren		
	Channel ['tʃænl]	Ärmelkanal		
	tunnel ['tʌnl]	Tunnel		
	complicated ['kɒmplɪkeɪtɪd]	kompliziert	◆▶	simple – einfach
	anyway ['eniweɪ]	jedenfalls		
	explore [ɪk'splɔː]	erforschen, erkunden		
	a couple of [ə 'kʌpl əv]	ein paar		for ~ days – ein paar Tage lang
	found [faʊnd]	simple past: find	⚠	unregelmäßig
	seem [siːm]	scheinen		
	incredibly [ɪn'kredəbl]	unglaublich		Adverb
	lots of ['lɒts əv]	viele		~ mountains
	although [ɔːl'ðəʊ]	obwohl		
	travel sick ['trævl sɪk]	reisekrank		I often get ~
	flew [fluː]	simple past: fly	⚠	unregelmäßig
35	enjoyable [ɪn'dʒɔɪəbl]	angenehm		
	attractive [ə'træktɪv]	attraktiv, anziehend		
	beach holiday ['biːtʃ hɒlədeɪ]	Strandurlaub		
	city holiday ['sɪti hɒlədeɪ]	Urlaub in der Stadt		
	camping holiday ['kæmpɪŋ hɒlədeɪ]	Campingurlaub		
	quiet ['kwaɪət]	still, ruhig	◆▶	noisy, busy – laut, belebt
	busy ['bɪzi]	belebt	◆▶	quiet – still, ruhig
36	travel enquiry [ˌtrævl ɪn'kwaɪəri]	Reiseauskunft		
	reservation [ˌrezə'veɪʃn]	Reservierung		
	cash [kæʃ]	einlösen		~ a cheque – einen Scheck einlösen
	traveller's cheque ['trævələz tʃek]	Reisescheck		
	flight [flaɪt]	Flug		
	sure [ʃʊə]	natürlich		lässig/umgangssprachlich, als Antwort auf eine Frage oder Bitte
	passport ['pɑːspɔːt]	Reisepass		
	the week of ... to ... [ðə 'wiːk əv ... tu]	die Woche zwischen ... und ...		~ June 5 ~ June 12
	return [rɪ'tɜːn]	Rückfahrkarte		single – einfache Fahrt
	what kind of ...? [wɒt 'kaɪnd əv]	was für ein(e) ...?		~ room do you want?
	following ['ðə 'fɒləʊɪŋ]	folgend		the ~ Friday – den Freitag darauf
	credit card ['kredɪt kɑːd]	Kreditkarte	⚠	Aussprache

tʃ	dʒ	ʃ	ʒ	θ	ð	ŋ	s	z	v	w
chips	jet	ship	garage	thing	the	ring	ice	as	very	wet

single ['sɪŋgl] — Einzelzimmer — je nach Zusammenhang auch: *einfache Fahrt* usw.

bathroom ['bɑ:θru:m] — Badezimmer

37 choose [tʃu:z] — wählen, aussuchen — ⚠ unregelmäßig
apartment [ə'pɑ:tmənt] — Wohnung — ≈ **flat**
no. ['nʌmbə] — Nr. — Abkürzung: **number**
per [pə] — pro, per
min. ['mɪnɪt] — Min. — Abkürzung: **minute**
night life ['naɪt laɪf] — Nachtleben
town centre [ˌtaʊn 'sentə] — Stadtzentrum, City
comfortable ['kʌmftəbl] — bequem
near [nɪə] — nahe — ◆ **far** – *weit*
noisy ['nɔɪzi] — laut, geräuschvoll, lärmend — ◆ **quiet** – *still, ruhig*

convenient [kən'vi:niənt] — günstig, praktisch — ◆ **inconvenient**
peaceful ['pi:sfl] — friedlich — ◆ **noisy, busy** – *laut, lebhaft*
simple ['sɪmpl] — einfach, schlicht — ◆ **luxurious** – *luxuriös*
centre of town [ˌsentər əv 'taʊn] — Stadtzentrum, City
this is ... speaking [ðɪs ɪz ... 'spi:kɪŋ] — hier spricht ... — Telefonsprache
study ['stʌdi] — (eingehend) lesen — sonst auch: *studieren* usw.
decide [dɪ'saɪd] — (sich) entscheiden
hotel receptionist [həʊˌtel rɪ'sepʃənɪst] — Empfangsherr/-dame in einem Hotel

tourist information [ˌtʊərɪst ɪnfə'meɪʃn] — Fremdenverkehrsamt
employee [ɪm'plɔɪi:] — Arbeitnehmer/in
greet [gri:t] — begrüßen
arrival [ə'raɪvl] — Ankunft — **on your ~**
check in [ˌtʃek 'ɪn] — anmelden — sonst auch intransitiv: *einchecken*
make a booking [meɪk ə 'bʊkɪŋ] — eine Reservierung vornehmen

look after [ˌlʊk 'ɑ:ftə] — sich kümmern um — **she looks after tourists**
while [waɪl] — während — **~ you are on holiday**
excursion [ɪk'skɜ:ʃn] — Ausflug, Exkursion — ⚠ Aussprache
local ['ləʊkl] — örtlich
tourist office [ˌtʊərɪst 'ɒfɪs] — Fremdenverkehrsbüro

UNIT 5 His job or hers?

38 hers [hɜ:z] — ihre(r, s) — Pronomen: **that's ~** – *das ist ihre(r, s), das gehört ihr*

unequal [ʌn'i:kwəl] — ungleich — ◆ **equal** – *gleich*
opportunity [ˌɒpə'tju:nəti] — Gelegenheit, Chance
area ['eəriə] — Gebiet, Bereich — **in this ~ of work** – *in diesem Arbeitsbereich*

earn [ɜ:n] — verdienen
possibly ['pɒsəbl] — möglicherweise
a few [ə 'fju:] — ein paar
however [haʊ'evə] — doch, jedoch, aber
model ['mɒdl] — Mannequin, Dressman
things are different [ˌθɪŋz ə 'dɪfrənt] — die Lage ist anders
few ['fju:ə] — wenige — ◆ **many** – *viele*
male [meɪl] — männlich
female ['fi:meɪl] — weiblich
modelling job ['mɒdlɪŋ dʒɒb] — Auftrag als Mannequin/Dressman — **she's looking for a ~**

a year [ə 'jɪə] — im Jahr — **£20,000 ~**
case [keɪs] — Fall — **this is a ~ of sexism**
not only ... but also [nɒt ˌəʊnli ... bət ɑ:'lsəʊ] — nicht nur ..., sondern auch
sexism ['seksɪzəm] — Sexismus
towards [tə'wɔ:dz] — gegenüber — sonst auch: *auf ... zu, in Richtung auf* **in the ~**
past [pɑ:st] — Vergangenheit
business ['bɪznəs] — Unternehmen

iː	ɪ	e	æ	ɑː	ɒ	ɔː	ʊ	uː	ʌ	ɜː	ə
see	sit	ten	bad	arm	got	saw	put	too	cut	bird	about

	advertise ['ædvətaɪz]	werben für	~ a product
	product ['prɒdʌkt]	Produkt, Erzeugnis	
	for this reason [fə ðɪs 'riːzn]	aus diesem Grund	⚠ for, nicht out of
	interested in ['ɪntrəstɪd ɪn]	interessiert an	⚠ in, nicht on
	cosmetics [kɒz'metɪks]	Kosmetika	Plural
	female ['fiːmeɪl]	Frau	
	male [meɪl]	Mann	
	model ['mɒdl]	vorführen	
39	in demand [ɪn dɪ'mɑːnd]	gefragt	good models are ~
	market ['mɑːkɪt]	vermarkten	
	not just [nɒt 'dʒʌst]	nicht nur	
	handsome ['hænsəm]	gutaussehend	◆ ugly – hässlich
	nowadays ['naʊədeɪz]	heutzutage	
	plain [pleɪn]	alltäglich, nicht schön	
	ordinary-looking ['ɔːdnri lʊkɪŋ]	durchschnittlich aussehend	
	About time! [ə'baʊt 'taɪm]	Es wird Zeit!	
	at last [ət 'lɑːst]	endlich	
	future ['fjuːtʃə]	Zukunft	
	business ['bɪznəs]	Branche	
	… is ours [ɪz 'aʊəz]	… gehört uns	
	ours ['aʊəz]	unsere(r, s)	Pronomen
	modelling work ['mɒdlɪŋ wɜːk]	Arbeit als Mannequin/ Dressman	
	Why is this?	Warum ist das so?	
	feminist ['femənɪst]	feministisch	
	movement ['muːvmənt]	Bewegung	the feminist ~
	sexist ['seksɪst]	sexistisch	
	manufacturer [ˌmænju'fæktʃərə]	Hersteller/in, Produzent/in	
	target s.th. at s.o. ['tɑːgɪt]	mit etw. auf jmdn. zielen	
	as well as [əz 'wel əz]	ebenso wie, sowohl … als auch …	men ~ women
	educated ['edʒukeɪtɪd]	gebildet	
	intelligent [ɪn'telɪdʒənt]	intelligent	⚠ Aussprache
	looks [lʊks]	Aussehen	Plural
	of course [əf 'kɔːs]	natürlich	
	equal ['iːkwəl]	gleich	
	sex object ['seks ɒbdʒɪkt]	Sexobjekt	
40	important [ɪm'pɔːtnt]	wichtig	
	yourself [jɔː'self]	sich	Can you describe ~? – Können Sie sich beschreiben?
	call [kɔːl]	nennen	
	become [bɪ'kʌm]	werden	⚠ nicht bekommen
	popular ['pɒpjələ]	beliebt, populär	
	have to ['hæv tə]	müssen	≈ must (unvollständiges Verb)
	both … and [bəʊθ, ənd]	sowohl … als auch	
	well-known [ˌwel'nəʊn]	sehr bekannt	
	advertising ['ædvətaɪzɪŋ]	Werbung	
41	mine [maɪn]	meine(r, s)	Pronomen
	yours [jɔːz]	deine(r, s), Ihre(r, s)	Pronomen
	theirs [ðeəz]	ihre(r, s)	Pronomen
	no longer [nəʊ 'lɒŋə]	nicht länger	it's ~ mine – es gehört mir nicht mehr
	sold [səʊld]	simple past: sell	⚠ unregelmäßig
42	I am afraid that … [aɪm ə'freɪd ðət]	leider …	~ he's not here
	position [pə'zɪʃn]	Stelle	
	italic [ɪ'tælɪks]	Kursivschrift	
	management ['mænɪdʒmənt]	Management, Führung	
	collection [kə'lekʃn]	Sammlung	
	job interview ['dʒɒb ɪntəvjuː]	Vorstellungsgespräch	
	lose weight [luːz 'weɪt]	abnehmen	⚠ unregelmäßiges Verb
43	compare [kəm'peə]	vergleichen	
	amount [ə'maʊnt]	Menge	

tʃ	dʒ	ʃ	ʒ	θ	ð	ŋ	s	z	v	w
chips	**j**et	**sh**ip	gara**g**e	**th**ing	**th**e	ri**ng**	i**c**e	a**s**	**v**ery	**w**et

    it's your fault [ɪts jɔː 'fɔːlt]   es ist deine Schuld
    began [bɪ'gæn]   simple past: **begin**   ⚠ unregelmäßig
    catalogue ['kætəlɒg]   Katalog   ⚠ Aussprache
    famous ['feɪməs]   berühmt
    photographer [fə'tɒgrəfə]   Fotograf/in
    discover [dɪ'skʌvə]   entdecken
    various different [ˌveəriəs 'dɪfrənt]   verschiedene
    feel about ['fiːl əbaʊt]   halten von
    mean [miːn]   meinen, sagen wollen   **what I ~ is, ...**
    advertiser ['ædvətaɪzə]   Werbekunde, -firma
    exploit [ɪk'splɔɪt]   ausbeuten
    decision [dɪ'sɪʒn]   Entscheidung   **the ~ is mine** – *ich entscheide*
    career [kə'rɪə]   Karriere
    a bit [ə 'bɪt]   ein wenig, etwas   ≈ **a little**
    unfair [ˌʌn'feə]   unfair, ungerecht
    not at all [nɒt ət 'ɔːl]   überhaupt nicht
    media job ['miːdiə dʒɒb]   Medienarbeit
    advert ['ædvɜːt]   Werbung   Verkürzung: **advertisement**
    more and more [ˌmɔːr ənd 'mɔː]   immer mehr
    these days ['ðiːz ˌdeɪz]   heutzutage
    keep s.o. happy [kiːp 'hæpi]   jmdn. glücklich machen

44   **advertisement** [əd'vɜːtɪsmənt]   Reklame
    slogan ['sləʊgən]   Werbespruch, Slogan
    on time [ɒn 'taɪm]   pünktlich
    look after (yourself) [ˌlʊk 'ɑːftə (jɔːˌself)]   pass gut auf (dich) auf
    smooth [smuːð]   glatt   umgangssprachlich: *cool*

45   **look up** [ˌlʊk 'ʌp]   nachschlagen
    in the back of [ɪn ðə 'bæk əv]   hinten in
    mail shot ['meɪlʃɒt]   Postwurfsendung
    commercial [kə'mɜːʃl]   (Fernseh-)Reklame   ≈ **ad, advert, advertisement**
    gift [gɪft]   Geschenk   ≈ **present**
    competition [ˌkɒmpə'tɪʃn]   Wettbewerb
    discount offer ['dɪskaʊnt ɒfə]   Sonderangebot
    sponsorship ['spɒnsəʃɪp]   finanzielle Unterstützung
    snack food ['snæk fuːd]   Häppchen
    gimmick ['gɪmɪk]   Verkaufstrick
    type [taɪp]   Art   ≈ **sort, kind**
    letter box ['letəbɒks]   Briefkasten
    sports event ['spɔːts ɪvent]   Sportereignis
    enter ['entə]   teilnehmen an
    persuade [pə'sweɪd]   überzeugen, überreden
    feel [fiːl]   sich fühlen
    especially [ɪ'speʃəli]   besonders
    like it or not [ˌlaɪk ɪt ɔː 'nɒt]   ob man will oder nicht
    ... is here to stay [ɪz ˌhɪə tə 'steɪ]   ... wird bleiben   **advertising is ~**
    trainer ['treɪnə]   Turnschuh
    fill in [fɪl ɪn]   eintragen   **~ the missing word**
    missing ['mɪsɪŋ]   fehlend   **one word's ~** – *ein Wort fehlt*
    department [dɪ'pɑːtmənt]   Abteilung
    responsible [rɪ'spɒnsəbl]   verantwortlich
    publicity campaign [pʌb'lɪsəti kæmpeɪn]   Werbekampagne
    mainly ['meɪnli]   hauptsächlich
    brochure ['brəʊʃə]   Broschüre, Prospekt
    ad [æd]   Reklame, Anzeige   Verkürzung: **advertisement**
    design [dɪ'zaɪn]   Entwurf, Design
    rest [rest]   Rest
    do well [duː 'wel]   Erfolg haben   **she's doing well in her new job**

UNIT 6   Food and diet

46   **diet** ['daɪət]   Diät, Ernährung
    experiment [ɪk'sperɪmənt]   Versuch, Experiment

i:	ɪ	e	æ	ɑ:	ɒ	ɔ:	ʊ	u:	ʌ	ɜ:	ə
see	sit	ten	bad	arm	got	saw	put	too	cut	bird	about

	pupil ['pju:pl]	Schüler/in	
	have lunch [həv 'lʌntʃ]	zu Mittag essen	
	at school [ət 'sku:l]	in der Schule	they have lunch ~
	menu ['menju:]	Speisekarte	⚠ nicht: *Menü*
	ostrich ['ɒstrɪtʃ]	Strauß (Vogel)	
	burger ['bɜ:gə]	Hamburger	
	catering manager ['keɪtərɪŋ mænɪdʒə]	Gastronom/in	
	understand [ˌʌndə'stænd]	verstehen, begreifen	⚠ unregelmäßig
	chicken ['tʃɪkɪn]	Huhn, Hähnchen	
	taste [teɪst]	schmecken	
	beef [bi:f]	Rindfleisch	
	stop [stɒp]	aufhören	we stopped eating beef
	scare [skeə]	Schrecken	the BSE ~
	animal lover ['ænɪml lʌvə]	Tierfreund/in	
	anybody ['enibɒdi]	jemand	how can ~ do that?
	fact [fækt]	Tatsache	
	Japan [dʒə'pæn]	Japan	⚠ Aussprache
	poisonous ['pɔɪzənəs]	giftig	
	qualified ['kwɒlɪfaɪd]	ausgebildet	a ~ chef
	correctly [kə'rektli]	richtig	Adverb
			◆▶ incorrectly
47	order ['ɔ:də]	bestellen	we'd like to ~, please
	What can I get you? [ˌwɒt kən aɪ 'get ju:]	Was darf ich Ihnen bringen?	
	dish [dɪʃ]	Gericht	sonst auch: *Teller*
	dish of the day [ˌdɪʃ əv ðə 'deɪ]	Tagesgericht	what's the ~?
	shepherd's pie [ˌʃepədz 'paɪ]	Auflauf aus Hackfleisch und Kartoffelbrei	
	pie [paɪ]	Pastete	hier eigentlich ein Auflauf
	hot [hɒt]	heiß, warm	sonst auch: *scharf (gewürzt)*
	not too [nɒt tu:]	nicht besonders	I'm ~ keen on beef
	salmon ['sæmən]	Lachs	⚠ Aussprache
	green bean [ˌgri:n 'bi:n]	grüne Bohne	
	Anything to start with? [ˌeniθɪŋ tə 'stɑ:t wɪð]	Eine Vorspeise?	
	be on a diet [bi ˌɒn ə 'daɪət]	eine Schlankheitskur machen	I'm on a diet
	low-calorie [ˌləʊ'kæləri]	mit wenig Kalorien	a ~ dish
	fat [fæt]	Fett	with no ~ – *ohne Fett*
	serve [sɜ:v]	servieren	
	choice [tʃɔɪs]	Auswahl	we have a ~ of salads
	pasta ['pæstə]	Nudeln	
	french fries [ˌfrentʃ 'fraɪz]	Pommes frites	≈ chips
	Anything to follow? [ˌeniθɪŋ tə 'fɒləʊ]	Und danach?	
	grilled [grɪld]	gegrillt	von **grill** – *grillen*
	tomato [tə'mɑ:təʊ]	Tomate	⚠ Plural: **tomatoes**
	dessert [dɪ'zɜ:t]	Nachspeise	⚠ Aussprache u. Schreibung: **desert** ['dezət] – *Wüste*
	starter ['stɑ:tə]	Vorspeise	
	Japanese [ˌdʒæpə'ni:z]	japanisch	⚠ Aussprache
	strange [streɪndʒ]	fremdartig, seltsam	
48	meal [mi:l]	Essen, Mahlzeit	enjoy your ~ – *guten Appetit!*
	main [meɪn]	Haupt-	main course – *Hauptgericht*
49	bought [bɔ:t]	simple past: buy	⚠ unregelmäßig
50	knew [nju:]	simple past: know	⚠ unregelmäßig
	make ... better [ˌmeɪk 'betə]	wiedergutmachen	
51	school lunch ['sku:l lʌntʃ]	Mittagessen in der Schule	
	just now [dʒʌst 'naʊ]	im Moment	≈ I'm busy ~ right now
	well-balanced [ˌwel'bælənst]	ausgeglichen	
	fast food [ˌfɑ:st 'fu:d]	Schnellgerichte	
	get ready (for) [get 'redi]	Vorbereitungen treffen (für)	

tʃ	dʒ	ʃ	ʒ	θ	ð	ŋ	s	z	v	w
chips	jet	ship	garage	thing	the	ring	ice	as	very	wet

vodka [ˈvɒdkə] — Wodka — ⚠ Schreibung

soft drink [ˌsɒft ˈdrɪŋk] — alkoholfreies Getränk — ≈ **non-alcoholic drink**
alcohol [ˈælkəhɒl] — Alkohol — ⚠ Schreibung
crisp [krɪsp] — Chip
nut [nʌt] — Nuss
things like that [θɪŋz ˌlaɪk ˈðæt] — derartige Sachen — **nuts, crisps and ~**
enough [ɪˈnʌf] — ausreichend, genug — **there's not ~ bread**
say [seɪ] — sagen wir … — **we need, ~, twelve bottles of wine**
baguette [bæˈget] — Baguette
loaf [ləʊf] — Brotlaib — ⚠ unregelmäßiger Plural: **loaves**
brown bread [ˌbraʊn ˈbred] — Grau-, Mischbrot
main dish [ˌmeɪn ˈdɪʃ] — Hauptgericht
vegetarian [ˌvedʒəˈteəriən] — vegetarisch — **are you ~?** – *sind Sie Vegetarier/in?*
as far as [əz ˈfɑːr əs] — so weit
put down [ˌpʊt ˈdaʊn] — niederschreiben
fresh [freʃ] — frisch — ◆▶ **frozen, tinned** – *tiefgefroren, aus der Dose*

lettuce [ˈletɪs] — Kopfsalat
avocado [ˌævəˈkɑːdəʊ] — Avocado
breakfast cereal [ˈbrekfəst sɪəriəl] — Frühstücksflocken
thought [θɔːt] — simple past: **think** — ⚠ unregelmäßig
rather than [ˈrɑːðə] — lieber als, anstatt — **we should eat fish ~ meat**
save [seɪv] — sparen — **I need to ~ money**

52
dietician [ˌdaɪəˈtɪʃn] — Diätberater/in
advise [ədˈvaɪz ɒn] — beraten
food scientist [ˈfuːd saɪəntɪst] — Nahrungswissen- schaftler/in

scientist [ˈsaɪəntɪst] — (Natur-)Wissen- schaftler/in

study [ˈstʌdi] — erforschen
food product [ˈfuːd prɒdʌkt] — Nahrungsmittel
take orders [teɪk ˈɔːdəz] — die Bestellung aufnehmen
health centre [ˈhelθ sentə] — Ärztezentrum
company [ˈkʌmpəni] — Unternehmen, Firma — ≈ **firm, company, business**

53
avoid [əˈvɔɪd] — vermeiden — **I try to ~ fat and sugar**
disease [dɪˈziːz] — Krankheit — **he got a terrible ~**
smoking [ˈsməʊkɪŋ] — Rauchen
lean [liːn] — fettarm — bes. Fleisch
balance [ˈbæləns] — Gleichgewicht — **you need to get the right ~**
go without [ˌgəʊ wɪðˈaʊt] — verzichten auf — **you don't have to ~ good food**
stop [stɒp] — verhindern — **exercise can ~ you getting fat**
ice cream [ˌaɪsˈkriːm] — Speiseeis
protein [ˈprəʊtiːn] — Protein — ⚠ Aussprache
dairy food [ˈdeəri fuːd] — Molkereiprodukt(e)
cereal [ˈsɪəriəl] — Getreide — sonst auch: *Frühstücksflocken*
vitamin [ˈvɪtəmɪn] — Vitamin — ⚠ Aussprache
fibre [ˈfaɪbə] — Ballaststoffe
content [kənˈtent] — Gehalt — **fat content** – *Fettgehalt*
speaker [ˈspiːkə] — Sprecher
upset [ʌpˈset] — betrübt — **don't get ~** – *reg dich nicht auf*
balanced [ˈbælənst] — ausgeglichen
get used to [get ˈjuːst tə] — sich gewöhnen an
educate [ˈedʒukeɪt] — erziehen
rubbish [ˈrʌbɪʃ] — Mist — eigentlich: *Abfälle, Müll*
put s.o. off s.th. [ˌpʊt ˈɒf] — jmdm. die Lust an etw. nehmen — **it puts you off eating**

basic [ˈbeɪsɪk] — einfach
even so [ˌiːvən ˈsəʊ] — trotzdem — **~, he lived to the age of 93**
fair [feə] — gerecht
for ever [fɔː ˈevə] — (für immer und) ewig — **nobody lives ~**
fry [fraɪ] — braten, frittieren

i:	ɪ	e	æ	ɑ:	ɒ	ɔ:	ʊ	u:	ʌ	ɜ:	ə
see	sit	ten	bad	arm	got	saw	put	too	cut	bird	about

grill [grɪl] — grillen
boil [bɔɪl] — kochen
carbohydrates [ˌkɑ:bəʊ'haɪdreɪts] — Kohlenhydrate

UNIT 7 Problems and anxieties

54
anxiety [æŋ'zaɪəti] — Besorgnis
mailbag ['meɪlbæg] — Posttasche
depressed [dɪ'prest] — deprimiert
awkward ['ɔ:kwəd] — unbeholfen, ungeschickt
stupid ['stju:pɪd] — dumm, blöde
laugh at ['lɑ:f ət] — lachen über, auslachen — they're always laughing at me
pick on ['pɪk ɒn] — kritisieren
the other day [ðə ˌʌðə 'deɪ] — neulich — I saw her ~
mark [mɑ:k] — Note — I got bad ~s in the exam
complain [kəm'pleɪn] — sich beklagen
should [ʃʊd] — sollten △ unregelmäßig
treat [tri:t] — behandeln — don't ~ her like a baby
argue ['ɑ:gju:] — sich streiten
all the time [ˌɔ:l ðə 'taɪm] — stets — we argue ~
even though ['i:vn ðəʊ] — obwohl
frustrated [frʌ'streɪtɪd] — frustriert
drive s.o. crazy [draɪv 'kreɪzi] — jmdn. zur Verzweiflung treiben

bored [bɔ:d] — gelangweilt ◆▶ excited – *aufgeregt, begeistert*
shy [ʃaɪ] — schüchtern, scheu ◆▶ outgoing – *kontaktfreudig*

55
reply [rɪ'plaɪ] — antworten — auch Nomen: *Antwort*
reply [rɪ'plaɪ] — Antwort — auch Verb: *antworten*
low [ləʊ] — elend — I'm feeling ~
pretty ['prɪti] — ziemlich — I felt ~ stupid – *ich kam mir ziemlich doof vor*

quite [kwaɪt] — völlig, ziemlich — that's ~ normal
of your age [əv jɔ: 'eɪdʒ] — deines/Ihres Alters — it's normal for someone ~
tell (from) [tel (frəm)] — erkennen (an) — I can ~ from your letter that …
mirror ['mɪrə] — Spiegel — look in/into the ~
point of view [ˌpɔɪnt əv 'vju:] — Standpunkt — try to see it from their ~
be to blame [bi tə 'bleɪm] — schuld sein — she isn't to blame
at least [ət 'li:st] — wenigstens — you can ~ try
reasonable ['ri:znəbl] — vernünftig
there's no harm in [ðeəz ˌnəʊ 'hɑ:m ɪn] — es kann nichts schaden, ~ wenn man — trying … – *es kann nichts schaden, wenn man versucht …*
work [wɜ:k] — klappen — it may ~ – *es könnte klappen*

56
advice [əd'vaɪs] — Ratschlag, Ratschläge — Plural: pieces of ~
in what way [ɪn ˌwɒt 'weɪ] — in welcher Weise ≈ how – *wie*
suggest [sə'dʒest] — nahelegen
the same [ðə 'seɪm] — gleich — they're both ~
give in (to s.o.) [ˌgɪv 'ɪn] — (jmdm.) nachgeben — he won't ~ to his parents
make the first move [meɪk ðə fɜ:st 'mu:v] — den ersten Schritt tun — you must ~
the ones [ðə 'wʌnz] — diejenigen — ~ underlined – *die unterstrichenen*
clever ['klevə] — begabt ≈ intelligent
confident ['kɒnfɪdənt] — zuversichtlich

57
make s.o. do s.th. [meɪk 'du:] — jmdn. etw. tun lassen (= veranlassen) — you can't ~ me ~ it – *du kannst mich nicht zwingen, es zu tun*
let s.o. do s.th. [let 'du:] — jmdn. etw. tun lassen (= erlauben) — please ~ me ~ it myself – *lass es mich bitte selbst machen*
realise ['rɪəlaɪz] — erkennen, feststellen — do you ~ that … ? – *ist es Ihnen klar, dass … ?*

58
marry ['mæri] — heiraten — will you ~ me?
study ['stʌdi] — (eingehend) betrachten — ~ the picture
get away with it [get ə'weɪ wɪð ɪt] — ungestraft davonkommen — don't let them ~
accept [ək'sept] — hinnehmen — you don't have to ~ it

tʃ	dʒ	ʃ	ʒ	θ	ð	ŋ	s	z	v	w
chips	jet	ship	garage	thing	the	ring	ice	as	very	wet

    service ['sɜːvɪs]   Bedienung
    secret ['siːkrɪt]   Geheimnis

59 turn s.th. into s.th. ['tɜːn ˌɪntʊ]   etw. in etw. verwandeln
    remember [rɪ'membə]   denken an   did you ~ to phone her?
    meet [miːt]   kennen lernen
    brought [brɔːt]   simple past: **bring** ⚠ unregelmäßig
    right [raɪt]   Recht   you don't have the ~ to say that
    awful ['ɔːfl]   furchtbar ⬌ great, wonderful – *großartig*
    truth [truːθ]   Wahrheit   tell her the ~
    frighten ['fraɪtn]   Angst einjagen

60 unemployment [ˌʌnɪm'plɔɪmənt]   Arbeitslosigkeit
    health and safety [ˌhelθ ənd 'seɪfti]   Arbeitsschutz   ~ regulations –
                                                               Arbeitsschutzvorschriften
    stress [stres]   Stress ⚠ Aussprache
    racial discrimination [ˌreɪʃl dɪˌskrɪmɪ'neɪʃn]   Rassendiskriminierung
    pension ['penʃn]   Rente, Pension ⚠ Aussprache
    redundancy [rɪ'dʌndənsi]   Entlassung (wegen   there were 300 redundancies – *es*
                                      Überkapazität)   *gab 300 Entlassungen*
    sexual harassment [ˌsekʃuəl 'hærəsmənt]   sexuelle Belästigung
    'A' level ['eɪ levl]   ≈ Abitur   = **Advanced Level** – wörtl.
                                                                    fortgeschrittene Stufe

    factory ['fæktəri]   Fabrik
    frustrating [frʌ'streɪtɪŋ]   frustrierend
    employer [ɪm'plɔɪə]   Arbeitgeber/in   gleiche Form für beide Geschlechter
    Pakistani [ˌpɑːkɪ'stɑːni]   Pakistani
    amount [ə'maʊnt]   Menge
    less and less [les ənd 'les]   immer weniger   ebenso: **more and more**
    rat [ræt]   Ratte
    chairperson ['tʃeəpɜːsn]   Vorsitzende/r
    keep ...ing [kiːp]   ständig ...   why do you keep doing that? –
                                                             warum machst du das ständig?

    touch [tʌtʃ]   anfassen, berühren
    bottom ['bɒtəm]   Hintern   sonst auch: *unteres Ende, Fuß*
    agree [ə'griː]   übereinstimmen   does that ~ with what he said?
    unemployed [ˌʌnɪm'plɔɪd]   arbeitslos
    explain [ɪk'spleɪn]   erklären
    deliberately [dɪ'lɪbərət]   absichtlich   Adverb
    graduate ['grædʒuət]   (Hochschul-)Absolvent/in   vgl. **graduate** ['grædjueɪt] – *die*
                                                                    Hochschule absolvieren
    degree [dɪ'griː]   akademischer Grad   she's got a good ~ in German
    live on the dole [ˌlɪv ɒn ðə 'dəʊl]   Arbeitslosengeld   I'm living on the dole – *ich bin*
                                                  bekommen   *arbeitslos/bekomme Arbeitslosengeld*
    stressful ['stresfl]   stressig ⬌ relaxing – *entspannend*
    positive ['pɒzətɪv]   positiv ⬌ negative
    blame [bleɪm]   die Schuld geben   don't ~ me!
    active ['æktɪv]   aktiv ⬌ passive
    training course ['treɪnɪŋ kɔːs]   Lehrgang, Ausbildung
    add [æd]   hinzufügen
    work out [ˌwɜːk 'aʊt]   gut gehen, klappen

61 go with ['gəʊ wɪð]   passen zu
    sexually ['sekʃuəli]   sexuell   Adverb
    harass ['hærəs]   belästigen   vgl. **harassment** – *Belästigung*
    stress [stres]   belasten   gewöhnlich passiv: I'm really ~ed
                                                                         by my work
    leave out [ˌliːv 'aʊt]   auslassen   can you leave anything out?
    careers adviser [kə'rɪəz ədvaɪzə]   Berufsberater/in
    letter of application [ˌletər əv æplɪ'keɪʃn]   Bewerbungsschreiben   vgl. **apply** – *sich bewerben*
    application [ˌæplɪ'keɪʃn]   Bewerbung
    mistake [mɪ'steɪk]   Fehler
    model ['mɒdl]   Muster   use her letter as a ~
    apply (for) [ə'plaɪ (fɔː)]   sich bewerben (um)   I would like to apply for the job ...
    secretarial [ˌsekrə'teəriəl]   Sekretariats-   a ~ job

iː	ɪ	e	æ	ɑː	ɒ	ɔː	ʊ	uː	ʌ	ɜː	ə
see	sit	ten	bad	arm	got	saw	put	too	cut	bird	about

employment [ɪmˈplɔɪmənt]	Arbeit, Beschäftigung		
cover [ˈkʌvə]	behandeln, erfassen		
enclose [ɪnˈkləʊz]	beilegen		I enclose a CV
CV [ˌsiː ˈviː]	Lebenslauf		Abkürzung: **curriculum vitae**
consideration [kənˌsɪdəˈreɪʃn]	Erwägung		
look forward to [ˌlʊk ˈfɔːwəd tə]	sich freuen auf		I ~ hearing from you – *ich hoffe, bald von Ihnen zu hören*
		⚠	+ ing- Form, nicht Infinitiv
Yours sincerely [jɔːz sɪnˈsɪəli]	Mit freundlichen Grüßen		

UNIT 8 On the road!

62
on the road [ɒn ðə ˈrəʊd]	unterwegs		
likely [ˈlaɪkli]	wahrscheinlich	⚠	Adjektiv, nicht Adverb
accident [ˈæksɪdənt]	Unfall		
differently [ˈdɪfrənt]	anders		why do they do everything ~?
Roman [ˈrəʊmən]	römisch		
drove [drəʊv]	simple past: **drive**	⚠	unregelmäßig
chariot [ˈtʃæriət]	Kampfwagen		
rode [rəʊd]	simple past: **ride**	⚠	unregelmäßig
right-handed [ˌraɪtˈhændɪd]	rechtshändig		
protect [prəˈtekt]	schützen		
opposite [ˈɒpəzɪt]	entgegengesetzt		in the ~ direction
direction [dəˈrekʃn]	Richtung		
could [kʊd]	simple past: **can**	⚠	unregelmäßig
fight [faɪt]	kämpfen (mit)	⚠	unregelmäßig
defend [dɪˈfend]	verteidigen		
fought [fɔːt]	simple past: **fight**	⚠	unregelmäßig
kept [kept]	simple past: **keep**	⚠	unregelmäßig
pull s.o.'s leg [pʊl ... ˈleg]	jmdn. auf den		are you pulling my leg? – *willst du mich auf den Arm nehmen?*
at what point [ət wɒt ˈpɔɪnt]	an welchem Punkt		

63
road sign [ˈrəʊd saɪn]	Verkehrszeichen		
Roman [ˈrəʊmən]	Römer/in		
mark [mɑːk]	markieren		
stone [stəʊn]	Stein		
place [pleɪs]	setzen, stellen		
pace [peɪs]	Schritt		every 20 paces
became [bɪˈkeɪm]	simple past: **become**	⚠	unregelmäßig
century [ˈsentʃəri]	Jahrhundert		
warn (about) [ˈwɔːn əbaʊt]	warnen (vor)		
bend [bend]	Kurve		
introduce [ˌɪntrəˈdjuːs]	einführen		
appear [əˈpɪə]	erscheinen		
junction [ˈdʒʌŋkʃn]	Kreuzung, Abfahrt		turn left at the next ~
cat's eye [ˈkæts aɪ]	Katzenauge		
invent [ɪnˈvent]	erfinden		
millionaire [ˌmɪljəˈneə]	Millionär/in		auch: **millionairess** – *Millionärin*
lane [leɪn]	Spur		this road only has two ~s
overtake [ˌəʊvəˈteɪkɪŋ]	überholen	⚠	unregelmäßig
finally [ˈfaɪnəli]	schließlich		
in line with [ɪn ˈlaɪn wɪð]	in Übereinstimmung mit		~ European laws
class [klɑːs]	Kategorie		
order [ˈɔːdə]	Befehl		sonst auch Verb: *befehlen*
warning [ˈwɔːnɪŋ]	Warnung		
rectangle [ˈrektæŋgl]	Rechteck		

64
motor car [ˈməʊtəkɑː]	Auto		
arrive [əˈraɪv]	ankommen		
probable [ˈprɒbəbl]	wahrscheinlich		
fashionable [ˈfæʃnəbl]	modisch, modern		
category [ˈkætəgəri]	Kategorie, Klasse	≈	**class**

tʃ	dʒ	ʃ	ʒ	θ	ð	ŋ	s	z	v	w
chips	**j**et	**sh**ip	gara**g**e	**th**ing	**th**e	ri**ng**	i**c**e	a**s**	**v**ery	**w**et

65 enjoy oneself [ɪn'dʒɔɪ wʌnself] — sich amüsieren

66 mph [ˌmaɪlz pər 'aʊr] — Abkürzung: **miles per hour**
seatbelt ['siːtbelt] — Sicherheitsgurt
roundabout ['raʊndəbaʊt] — Kreisverkehr, Kreisel
clockwise ['klɒkwaɪz] — im Uhrzeigersinn ◄► **anticlockwise**
turn right/left [ˌtɜːn 'left 'raɪt] — rechts/links abbiegen
give way [gɪv 'weɪ] — Vorfahrt einräumen — you have to ~ here
express [ɪk'spres] — ausdrücken — how do you ~ that in English?
drink and drive [ˌdrɪŋk ən 'draɪv] — unter Alkoholeinfluss Auto fahren — don't ~

necessary ['nesəsəri] — nötig, notwendig
light [laɪt] — Scheinwerfer — don't leave your ~s on
light [laɪt] — Ampel — they didn't stop at the ~
pass [pɑːs] — bestehen
driving test ['draɪvɪŋtest] — Fahrprüfung
hand signal ['hænd sɪgnəl] — Handsignal
hurt [hɜːt] — verletzen ⚠ unregelmäßig
change [tʃeɪndʒ] — sich umziehen
teach s.o. s.th. [tiːtʃ] — jmdm. etw. beibringen ⚠ unregelmäßig

67 learner driver [ˌlɜːnə 'draɪvə] — Fahrschüler/in
special ['speʃl] — besondere(r, s)
plate [pleɪt] — Nummernschild — Verkürzung: **number plate**
driving licence ['draɪvɪŋ laɪsns] — Führerschein
skier ['skiːə] — Skiläufer/in
in those days [ɪn ðəʊz 'deɪz] — damals — ~ everything was different
taught [tɔːt] — simple past: **teach** ⚠ unregelmäßig
felt [felt] — simple past: **feel** ⚠ unregelmäßig
whistle ['wɪsl] — sausen, pfeifen
crash helmet ['kræʃ helmɪt] — Sturzhelm
polite [pə'laɪt] — höflich ◄► **impolite, rude** – unhöflich, grob
borrow ['bɒrəʊ] — sich etwas borgen — can I ~ your car?
though [ðəʊ] — obwohl, doch
get cross with [ˌget 'krɒs wɪð] — böse werden über
nightmare ['naɪtmeə] — Alptraum
anywhere ['eniweə] — irgendwo — I couldn't find ~ to park
inch [ɪntʃ] — Inch, Zoll — ca. 2,5 cm
motorway ['məʊtəweɪ] — Autobahn
speed freak ['spiːd friːk] — Raser

68 motoring ['məʊtərɪŋ] — Autofahren
driving instructor ['draɪvɪŋ ɪnstrʌktə] — Fahrlehrer/in
family saloon [ˌfæməli sə'luːn] — Limousine ⚠ **Limousine** – Prunkwagen mit Chauffeur
...-year-old ['jɪərəʊld] — ...jährig
racing driver ['reɪsɪŋ draɪvə] — Rennfahrer/in
PC [ˌpiː 'siː] — ≈ Wachtmeister — Abkürzung: **police constable** (männlich); WPC = **woman police constable**

traffic policeman ['træfɪk pəliːsmən] — Verkehrspolizist — auch: **traffic policewoman/police officer**

high-speed [ˌhaɪ'spiːd] — Hochgeschwindigkeits- — a ~ car
car showroom [ˌkɑː 'ʃəʊəʊːm] — Autosalon
salesperson ['seɪlzpɜːsn] — Verkäufer/in — auch: **salesman/woman**
have in mind [həv ɪn 'maɪnd] — denken an
test-drive ['testdraɪv] — Probe fahren — may I test-drive this car?
model ['mɒdl] — Modell
family man ['fæməli mən] — Familienvater
business woman ['bɪznəswʊmən] — Geschäftsfrau — **businessman** – Geschäftsmann
house husband ['haʊs hʌzbənd] — Hausmann — **housewife** – Hausfrau
executive model [ɪg'zekjətɪv mɒdl] — Modell für Anspruchsvolle — eigentlich: Modell für Manager

hatchback ['hætʃbæk] — Hecktürmodell
4-wheel drive [ˌfɔːwiːl 'draɪv] — Vierradantrieb
off-road vehicle [ˌɒfrəʊd 'viːəkl] — Geländewagen

iː	ɪ	e	æ	ɑː	ɒ	ɔː	ʊ	uː	ʌ	ɜː	ə
see	sit	ten	bad	arm	got	saw	put	too	cut	bird	about

	vehicle ['viːəkl]	Fahrzeug	
	sports car ['spɔːts kɑː]	Sportwagen	
69	sound [saʊnd]	Geräusch	sonst auch Verb: *sich anhören*
	start [stɑːt]	starten, anlassen	**I couldn't ~ the car this morning**
	accelerate [əkˈseləreɪt]	beschleunigen	⇔ **slow down, decelerate** (förmlich)
	change gear [tʃeɪndʒ 'gɪə]	in einen anderen Gang schalten	**you need to ~ now**
	brake [breɪk]	bremsen	sonst auch Nomen: *Bremse*
	crash into [kræʃ]	prallen gegen	**we crashed into a tree**
	order ['ɔːdə]	Reihenfolge	**put them in the right ~**
	change a tyre [tʃeɪndʒ ə 'taɪə]	einen Reifen wechseln	
	take off [ˌteɪk 'ɒf]	entfernen	≈ **remove**
	make sure [ˌmeɪk 'ʃʊə]	sich vergewissern	**~ the brake is on**
	brake [breɪk]	Bremse	sonst auch Verb: *bremsen*
	jack [dʒæk]	Wagenheber	
	lower ['ləʊə]	herunterlassen	**~ the car**
	do up [ˌduː 'ʌp]	fest schrauben	**~ the nuts**
	nut [nʌt]	Schraubenmutter	
	hubcap ['hʌbkæp]	Radkappe	
	fail [feɪl]	nicht bestehen, durchfallen	mit oder ohne Objekt: **he ~ed (his test)**
	eyesight ['aɪsaɪt]	Sehvermögen	
	Highway Code [ˌhaɪweɪ 'kəʊd]	Straßenverkehrsordnung	
	emergency [ɪ'mɜːdʒənsi]	Notfall	**in an ~** – *im Notfall*
	reverse [rɪ'vɜːs]	zurücksetzen, rückwärts fahren	mit oder ohne Objekt: **she ~ed (the car)**
	signal ['sɪgnəl]	blinken	
	speed limit ['spiːd lɪmɪt]	Geschwindigkeitsbegrenzung	**keep to the ~**
	distance ['dɪstəns]	Entfernung	**at a correct ~**
	act [ækt]	sich verhalten	
	properly ['prɒpəli]	richtig, korrekt	Adverb ≈ **correctly**

UNIT 9 The USA and the Big Apple

70	visitor ['vɪzɪtə]	Besucher/in	
	over here [ˌəʊvə 'hɪə]	hier, hierzulande	**how long have you been ~?**
	for three days [fɔː θriː deɪz]	seit drei Tagen	
	since [sɪns]	seit(dem)	**~ you've been here**
	quite a lot [kwaɪt ə 'lɒt]	ziemlich viel	**I've done ~**
	trade [treɪd]	Handel	
	liberty ['lɪbəti]	Freiheit	
	yet [jet]	schon, bereits	**have you seen the park ~ ?**
	forget [fə'get]	vergessen	△ unregelmäßig
	play [pleɪ]	Theaterstück	
	this morning [ðɪs mɔːnɪŋ]	heute früh	
	building ['bɪldɪŋ]	Gebäude	
	loud [laʊd]	laut	
	sense of humour [ˌsens əv 'hjuːmə]	Sinn für Humor	**he has no ~**
71	sergeant ['sɑːdʒənt]	≈ Polizeimeister/in	
	interviewer ['ɪntəvjuːə]	Interviewer/in	
	I guess [aɪ 'ges]	ich meine	US **~ so** – *ich glaube schon*
	work the streets [wɜːk ðə 'striːts]	Streife fahren/gehen	
	patrol car [pə'trəʊl kɑː]	Streifenwagen	
	recently ['riːsntli]	neulich, in letzter Zeit	
	or so [ɔː 'səʊ]	so ungefähr	**in a couple of hours ~**
	fill out [ˌfɪl 'aʊt]	ausfüllen	**please ~ this form**
	report [rɪ'pɔːt]	Bericht	
	drug dealing ['drʌg diːlɪŋ]	Drogenhandel	**~ is a big problem here**
	arrest [ə'rest]	festnehmen	
	pickpocket ['pɪkpɒkɪt]	Taschendieb	
	ever ['evə]	jemals	**have you ~ seen this man?**

tʃ	dʒ	ʃ	ʒ	θ	ð	ŋ	s	z	v	w
chips	**j**et	**sh**ip	gara**g**e	**th**ing	**th**e	ri**ng**	**i**ce	a**s**	**v**ery	**w**et

the night before last [ðə ˌnaɪt bɪfɔː ˈlɑːst] — vorgestern abend
violent [ˈvaɪələnt] — gewalttätig
You kidding? [ju ˈkɪdɪŋ] — Machen Sie Witze? US
practically [ˈpræktɪkli] — fast — sonst auch: *praktisch*
gotten [ˈgɒtn] — = got (past participle) US
armed robbery [ˌɑːmd ˈrɒbəri] — bewaffneter Raubüberfall

knife wound [ˈnaɪf wuːnd] — Schnitt-/Stichwunde
tourist [ˈtʊərɪst] — Tourist/in — ⚠ Aussprache
for a start [fər ə ˈstɑːt] — zunächst einmal
walk the streets [ˌwɔːk ðə ˈstriːts] — auf die Straße gehen
at night [ət ˈnaɪt] — nachts
advisable [ədˈvaɪsəbl] — ratsam — von **advise** – *raten*
murder [ˈmɜːdə] — Mord — sonst auch Verb: *ermorden* — **the murder took place in the park**
take place [teɪk ˈpleɪs] — stattfinden
mean [miːn] — heißen — **that doesn't mean that ...** – *das heißt nicht, dass*

night life [ˈnaɪtlaɪf] — Nachtleben
that's what ... is all about — das ist das Wesentliche an ...

get around [ˌget əˈraʊnd] — herumkommen — ≈ **get about**
cab [kæb] — Taxi — ≈ **taxi** (GB)
during [ˈdjʊərɪŋ] — während — **~ the day** – *während des Tages*
subway [ˈsʌbweɪ] — U-Bahn — US = **underground, tube** (GB)
cheap [tʃiːp] — billig, günstig — ◄► **expensive, dear** – *teuer*
take a ride [ˌteɪk ə ˈraɪd] — eine Fahrt unternehmen — **let's ~ in a cab**
car [kɑː] — (Eisenbahn-)Wagen — US = **carriage** (GB)
frightening [ˈfraɪtnɪŋ] — furchterregend
don't get me wrong [ˌdəʊnt get miː ˈrɒŋ] — verstehen Sie mich nicht falsch — umgangssprachlich

you just got to [ju ˈdʒʌst ˌgɒt tə] — Sie müssen einfach — US **~ be careful**

careful [ˈkeəfl] — vorsichtig
list [lɪst] — auflisten — sonst auch Nomen: *Liste*
so far [ˌsəʊ ˈfɑː] — bisher — **she's visited three places ~**

72 rescue [ˈreskjuː] — retten — ≈ **save**
chase [tʃeɪs] — verfolgen
attend [əˈtend] — versorgen (Verletzte/n) — sonst auch: *anwesend sein (bei)*
wounded [ˈwuːndɪd] — verwundet
shoot [ʃuːt] — (an)schießen, erschießen
murderer [ˈmɜːdərə] — Mörder — ⚠ **murder** – *Mord*, nicht *Mörder*
violence [ˈvaɪələns] — Gewalt — vgl. **violent** – *gewalttätig*

73 already [ɔːlˈredi] — schon, bereits

74 felt [ˈpəʊstkɑːd] — past participle: **feel** — ⚠ unregelmäßig
postcard [ɪkˈsaɪtɪd] — Postkarte
excited [ɪkˈsaɪtɪd] — (freudig) aufgeregt
be in love with [biː ɪn ˈlʌv wɪð] — lieben, verliebt sein in — **I'm in love with her**
for ages [fər ˈeɪdʒɪz] — ewig, eine Ewigkeit — **I've been waiting here ~** – *ich warte hier schon eine Ewigkeit*

president [ˈprezɪdənt] — Präsident/in
have ... left [hæv ˈleft] — noch haben — **she has one day left** – *es bleibt ihr noch ein Tag übrig*

trip [trɪp] — Ausflug, Reise — **let's take a ~ to Fisherman's Wharf**
redwood [ˈredwʊd] — Redwood (Baum)

75 several [ˈsevrəl] — einige, mehrere
honestly [ˈɒnɪstli] — ehrlich — Adverb
exactly [ɪgˈzæktli] — exakt, genau — Adverb
look at [ˈlʊk ət] — sich anschauen
avenue [ˈævənjuː] — Allee, Boulevard
message [ˈmesɪdʒ] — Mitteilung, Nachricht
it was a shame [ɪt wɒz ə ˈʃeɪm] — schade

iː	ɪ	e	æ	ɑː	ɒ	ɔː	ʊ	uː	ʌ	ɜː	ə
see	sit	ten	bad	arm	got	saw	put	too	cut	bird	about

	news [njuːz]	Neuigkeiten	sonst auch: *Nachrichten*
	love to ['lʌv tə]	liebe Grüße an	**(give my) ~ John**
	independent [ˌɪndɪ'pendənt]	unabhängig	◆ **dependent** – *abhängig*
	lecture ['lektʃə]	Vorlesung	
	surfer ['sɜːfə]	Surfer/in	
	brain [breɪn]	Gehirn	
	certainly ['sɜːtnli]	sicherlich, gewiss	
	the States [steɪts]	die Staaten	**the United States of America**
76	borough ['bʌrə]	Stadtbezirk	US = **district** (GB)
	window-shopping ['wɪndəʊˌʃɒpɪŋ]	Schaufensterbummel	
	baseball ['beɪsbɔːl]	Baseball	
	stadium ['steɪdiəm]	Stadion	
	elevator ['elɪveɪtə]	Aufzug	US = **lift** (GB)
	delicatessen [ˌdelɪkə'tesn]	Feinkost(geschäft)	
	accent ['æksent]	Akzent	⚠ Aussprache und Schreibung
	world-famous [ˌwɜːld'feɪməs]	weltberühmt	
	skyline ['skaɪlaɪn]	Silhouette, Skyline	
77	but [bʌt]	außer	**everything ~ Central Park**
	delicatessen [ˌdelɪkə'tesn]	Feinkostgeschäft	
	imagine [ɪ'mædʒɪn]	sich vorstellen	
	downtown ['daʊntaʊn]	ins Zentrum	US = **into town** (GB)
	round trip ticket [ˌraʊndtrɪp 'tɪkɪt]	Rückfahrkarte	US = **return ticket** (GB)
	one way ticket [ˌwʌnweɪ 'tɪkɪt]	einfache Fahrkarte	US = **single ticket** (GB)
	gas [gæs]	Benzin	US = **petrol** (GB)
	gas station ['gæs steɪʃn]	Tankstelle	US = **petrol station** (GB)
	mailbox ['meɪlbɒks]	Briefkasten	US = **postbox** (GB)
	drugstore ['drʌgstɔː]	Drogerie	US = **chemist's** (GB)
	madam ['mædəm]	gnädige Frau	
	departure gate [dɪ'pɑːtʃə geɪt]	Flugsteig	
	sidewalk ['saɪdwɔːk]	Bürgersteig	US = **pavement** (GB)
	chemist's ['kemɪsts]	Drogerie, Apotheke	
	return ticket [rɪ'tɜːn 'tɪkɪt]	Rückfahrkarte	
	single ticket [ˌsɪŋgl 'tɪkɪt]	einfache Fahrkarte	
	petrol ['petrəl]	Benzin	
	pavement ['peɪvmənt]	Bürgersteig	
	postbox ['letəbɒks]	Briefkasten	
	secondary school ['sekəndri skuːl]	Schule der Sekundarstufe	
	hang (a)round [ˌhæŋ ə'raʊnd]	herumhängen	
	shopping arcade ['ʃɒpɪŋ ɑːkeɪd]	Einkaufspassage	
	on the tube [ɒn ðə 'tjuːb]	mit der U-Bahn	
	lawyer ['lɔːjə]	Rechtsanwalt, Rechtsanwältin	
	folks [fəʊks]	Familie	US = **family**
	high school [haɪ skuːl]	Schule der Sekundarstufe	US ≈ **secondary school** (GB)
	a whole lot [ə həʊl 'lɒt]	viel	US
	math [mæθ]	Mathe(matik)	US = **maths** (GB)
	on the weekend [ɒn ðə ˌwiːk'end]	am Wochenende	US = **at the weekend** (GB)
	hang out [ˌhæŋ 'aʊt]	herumhängen	US = **hang (a)round** (GB)
	mall [mæl]	überdachtes Einkaufszentrum	US ≈ **shopping arcade/shopping centre** (GB)
	movie ['muːvi]	Spielfilm	US = **film** (GB)
	attorney [ə'tɜːni]	Rechtsanwalt, Rechtsanwältin	US = **lawyer** (GB)
	grade [greɪd]	Note	US = **mark** (GB)
	store clerk ['stɔː klɜːrk]	Verkäufer/in	US = **shop assistant** (GB)
	more like it [ˌmɔː 'laɪk ɪt]	wahrscheinlicher	
	someday ['sʌmdeɪ]	eines Tages	US

tʃ	dʒ	ʃ	ʒ	θ	ð	ŋ	s	z	v	w
chips	jet	ship	garage	thing	the	ring	ice	as	very	wet

UNIT 10 Europe and the Europeans

78 hate [heɪt] — hassen — I ~ learning English
◆ love – *lieben*

I'll [aɪl] — = I will
end up (...ing) [ˌend 'ʌp] — schließlich ... — you'll ~ working here – *du wirst schließlich hier arbeiten*
~ they go – *wohin sie auch gehen*
wherever [weər'evə] — wohin (auch immer)
useful ['juːsfl] — nützlich — ◆ useless – *nutzlos*
Spanish ['spænɪʃ] — Spanisch — ⚠ Aussprache und Schreibung
Italian [ɪ'tæljən] — Italienisch
Dutch [dʌtʃ] — Holländisch
on and on [ˌɒn ənd 'ɒn] — immer weiter — it goes ~ – *es hört nicht mehr auf*
be going to ... [bi 'gəʊɪŋ tə] — werden — I'm going to learn Italian
nanny ['næni] — Kindermädchen
be able to [bi 'eɪbl tə] — können — I'll ~ learn the language
mostly ['məʊstli] — hauptsächlich, größtenteils — they are ~ like us – *sie sind größtenteils wie wir*
stereotype ['steriətaɪp] — Stereotyp — ⚠ Aussprache und Schreibung
nationality [ˌnæʃə'næləti] — Staatsangehörigkeit — hier: *Menschen einer bestimmten Nationalität*

unfriendly [ʌn'frendli] — unfreundlich — ⚠ Adjektiv, nicht Adverb
eccentric [ɪk'sentrɪk] — exzentrisch — ⚠ Schreibung
Italian [ɪ'tæljən] — italienisch
Swedish ['swiːdɪʃ] — schwedisch — ⚠ Aussprache und Schreibung

79 difference ['dɪfrəns] — Unterschied — vgl. Adjektiv: **different** – *unterschiedlich, anders*

efficient [ɪ'fɪʃnt] — effizient — ◆ inefficient – *ineffizient, unfähig*
snobby ['snɒbi] — snobistisch, versnobt
passionate ['pæʃənət] — leidenschaftlich
wonder ['wʌndə] — sich fragen
in other words [ɪn ˌʌðə 'wɜːdz] — mit anderen Worten — ⚠ **in**, nicht **with**
Scottish ['skɒtɪʃ] — schottisch — ⚠ Aussprache und Schreibung
Welsh [welʃ] — Waliser — ⚠ nur im Plural: **the ~** – *die Waliser*
im Singular: **a Welshman/woman**
Irish ['aɪrɪʃ] — Iren — ⚠ nur im Plural: **the ~** – *die Iren*
im Singular: **an Irishman/woman**

such [sʌtʃ] — solche(r,s)
Basque [bæsk] — Baske/Baskin
Spain [speɪn] — Spanien
Bavarian [bə'veəriən] — Bayer/in
bet [bet] — wetten — I ~ that ... – *wetten, dass ...*
just like ['dʒʌst ˌlaɪk] — genau wie
UK [ˌjuː 'keɪ] — = United Kingdom
loads of ['ləʊdz əv] — eine ganze Menge — umgangssprachlich

80 map [mæp] — Landkarte — sonst auch: *(Stadt-)Plan*
European Union [ˌjʊərəpiːən 'juːniən] — Europäische Union — Abkürzung: EU
Republic of Ireland [rɪˌpʌblɪk əv 'aɪələnd] — Republik Irland
Northern Ireland [ˌnɔːðən 'aɪələnd] — Nordirland
Wales [weɪlz] — Wales
United Kingdom [juːˌnaɪtɪd 'kɪŋdəm] — Vereinigtes Königreich — = *Großbritannien und Nordirland*
Sweden ['swiːdn] — Schweden — ⚠ Aussprache und Schreibung
Finland ['fɪnlənd] — Finnland — ⚠ Schreibung
Denmark ['denmɑːk] — Dänemark
The Netherlands [ðə 'neðələndz] — die Niederlande
Belgium ['beldʒəm] — Belgien
Luxembourg ['lʌksəmbɜːg] — Luxemburg — ⚠ Schreibung
Italy ['ɪtəli] — Italien
Greece [griːs] — Griechenland
tulip ['tjuːlɪp] — Tulpe
make up [ˌmeɪk 'ʌp] — bilden — three countries ~ Britain
rather ['rɑːðə] — ziemlich — ≈ quite

iː	ɪ	e	æ	ɑː	ɒ	ɔː	ʊ	uː	ʌ	ɜː	ə
see	sit	ten	bad	arm	got	saw	put	too	cut	bird	about

	snobbish ['snɒbɪʃ]	snobistisch, versnobt	≈	snobby
	foreign ['fɒrən]	Auslands-, Außen-, ausländisch		~ language – Fremdsprache
	abroad [ə'brɔːd]	im Ausland, ins Ausland		are you going ~ for your holiday?
81	meaning ['miːnɪŋ]	Bedeutung, Sinn		
	performance [pə'fɔːməns]	Veranstaltung		
	start [stɑːt]	anfangen, beginnen	≈	begin
	run [rʌn]	fahren		the buses ~ every hour
	land [lænd]	landen		when do we ~ in London?
	schedule ['ʃedjuːl]	Programm		we have a busy ~
	check in [ˌtʃek 'ɪn]	sich anmelden	◆	check out – sich abmelden
82	suntan ['sʌntæn]	Sonnenbräune		with a ~ – braungebrannt
	theatre ['θɪətə]	Theater	⚠	Aussprache und Schreibung
	currency ['kʌrənsi]	Währung		
	Russia ['rʌʃə]	Russland		
	police force [pə'liːs fɔːs]	Polizei(truppe)		a European ~
	learnt [lɜːnt]	simple past: learn	⚠	unregelmäßig
	travel courier ['trævl kʊriə]	Reiseführer/in		
	Portuguese [ˌpɔːtʃu'giːz]	Portugiesisch	⚠	Schreibung
	business ['bɪznəs]	Geschäft, Firma	≈	firm, company
	won't [wəʊnt]	= will not		
	leisure activity ['leʒə æktɪvəti]	Freizeitbeschäftigung		
83	shown [ʃəʊn]	past participle: show		
	delicious [dɪ'lɪʃəs]	köstlich, lecker		
	city break ['sɪti breɪk]	(kurzer) Städteurlaub		
	skiing holiday ['skiːɪŋ hɒlədeɪ]	Skiurlaub	⚠	Aussprache: [skiː-]
	walking holiday ['wɔːkɪŋ hɒlədeɪ]	Wanderurlaub		
	camp [kæmp]	zelten, campen		
	change [tʃeɪndʒ]	wechseln, tauschen	≈	exchange
	go on [ˌgəʊ 'ɒn]	dauern		the party went on for 24 hours
	Turkey ['tɜːki]	die Türkei	⚠	ohne Artikel: to ~ – in die Türkei
4ww	worker ['wɜːkə]	Arbeiter/in		
ww	quality control ['kwɒləti kən'trəʊl]	Qualitätskontrolle		
ww	plant [plɑːnt]	Fabrik	≈	factory
ww	production-line [prə'dʌkʃn laɪn]	Fertigungsstraße		
ww	shopfloor [ˌʃɒp'flɔː]	Werkstatt, Produktion(sstätte)		a ~ worker – Arbeiter/in in der Produktion
ww	if you like [ɪf ju 'laɪk]	wenn Sie so wollen		
ww	well-paid [ˌwel'peɪd]	gut bezahlt		a ~ job/worker
			◆	badly-paid – schlecht bezahlt
ww	take over [ˌteɪk 'əʊvə]	übernehmen		BMW wants to ~ the company
ww	Bavaria [bə'veərɪə]	Bayern		
ww	design technician [dɪ'zaɪn teknɪʃn]	Konstruktionstechniker/in		
ww	design [dɪ'zaɪn]	Konstruktion		
ww	involve [ɪn'vɒlv]	mit sich bringen		most of my work ~s using a computer
ww	project ['prɒdʒekt]	Projekt	⚠	Aussprache und Schreibung
ww	designer [dɪ'zaɪnə]	Konstrukteur/in		sonst auch: Grafiker/in
ww	apprentice [ə'prentɪs]	Auszubildende/r		gleiche Form für beide Geschlechter
ww	canteen [kæn'tiːn]	Kantine		
ww	managing director [ˌmænɪdʒɪŋ də'rektə]	Geschäftsführer/in		
ww	introduction [ˌɪntrə'dʌkʃn]	Einleitung, Einführung		
ww	host [həʊst]	Gastgeber-		the ~ family – die Gastgeberfamilie
ww	team [tiːm]	Mannschaft, Team		
ww	radio-controlled [ˌreɪdɪəʊ kən'trəʊld]	ferngesteuert		~ cars
ww	demonstration [ˌdemən'streɪʃn]	Vorführung		
ww	prize-giving ['praɪzgɪvɪŋ]	Preisverleihung		
ww	farewell [ˌfeə'wel]	Abschieds-		~ dinner – Abschiedsessen
5ww	curriculum vitae [kəˌrɪkjələm 'viːtaɪ]	Lebenslauf		Abkürzung: CV
ww	educational [ˌedʒu'keɪʃənl]	Ausbildungs-		~ qualifications – Ausbildung
ww	comprehensive [ˌkɒmprɪ'hensɪv]	Gesamtschule		Verkürzung von: school

tʃ	dʒ	ʃ	ʒ	θ	ð	ŋ	s	z	v	w
chips	jet	ship	garage	thing	the	ring	ice	as	very	wet

ww	science ['saɪəns]	Naturwissenschaften	we're doing ~ this afternoon
ww	history ['hɪstri]	Geschichte	
ww	geography [dʒi'ɒgrəfi]	Erdkunde	
ww	referee [ˌrefə'riː]	Referenz	sonst auch: *Schiedsrichter*
ww	personal tutor [ˌpɜːsənl 'tjuːtə]	Tutor	
ww	outdoor pursuit [ˌaʊtdɔː pə'sjuːt]	Aktivitäten im Freien	~s like walking and skiing –
ww	belong to [bɪ'lɒŋ tə]	angehören, Mitglied sein in	I ~ a climbing club
ww	climbing club ['klaɪmɪŋ klʌb]	Bergsteiger-/Kletterverein	
ww	water-skiing ['wɔːtəskiːɪŋ]	Wasserski	I like doing ~
ww	captain ['kæptɪn]	Kapitän	
ww	athletics [æθ'letɪks]	Leichtathletik	als Singular behandelt: **athletics is exciting**
ww	chance [tʃɑːns]	Gelegenheit	
ww	favourite ['feɪvərɪt]	liebste(r,s), Lieblings-	
ww	band [bænd]	Band, Gruppe	my ~ band
86	workout ['wɜːkaʊt]	Training	
	revision exercise [rɪ'vɪʒn eksəsaɪz]	Wiederholungsübung	
	lovely ['lʌvli]	schön, hübsch, reizend	⚠ Adjektiv nicht Adverb ⬌ **horrible, ugly** – *entsetzlich, hässlich*
	view [vjuː]	Aussicht, Blick	a ~ of the lake
	across [ə'krɒs]	über (... hinweg)	a view ~ the mountains
	cooker ['kʊkə]	Herd	
	video ['vɪdiəʊ]	Videorecorder	sonst auch: *Videokassette; (auf Video) aufnehmen*
	ideal [aɪ'dɪəl]	ideal	⚠ Aussprache
	perfect ['pɜːfɪkt]	vollkommen, perfekt	⚠ Aussprache
	horrible ['hɒrəbl]	entsetzlich	⬌ **lovely** – *schön, reizend*
	hi-fi ['haɪfaɪ]	Hi-Fi-Gerät	Verkürzung von: **high-fidelity**
	Christmas ['krɪsməs]	Weihnachten	
	prefer [prɪ'fɜː]	vorziehen, lieber mögen, bevorzugen	I ~ cities to the countryside – *ich ziehe Städte dem Land vor*
	eat out [ˌiːt 'aʊt]	zum Essen gehen	let's ~ – *gehen wir auswärts essen*
	odd one out [ɒd wʌn 'aʊt]	etwas, das nicht dazugehört	which word is the ~ ? – *welches Wort gehört nicht dazu?*
	village ['vɪlɪdʒ]	Dorf	
87	living room ['lɪvɪŋruːm]	Wohnzimmer	
	writing ['raɪtɪŋ]	Schreiben	
	penfriend ['penfrend]	Brieffreund/in	gleiche Form für beide Geschlechter
	back [bæk]	zurück	please write ~
	result [rɪ'zʌlt]	Ergebnis; Note	
	afterwards ['ɑːftəwədz]	nachher, hinterher	she'll get a good job ~

UNIT 11 It's not a bad place to live

88	ask the way [ˌɑːsk ðə 'weɪ]	nach dem Weg fragen	
	Excuse me. [ɪk'skjuːz mi]	Verzeihung.	
	round here [raʊnd 'hɪə]	hier in der Nähe	is there a post office ~?
	Let me see. [ˌlet miː 'siː]	Lassen Sie mich mal überlegen.	
	newsagent ['njuːzeɪdʒənt]	Zeitungshändler	~'s – *Zeitungsladen*
	photo booth ['fəʊtəʊ buːð]	Fotokabine	
	inside [ˌɪn'saɪd]	innen	
	at the back [ət ðə 'bæk]	hinten	
	till [tɪl]	bis	Verkürzung von: **until**
	optician [ɒp'tɪʃn]	Optiker/in	~'s – *der Laden ist gemeint, nicht der Mensch*
	crossroads ['krɒsrəʊdz]	Kreuzung	⚠ Plural
	post office ['pəʊst ɒfɪs]	Postamt	
	half way down [ˌhɑːf weɪ 'daʊn]	auf halbem Weg	
	launderette [ˌlɔːndə'ret]	Waschsalon	
	post box ['pəʊstbɒks]	Briefkasten	

iː	ɪ	e	æ	ɑː	ɒ	ɔː	ʊ	uː	ʌ	ɜː	ə
see	sit	ten	bad	arm	got	saw	put	too	cut	bird	about

	miss [mɪs]	verfehlen	you can't ~ it
	double yellow lines [ˌdʌbl ˌjeləʊ 'laɪnz]	absolutes Halteverbot	
	multi-storey car park [ˌmʌltistɔːri 'kɑː pɑːk]	Parkhaus	
	facility [fə'sɪləti]	Einrichtung	
	library ['laɪbrəri]	Bücherei, Bibliothek	
	leisure centre ['leʒə sentə]	Freizeitzentrum	
89	atmosphere ['ætməsfɪə]	Atmosphäre, Stimmung	
	appeal (to) [ə'piːl]	(jmdm.) gefallen	it doesn't ~ to me – es gefällt mir nicht/spricht mich nicht an
	that's it [ðæts 'ɪt]	das ist alles	
	not even ... [nɒt 'iːvən]	nicht einmal ...	there isn't even a pub
	bus route ['bʌs ruːt]	Busstrecke	
	a bit of a problem [ə ˌbɪt əv ə 'prɒbləm]	ein ziemliches Problem	
	suburb ['sʌbɜːb]	Vorort, Außenbezirk	in the ~s – am Stadtrand
	chance [tʃɑːns]	Gelegenheit	if I get the ~
	move [muːv]	umziehen	sonst auch: (sich) bewegen
	somewhere ['sʌmweə]	irgendwohin	sonst auch: irgendwo
	handy ['hændi]	in der Nähe, praktisch	the post office is very ~
	more or less [ˌmɔːr ɔː 'les]	mehr oder weniger	~ everything – so ziemlich alles
	swimming pool ['swɪmɪŋ puːl]	Schwimmbad	
	squash court ['skwɒʃ kɔːt]	Squashplatz	
	bus service ['bʌs sɜːvɪs]	Busverbindung	
	rail service ['reɪl sɜːvɪs]	Zugverbindung	
	be a pain [ə 'peɪn]	lästig/ärgerlich/ schwierig sein	he's such a pain – er ist so eine Plage
	at times [ət 'taɪmz]	manchmal	≈ sometimes
	on the whole [ɒn ðə 'həʊl]	im Großen und Ganzen	~ it's OK
90	directions [də'rekʃnz]	Wegbeschreibung	⚠ Plural
	bookshop ['bʊkʃɒp]	Buchhandlung	
	disadvantage [ˌdɪsəd'vɑːntɪdʒ]	Nachteil	◆ advantage – Vorteil
	satisfied ['sætɪsfaɪd]	zufrieden	
	entertainment [ˌentə'teɪnmənt]	Unterhaltung	
	else [els]	sonst	and not much ~ – und sonst nicht viel
	test [test]	untersuchen	get your eyes ~ed!
	above ground [ə'bʌv graʊnd]	über der Erde	⚠ ohne Artikel
	under ground ['ʌndə graʊnd]	unter der Erde	⚠ ohne Artikel
	outside [aut'saɪd]	außerhalb von	~ (of) town – außerhalb der Stadt
91	petrol station ['petrəl steɪʃn]	Tankstelle	⚠ Aussprache: [steɪʃn]
92	railway station ['reɪlweɪ steɪʃn]	Bahnhof	⚠ Aussprache: [steɪʃn]
	turning ['tɜːnɪŋ]	Abfahrt, Abzweigung	it's the first ~ on the left
	health centre ['helθ sentə]	Ärztezentrum	
	direct (s.o. to somewhere) [də'rekt]	(jmdm.) den Weg (zu/nach) sagen	can you ~ me to the station?
93	peace [piːs]	Frieden, Ruhe	~ and quiet – Ruhe und Frieden
	quiet ['kwaɪət]	Stille	
	hurry up [ˌhʌri 'ʌp]	sich beeilen	
	street map ['striːt mæp]	Stadtplan	⚠ road map – Straßenkarte
	by car [baɪ 'kɑː]	mit dem Wagen	ebenso: by plane, by train, by bike usw. aber: on foot
	member ['membə]	Mitglied	
	estate agent [ɪ'steɪt eɪdʒənt]	Immobilienmakler/in	gleiche Form für beide Geschlechter
	detail ['diːteɪl]	Einzelheit	
	built [bɪlt]	past participle: build	
	balcony ['bælkəni]	Balkon	
	dining room ['daɪnɪŋruːm]	Esszimmer	
ww	suited to ['suːtɪd tə]	geeignet für	what job do you think you are ~?
ww	district nurse ['dɪstrɪkt nɜːs]	Gemeindeschwester	
ww	favourite ['feɪvərɪt]	liebste(r, s), Lieblings-	
ww	biology [baɪ'ɒlədʒi]	Biologie	
ww	first aid [ˌfɜːst 'eɪd]	erste Hilfe	

tʃ	dʒ	ʃ	ʒ	θ	ð	ŋ	s	z	v	w
chips	jet	ship	garage	thing	the	ring	ice	as	very	wet

ww	gentle ['dʒentl]	sanft	◆▶	rough – *grob, roh*
ww	others ['ʌðəz]	andere		she wants to help ~
ww	patient ['peɪʃnt]	geduldig	◆▶	impatient
ww	concerned about [kən'sɜːnd əbaʊt]	besorgt um		
ww	elderly ['eldəli]	älter		~ people – *ältere Leute*
ww	cleaning ['kliːnɪŋ]	Saubermachen		she helps with the ~
ww	quality ['kwɒləti]	Eigenschaft		sonst auch: *Qualität*
ww	development [dɪ'veləpmənt]	Entwicklung		vgl. Verb: **develop** – *(sich) entwickeln*
ww	impatient [ɪm'peɪʃnt]	ungeduldig	◆▶	**patient** – *geduldig*
ww	nervous ['nɜːvəs]	nervös	◆▶	**calm** – *ruhig*
ww	faint [feɪnt]	ohnmächtig werden		
ww	needle ['niːdl]	Nadel		
95 ww	need [niːd]	Bedürfnis		sonst auch Verb: *brauchen*
ww	leaflet ['liːflət]	Broschüre, Prospekt		
ww	community centre [kə'mjuːnəti sentə]	Bürgerzentrum		
ww	drug [drʌg]	Droge, Rauschgift		
ww	crack [kræk]	Crack		
ww	ecstasy ['ekstəsi]	Ecstasy (Droge)		
ww	addict ['ædɪkt]	Süchtige/r, Abhängige/r		drug ~ – *Drogenabhängige/r*
ww	sex education [,seks edʒu'keɪʃn]	sexuelle Aufklärung		
ww	suddenly ['sʌdnli]	plötzlich		Adverb; vgl. Adjektiv: **sudden**
ww	all sorts of [ɔːl 'sɔːts əv]	allerlei		
ww	might [maɪt]	könnte	⚠	unregelmäßig
ww	attract [ə'trækt]	anziehen		
ww	burglar ['bɜːglə]	Einbrecher/in		
ww	secure [sɪ'kjʊə]	sicher, fest		our house isn't very ~
ww	bother ['bɒðə]	stören		sorry to ~ you, but ...
ww	willing ['wɪlɪŋ]	gewillt, bereitwillig		they are ~ to help
ww	home security [həʊm sɪ'kjʊərəti]	Sicherheit im Haushalt		
ww	crack [kræk]	(erfolgreich) bekämpfen		I've ~ed it! – *ich habe die Lösung gefunden!*
ww	crime [kraɪm]	Verbrechen		
ww	provide [prə'vaɪd]	zur Verfügung stellen		
ww	care for ['keə fə]	versorgen		
ww	claim [kleɪm]	beantragen, beanspruchen		sonst auch: *behaupten*
ww	kind [kaɪnd]	Art	≈	sort, type
ww	caring ['keərɪŋ]	rücksichtsvoll	◆▶	**uncaring** – *rücksichtslos, hartherzig*
ww	motorist ['məʊtərɪst]	Autofahrer/in		
ww	energy ['enədʒi]	Energie	⚠	Aussprache und Schreibung
ww	environment [ɪn'vaɪrənmənt]	Umwelt		
ww	cassette [kə'set]	Cassette	⚠	Aussprache und Schreibung
ww	connected with [kə'nektɪd wɪð]	verbunden mit		
ww	dental nurse ['dentl nɜːs]	Zahnarzthelfer/in		
ww	traffic warden ['træfɪk wɔːdn]	≈ Verkehrspolizist/in		
ww	prison officer ['prɪzn ɒfɪsə]	Gefängnisaufseher/in		
96	sign [saɪn]	(Verkehrs)Zeichen		sonst auch *Zeichen* oder *Schild* im Allgemeinen
	second ['sekənd]	Sekunde		
	latest ['leɪtɪst]	neueste(r, s)		the ~ model
	test drive ['test draɪv]	Probefahrt		
	carefully ['keəfəli]	sorgfältig		Adverb; vgl. Adjektiv: **careful**
	ignore [ɪg'nɔː]	ignorieren,	◆▶	**pay attention to** – *beachten*
	suddenly ['sʌdnli]	plötzlich		Adverb; vgl. Adjektiv: **sudden**
	onto ['ɒntə]	auf (+ Akk.)		auch getrennt: **on to**
	gently ['dʒentli]	behutsam, sanft		Adverb; vgl. Adjektiv: **gentle**
97	drawing ['drɔːɪŋ]	Zeichnung		vgl. Verb: **draw** – *zeichnen*
	description [dɪ'skrɪpʃn]	Beschreibung		vgl. Verb: **describe** – *beschreiben*
	expression [ɪk'spreʃn]	Ausdruck		sonst auch: *Gesichtsausdruck*
	given ['gɪvn]	past participle: **give**	⚠	unregelmäßig

iː	ɪ	e	æ	ɑː	ɒ	ɔː	ʊ	uː	ʌ	ɜː	ə
see	sit	ten	bad	arm	got	saw	put	too	cut	bird	about

UNIT 12 The best way to travel

98

except [ɪk'sept]	außer	~ that – *außer, dass*
cc [ˌsiː 'siː]	Kubikzentimeter	Abkürzung von: **cubic centimeter**
top speed [ˌtɒp 'spiːd]	Höchstgeschwindigkeit	
kph [ˌkeɪ piː 'eɪtʃ]	km/h (Kilometer pro Stunde)	Abkürzung von: **kilometres per hour**
total ['təʊtl]	Gesamt-	a ~ distance of …
desert ['dezət]	Wüste	⚠ Aussprache und Schreibung: dessert [dɪ'zɜːt] – *Nachtisch*
even if ['iːvn ɪf]	selbst wenn	
reliable [rɪ'laɪəbl]	zuverlässig	
economical [ˌiːkə'nɒmɪkl]	wirtschaftlich	
fifties ['fɪftiz]	fünfziger Jahre	a song from the ~
go wrong [ˌgəʊ 'rɒŋ]	kaputt gehen	sonst auch: *schief gehen*
chose [tʃəʊz]	simple past: **choose**	⚠ unregelmäßig
save up [ˌseɪv 'ʌp]	sparen	she has saved up a lot of money
after all [ˌɑːftər 'ɔːl]	schließlich doch	~, he is rich

99

approximately [ə'prɒksɪmətli]	ungefähr, etwa, circa	◆ exactly – *genau*
apart from [ə'pɑːt frəm]	abgesehen von	
pollution [pə'luːʃn]	Umweltverschmutzung	
face [feɪs]	ausgesetzt sein	we are facing serious problems
serious ['sɪəriəs]	schlimm, schwer, ernst	
congestion [kən'dʒestʃən]	Stockungen, Verkehrsstaus	im Allgemeinen; **traffic jam** – *(einzelner) Verkehrsstau*
government ['gʌvənmənt]	Regierung	
charge [tʃɑːdʒ]	erheben	~ tax – *Steuer erheben*
tax [tæks]	Steuer	
solve [sɒlv]	lösen	~ a problem
improve [ɪm'pruːv]	verbessern	
public transport [ˌpʌblɪk 'trænspɔːt]	öffentliche Verkehrsmittel	by ~ – *mit öffentlichen Verkehrsmitteln*
commute [kə'mjuːt]	pendeln	
surely ['ʃʊəli]	sicherlich	
micro-light ['maɪkrəʊlaɪt]	superleicht	
machine [mə'ʃiːn]	Maschine	hier: *Flugzeug*
destination [ˌdestɪ'neɪʃn]	Fahrtziel, Reiseziel	
traffic jam ['træfɪk dʒæm]	Verkehrsstau	
on horseback [ɒn 'hɔːsbæk]	zu Pferde	
favourite ['feɪvərɪt]	liebste(r, s), Lieblings-	

100

definition [ˌdefɪ'nɪʃn]	Definition	⚠ Aussprache
fit [fɪt]	passen zu	which definition ~s which word?
depend on [dɪ'pend ɒn]	sich verlassen auf	you can ~ me
common ['kɒmən]	gewöhnlich	◆ unusual, rare – *ungewöhnlich*
solution [sə'luːʃn]	Lösung	vgl. Verb: **solve** – *lösen*
might [maɪt]	könnte	⚠ unregelmäßig
writer ['raɪtə]	Schriftsteller/in	≈ author
totally ['təʊtəli]	völlig	◆ partially – *teilweise*

101

paid [peɪd]	conditional: **pay**	⚠ unregelmäßig
adventurous [əd'ventʃərəs]	abenteuerlich	
definitely ['defɪnətli]	bestimmt, sicher	it would ~ work – *es würde bestimmt klappen*

102

destroy [dɪ'strɔɪ]	zerstören, vernichten	pollution is ~ing the environment
pleasant ['pleznt]	angenehm	
spaceship ['speɪsʃɪp]	Raumschiff	
reach [riːtʃ]	erreichen	
star [stɑː]	Stern	
angry ['æŋgri]	böse, ärgerlich	don't get ~ with us – *werd nicht böse auf uns*
instruction [ɪn'strʌkʃnz]	Anweisung	read the ~s carefully
secret agent [ˌsiːkrət 'eɪdʒənt]	Geheimagent/in	
mission ['mɪʃn]	Auftrag	
notes [nəʊts]	Notizen	are you taking ~?

tʃ	dʒ	ʃ	ʒ	θ	ð	ŋ	s	z	v	w
chips	**j**et	**sh**ip	gara**g**e	**th**ing	**th**e	ri**ng**	i**c**e	a**s**	**v**ery	**w**et

	Right. [raɪt]	Gut.	eigentlich nur, um den Hörer aufmerksam zu machen
	meeting point ['miːtɪŋ pɔɪnt]	Treffpunkt	
	... hours ['aʊəz]	... Uhr	Militärsprache: **at 1500 (fifteen hundred)** ~ – *um 15.00 Uhr*
	motorbike ['məʊtəbaɪk]	Motorrad	≈ **motorcycle**
	platform ['plætfɔːm]	Bahnsteig, Gleis	
	jump off [ˌdʒʌmp 'ɒf]	abspringen	
	hill [hɪl]	Hügel	
	spy [spaɪ]	Spion/in	
	microfilm ['maɪkrəʊfɪlm]	Mikrofilm	
	password ['pɑːswɜːd]	Kennwort	
	impossible [ɪm'pɒsəbl]	unmöglich	◆ **possible** – *möglich*
	invite [ɪn'vaɪt]	einladen	
	lottery ['lɒtəri]	Lotterie	
	moon [muːn]	Mond	
103	**be stuck** [bi 'stʌk]	festsitzen	**she's stuck in a traffic jam**
	parking space ['pɑːkɪŋ speɪs]	Parkplatz, Parklücke	
	island ['aɪlənd]	Insel	△ Aussprache
	luxury item ['lʌkʃəri aɪtəm]	Luxusgut	
104ww	**cabin attendant** [ˌkæbɪn ə'tendənt]	Flugbegleiter/in	≈ (air) steward/ess
ww	**independently** [ˌɪndɪ'pendəntli]	unabhängig	**work** ~ – *freiberuflich arbeiten*
ww	**lunchtime** ['lʌntʃtaɪm]	Mittagszeit, Mittagspause	**at** ~ – *in der Mittagszeit*
ww	**on average** [ɒn 'ævərɪdʒ]	im Durchschnitt	
ww	**remain** [rɪ'meɪn]	bleiben	≈ **stay**
ww	**calm** [kɑːm]	ruhig	
ww	**connection** [kə'nekʃn]	Anschluss	
ww	**satisfaction** [ˌsætɪs'fækʃn]	Befriedigung	
ww	**agency** ['eɪdʒənsi]	(Reise)Büro	
ww	**tiring** ['taɪərɪŋ]	anstrengend	
ww	**actually** ['æktʃuəli]	eigentlich, wirklich	**it's quite interesting** ~
ww	**fare** [feə]	Fahrgast	sonst auch: *Flugpreis, Fahrpreis*
ww	**character** ['kærəktə]	Original	**he's a real** ~
ww	**rich** [rɪtʃ]	reich, wohlhabend	◆ **poor** – *arm*
ww	**tip** [tɪp]	Trinkgeld geben	~ **well** – *ein großzügiges Trinkgeld geben*
105ww	**seat** [siːt]	Sitz	
ww	**upright** ['ʌpraɪt]	aufrecht	
ww	**fare** [feə]	Fahrpreis	sonst auch: *Fahrgast*
ww	**get in** [ˌget 'ɪn]	ankommen	sonst auch: *einsteigen*
ww	**client** ['klaɪənt]	Kunde, Kundin	≈ **customer**
ww	**local time** ['ləʊkl taɪm]	Ortszeit	
ww	**annoying** [ə'nɔɪɪŋ]	ärgerlich, lästig	
ww	**coach** [kəʊtʃ]	Reisebus	
ww	**holiday destination** [ˌhɒlədeɪ ˌdestɪ'neɪʃn]	Urlaubsziel	
ww	**attraction** [ə'trækʃn]	Reiz, Attraktion	**what are the** ~**s of this place?**
ww	**chosen** ['tʃəʊzn]	past participle: **choose**	**are you an** ~ **type?** – *sind Sie gern im Freien?*
ww	**outdoor** ['aʊtdɔː]	gern im Freien	
106	**translate** [træns'leɪt]	übersetzen	~ **it into German**
	enormous [ɪ'nɔːməs]	enorm, gewaltig	≈ **huge**
	New Yorker [ˌnjuː 'jɔːkə]	New-Yorker/in	ebenso nur: **Londoner, Berliner**
	leave [liːv]	abfliegen	~ **for home** – *nach Hause abfliegen*
	ring [rɪŋ]	anrufen	
	use [juːs]	Gebrauch	△ Aussprache; vgl. Verb **use** [juːz] – *gebrauchen, benutzen*
107	**synonym** ['sɪnənɪm]	Synonym	△ Aussprache
	last [lɑːst]	dauern	

iː	ɪ	e	æ	ɑː	ɒ	ɔː	ʊ	uː	ʌ	ɜː	ə
see	sit	ten	bad	arm	got	saw	put	too	cut	bird	about

UNIT 13 Technology old and new

108
- quiz [kwɪz] — Quiz — ⚠ Aussprache
- in progress [ɪn 'prəʊgres] — im Gange
- zip fastener ['zɪp fɑːsnə] — Reißverschluss
- Sorry! ['sɒri] — Tut mir leid! — hier: *Leider falsch!*
- Ready? ['redi] — Fertig? — **are you ~?** – *bist du fertig/soweit?*
- civil war [ˌsɪvl 'wɔː] — Bürgerkrieg
- invention [ɪn'venʃn] — Erfindung — vgl. Verb: **invent** – *erfinden*
- machine gun [məˈʃiːngʌn] — Maschinengewehr
- construction [kən'strʌkʃn] — Bauwerk — **bridges, tunnels and other ~s**
- used to ['juːs tə] — gewöhnt an
- forgotten [fə'gɒtn] — past participle: **forget** — ⚠ unregelmäßig
- nylon ['naɪlɒn] — Nylon — **made of ~** – *aus Nylon*
- aerosol spray ['eərəsɒl spreɪ] — Aerosolspray
- instant coffee [ˌɪnstənt 'kɒfi] — Pulverkaffee
- artificial [ˌɑːtɪ'fɪʃl] — künstlich — ◆ **natural** – *natürlich*
- heart [hɑːt] — Herz
- clue [kluː] — *hier:* Ahnung — **I haven't got a ~** – *ich habe keine Ahnung*

- World War II [ˌwɜːld 'wɔː tuː] — der Zweite Weltkrieg — **in ~** – *im Zweiten Weltkrieg*
- it's your turn [ɪts jɔː 'tɜːn] — du bist dran
- within [wɪ'ðɪn] — innerhalb von — **~ three years**
- sewing machine ['səʊɪŋ məʃiːn] — Nähmaschine
- major ['meɪdʒə] — Haupt-, bedeutend
- innovation [ˌɪnə'veɪʃn] — Neuerung
- in recent times [ɪn 'riːsnt taɪmz] — in den letzten Jahren
- silicon chip [ˌsɪlɪkən 'tʃɪp] — Siliziumchip
- allow [ə'laʊ] — ermöglichen — sonst: *erlauben, gestatten* ≈ **make possible**

- all sorts of [ɔːl 'sɔːts əv] — allerlei
- appliance [ə'plaɪəns] — Gerät
- smart [smɑːt] — intelligent — **~ technology**
- contain [kən'teɪn] — enthalten
- microwave ['maɪkrəweɪv] — Mikrowellenherd — Verkürzung von: **microwave oven**
- iron ['aɪən] — Bügeleisen — sonst auch: *Eisen* auch Verb: *bügeln*

109
- Well done! [ˌwel 'dʌn] — Gut gemacht!, Bravo!
- fortune ['fɔːtʃuːn] — Vermögen — **make s.o.'s ~** – *jmdn. reich machen*
- award [ə'wɔːd] — verleihen — **~ a prize** sonst auch Nomen: *Preis, Auszeichnung*

- prize [praɪz] — Preis — im Sinne: *Gewinn, Auszeichnung* ⚠ Aussprache; vgl. **price** [praɪs] – *(Verkaufs-)Preis*

- explosive [ɪk'spləʊsɪv] — Sprengstoff
- dynamite ['daɪnəmaɪt] — Dynamit — **this story is ~!** – *diese Geschichte ist der reinste Zündstoff!*
- absolutely ['æbsəluːtli] — absolut, völlig — **~ right**
- inexpensive [ˌɪnɪk'spensɪv] — preiswert — ◆ **expensive** – *teuer*
- weapon ['wepən] — Waffe
- manufacture [ˌmænju'fæktʃə] — herstellen — ≈ **make**
- score [skɔː] — Spielstand — **what's the ~?** – *wie steht das Spiel?*
- come along [ˌkʌm ə'lɒŋ] — erscheinen, auftauchen — **before cars came along** – *bevor es Autos gab*

110
- chronological [ˌkrɒnə'lɒdʒɪkl] — zeitlich — **in ~ order**
- surprise [sə'praɪz] — überraschen

111
- rang [ræŋ] — simple past: **ring** — ⚠ unregelmäßig
- set up [ˌset 'ʌp] — gründen

112
- earthquake ['ɜːθkweɪk] — Erdbeben
- do the ironing [ˌduː ði 'aɪənɪŋ] — bügeln
- go for lunch [ˌgəʊ fə 'lʌntʃ] — zu Mittag essen gehen

tʃ	dʒ	ʃ	ʒ	θ	ð	ŋ	s	z	v	w
chips	jet	ship	garage	thing	the	ring	ice	as	very	wet

113	wrote [rəʊt]	simple past: **write**	⚠	unregelmäßig
	assignment [ə'saɪnmənt]	Hausaufgabe		
	wallet ['wɒlɪt]	Brieftasche	⚠	**briefcase** – *Aktentasche*
	ages ['eɪdʒɪz]	eine Ewigkeit		**they waited ~ for the bus**
	fed up [ˌfed 'ʌp]	satt		**I'm ~ with you** – *ich habe dich satt*
	share [ʃeə]	teilen		
	keep [kiːp]	halten		**fridges ~ food fresh**
	be around [bi ə'raʊnd]	existieren		**before cars were around**
	sound effect ['saʊnd ɪfekt]	Geräuscheffekt		
	have a shower [həv ə 'ʃaʊə]	duschen		
	storm [stɔːm]	Unwetter, Gewitter		
	broke [brəʊk]	simple past: **break**	⚠	unregelmäßig
	break [breɪk]	(los)brechen	⚠	unregelmäßig
	catch [kætʃ]	erreichen		**she was waiting to ~ her plane** – *sie wartete auf ihren Flug*
	explosion [ɪk'spləʊʒn]	Explosion, Sprengung	⚠	Aussprache
	alarm [ə'lɑːm]	Alarmanlage		
	go off [ˌgəʊ 'ɒf]	losgehen		
	pay attention to [peɪ ə'tenʃn tə]	beachten		
	born [bɔːn]	geboren		**when were you ~?**
	nervous ['nɜːvəs]	nervös	↔	**calm** – *ruhig*
	interrupt [ˌɪntə'rʌpt]	unterbrechen		**don't ~ me when I'm talking!**
	clean [kliːn]	putzen		**he's ~ing his teeth** – *er putzt sich (gerade) die Zähne*
	wash one's hair [ˌwɒʃ wʌnz 'heə]	sich die Haare waschen		
	into the middle [ˌɪntə ðə 'mɪdl]	in die Mitte		
	pick out [ˌpɪk 'aʊt]	herausnehmen		
	guess [ges]	raten		
114ww	**everyday** ['evrɪdeɪ]	alltäglich, Alltags-		
ww	**tool** [tuːl]	Werkzeug		
ww	**screwdriver** ['skruːdraɪvə]	Schraubenzieher		
ww	**put in** [ˌpʊt 'ɪn]	einsetzen		
ww	**screw** [skruː]	Schraube		sonst auch Verb: *schrauben*
ww	**electric** [ɪ'lektrɪk]	elektrisch, Elektro-		
ww	**work out** [ˌwɜːk 'aʊt]	ausrechnen	≈	**calculate**
ww	**calculation** [ˌkælkju'leɪʃn]	Berechnung		
ww	**copy** ['kɒpi]	fotokopieren		
ww	**document** ['dɒkjumənt]	Dokument		sonst auch Nomen: *Kopie, Exemplar*
ww	**hole** [həʊl]	Loch		
ww	**blow** [bləʊ]	blasen		
ww	**carpet** ['kɑːpɪt]	Teppich		
ww	**fan** [fæn]	Ventilator		
ww	**drill** [drɪl]	Bohrer, Bohrmaschine		sonst auch Verb: *bohren*
ww	**calculator** ['kælkjuleɪtə]	Taschenrechner		
ww	**abacus** ['æbəkəs]	Abakus, Rechenbrett		
ww	**hoover** ['huːvə]	Staubsauger		eigentlich ein Staubsauger der Marke Hoover® sonst auch Verb: *staubsaugen*
ww	**carpet beater** ['kɑːpɪt biːtə]	Teppichklopfer		
ww	**photocopier** ['fəʊtəʊkɒpɪə]	Fotokopierer	⚠	Schreibung
ww	**scribe** [skraɪb]	Schreiber		veraltet
115ww	**film** [fɪlm]	(ver)filmen		sonst auch Nomen: *Film*
ww	**press** [pres]	drücken (auf)		
ww	**button** ['bʌtn]	Taste, Knopf		**press the ~**
ww	**enable** [ɪ'neɪbl]	ermöglichen	≈	**allow**
ww	**cassette** [kə'set]	Cassette	⚠	Aussprache
ww	**earphones** ['ɪəfəʊnz]	Kopfhörer		**a pair of ~**
ww	**clip s.th. to s.th.** [klɪp]	etw. an etw. anklemmen		**~ it ~ your belt** – *klemm es an deinen Gürtel an*
ww	**belt** [belt]	Gürtel		
ww	**cycle** ['saɪkl]	Rad fahren		

i: see	ɪ sit	e ten	æ bad
ɑ: arm	ɒ got	ɔ: saw	ʊ put
u: too	ʌ cut	ɜ: bird	ə about

ww	receive [rɪ'si:v]	empfangen		sonst auch: *erhalten*
ww	call [kɔ:l]	Anruf		sonst auch Verb: *(an)rufen*
ww	almost ['ɔ:lməʊst]	fast	≈	nearly
ww	record [rɪ'kɔ:d]	aufnehmen		
ww	switch [swɪtʃ]	Schalter, Knopf		
ww	rewind [ˌri:'waɪnd]	zurückspulen		
ww	eject [i'dʒekt]	auswerfen		rewind, then ~ the cassette
ww	part [pɑ:t]	Teil		
ww	set up [ˌset 'ʌp]	aufbauen		have you ~ the computer properly?
ww	monitor ['mɒnɪtə]	Monitor		
ww	cable ['keɪbl]	Kabel		
ww	CPU [ˌsi: pi: 'ju:]	Prozessor		
ww	plug [plʌg]	Stecker		
ww	keyboard ['ki:bɔ:d]	Tastatur		
ww	mouse [maʊs]	Maus		
ww	plug in [ˌplʌg 'ɪn]	einstöpseln, anschließen	≈	~ the monitor/computer attach, connect
ww	turn on [ˌtɜ:n 'ɒn]	einschalten		
ww	attach [ə'tætʃ]	anschließen		
ww	install [ɪn'stɔ:l]	installieren		
ww	software ['sɒftweə]	Computerprogramm(e)		
ww	chapter ['tʃæptə]	Kapitel		
ww	connect [kə'nekt]	einstöpseln, anschließen		sonst auch: *verbinden*
ww	difference ['dɪfrəns]	Unterschied		vgl. Adjektiv: **different** – *anders, unterschiedlich*
ww	computing [kəm'pju:tɪŋ]	Computertechnik		
116	soup [su:p]	Suppe		
	beefburger ['bi:fbɜ:gə]	Hamburger		
	either ... or [ˌaɪðə 'ɔ:]	entweder ... oder		
	bill [bɪl]	Rechnung		
	Waiter! ['weɪtə]	Herr Ober!		
	Indian ['ɪndiən]	indisch		
	eaten ['i:tn]	past participle: **eat**	⚠	unregelmäßig
	It's all gone. [ɪts ɔ:l 'gɒn]	Es ist alle.		
	That's a pity. [ˌðæts ə 'pɪti]	Das ist schade.		
117	margarine [ˌmɑ:dʒə'ri:n]	Margarine	⚠	Aussprache
	electric [ɪ'lektrɪk]	elektrisch, Elektro-		
	food mixer ['fu:d mɪksə]	Mixer, Mixgerät	≈	(food) blender, food processor
	ingredient [ɪn'gri:diənt]	Zutat		
	mix [mɪks]	verrühren, mixen		
	mixing bowl ['mɪksɪŋ bəʊl]	Rührschüssel		
	bowl [bəʊl]	Schüssel		

UNIT 14 Uses and abuses

118	abuse [ə'bju:s]	Missbrauch	⚠	Aussprache; vgl. Verb: **abuse** [ə'bju:z] – *missbrauchen*
	drug [drʌg]	Droge, Rauschgift		
	be terrified ['terɪfaɪd]	schreckliche Angst haben		he's ~ of flying – *er hat schreckliche Angst vor dem Fliegen*
	for no reason [fə nəʊ 'ri:zn]	grundlos		
	estimate ['estɪˌmeɪt]	schätzen	⚠	Aussprache
	against the law [əˌgenst ðə 'lɔ:]	illegal, gesetzeswidrig		nur nach dem Nomen: **stealing is ~** – *Stehlen ist gesetzeswidrig*
	long-term [ˌlɒŋ'tɜ:m]	langfristig	↔	short-term – *kurzfristig*
	effect [ɪ'fekt]	Wirkung, Auswirkung		
	illegal [ɪ'li:gl]	illegal, gesetzeswidrig	≈	against the law
			⚠	Aussprache
	politician [ˌpɒlə'tɪʃn]	Politiker/in		
	discuss [dɪ'skʌs]	besprechen		
	youth culture ['ju:θ kʌltʃə]	Jugendkultur		
	repeat [rɪ'pi:t]	wiederholen		
	death [deθ]	Tod(esfall)		

tʃ	dʒ	ʃ	ʒ	θ	ð	ŋ	s	z	v	w
chips	jet	ship	garage	thing	the	ring	ice	as	very	wet

	dose [dəʊs]	Dosis	
	record [rɪˈkɔːd]	aufzeichnen, belegen	300 deaths were ~ed – *300 Todesfälle wurden registriert*
	threat [θret]	Gefahr	a ~ to society
	society [səˈsaɪəti]	Gesellschaft	
	suspected [səˈspektɪd]	mutmaßlich	◆ proven – *bewiesen*
	suicide [ˈsuːɪsaɪd]	Selbstmord	commit ~ – *Selbstmord begehen*
	footballer [ˈfʊtbɔːlə]	Fußballspieler/in	
	season [ˈsiːzn]	Saison	the football ~
	cup-winning [ˈkʌpwɪnɪŋ]	im Pokal siegreich	
	team [tiːm]	Mannschaft	
	suspect [səˈspekt]	vermuten	
	overdose [ˈəʊvədəʊs]	Überdosis	he took an ~
	sleeping tablet [ˈsliːpɪŋ tæblət]	Schlaftablette	
	brilliant [ˈbrɪliənt]	großartig glänzend	a ~ career/footballer
	ahead of [əˈhed əv]	vor	
	pressure [ˈpreʃə]	Druck	
	succeed [səkˈsiːd]	Erfolg haben	◆ fail – *scheitern*
119	soft drug [ˌsɒft ˈdrʌg]	weiche Droge	◆ hard drug – *harte Droge*
	addicted to [əˈdɪktɪd tə]	-süchtig	~ drugs – *drogensüchtig*
	tobacco [təˈbækəʊ]	Tabak	
	regret [rɪˈgret]	bereuen	you'll ~ it! – *das wirst du bereuen!*
	liberal [ˈlɪbərəl]	liberal	⚠ Aussprache
	strict [strɪkt]	streng	◆ liberal
	completely [kəmˈpliːtli]	völlig	Adverb
	crazy [ˈkreɪzi]	verrückt	≈ mad
	unfit [ʌnˈfɪt]	unfähig, ungeeignet	
	cough [kɒf]	Husten	sonst auch Verb: husten
	cancer [ˈkænsə]	Krebs	medizinisch und auch astronomisch; als Schalentier jedoch: crab
	old age [ˌəʊld ˈeɪdʒ]	(hohes) Alter	◆ youth – *Jugend*
	danger [ˈdeɪndʒə]	Gefahr	vgl. Adjektiv: dangerous
	ban [bæn]	verbieten	sonst auch Nomen: Verbot
	in the first place [ɪn ðə ˈfɜːst pleɪs]	von vornherein	sonst auch: erstens
	think straight [θɪŋk ˈstreɪt]	klar denken	
	legal [ˈliːgl]	gesetzlich, legal	◆ illegal, against the law
	hysterical [hɪˈsterɪkl]	hysterisch	
	reaction [rɪˈækʃn]	Reaktion	⚠ Aussprache und Schreibung
	generation [ˌdʒenəˈreɪʃn]	Generation	⚠ Aussprache
	caffeine [ˈkæfiːn]	Koffein	
120	whether [ˈweðə]	ob	say ~ it's true
	broken home [ˌbrəʊkən ˈhəʊm]	zerrüttete Familienverhältnisse	they come from a ~
	successful [səkˈsesfl]	erfolgreich	
	look [lʊk]	aussehen	it ~s promising
	promising [ˈprɒmɪsɪŋ]	vielversprechend	vgl. Verb: promise – *versprechen*
	relieve [rɪˈliːv]	lindern	this will ~ the pain
	addictive [əˈdɪktɪv]	süchtig machend	it's very ~
	illness [ˈɪlnəs]	Krankheit	≈ disease
	addict [ˈædɪkt]	Süchtige/r	⚠ Aussprache; vgl. addictive [əˈdɪktɪv]
	dependent on [dɪˈpendənt ɒn]	abhängig von	
121	get into trouble [ˌget ɪntə ˈtrʌbl]	Schwierigkeiten bekommen	you'll ~ with the police – *du wirst Ärger mit der Polizei bekommen*
122	light [laɪt]	Licht	sonst auch Adjektiv: hell
	off [ɒf]	aus	the lights are ~
			◆ on – *an*
	ran [ræn]	simple past: run	⚠ unregelmäßig
	run away [ˌrʌn əˈweɪ]	weglaufen	~ from home
	childhood [ˈtʃaɪldhʊd]	Kindheit	
	alone [əˈləʊn]	allein(e)	
	on the streets [ɒn ðə ˈstriːts]	auf der Straße	he lives ~

iː	ɪ	e	æ	ɑː	ɒ	ɔː	ʊ	uː	ʌ	ɜː	ə
see	sit	ten	bad	arm	got	saw	put	too	cut	bird	about

	possibility [ˌpɒsəˈbɪləti]	Möglichkeit		vgl. Adjektiv: **possible** – *möglich*
	I'm in a bad way [ɪn ə ˌbæd ˈweɪ]	mir geht es schlecht		
	on top of that [ɒn ˌtɒp əv ˈðæt]	obendrein		
	worth [wɜːθ]	wert		he says life isn't ~ living
	face up to [ˌfeɪs ˈʌp tə]	sich abfinden mit		you must ~ it – *du musst der Tatsache ins Gesicht sehen*
	no matter … [nəʊ ˈmætə]	egal …		~ how bad things are – *egal, wie schlecht es einem geht*
	I suppose … [aɪ səˈpəʊz]	eigentlich		~ you'd say … – *eigentlich könnte man sagen …*
	homeless [ˈhəʊmləs]	obdachlos		
	drop-out [ˈdrɒpaʊt]	Aussteiger/in		
	bridge [brɪdʒ]	Brücke		
	shelter [ˈʃeltə]	Unterkunft		
	well-off [ˌwel ˈɒf]	wohlhabend		
	luckily [ˈlʌkɪli]	glücklicherweise		
	save [seɪv]	retten	≈	rescue
	in the end [ɪn ði ˈend]	zum Schluss	◆▶	at first – *am Anfang*
	brave [breɪv]	mutig, tapfer	◆▶	cowardly – *feige*
	spoil [spɔɪl]	verwöhnen		sonst auch: *verderben*
	miserable [ˈmɪzrəbl]	unglücklich, elend		I feel ~
	optimistic [ˌɒptɪˈmɪstɪk]	optimistisch	◆▶	pessimistic
	breakdown [ˈbreɪkdaʊn]	(Nerven-)Zusammenbruch		
123	drop out [ˌdrɒp ˈaʊt]	sein Studium abbrechen		he dropped out of his course – *er brach sein Studium ab*
	wise [waɪz]	weise	◆▶	foolish – *dumm, töricht*
	crash [kræʃ]	Unfall		sonst auch Verb: *einen Unfall haben*
	be involved in [bi ɪnˈvɒlvd ɪn]	beteiligt sein in, verwickelt sein in		
	awake [əˈweɪk]	wach	◆▶	asleep – *schlafend*
	alive [əˈlaɪv]	lebend, lebendig	◆▶	dead – *tot*
	unlucky [ʌnˈlʌki]	unglückselig		be ~ – *Pech haben*
4ww	project [ˈprɒdʒekt]	Projekt	△	Aussprache und Schreibung
ww	drug-related [ˈdrʌɡ rɪleɪtɪd]	mit Drogen verbunden	△	Aussprache
ww	heroin [ˈherəʊɪn]	Heroin		she's got a drug ~ – *sie ist drogensüchtig*
ww	habit [ˈhæbɪt]	Abhängigkeit		
ww	alcoholic [ˌælkəˈhɒlɪk]	Alkoholiker/in		sonst auch Adjektiv: *alkoholisch*
ww	counsellor [ˈkaʊnsələ]	Berater/in		
ww	diploma [dɪˈpləʊmə]	Diplom		
ww	dry out [ˌdraɪ ˈaʊt]	eine Entziehungskur machen		nur bei Alkoholikern
ww	counsel [ˈkaʊnsl]	beraten		
ww	homelessness [ˈhəʊmləsnəs]	Obdachlosigkeit		
ww	poverty [ˈpɒvəti]	Armut		vgl. Adjektiv: **poor** – *arm*
ww	full-time [ˌfʊl ˈtaɪm]	ganztags		do you work here ~?
ww	satisfy [ˈsætɪsfaɪ]	befriedigen		
ww	give up [ˌɡɪv ˈʌp]	aufgeben		
ww	nowhere [ˈnəʊweə]	nirgends, nirgendwo		
ww	poor [pʊə]	arm	◆▶	rich – *reich*
ww	suffer [ˈsʌfə]	leiden unter		they ~ed stress after the accident auch: **suffer from** – *leiden an*
ww	counselling [ˈkaʊnsəlɪŋ]	Beratung		
ww	psychiatric [ˌsaɪkiˈætrɪk]	psychiatrisch	△	Aussprache
ww	psychological [ˌsaɪkəˈlɒdʒɪkl]	psychologisch	△	Aussprache
ww	debt [det]	Schulden	△	Aussprache
ww	disaster [dɪˈzɑːstə]	Katastrophe		
ww	cope with [ˈkəʊp wɪð]	fertig werden mit		
ww	problematic [ˌprɒbləˈmætɪk]	problematisch		
ww	relationship [rɪˈleɪʃnʃɪp]	Beziehung, Verhältnis		
ww	lost [lɒst]	past participle: **lose**	△	unregelmäßig
ww	outline [ˈaʊtlaɪn]	umreißen, skizzieren		can you ~ what the problem is?

tʃ	dʒ	ʃ	ʒ	θ	ð	ŋ	s	z	v	w
chips	jet	ship	garage	thing	the	ring	ice	as	very	wet

125ww charity ['tʃærəti] — Wohltätigkeits-organisation

ww comedian [kə'mi:diən] — Komiker/in
ww Africa ['æfrikə] — Afrika — ⚠ Schreibung
ww silly ['sɪli] — töricht, albern — ◀▶ serious – *ernsthaft*
ww purpose ['pɜ:pəs] — Zweck, Absicht — it's for a serious ~
ww raise [reɪz] — auftreiben — how did you ~ the money?
ww suffer ['sʌfə] — leiden
ww disabled [dɪs'eɪbld] — behindert — physically/mentally ~ – *körperlich/geistig* ~
ww organisation [ˌɔ:gənaɪ'zeɪʃn] — Organisation — ⚠ Aussprache
ww overseas aid [ˌəʊvə'si:z] — Entwicklungshilfe
ww rebuild [ˌri:'bɪld] — wieder aufbauen
ww clothing ['kləʊðɪŋ] — Kleidung
ww satisfying ['sætɪsfaɪɪŋ] — befriedigend
ww otherwise ['ʌðəwaɪz] — sonst
ww organise ['ɔ:gənaɪz] — organisieren
ww scheme [ski:m] — Plan, Programm
ww deprived [dɪ'praɪvd] — benachteiligt — ◀▶ privileged – *privilegiert*
ww authority [ɔ:'θɒrəti] — Behörde
ww ethnic ['eθnɪk] — ethnisch — ~ minority
ww minority [maɪ'nɒrəti] — Minderheit — ◀▶ majority – *Mehrheit*
ww housing ['haʊzɪŋ] — Wohnungen
ww particular [pə'tɪkjələ] — besondere(r, s) — the right job for your ~ skills
ww ability [ə'bɪləti] — Fähigkeit
ww job market ['dʒɒb mɑ:kɪt] — Arbeitsmarkt
ww changeable ['tʃeɪndʒəbl] — veränderlich — ◀▶ stable – *beständig*
ww up to date [ˌʌp tə 'deɪt] — auf dem neusten Stand — keep ~

126 transport company ['trænspɔ:t kʌmpəni] — Transportunternehmen
fall in love [ˌfɔ:l ɪn 'lʌv] — sich verlieben
all alone [ˌɔ:l ə'ləʊn] — ganz allein

127 critical ['krɪtɪkl] — kritisch
problem page ['prɒbləm peɪdʒ] — Problemseite

UNIT 15 Do you shop till you drop?

128 shop [ʃɒp] — einkaufen — sonst auch Nomen: *Laden, Geschäft*
drop [drɒp] — umfallen — till you ~ – *bis zum Gehtnichtmehr*
revolution [ˌrevə'lu:ʃn] — Revolution — ⚠ Aussprache
open late [ˌəʊpən 'leɪt] — länger öffnen — many shops ~ on Thursdays
law [lɔ:] — Gesetz
Sunday shopping ['sʌndeɪ ʃɒpɪŋ] — Einkaufen am Sonntag
store [stɔ:] — Laden, Geschäft — ≈ shop bes. *größerer Laden, Warenhaus*

High Street shop ['haɪ stri:t ʃɒp] — Geschäft in der Innenstadt

Bank Holiday [ˌbæŋk 'hɒlədeɪ] — öffentlicher Feiertag
advantage [əd'vɑ:ntɪdʒ] — Vorteil — ◀▶ disadvantage – *Nachteil*
all-night [ˌɔ:l'naɪt] — 24-stündig — ~ shopping
Christmas Day [ˌkrɪsməs 'deɪ] — der erste Weihnachtstag
shopping hours ['ʃɒpɪŋ aʊəz] — Ladenöffnungszeiten
dramatically [drə'mætɪkli] — dramatisch — Adverb; vgl. Adjektiv: **dramatic**
shut [ʃʌt] — zumachen — ◀▶ open – *aufmachen*
drunken ['drʌŋkən] — betrunken — ◀▶ sober – *nüchtern*
youth [ju:θ] — Jugendliche/r — sonst auch: *Jugend*

129 increase [ɪn'kri:s] — erweitern — ◀▶ decrease – *einschränken*
consumerist [kən'sju:mərɪst] — Verbraucher-
channel [tʃænl] — Kanal, Programm
sophisticated [sə'fɪstɪkeɪtɪd] — hochentwickelt
goods [gʊdz] — Waren — Plural; selten im Singular
screen [skri:n] — Bildschirm
deliver [dɪ'lɪvə] — liefern — we'll ~ it to your door

iː	ɪ	e	æ	ɑː	ɒ	ɔː	ʊ	uː	ʌ	ɜː	ə
see	sit	ten	bad	arm	got	saw	put	too	cut	bird	about

	development [dɪ'veləpmənt]	Entwicklung	new ~ – *Neuerung*
	virtual ['vɜːtʃuəl]	virtuell	
	key in [ˌkiː 'ɪn]	eingeben	
	weekly ['wiːkli]	wöchentlich	ebenso: **daily, monthly, yearly**
	order ['ɔːdə]	Bestellung	sonst auch Verb: *bestellen*
	mail order catalogue [meɪl'ɔːdə kætəlɒg]	Versandhauskatalog	
	old-fashioned [ˌəʊld'fæʃənd]	altmodisch	◆▶ **modern**
	method ['meθəd]	Methode, Verfahren	
	encourage [ɪn'kʌrɪdʒ]	ermuntern	◆▶ **discourage** – *abhalten, abbringen*
130	specialist ['speʃəlɪst]	spezial, Fach-	
	home delivery [ˌhəʊm dɪ'lɪvəri]	Lieferung ins Haus	
	late night shopping [ˌleɪt naɪt 'ʃɒpɪŋ]	Einkaufen spät am Abend	
	opening times ['əʊpnɪŋ taɪmz]	Öffnungszeiten	what are the ~?
	home shopping ['həʊm ʃɒpɪŋ]	Einkaufen von zu Hause aus	
	all night [ɔːl 'naɪt]	die ganze Nacht	ebenso: **all day, all morning** usw.
	event [ɪ'vent]	Ereignis	
	introduce [ˌɪntrə'djuːs]	einführen	sonst auch: *vorstellen*
131	packet ['pækɪt]	Päckchen, Packung, Schachtel	a ~ of cigarettes
132	cassette [kə'set]	Cassette	⚠ Aussprache
	butter ['bʌtə]	Butter	⚠ Aussprache
	detective story [dɪ'tektɪv stɔːri]	Detektivgeschichte	
	video tape ['vɪdiəʊ teɪp]	Videoband	
	as well [əz 'wel]	auch	≈ **too**
	soap [səʊp]	Seife	
	medicine ['medsn]	Medikament	
	at the same time [ət ðə ˌseɪm 'taɪm]	gleichzeitig	
	bouquet [bu'keɪ]	(Blumen-)Strauß	⚠ Aussprache
	flower ['flaʊə]	Blume	
	plant [plɑːnt]	Pflanze	sonst auch Verb: *pflanzen*
	toy car ['tɔɪ kɑː]	Spielzeugauto	
	nail [neɪl]	Nagel	
	hammer ['hæmə]	Hammer	
	baker's ['beɪkəz]	Bäckerei	
	toy shop ['tɔɪ ʃɒp]	Spielzeugladen	
	do-it-yourself shop [ˌduː ɪt jɔː'self ʃɒp]	Baumarkt	Abkürzung: **DIY shop**
	florist's ['flɒrɪsts]	Blumengeschäft	
	penicillin [ˌpenɪ'sɪlɪn]	Penizillin	⚠ Aussprache und Schreibung
	soap powder ['səʊp paʊdə]	Seifenpulver	
	aspirin ['æsprɪn]	Aspirin	
	mini- ['mɪni]	Mini-	~dialogue – *kurzer Dialog*
	tea bag ['tiːbæg]	Teebeutel	
	petrol-driven ['petrəl drɪvn]	mit Benzinmotor	~ car
	biro ['baɪrəʊ]	Kuli, Kugelschreiber	eigentlich: ein Kugelschreiber der Marke Biro®
	hidden ['hɪdn]	versteckt	past participle von: **hide** – *verstecken*
	same day delivery [ˌseɪm deɪ dɪ'lɪvəri]	Lieferung am selben Tag	
	guarantee [ˌgærən'tiː]	garantieren	
	photography [fə'tɒgrəfi]	Fotografie	
	forbidden [fə'bɪdn]	verboten	past participle von: **forbid** – *verbieten*
	pet [pet]	Haustier	
	credit ['kredɪt]	Kredit	
133	milkman ['mɪlkmən]	Milchmann	
	How are you doing? [ˌhaʊ ə ju 'duːɪŋ]	Wie geht's?	
	extra ['ekstrə]	zusätzlich	
	time off [ˌtaɪm 'ɒf]	freie Zeit	
	at all [ət 'ɔːl]	überhaupt	nothing ~
	tiring ['taɪərɪŋ]	anstrengend, ermüdend	
	kiss [kɪs]	Kuss	sonst auch Verb: *küssen*

tʃ	dʒ	ʃ	ʒ	θ	ð	ŋ	s	z	v	w
chips	jet	ship	garage	thing	the	ring	ice	as	very	wet

134ww	banking ['bæŋkɪŋ]	Bankwesen		
ww	open ['əʊpən]	eröffnen		I'd like to ~ an account – *ich möchte ein Konto eröffnen*
ww	bank account ['bæŋk əkaʊnt]	Bankkonto		
ww	pay cheque ['peɪ tʃek]	Lohn-/Gehaltsüberweisung		
ww	identification [aɪˌdentɪfɪ'keɪʃn]	Ausweispapiere		do you have any ~?
ww	overdraft ['əʊvədrɑːft]	Kontoüberziehung		have an ~ (of £20) – *sein Konto (um £20) überzogen haben*
ww	bank manager ['bæŋk mænɪdʒə]	Bankmanager/in		
ww	bank clerk ['bæŋk klɑːk]	Bankangestellte/r		
ww	banker's card ['bæŋkəz kɑːd]	Scheckkarte	≈	cheque card
ww	cheque book ['tʃek bʊk]	Scheckbuch		
ww	cash dispenser ['kæʃ dɪspensə]	Geldautomat		
ww	loan [ləʊn]	Kredit, Darlehen		
ww	insert [ɪn'sɜːt]	einfügen	◆	remove – *entfernen*
ww	statement of account [ˌsteɪtmənt əv ə'kaʊnt]	Kontoauszug		
135ww	take turns [teɪk 'tɜːnz]	sich abwechseln		~ at being the manager
ww	pay in [ˌpeɪ 'ɪn]	einzahlen	◆	I'd like to pay £10 into my account take out – *abheben*
ww	pass [pɑːs]	überreichen		please ~ me the money
ww	find out about [ˌfaɪnd 'aʊt əbaʊt]	sich erkundigen nach		
ww	fill in [ˌfɪl 'ɪn]	ausfüllen		sonst auch: *eintragen*
ww	withdraw [wɪð'drɔː]	abheben	≈	take out
ww	to self [ˌraɪt ə 'tʃek tə self]	an selbst	◆	pay in/deposit – *einzahlen* nur in der Verbindung: **write a cheque ~** –
ww	pay out [ˌpeɪ 'aʊt]	auszahlen		
ww	debit ['debɪt]	Soll		~ and credit – *Soll und Haben*
ww	credit ['kredɪt]	Haben		debit and ~ – *Soll und Haben*
ww	balance ['bæləns]	Kontostand, Saldo		
ww	bring forward [ˌbrɪŋ 'fɔːwəd]	übertragen		
ww	boutique [buː'tiːk]	Boutique		
ww	salary ['sæləri]	Gehalt		
ww	carry forward [ˌkæri 'fɔːwəd]	übertragen		
ww	in the black [ɪn ðə 'blæk]	in den schwarzen Zahlen	◆	in the red
ww	in the red [ɪn ðə 'red]	in den roten Zahlen	◆	in the black
ww	luxury ['lʌkʃəri]	Luxus		oft Plural: *Luxusgüter*
ww	necessity [nə'sesəti]	Notwendigkeit		
136	huge [hjuːdʒ]	riesig	◆	tiny – *winzig*
	influence ['ɪnfluəns]	beeinflussen		sonst auch Nomen: *Einfluss*
	peach [piːtʃ]	Pfirsich		
	grocer's ['grəʊsəz]	Lebensmittelgeschäft		
	quality ['kwɒləti]	Qualität		
	for the same price [fə ðə seɪm 'praɪs]	zum gleichen Preis		
	showroom ['ʃəʊruːm]	Ausstellungsraum		
	... off [ɒf]	... Rabatt	≈	25 per cent ~ discount
137	rich [rɪtʃ]	reich, wohlhabend	≈	well-off, wealthy
			◆	poor – *arm*
	dream [driːm]	träumen		
	dream [driːm]	Traum		

UNIT 16 Reduce, repair, reuse, recycle

138	reduce [rɪ'djuːs]	reduzieren, verringern		~ by 50 per cent – *um 50 Prozent reduzieren*
			◆	increase – *vermehren*
	reuse [ˌriː'juːz]	wieder verwenden	△	Aussprache
	recycle [ˌriː'saɪkl]	recyceln		

iː	ɪ	e	æ	ɑː	ɒ	ɔː	ʊ	uː	ʌ	ɜː	ə
see	sit	ten	bad	arm	got	saw	put	too	cut	bird	about

produce [prəˈdjuːs]	produzieren	
waste [weɪst]	Abfall, Müll	
developed country [dɪˌveləpt ˈkʌntri]	Industrieland	household ~, nuclear ~ vgl. developing country – *Entwicklungsland*
environment [ɪnˈvaɪrənmənt]	Umwelt	
clear [klɪə]	klar	it's ~ that …
household [ˈhaʊshəʊld]	Haushalts-	~ waste
throw away [ˌθrəʊ əˈweɪ]	wegwerfen	
purpose [ˈpɜːpəs]	Zweck	for another ~
packaging [ˈpækɪdʒɪŋ]	Verpackung	
great [greɪt]	groß	
percentage [pəˈsentɪdʒ]	Prozentsatz	
Earth [ɜːθ]	Erde	(the) Earth – *die Erde* auch eines Berges
summit [ˈsʌmɪt]	Gipfel	you must ~ the problem ~
take seriously [teɪk ˈsɪəriəsli]	ernst nehmen	plastic ~ – *Plastiktüte*
bag [bæg]	Tasche, Tüte	
plastic [ˈplæstɪk]	Kunststoff	
cool [kuːl]	kühlen	sonst auch Adjektiv: *kühl*
can [kæn]	Dose	◆ tin
California [ˌkæləˈfɔːniə]	Kalifornien	
unfortunately [ʌnˈfɔːtʃənətli]	leider	
gas [gæs]	Gas	△ Aussprache
global warming [ˌgləʊbl ˈwɔːmɪŋ]	Erderwärmung	
CFCs [ˌsiː ef ˈsiːz]	FCKWs	
methane [ˈmiːθeɪn]	Methan	△ Aussprache und Schreibung
greenhouse gas [ˌgriːnhaʊs ˈgæs]	Treibhausgas	
forbid [fəˈbɪd]	verbieten	△ unregelmäßig
pizza [ˈpiːtsə]	Pizza	△ Aussprache
employ [ɪmˈplɔɪ]	einstellen	
pick up [ˌpɪk ˈʌp]	aufheben	
count [kaʊnt]	zählen	
the more … the better [ðə ˌmɔː ðə ˈbetə]	je mehr …, desto besser	
tiger [ˈtaɪgə]	Tiger	△ Aussprache
air pollution [ˌeə pəˈluːʃn]	Luftverschmutzung	
rainforest [ˈreɪnfɒrɪst]	Regenwald	
third world [ˌθɜːd ˈwɜːld]	Dritte Welt	~ poverty – *Armut in der Dritten Welt* vgl. Adjektiv: poor – *arm*
poverty [ˈpɒvəti]	Armut	◆ wealth – *Reichtum*
kind [kaɪnd]	Art	≈ sort, type
figure [ˈfɪgə]	Zahl	
refer to [rɪˈfɜː tə]	sich beziehen auf	
recycling [ˌriːˈsaɪklɪŋ]	Recycling	vgl. Verb recycle – *recyceln*
according to [əˈkɔːdɪŋ tə]	zufolge, laut, nach	~ the text can you ~ three types of fast food?
name [neɪm]	nennen	
collect [kəˈlekt]	sammeln	
fix [fɪks]	reparieren	≈ repair
glass [glɑːs]	Glas	△ Aussprache und Schreibung
metal [ˈmetl]	Metall	△ Aussprache und Schreibung
bread roll [ˌbred ˈrəʊl]	Brötchen, Semmel	auch einfach: roll
add to [ˈæd tə]	beitragen zu	
human [ˈhjuːmən]	menschlich	vgl. human being – *Mensch*
refrigerator [rɪˈfrɪdʒəreɪtə]	Kühlschrank	Verkürzung: fridge
organic [ɔːˈgænɪk]	organisch	~ farming – *organische Landwirtschaft*
protest [prəˈtest]	protestieren	vgl. Nomen: protest [ˈprəʊtest]
pollute [pəˈluːt]	verschmutzen, verunreinigen	vgl. Nomen: pollution
planet [ˈplænɪt]	Planet	△ Aussprache
harmful [ˈhɑːmfl]	schädlich	◆ harmless – *unschädlich*
chemical [ˈkemɪkl]	Chemikalie	
reduction [rɪˈdʌkʃn]	Reduzierung	vgl. Verb: reduce – *reduzieren*
firm [fɜːm]	Firma	≈ business, company

tʃ	dʒ	ʃ	ʒ	θ	ð	ŋ	s	z	v	w
chips	jet	ship	garage	thing	the	ring	ice	as	very	wet

142	solar power [ˌsəʊlə ˈpaʊə]	Sonnenkraft	ebenso: **nuclear power** – *Atomkraft*
	lie [laɪ]	liegen	
	waste [weɪst]	verschwenden	sonst auch Nomen: *Verschwendung*
	give up [ˌgɪv ˈʌp]	aufgeben	
143	illustrate [ˈɪləstreɪt]	illustrieren, veranschaulichen	
	nuclear power [ˌnjuːkliə ˈpaʊə]	Atomkraft	
	coal [kəʊl]	Kohle	
	damage [ˈdæmɪdʒ]	schaden, beschädigen	
	wind farm [ˈwɪnd fɑːm]	Windkraftanlage	
	poor [pʊə]	schlecht	sonst auch: *arm*
	cycle [ˈsaɪkl]	Rad fahren	sonst auch Nomen: *Rad*
	carry on [ˌkæri ˈɒn]	weitermachen	I'll ~ **eating them** – *ich werde sie auch weiterhin essen*
	whatever [wɒtˈevə]	was auch immer	~ **anyone says** – *egal, was man sagt*
	I can't be bothered [aɪ kɑːnt bi ˈbɒðəd]	ich habe einfach keine Lust	
	redundant [rɪˈdʌndənt]	arbeitslos	be made ~ - *(wegen Überkapazität) entlassen werden*
	environmentally friendly [ɪnˌvaɪrənˌmentəli ˈfrendli]	umweltfreundlich	
	change [tʃeɪndʒ]	Änderung	sonst auch Verb: *ändern*
	scooter [ˈskuːtə]	(Motor-)Roller	
	deposit [dɪˈpɒzɪt]	Pfand	
	turn down [ˌtɜːn ˈdaʊn]	drosseln (Heizung)	
	heating [ˈhiːtɪŋ]	Heizung	
144 ww	description [dɪˈskrɪpʃn]	Beschreibung	vgl. Verb: **describe** – *beschreiben*
ww	own [əʊn]	besitzen	
ww	wheat [wiːt]	Weizen	a field of ~ – *ein Acker Weizen*
ww	herd [hɜːd]	Herde	a ~ of cows – *eine Herde Kühe*
ww	tractor [ˈtræktə]	Traktor	⚠ Schreibung
ww	treat [triːt]	behandeln	vgl. Nomen: **treatment** – *Behandlung*
ww	pesticide [ˈpestɪsaɪd]	Pestizid	⚠ Aussprache und Schreibung
ww	fertiliser [ˈfɜːtəlaɪzə]	Dünger	
ww	profit [ˈprɒfɪt]	Profit, Gewinn	make a ~
ww	field [fiːld]	Feld, Acker	
ww	machinery [məˈʃiːnəri]	Maschinen	⚠ Schreibung
ww	mad [mæd]	wahnsinnig	
ww	traditional [trəˈdɪʃənl]	traditionell	⬌ modern
ww	permanent [ˈpɜːmənənt]	dauerhaft	
ww	it's all about … [ɪts ˌɔːl əˈbaʊt]	es ist eine Frage von	
ww	environmental [ɪnˌvaɪrənˈmentl]	Umwelt-	
ww	mixture [ˈmɪkstʃə]	Mischung	
ww	care [keə]	Betreuung	vgl. Verb: **care for** – *betreuen*
ww	herb [hɜːb]	(Heil-, Würz-)Kraut	
ww	fruit tree [ˈfruːt triː]	Obstbaum	
ww	woodland [ˈwʊdlənd]	Wald(gebiet)	
ww	catch [kætʃ]	einfangen	
ww	drinking water [ˈdrɪŋkɪŋ wɔːtə]	Trinkwasser	
ww	aim [eɪm]	Ziel, Absicht	
ww	rainfall [ˈreɪnfɔːl]	Regen	sonst einfach: **rain**
145 ww	tree surgeon [ˈtriː sɜːdʒən]	Baumdoktor/in	
ww	landscape contractor [ˌlændskeɪp kənˈtræktə]	Gartengestalter/in	
ww	cut down [ˌkʌt ˈdaʊn]	fällen	the trees were ~ – *die Bäume wurden gefällt*
ww	cut off [ˌkʌt ˈɒf]	abscheiden	please ~ that branch – *schneiden Sie bitte diesen Ast ab*
ww	saw [sɔː]	Säge	sonst auch Verb: *sägen*
ww	seed [siːd]	Saat	grow plants from ~
ww	greenhouse [ˈgriːnhaʊs]	Gewächshaus	
ww	landscape [ˈlændskeɪp]	Landschaft	
ww	design [dɪˈzaɪn]	entwerfen	sonst auch Nomen: *Entwurf*

i:	ɪ	e	æ	ɑː	ɒ	ɔː	ʊ	uː	ʌ	ɜː	ə
see	sit	ten	bad	arm	got	saw	put	too	cut	bird	about

ww	office development ['ɒfɪs dɪveləpmənt]	Bürogelände	
ww	golf course ['gɒlf kɔːs]	Golfplatz	
ww	housing ['haʊzɪŋ]	Häuser, Wohnungen	
ww	private ['praɪvət]	privat, Privat-	◄► public – öffentlich
ww	fence [fens]	Zaun	
ww	path [pɑːθ]	(Fuß-)Weg	
146	try out [ˌtraɪ 'aʊt]	ausprobieren	
	fantastic [fæn'tæstɪk]	fantastisch	
	talent ['tælənt]	Talent, Begabung	vgl. Adjektiv: talented – begabt
	fitness ['fɪtnəs]	Fitness, Kondition	
	control [kən'trəʊl]	beherrschen	
	press [pres]	Presse	≈ the newspapers
	live up to s.th. [ˌlɪv 'ʌp tə]	etw. gerecht werden	he couldn't ~ his image – er konnte seinem Image nicht gerecht werden
	over ['əʊvə]	vorbei	it's ~ now – es ist vorbei
	unlikely [ʌn'laɪkli]	unwahrscheinlich	it's ~ that he'll ever ... – er wird wahrscheinlich nie ...
	title ['taɪtl]	Titel	⚠ Aussprache und Schreibung
	nightclub ['naɪtklʌb]	Nachtklub	
	lifestyle ['laɪfstaɪl]	Lebensstil	
	consumerism [kən'sjuːmərɪzəm]	Konsumverhalten	
	caring ['keərɪŋ]	rücksichtsvoll	
	actually ['æktʃuəli]	eigentlich, wirklich	
	traveller ['trævələ]	Reisende/r	
	permanent ['pɜːmənənt]	dauerhaft	◄► temporary – vorläufig
	certainty ['sɜːtnti]	Gewissheit	
	prediction [prɪ'dɪkʃn]	Vorhersage	vgl. Verb: predict – vorhersagen
47	visa ['viːzə]	Visum	
	keep fit [ˌkiːp 'fɪt]	Fitnesstraining	
	tent [tent]	Zelt	
	get married [get 'mærɪd]	heiraten	◄► get divorced – sich scheiden lassen

UNIT 17 Virtual lives!

48	grow [grəʊ]	wachsen	⚠ unregelmäßig
	trend [trend]	Trend	
	involve [ɪn'vɒlv]	einschließen	
	data handling [ˌdeɪtə 'hændlɪŋ]	Datenverwaltung	
	graphic design [ˌgræfɪk dɪ'zaɪn]	Grafik	⚠ Schreibung
	attraction [ə'trækʃn]	Reiz, Attraktion	
	comfort ['kʌmfət]	Komfort	work in the ~ of your own home – arbeiten Sie bequem zu Hause
	office politics [ˌɒfɪs 'pɒlətɪks]	Büropolitik	Plural
	advantage [əd'vɑːntɪdʒ]	Vorteil	◄► disadvantage – Nachteil
	flexible ['fleksəbl]	flexibel	⚠ Aussprache und Schreibung
	childcare ['tʃaɪldkeə]	Beaufsichtigung von Kindern	
	run [rʌn]	führen	~ a home – einen Haushalt führen sonst auch: leiten
	manage ['mænɪdʒ]	bewältigen	
	tied to ['taɪd tə]	an ... gebunden	
	strictly ['strɪktli]	streng	Adverb
	envy ['envi]	beneiden	sonst auch Nomen: Neid
	implication [ˌɪmplɪ'keɪʃn]	Auswirkung	what are the ~s for ...?
	working practice ['wɜːkɪŋ præktɪs]	Arbeitspraxis, -weise	
	future ['fjuːtʃə]	(zu)künftig	sonst auch Nomen: Zukunft ◄► past – vergangen, der Vergangenheit
	(trade) union [ˌtreɪd 'juːnɪən]	Gewerkschaft	◄► rich, wealthy – reich, wohlhabend
	poor [pʊə]	arm	
49	romance [rəʊ'mæns]	Romanze, Liebe(sgeschichte)	she was looking for ~
	surf [sɜːf]	surfen	~ the Internet
	go online [gəʊ 'ɒnlaɪn]	sich ans Internet anschließen	

tʃ	dʒ	ʃ	ʒ	θ	ð	ŋ	s	z	v	w
chips	jet	ship	garage	thing	the	ring	ice	as	very	wet

	bedtime ['bedtaɪm]	Schlafenszeit	until ~
	roof [ruːf]	Dach	under the same ~
150	communication [kə,mjuːnɪ'keɪʃn]	Kommunikation	⚠ Aussprache und Schreibung
	mobile phone [,məʊbaɪl 'fəʊn]	Mobiltelefon, Handy	umgangssprachlich einfach: **mobile**
	answering machine ['ɑːnsərɪŋ məʃiːn]	Anrufbeantworter	≈ **answerphone**
	paragraph ['pærəgrɑːf]	Absatz, Abschnitt	
	communicate [kə'mjuːnɪkeɪt]	sich verständigen	
	self-employed [,self ɪm'plɔɪd]	selbständig	im Sinne: *für sich selbst arbeitend*
	particular [pə'tɪkjələ]	besondere(r, s)	nothing in ~ – *nichts Besonderes/Bestimmtes*
	office equipment ['ɒfɪs ɪkwɪpmənt]	Büroartikel, Büroeinrichtung	
	connect [kə'nekt]	verbinden	
	illustration [,ɪlə'streɪʃn]	Illustrierung	⚠ Aussprache
	look after [,lʊk 'ɑːftə]	betreuen, aufpassen auf	can you ~ the children for an hour?
	association [ə,səʊsi'eɪʃn]	Verband	
	aspect ['æspekt]	Aspekt, Seite	
151	admit [əd'mɪt]	zugeben, eingestehen	◆ deny – *leugnen*
	appreciate [ə'priːʃieɪt]	schätzen	
	dislike [dɪs'laɪk]	nicht mögen	◆ like – *mögen*
	certain ['sɜːtn]	bestimmt	
	arrange [ə'reɪndʒ]	arrangieren	
	intend [ɪn'tend]	beabsichtigen	
	promise ['prɒmɪs]	versprechen	sonst auch Nomen: *Versprechung*
	wish [wɪʃ]	wünschen	sonst auch Nomen: *Wunsch*
	think of ['θɪŋk əv]	denken an	
	up-to-date [,ʌp tə 'deɪt]	aktuell	~ information
	meeting ['miːtɪŋ]	Besprechung, Sitzung	go to a ~ – *an einer Besprechung teilnehmen*
152	rush hour ['rʌʃaʊə]	Hauptverkehrszeit	
	noise [nɔɪz]	Lärm	stop making so much ~!
153	typewriter ['taɪpraɪtə]	Schreibmaschine	
	spelling ['spelɪŋ]	Rechtschreibung	vgl. Verb: **spell** – *buchstabieren*
	computing [kəm'pjuːtɪŋ]	Computerwissenschaft	
	project ['prɒdʒekt]	Projekt	⚠ Aussprache und Schreibung
	photocopy ['fəʊtəʊkɒpɪə]	fotokopieren	⚠ Schreibung
	chat [tʃæt]	plaudern	I like to ~ with my colleagues
	colleague ['kɒliːg]	Kollege, Kollegin	
	surprised [sə'praɪzd]	erstaunt	
	like [laɪk]	das, was man mag	~ and dislikes
	dislike ['dɪslaɪk]	das, was man nicht mag	
154ww	call [kɔːl]	Anruf	sonst auch Verb: *(an)rufen*
ww	helpline ['helplaɪn]	Telefonseelsorge; Informationsdienst; Notruf	
ww	pick up [,pɪk 'ʌp]	(mit dem Auto) abholen	could you ~ me ~?
ww	split up [,splɪt 'ʌp]	sich voneinander trennen	we've just ~ – *wir haben uns gerade voneinander getrennt*
ww	end [end]	beenden	~ it all – *Schluss machen*
ww	ambulance ['æmbjələns]	Krankenwagen	
ww	collapse [kə'læps]	zusammenbrechen	
ww	heart attack ['hɑːt ətæk]	Herzinfarkt, Herzanfall	
ww	abuse [ə'bjuːz]	missbrauchen	vgl. Nomen: **abuse** [ə'bjuːs]
ww	adult ['ædʌlt]	Erwachsene/r	
ww	thorough ['θʌrə]	gründlich	
ww	emergency service [ɪ'mɜːdʒənsi sɜːvɪs]	Notdienst	
ww	fire brigade ['faɪə brɪgeɪd]	Feuerwehr	
ww	ambulance service ['æmbjələns sɜːvɪs]	Rettungsdienst	
ww	find out [,faɪnd 'aʊt]	ermitteln	
ww	chart [tʃɑːt]	Tabelle	≈ table

i:	ɪ	e	æ	ɑ:	ɒ	ɔ:	ʊ	u:	ʌ	ɜ:	ə
see	sit	ten	bad	arm	got	saw	put	too	cut	bird	about

ww	keep waiting [ki:p 'weɪtɪŋ]	warten lassen		sorry to ~ you ~
ww	go ahead [ˌgəʊ ə'hed]	anfangen		
ww	reception [rɪ'sepʃn]	Empfang		
ww	hold the line [ˌhəʊld ðə 'laɪn]	in der Leitung bleiben		please ~ – bitte warten
ww	line [laɪn]	(Telefon-)Leitung		sonst auch: Linie, Zeile, Streifen
ww	be to do with [bi tə du: wɪð]	um ... gehen		what is it to do with? – worum geht es?
ww	put through [ˌpʊt 'θru:]	verbinden		I'll ~ you ~ – ich verbinde
ww	engaged [ɪn'geɪdʒd]	besetzt	≈	busy
ww	spell [spel]	buchstabieren		
ww	apologise [ə'pɒlədʒaɪz]	entschuldigen		
ww	enquire [ɪn'kwaɪə]	anfragen		
ww	request [rɪ'kwest]	bitten		sonst auch Nomen: Bitte
ww	response [rɪ'spɒns]	Antwort	≈	answer, reply
ww	request [rɪ'kwest]	Bitte		sonst auch Verb: bitten
ww	dentist ['dentɪst]	Zahnarzt, Zahnärztin		gleiche Form für beide Geschlechter
ww	surgery ['sɜ:dʒəri]	Praxis		dental ~ – Zahnarztpraxis
ww	Social Services [ˌsəʊʃl 'sɜ:vɪsɪz]	Sozialamt		
ww	patient ['peɪʃnt]	Patient/in	⚠	Aussprache
ww	caller ['kɔ:lə]	Anrufer/in, Besucher/in		
ww	business ['bɪznəs]	Anliegen		sonst auch: Geschäft; Unternehmen
ww	return the call [rɪˌtɜ:n ðə 'kɔ:l]	zurückrufen		
ww	health visitor ['helθ ˌvɪzɪtə]	Sozialarbeiter/in		in der Gesundheitsfürsorge
ww	urgently ['ɜ:dʒəntli]	dringend		Adverb
ww	tone [təʊn]	Ton		please speak after the ~
56	misunderstand [ˌmɪsʌndə'stænd]	missverstehen	⚠	unregelmäßig
	long distance [ˌlɒŋ'dɪstəns]	über eine große Entfernung hinweg		~ love
	telephone ['telɪfəʊn]	anrufen		sonst auch Nomen: Telefon
	modern ['mɒdn]	modern	⚠	Aussprache
	relationship [rɪ'leɪʃnʃɪp]	Beziehung		
	keep going [ki:p 'gəʊɪŋ]	aufrechterhalten	⚠	unregelmäßig
	air ticket ['eə ˌtɪkɪt]	Flugschein		
	e-mail ['i:meɪl]	als elektronische Post senden		please ~ me your response
	long for ['lɒŋ fə]	sich sehnen nach		
	videophone ['vɪdiəʊfəʊn]	Fernsehtelefon		
	widely ['waɪdli]	weit		~ available – allgemein erhältlich
	face [feɪs]	Gesicht		
	body language ['bɒdi ˌlæŋgwɪdʒ]	Körpersprache		
	otherwise ['ʌðəwaɪz]	sonst		
	set up [ˌset 'ʌp]	installieren	⚠	unregelmäßig
	sent [sent]	simple past: send	⚠	unregelmäßig
	parcel ['pɑ:sl]	Paket, Päckchen		
	disk [dɪsk]	Diskette		
	keyboard ['ki:bɔ:d]	Tastatur		
	mouse [maʊs]	Maus		
57	incoming ['ɪnkʌmɪŋ]	ankommend	↔	outgoing – hinausgehend
	book [bʊk]	buchen		book a flight
	sauna ['sɔ:nə]	Sauna	⚠	Aussprache
	memo ['meməʊ]	Notiz, Aktennotiz		
	rate [reɪt]	Tarif		
	wedding ['wedɪŋ]	Hochzeit		

UNIT 18 Choosing a job

58	assure [ə'ʃʊə]	versichern		
	ambitious [æm'bɪʃəs]	ehrgeizig		vgl. Nomen: ambition – Ehrgeiz
	push [pʊʃ]	drängen		sonst auch: schieben
	unable [ʌn'eɪbl]	unfähig		
	strength [streŋθ]	Stärke		~s and weaknesses – Stärken und Schwächen vgl. Adjektiv: strong – stark

tʃ	dʒ	ʃ	ʒ	θ	ð	ŋ	s	z	v	w
chips	**j**et	**sh**ip	gara**ge**	**th**ing	**th**e	ri**ng**	i**c**e	a**s**	**v**ery	**w**et

	weakness ['wi:knəs]	Schwäche	vgl. Adjektiv: **weak** – *schwach*
	train [treɪn]	ausbilden	vgl. Nomen: **training** – *Ausbildung*
	sort out [ˌsɔːt 'aʊt]	klären	
	suitable ['suːtəbl]	geeignet	
	unsuitable [ʌn'suːtəbl]	ungeeignet	
	veterinary nurse [ˌvetrənri 'nɜːs]	Tierpfleger/in	
	allergic [ə'lɜːdʒɪk]	allergisch	~ **to** – *allergisch gegen*
	office worker ['ɒfɪs wɜːkə]	Büroangestellte/r	
	talk over [ˌtɔːk 'əʊvə]	besprechen	**why don't we talk it over?**
	discrimination [dɪˌskrɪmɪ'neɪʃn]	Diskriminierung	
	ability [ə'bɪləti]	Fähigkeit	vgl. Adjektiv: **able** – *fähig*
	race [reɪs]	Rasse	
	religion [rɪ'lɪdʒən]	Religion, Glaube	△ Aussprache
	experienced [ɪk'spɪəriənst]	erfahren	◆ **inexperienced** – *unerfahren*
159	careers officer [kə'rɪəz ɒfɪsə]	Berufsberater/in	
	computer-based [kəm'pjuːtə beɪst]	auf Computerbasis	**a ~ test**
	multiple choice [ˌmʌltɪpl 'tʃɔɪs]	mit Auswahlantworten	**a ~ questionnaire**
	questionnaire [ˌkwestʃə'neə]	Fragebogen	△ Schreibung
	psychometric test [ˌsaɪkəʊ'metrɪk test]	psychometrischer Test	
	wide [waɪd]	breit, groß	**a ~ range** – *eine große Auswahl*
			◆ **narrow** – *eng, klein*
	range (of) [reɪndʒ]	Auswahl (an)	**a wide ~ of jobs** – *eine große Auswahl an Berufen*
	compatible (with) [kəm'pætəbl]	passend (zu); (einer Sache) entsprechend	**a job ~ with my abilities** – *ein Beruf, der meinen Fähigkeiten entspricht*
			◆ **incompatible**
	list [lɪst]	auflisten	sonst auch Nomen: *Liste*
	almost ['ɔːlməʊst]	fast	≈ **nearly**
	overlook [ˌəʊvə'lʊk]	übersehen	
	incompatible [ˌɪnkəm'pætəbl]	nicht passend	
	mechanical [mɪ'kænɪkl]	mechanisch	
	final ['faɪnl]	endgültig	**the ~ decision is yours**
	neither ['naɪðə]	auch nicht	**I can't help you, and ~ can they**
	influence ['ɪnfluəns]	beeinflussen	sonst auch Nomen: *Einfluss*
	traditionally [trə'dɪʃənəli]	traditionell	Adverb
	break [breɪk]	überwinden	eigentlich: *(zer)brechen*
	deal with ['diːl wɪð]	lösen	**we must ~ the problem**
	mankind [mæn'kaɪnd]	Menschheit	besser: **humankind**
	chairman ['tʃeəmən]	Vorsitzender	△ nur männlich
			vgl. **chairperson** – *Vorsitzende/r*
	headmaster [ˌhed'mɑːstə]	Schulleiter, Direktor	△ nur männlich
			vgl. **headteacher** – *Schulleiter/in*
	exclude [ɪk'skluːd]	ausschließen	◆ *einschließen*
	rephrase [ˌriː'freɪz]	anders ausdrücken	**can you ~ that?**
	humankind ['hjuːmənkaɪnd]	Menschheit	
	headteacher [ˌhed'tiːtʃə]	Schulleiter/in	
160	select [sɪ'lekt]	auswählen	
	sensitive ['sensətɪv]	empfindlich	**he is very ~ to criticism**
	journalist ['dʒɜːnəlɪst]	Journalist/in	
	pop star ['pɒp stɑː]	Schlagersänger/in	
	politician [ˌpɒlə'tɪʃn]	Politiker/in	
	immediately [ɪ'miːdiətli]	sofort, umgehend	△ Schreibung
	happiness ['hæpinəs]	Glück, Zufriedenheit	vgl. Adjektiv: **happy** – *glücklich*
	environmental [ɪnˌvaɪrən'mentl]	Umwelt-	~ **problems** – *Umweltprobleme*
	overtime ['əʊvətaɪm]	Überstunden	**I do a lot of ~**
	housework ['haʊswɜːk]	Hausarbeit	
	cleaning lady ['kliːnɪŋ leɪdi]	Putzfrau	△ nur weiblich
			vgl. **cleaner** – *Reinigungskraft*
	businessman ['bɪznəsmən]	Geschäftsmann	△ nur männlich
			vgl. **businessperson**
	headmistress [ˌhed'mɪstrəs]	Schulleiterin	△ nur weiblich
			vgl. **headteacher**

i:	ɪ	e	æ	ɑ:	ɒ	ɔ:	ʊ	u:	ʌ	ɜ:	ə
see	sit	ten	bad	arm	got	saw	put	too	cut	bird	about

	fireman ['faɪəmən]	Feuerwehrmann	⚠	nur männlich vgl. **fire officer**
161	dissatisfied [dɪs'sætɪsfaɪd]	unzufrieden	◆▶	**satisfied** – *zufrieden*
	disagree [ˌdɪsə'gri:]	nicht einverstanden sein	◆▶	**agree** – *einverstanden sein*
	disappear [ˌdɪsə'pɪə]	verschwinden	◆▶	**appear** – *erscheinen*
	impolite [ˌɪmpə'laɪt]	unhöflich	◆▶	**polite** – *höflich*
	unimportant [ˌʌnɪm'pɔ:tənt]	unwichtig		
	unsuccessful [ˌʌnsək'sesfl]	erfolglos		
	drinkable ['drɪŋkəbl]	trinkbar		
	likeable ['laɪkəbl]	sympathisch		
	helpful ['helpfl]	hilfreich, hilfsbereit		
.62	unpleasant [ʌn'pleznt]	unangenehm		
	unpopular [ʌn'pɒpjələ]	unbeliebt		
	senior ['si:niə]	leitend/höher		~ **jobs** – *leitende/höhere Stellungen*
	boss [bɒs]	Chef/in		
	ever since [evə 'sɪns]	seitdem		~ **you became my boss**
	divorce [dɪ'vɔ:s]	sich scheiden lassen		
	treatment ['tri:tmənt]	Behandlung		vgl. Verb: *behandeln*
	cause [kɔ:z]	verursachen		vgl. Nomen: *Ursache*
	feminism ['femənɪzəm]	Feminismus		
	satisfy ['sætɪsfaɪ]	befriedigen		
	demand [dɪ'mɑ:nd]	Forderung		vgl. Verb: *fordern, verlangen*
	laughable ['lɑ:fəbl]	lächerlich		
63	respond to [rɪ'spɒnd]	reagieren auf		
	apologise [ə'pɒlədʒaɪz]	sich entschuldigen		
	shall [ʃəl]	sollen	⚠	unregelmäßig
	settled ['setl]	abgemacht		
	point [pɔɪnt]	Punkt		
ww	required [rɪ'kwaɪəd]	verlangt, gefordert		
ww	Ltd. ['lɪmɪtɪd]	≈ GmbH		Abkürzung von: **limited** – *beschränkt*
ww	closing date ['kləʊzɪŋ deɪt]	Einsendeschluss		**what's the ~?**
ww	office administrator [ˌɒfɪs əd'mɪnɪstreɪtə]	Büroleiter/in		
ww	educational [ˌedʒu'keɪʃənl]	Ausbildungs-		
ww	depending on [dɪ'pendɪŋ ɒn]	abhängig von		
ww	applicant ['æplɪkənt]	Bewerber/in		vgl. Verb: **apply** – *sich bewerben*
ww	ask for ['ɑ:sk fə]	bitten um		
ww	extract ['ekstrækt]	Auszug		
ww	efficient [ɪ'fɪʃnt]	tüchtig	◆▶	**inefficient** – *untüchtig*
ww	hardworking [ˌhɑ:d'wɜ:kɪŋ]	fleißig	◆▶	**lazy** – *faul*
ww	loyal ['lɔɪəl]	treu	◆▶	**disloyal** – *untreu*
ww	electronic engineering [ɪlek,trɒnɪk endʒɪ'nɪərɪŋ]	Elektronik		
ww	current ['kʌrənt]	gegenwärtig		
ww	join [dʒɔɪn]	anfangen bei		sonst auch: *verbinden; beitreten*
ww	deaf [def]	taub		
ww	understood [ˌʌndə'stʊd]	past participle: **understand**	⚠	unregelmäßig
ww	imaginative [ɪ'mædʒɪnətɪv]	fantasievoll		
ww	appoint [ə'pɔɪnt]	einstellen		**she was ~ed to the job**
ww	suited ['su:tɪd]	geeignet		
ww	experience [ɪk'spɪəriəns]	Erfahrung		sonst auch: *Erlebnis*
ww	apply for [ə'plaɪ fə]	sich bewerben um		
ww	suffer from ['sʌfə frəm]	leiden an		
ww	lie [laɪ]	lügen		
ww	computer programmer [kəm'pju:tə prəʊgræmə]	Programmierer/in		
ww	fill in [ˌfɪl 'ɪn]	ausfüllen		sonst auch: *eintragen*
ww	handwriting ['hændraɪtɪŋ]	Handschrift		

tʃ	dʒ	ʃ	ʒ	θ	ð	ŋ	s	z	v	w
chips	jet	ship	garage	thing	the	ring	ice	as	very	wet

ww **interview** ['ɪntəvjuː]   ein Vorstellungs-gespräch führen mit   he was ~ed on Monday

ww **impression** [ɪm'preʃn]   Eindruck

166 **Congratulations!** [kənˌgrætʃʊ'leɪʃnz]   Herzlichen Glückwunsch!
effort ['efət]   Mühe, Bemühung
thankful ['θæŋkfl]   dankbar ≈ grateful
stay with it ['steɪ wɪð ɪt]   nicht aufgeben
notice ['nəʊtɪs]   bemerken

167 **travel agency** ['trævl eɪdʒənsi]   Reisebüro
job application [ˌdʒɒb ˌæplɪ'keɪʃn]   Stellenbewerbung
voluntary work ['vɒləntri wɜːk]   freiwillige Arbeit

168 **electronics** [ˌɪlek'trɒnɪks]   Elektronik
come on [ˌkʌm 'ɒn]   los, komm schon   ~, let's go! – los, gehen wir!

Commercial Correspondence and Further reading

Die chronologische Wörterliste für diesen Teil setzt nur die Wörter voraus, die im **Grundwortschatz** und in den **Units 1–9** enthalten sind.

Commercial Correspondence

170 **commercial** [kə'mɜːʃl]   Handels-
correspondence [ˌkɒrɪ'spɒndəns]   Briefwechsel, Korrespondenz
reference (ref) ['refərəns]   Zeichen
supplier [sə'plaɪə]   Anbieter, Lieferant/in
optical ['ɒptɪkl]   optisch
instrument ['ɪnstrəmənt]   Instrument
enclosed [ɪn'kləʊzd]   (einem Brief) beigelegt
copy ['kɒpi]   Exemplar
company brochure [ˌkʌmpəni 'brəʊʃə]   Firmenprospekt
trade fair ['treɪd feə]   Handelsmesse
representative [ˌreprɪ'zentətɪv]   Vertreter/in
inspect [ɪn'spekt]   sich ansehen
range [reɪndʒ]   Sortiment
impressed [ɪm'prest]   beeindruckt
line [laɪn]   Produktgruppe
frame [freɪm]   Rahmen
reading glasses ['riːdɪŋ glɑːsɪz]   Lesebrille
order ['ɔːdə]   bestellen
firm [fɜːm]   Firma
at your earliest convenience [ət jɔːr ˌɜːliɪst kən'viːniəns]   möglichst bald
grateful ['greɪtfl]   dankbar
current ['kʌrənt]   aktuell
price list ['praɪs lɪst]   Preisliste
Yours faithfully [jɔːz 'feɪθfəli]   Mit freundlichen Grüßen, Hochachtungsvoll
per pro (pp) [ˌpɜː 'prəʊ]   im Auftrag (i.A.)
Ms [mɪz]   Frau/Fräulein
enclosure (enc) [ɪn'kləʊʒə]   Anlage
carbon copy (cc) [ˌkɑːbən 'kɒpi]   Durchschrift
letterhead ['letəhed]   Briefkopf
recipient [rɪ'sɪpiənt]   Empfänger/in
inside address [ˌɪnsaɪd ə'dres]   Innenadresse

salutation [ˌsæljuː'teɪʃn]   Anrede
introduction [ˌɪntrə'dʌkʃn]   Einleitung
request [rɪ'kwest]   Bitte
refer to [rɪ'fɜː tə]   hinweisen auf
contact ['kɒntækt]   Kontakt
complimentary close [ˌkɒmplɪˌmentri 'kləʊz]   Schlussformel
signature ['sɪgnətʃə]   Unterschrift

171 **layout** ['leɪaʊt]   Layout
vary ['veəri]   unterschiedlich sein
punctuation [ˌpʌŋktʃu'eɪʃn]   Zeichensetzung
abbreviation [əˌbriːvi'eɪʃn]   Abkürzung
contain [kən'teɪn]   enthalten
initial [ɪ'nɪʃl]   Initiale
wrote [rəʊt]   simple past: **write**
capital ['kæpɪtl]   Großbuchstabe
key in [ˌkiː 'ɪn]   eingeben
method ['meθəd]   Methode, Verfahren
Asian ['eɪʃn]   asiatisch
Best wishes [best 'wɪʃɪz]   Viele Grüße
whether ['weðə]   ob
directly [də'rektli]   direkt
sender ['sendə]   Absender
sign [saɪn]   unterschreiben
on behalf of [ɒn bɪ'hɑːf əv]   im Namen von
end [end]   Ende, Schluss
reader ['riːdə]   Leser/in
circulation [ˌsɜːkjə'leɪʃn]   Zirkulation
sent [sent]   past participle: **send**

Further Reading 1

172 **grass** [grɑːs]   Gras
fence [fens]   Zaun
plastic surgery [ˌplæstɪk 'sɜːdʒəri]   plastische Chirurgie
shape [ʃeɪp]   Form
lip [lɪp]   Lippe
instantly ['ɪnstəntli]   sofort
sign [saɪn]   (An)zeichen
current ['kʌrənt]   aktuell

i:	ɪ	e	æ	ɑː	ɒ	ɔː	ʊ	uː	ʌ	ɜː	ə
see	sit	ten	bad	arm	got	saw	put	too	cut	bird	about

breast [brest] — Brust
reduce [rɪˈdjuːs] — reduzieren
stomach [ˈstʌmək] — Magen
increasingly [ɪnˈkriːsɪŋli] — zunehmend
extreme [ɪkˈstriːm] — äußerst, extrem
look [lʊk] — aussehen
obvious [ˈɒbviəs] — offensichtlich
skin [skɪn] — Haut
completely [kəmˈpliːtli] — völlig
danger [ˈdeɪndʒə] — Gefahr
fall to pieces [fɔːl tə ˈpiːsɪz] — (in Stücke) zerfallen
whether [ˈweðə] — ob
in public [ɪn ˈpʌblɪk] — in der Öffentlichkeit
mask [mɑːsk] — Maske
report [rɪˈpɔːt] — Bericht
else [els] — sonst
face [feɪs] — Gesicht

173 **wonder about** [ˈwʌndər əbaʊt] — sich Gedanken machen über

Further Reading 2

cost [kɒst] — Kosten
rude [ruːd] — unhöflich
total [ˈtəʊtl] — Gesamt-
bring up [ˌbrɪŋ ˈʌp] — aufziehen
according to [əˈkɔːdɪŋ tə] — zufolge, laut, nach
recent [ˈriːsnt] — letzte(r, s), jüngste(r, s)
average [ˈævərɪdʒ] — Durchschnitts-
income [ˈɪnkʌm] — Einkommen
demand [dɪˈmɑːnd] — Forderung
keep [kiːp] — unterhalten
including [ɪnˈkluːdɪŋ] — einschließlich
enormous [ɪˈnɔːməs] — enorm, gewaltig
include [ɪnˈkluːd] — einbeziehen
electricity [ɪˌlekˈtrɪsəti] — Elektrizität, Strom
bill [bɪl] — Rechnung
Christmas [ˈkrɪsməs] — Weihnachts-
contribution [ˌkɒntrɪˈbjuːʃn] — Beitrag
marriage [ˈmærɪdʒ] — Ehe, Hochzeit
Caribbean [ˌkærəˈbiːən] — Karibik
round the world flight [ˌraʊnd ðə ˈwɜːld flaɪt] — Flug rund um die Welt
champagne [ʃæmˈpeɪn] — Champagner
comparison [kəmˈpærɪsn] — Vergleich

74 **finding** [ˈfaɪndɪŋ] — Ergebnis
figure [ˈfɪgə] — Zahl
name [neɪm] — nennen
meaning [ˈmiːnɪŋ] — Bedeutung, Sinn

Further Reading 3

scooter [ˈskuːtə] — (Motor-)Roller
rollerblades [ˈrəʊləbleɪdz] — Inline-Skates
seventies [ˈsevntiz] — Siebziger
eighties [ˈeɪtiz] — Achtziger
nineties [ˈnaɪntiz] — Neunziger
definitely [ˈdefɪnətli] — bestimmt
after all [ˌɑːftər ˈɔːl] — schließlich doch
band [bænd] — Band
design [dɪˈzaɪn] — entwerfen
remain [rɪˈmeɪn] — bleiben
more or less [ˌmɔːr ɔː ˈles] — mehr oder weniger
ever since [ˌevə ˈsɪns] — seitdem

handlebars [ˈhændlbɑːz] — Lenkstange
covered [ˈkʌvəd] — zugedeckt
wasp [wɒsp] — Wespe
Italian [ɪˈtæliən] — Italienisch
noise [nɔɪz] — Geräusch, Lärm
shape [ʃeɪp] — Form
within [wɪˈðɪn] — innerhalb von
rival [ˈraɪvl] — Rivale, Rivalin
arrive on the scene [əˌraɪv ɒn ðə ˈsiːn] — erscheinen
fifties [ˈfɪftiz] — Fünfziger
sixties [ˈsɪkstiz] — Sechziger
extremely [ɪkˈstriːmli] — sehr
advantage [ədˈvɑːntɪdʒ] — Vorteil
motorbike [ˈməʊtəbaɪk] — Motorrad
in particular [ɪn pəˈtɪkjələ] — insbesondere
sophisticated [səˈfɪstɪkeɪtɪd] — hochentwickelt
image [ˈɪmɪdʒ] — Image
on the other hand [ɒn ði ˈʌðə hænd] — andererseits
dress in [ˈdres ɪn] — sich kleiden in
leather [ˈleðə] — Leder
boot [buːt] — Stiefel

175 **disappear** [ˌdɪsəˈpɪə] — verschwinden
almost [ˈɔːlməʊst] — fast
mid- [mɪd] — Mittel-
production [prəˈdʌkʃn] — Produktion
end [end] — aufhören
else [els] — andere(r, s)
prefer [prɪˈfɜː] — vorziehen

Further Reading 4

176 **glory** [ˈglɔːri] — Herrlichkeit
vast [vɑːst] — riesig
region [ˈriːdʒən] — Gebiet, Gegend
attraction [əˈtrækʃn] — Reiz, Attraktion
tend to [ˈtend tə] — neigen zu
concentrate [ˈkɒnsntreɪt] — sich konzentrieren
else [els] — sonst
on offer [ɒn ˈɒfə] — im Angebot
theme park [ˈθiːm pɑːk] — Freizeitpark
capital [ˈkæpɪtl] — Hauptstadt
relax [rɪˈlæks] — sich entspannen
palm tree [ˈpɑːmtriː] — Palme
sandy [ˈsændi] — sandig
clear [klɪə] — klar, durchsichtig
warm [wɔːm] — warm
perfect [ˈpɜːfɪkt] — vollkommen
paradise [ˈpærədaɪs] — Paradies
criminal [ˈkrɪmɪnl] — Verbrecher/in
rob [rɒb] — berauben
murder [ˈmɜːdə] — ermorden
familiar [fəˈmɪliə] — vertraut, bekannt
programme [ˈprəʊgræm] — Sendung
be set [bi ˈset] — spielen
studio [ˈstjuːdiəʊ] — Studio
wine producer [ˌwaɪn prəˈdjuːsə] — Winzer
lifestyle [ˈlaɪfstaɪl] — Lebensstil
religion [rɪˈlɪdʒən] — Religion, Glaube
completely [kəmˈpliːtli] — völlig
born [bɔːn] — geboren
historic [hɪˈstɒrɪk] — historische(r, s)

tʃ	dʒ	ʃ	ʒ	θ	ð	ŋ	s	z	v	w
chips	**j**et	**sh**ip	gara**g**e	**th**ing	**th**e	ri**ng**	i**c**e	a**s**	**v**ery	**w**et

monument ['mɒnjumənt] — Denkmal, Monument
civil war [ˌsɪvl 'wɔː] — Bürgerkrieg
land [lænd] — Land
snowy ['snəʊi] — verschneit
peak [piːk] — Gipfel
dark [dɑːk] — düster
forest ['fɒrɪst] — Wald
endless ['endləs] — endlos
hire ['haɪə] — mieten
wild [waɪld] — wild

177 ideal [aɪ'dɪəl] — ideal

Further Reading 5

packaging ['pækɪdʒɪŋ] — Verpackung
carefully ['keəfəli] — sorgfältig
design [dɪ'zaɪn] — entwerfen
can [kæn] — Dose
packet ['pækɪt] — Packung, Schachtel
specialist ['speʃəlɪst] — Fachmann/Frau
test [test] — ausprobieren, testen
prefer [prɪ'fɜː] — vorziehen
chose [tʃəʊz] — simple past: **choose**
particular [pə'tɪkjələ] — bestimmte(r, s)
conclusion [kən'kluːʒn] — (Schluss-)Folgerung
deodorant [di'əʊdərənt] — Deodorant
ranging from ... to ['reɪndʒɪŋ] — von ... bis
according to [ə'kɔːdɪŋ tə] — je nach
power ['paʊə] — Macht
depend on [dɪ'pend ɒn] — abhängig sein von
combination [ˌkɒmbɪ'neɪʃn] — Kombination
element ['elɪmənt] — Element
attract [ə'trækt] — anziehen
attention [ə'tenʃn] — Aufmerksamkeit
immediately [ɪ'miːdiətli] — sofort, umgehend
closely ['kləʊsli] — genau
sharp [ʃɑːp] — spitz
angular ['æŋɡjələ] — eckig
shape [ʃeɪp] — Form
slogan ['sləʊɡən] — (Werbe-)Spruch
improve [ɪm'pruːv] — verbessern
environmentally [ɪnˌvaɪrən'mentəli] — Umwelt-, umwelt-
friendly ['frendli] — freundlich
print [prɪnt] — drucken
feminine ['femənɪn] — weiblich
circle ['sɜːkl] — Kreis
curve [kɜːv] — Kurve
association [əˌsəʊsi'eɪʃn] — Assoziation
package ['pækɪdʒ] — Verpackung
wonder ['wʌndə] — sich fragen
whether ['weðə] — ob
golden ['ɡəʊldən] — golden
arch [ɑːtʃ] — Bogen
eventually [ɪ'ventʃuəli] — schließlich, endlich

178 find out [ˌfaɪnd 'aʊt] — herausfinden
designer [dɪ'zaɪnə] — Grafiker/in
combine [kəm'baɪn] — zusammenfügen
perfume ['pɜːfjuːm] — Parfüm
horrible ['hɒrəbl] — entsetzlich, schrecklich
personal ['pɜːsənl] — persönlich
particularly [pə'tɪkjələli] — besonders

Further Reading 6

freedom ['friːdəm] — Freiheit
adolescent [ˌædə'lesnt] — Jugendliche/r
stranger ['streɪndʒə] — Fremde/r
according to [ə'kɔːdɪŋ tə] — zufolge, laut
expert ['ekspɜːt] — Fachmann/frau
increasingly [ɪn'kriːsɪŋli] — zunehmend

179 either ['aɪðə] — entweder
control [kən'trəʊl] — Kontrolle
society [sə'saɪəti] — Gesellschaft
case [keɪs] — Fall
victim ['vɪktɪm] — Opfer
attack [ə'tæk] — angreifen
modern ['mɒdn] — modern

180 asleep [ə'sliːp] — schlafend

Further Reading 7

recent ['riːsnt] — letzte(r, s), jüngste(r, s)
difference ['dɪfrəns] — Unterschied
everyday ['evrideɪ] — alltäglich, Alltags-
habit ['hæbɪt] — Gewohnheit
European [ˌjʊərə'piːən] — Europäer/in
based on ['beɪst ɒn] — basierend auf
activity [æk'tɪvəti] — Aktivität
period ['pɪərɪəd] — Zeit(raum)
result [rɪ'zʌlt] — Ergebnis
whether ['weðə] — ob
stereotyped ['steriətaɪpt] — stereotyp
image ['ɪmɪdʒ] — Bild, Vorstellung
nationality [ˌnæʃə'næləti] — (Menschen einer bestimmten) Nationalität
surprising [sə'praɪzɪŋ] — überraschend
Czech [tʃek] — Tscheche/Tschechin
Hungarian [hʌŋ'ɡeərɪən] — Ungar/in
Spanish ['spænɪʃ] — Spanier (Plural)
Irish ['aɪrɪʃ] — Iren
tend to ['tend tə] — neigen zu
Russian ['rʌʃn] — Russe/Russin
Italian [ɪ'tælɪən] — Italiener/in
Turkey ['tɜːki] — Türkei
have a hot temper [hæv ə ˌhɒt 'tempə] — jähzornig sein
support [sə'pɔːt] — unterstützen
Turk [tɜːk] — Türke/Türkin
shout [ʃaʊt] — (laut) rufen, schreien
controlled [kən'trəʊld] — beherrscht
accurate ['ækjərət] — genau
Latin ['lætɪn] — südländisch
character ['kærəktə] — Charakter, Wesen
Dutch [dʌtʃ] — Holländer (Plural)
Holland ['hɒlənd] — Holland
surprise [sə'praɪz] — Überraschung
Dane [deɪn] — Däne/Dänin
Finn [fɪn] — Finne/Finnin
Scandinavian [ˌskændɪ'neɪvɪən] — skandinavisch
Swede [swiːd] — Schwede/Schwedin
reserved [rɪ'zɜːvd] — zurückhaltend
conclude [kən'kluːd] — schließen, folgern
statistics [stə'tɪstɪks] — Statistiken
stereotype ['steriətaɪp] — Stereotyp

iː	ɪ	e	æ	ɑː	ɒ	ɔː	ʊ	uː	ʌ	ɜː	ə
see	sit	ten	bad	arm	got	saw	put	too	cut	bird	about

nation	['neɪʃn]	Nation
existing	[ɪg'zɪstɪŋ]	bestehend
incorrect	[ˌɪnkə'rekt]	falsch, unrichtig
conclusion	[kən'kluːʒn]	(Schluss-)Folgerung
individual	[ˌɪndɪ'vɪdʒuəl]	Individuum
according to	[ə'kɔːdɪŋ tə]	zufolge, laut, nach
181 behave	[bɪ'heɪv]	sich verhalten

Further Reading 8

candle	['kændl]	Kerze
tragically	['trædʒɪkli]	tragisch
car crash	['kɑː kræʃ]	Autounfall
shock	[ʃɒk]	erschüttern
impossible	[ɪm'pɒsəbl]	unmöglich
glamorous	['glæmərəs]	glanzvoll
screen	[skriːn]	Bildschirm
South Africa	[ˌsaʊθ 'æfrɪkə]	Südafrika
Australia	[ɒ'streɪliə]	Australien
sent	[sent]	simple past: send
flower	['flaʊə]	Blume
funeral	['fjuːnərəl]	Beerdigung
182 ever since	[ˌevə 'sɪns]	seitdem
death	[deθ]	Tod
wonder	['wʌndə]	sich fragen
cause	[kɔːz]	verursachen
public	['pʌblɪk]	Öffentlichkeit
intrude on	[ɪn'truːd ɒn]	sich eindrängen in
surprising	[sə'praɪzɪŋ]	überraschend
fortune	['fɔːtʃuːn]	Vermögen
strongly	['strɒŋgli]	heftig
interest	['ɪntrəst]	Interesse
concentrate	['kɒnsntreɪt]	sich konzentrieren
whatever	[wɒt'evə]	was auch immer
might	[maɪt]	könnte
certain	['sɜːtn]	sicher, gewiss
legend	['ledʒənd]	Legende
brief	[briːf]	kurz
worth	[wɜːθ]	wert
according to	[ə'kɔːdɪŋ tə]	zufolge, laut, nach
183 admire	[əd'maɪə]	bewundern

Further Reading 9

drug	[drʌg]	Droge, Rauschgift
war	[wɔː]	Krieg
addict	['ædɪkt]	Süchtige/r
Sweden	['swiːdn]	Schweden
manage	['mænɪdʒ]	zurechtkommen mit, bewältigen
chance	[tʃɑːns]	Chance
former	['fɔːmə]	ehemalig
obviously	['ɒbviəsli]	offensichtlich
keep s.o. away from s.th.	[ˌkiːp ə'weɪ frəm]	jmdn. von etw. fernhalten
above all	[əbʌv 'ɔːl]	vor allem
success	[sək'ses]	Erfolg
well-being	['welbiːɪŋ]	Wohlergehen, Behaglichkeit
period	['pɪəriəd]	Zeit(raum)
come off	[ˌkʌm 'ɒf]	sich entwöhnen von
completely	[kəm'pliːtli]	völlig
life skill	['laɪf skɪl]	lebenswichtige Fähigkeit
academic	[ˌækə'demɪk]	akademisch
joy	[dʒɔɪ]	Freude
nature	['neɪtʃə]	Natur
treatment	['triːtmənt]	Behandlung
policy	['pɒləsi]	(praktische) Politik
Holland	['hɒlənd]	Holland
Spain	[speɪn]	Spanien
cannabis	['kænəbɪs]	Haschisch
heroin	['herəʊɪn]	Heroin
use	[juːz]	Gebrauch
legal	['liːgl]	legal
Greece	[griːs]	Griechenland
tough	[tʌf]	hart
Swede	[swiːd]	Schwede/Schwedin
control	[kən'trəʊl]	kontrollieren
create	[kriː'eɪt]	(er)schaffen, hervorrufen, verursachen
huge	[hjuːdʒ]	riesig
black market	[ˌblæk 'mɑːkɪt]	Schwarzmarkt
led	[led]	simple past: lead
increase	[ɪn'kriːs]	Zunahme
illegal	[ɪ'liːgl]	gesetzeswidrig
strict	[strɪkt]	streng
user	['juːzə]	Benutzer/in
community	[kə'mjuːnəti]	Gemeinde
contribute	[kən'trɪbjuːt]	beitragen
success rate	[sək'ses reɪt]	Erfolgsrate

Further Reading 10

craze	[kreɪz]	Fimmel
unfit	[ʌn'fɪt]	schlecht in Form
unhealthy	[ʌn'helθi]	ungesund
surprising	[sə'praɪzɪŋ]	überraschend
solve	[sɒlv]	lösen
forever	[fə'revə]	für immer
exercise	['eksəsaɪz]	Übung
video	['vɪdiəʊ]	Video
machine	[mə'ʃiːn]	Gerät
achieve	[ə'tʃiːv]	erreichen, erlangen
ideal	[aɪ'dɪəl]	ideal
shape	[ʃeɪp]	Form
latest	['leɪtɪst]	neueste(r, s)
billion	['bɪliən]	Milliarde
rich	[rɪtʃ]	reich, wohlhabend
obsession	[əb'seʃn]	fixe Idee
organic	[ɔː'gænɪk]	organisch
health-conscious	['helθkɒnʃəs]	gesundheitsbewusst
undernourished	[ˌʌndə'nʌrɪʃt]	unterernährt
given	['gɪvn]	past participle: give
185 effort	['efət]	Mühe, Anstrengung
difference	['dɪfrəns]	Unterschied
thin	[θɪn]	dünn
biscuit	['bɪskɪt]	Keks
stairs	[steəz]	Treppe
change	[tʃeɪndʒ]	(Ver-)Änderung
mention	['menʃn]	erwähnen, nennen
benefit	['benɪfɪt]	Vorteil, Nutzen
slim	[slɪm]	schlank
186 favourite	['feɪvərɪt]	liebste(r, s), Lieblings-

tʃ	dʒ	ʃ	ʒ	θ	ð	ŋ	s	z	v	w
chips	**j**et	**sh**ip	gara**g**e	**th**ing	**th**e	ri**ng**	**ice**	a**s**	**v**ery	**w**et

Further Reading 11

equality [ɪˈkwɒləti]		Gleichberechtigung
'A' level [ˈeɪ levl]		≈ Abitur
personal [ˈpɜːsənl]		persönlich
tutor [ˈtjuːtə]		Tutor
need [niːd]		Bedürfnis
might [maɪt]		könnte
tend to [ˈtend tə]		neigen zu
organise [ˈɔːɡənaɪz]		organisieren
institution [ˌɪnstɪˈtjuːʃn]		Institution
with s.o. in mind [ɪn ˈmaɪnd]		im Hinblick auf jmdn.
pregnant [ˈpreɡnənt]		schwanger
injured [ˈɪndʒəd]		verletzt
interest [ˈɪntrəst]		Interesse
include [ɪnˈkluːd]		einbeziehen
society [səˈsaɪəti]		Gesellschaft
disabled [dɪsˈeɪbld]		behindert
stairs [steəz]		Treppe
injury [ˈɪndʒəri]		Verletzung
such as [ˈsʌtʃ əz]		wie zum Beispiel
broken [ˈbrəʊkən]		past participle: **break**
difficulty [ˈdɪfɪkəlti]		Schwierigkeit
neither [ˈnaɪðə]		auch nicht
extra [ˈekstrə]		zusätzlich, extra
project work [ˈprɒdʒekt wɜːk]		Projektarbeit
examination [ɪɡˌzæmɪˈneɪʃn]		(Abschluss-)Prüfung
disability [ˌdɪsəˈbɪləti]		Behinderung
care for [ˈkeə fə]		versorgen
relative [ˈrelətɪv]		Verwandte/r
photography [fəˈtɒɡrəfi]		Fotografie
blind [blaɪnd]		blind
form [fɔːm]		Form, Gestalt
take [teɪk]		(sich Notizen) machen
note [nəʊt]		Notiz
textbook [ˈtekstbʊk]		Lehrbuch
onto [ˈɒntə]		auf
tape [teɪp]		(Ton-)Band
otherwise [ˈʌðəwaɪz]		sonst
get around [ˌɡet əˈraʊnd]		herumkommen
learnt [lɜːnt]		past participle: **learn**

187

private [ˈpraɪvət]	privat, Privat-
given [ˈɡɪvn]	past participle: **give**
treatment [ˈtriːtmənt]	Behandlung

Further Reading 12

technique [tekˈniːk]	Methode
dream [driːm]	Traum
nervously [ˈnɜːvəsli]	nervös
wonder [ˈwʌndə]	sich fragen
whether [ˈweðə]	ob
suddenly [ˈsʌdnli]	plötzlich
golden [ˈɡəʊldən]	golden
might [maɪt]	könnte
prepare oneself [prɪˈpeə]	sich vorbereiten
impression [ɪmˈpreʃn]	Eindruck
given [ˈɡɪvn]	past participle: **give**
firstly [ˈfɜːstli]	zuerst
claim [kleɪm]	behaupten
face [feɪs]	Gesicht
fit [fɪt]	passen
colleague [ˈkɒliːɡ]	Kollege, Kollegin

188

secondly [ˈsekəndli]	zweitens
impress [ɪmˈpres]	beeindrucken
future [ˈfjuːtʃə]	(zu)künftig
carefully [ˈkeəfəli]	sorgfältig
tight [taɪt]	eng
skirt [skɜːt]	Rock
heel [hiːl]	Absatz
unless [ənˈles]	wenn ... nicht
direct [dəˈrekt]	direkt
required [rɪˈkwaɪəd]	verlangt, gefordert
nervous [ˈnɜːvəs]	nervös
get to the point [ˌɡet tə ðə ˈpɔɪnt]	auf den Punkt kommen
personality [ˌpɜːsəˈnæləti]	Persönlichkeit
natural [ˈnætʃrəl]	natürlich, echt
in the end [ɪn ði ˈend]	schließlich
mysterious [mɪˈstɪəriəs]	geheimnisvoll
make friends with [meɪk ˈfrendz wɪð]	sich anfreunden mit
last [lɑːst]	dauern
almost [ˈɔːlməʊst]	fast

ALPHABETISCHES WÖRTERVERZEICHNIS

Diese Liste enthält alle Wörter in WORK WITH ENGLISH in alphabetischer Reihenfolge. Hier jedoch nicht aufgeführt sind die Wörter, die zum Grundwortschatz gehören.
Ein Sternchen * vor der Seitenzahl bedeutet, dass das Stichwort auf der Kassette und nicht im Buch vorkommt.

'A' level *60* ≈ Abitur
abacus *114* Abakus, Rechenbrett
abbreviation *171* Abkürzung
ability *125* Fähigkeit
able: be ~ to *78* können
About time! *39* Es wird Zeit!
above all *183* vor allem
above ground *90* über der Erde
abroad *80* im Ausland, ins Ausland
absolutely *109* absolut, völlig
abuse *118* Missbrauch
abuse *154* missbrauchen
academic *183* akademisch
accelerate *69* beschleunigen, Gas geben
accent *76* Akzent
accept *58* hinnehmen
accident *62* Unfall
according to *140; 177* zufolge, laut, nach; je nach
accounts clerk *12* Buchhalter/in
accurate *180* genau
achieve *184* erreichen, erlangen
across *86* über (... hinweg)
act *69* sich verhalten
active **60* aktiv
activity *180* Aktivität
actually *104* eigentlich, wirklich
ad **45* Reklame, Anzeige
add **60* hinzufügen
add to *140* beitragen zu
addict **95* Süchtige/r
addicted to *119* -süchtig
addictive *120* süchtig machend
admire *183* bewundern
admit *151* zugeben, eingestehen
adolescent *178* Jugendliche/r
adult *154* Erwachsene/r
advanced *23* fortgeschritten
advantage *128* Vorteil
adventurous *101* abenteuerlich
advert **43* Werbung
advertise *38* werben für
advertisement *44* Reklame
advertiser **43* Werbekunde, -firma
advertising *40* Werbung
advice *56* Ratschlag, (guter) Rat, Ratschläge
advisable *71* ratsam
advise *52* beraten
aerosol spray *108* Aerosolspray
afraid: I am ~ that ... *42* leider ...
afraid: I'm ~ not **27* leider nicht
Africa **125* Afrika

after all *98* schließlich doch
after work *18* nach der Arbeit
afterwards *87* nachher, hinterher
against the law *118* illegal, gesetzeswidrig
agency *104* (Reise-)Büro
ages *113* eine Ewigkeit
ages: for ~ *74* ewig, eine Ewigkeit
ago *30* vor
agree *60* übereinstimmen
agriculture *28* Landwirtschaft
ahead of *118* vor
aim *144* Ziel, Absicht
air pollution *139* Luftverschmutzung
air ticket *156* Flugschein
alarm *113* Alarmanlage
alcohol **51* Alkohol
alcoholic **124* Alkoholiker/in
alive *123* lebend, lebendig
all alone *126* ganz allein
all night *130* die ganze Nacht
all sorts of **95* allerlei
all the time *54* stets
all through the year *32* das ganze Jahr über
all-night *128* 24-stündig
allergic *158* allergisch
allow *108* ermöglichen
almost **115* fast
alone *122* allein(e)
already *73* schon, bereits
although **34* obwohl
ambitious *158* ehrgeizig
ambulance **154* Krankenwagen
ambulance service *154* Rettungsdienst
amount *43* Menge
angry *102* böse, ärgerlich
angular *177* eckig
animal lover *46* Tierfreund/in
annoying **105* ärgerlich, lästig
another *13* ein(e) andere(r, s)
answering machine *150* Anrufbeantworter
anxiety *54* Besorgnis
any more *10* weitere(r, s)
anybody *46* jemand
Anything to follow? *47* Und danach?
Anything to start with? *47* Eine Vorspeise?
anyway **34* jedenfalls
anywhere **67* irgendwo
apart from *99* abgesehen von
apartment *37* Wohnung
apologise *154* sich entschuldigen

appeal (to) *89* (jmdm.) gefallen
appear *63* erscheinen
appliance *108* Gerät
applicant *164* Bewerber/in
application *61* Bewerbung
apply (for) *61* sich bewerben (um)
appoint *164* einstellen
appointment **13* Termin
appreciate *151* schätzen
apprentice *84* Auszubildende/r
approximately *99* ungefähr, etwa, circa
arch *177* Bogen
area *38* Gebiet, Bereich
argue *54* sich streiten
armed robbery *71* bewaffneter Raubüberfall
around the clock *31* rund um die Uhr
around: be ~ *113* existieren
arrange *151* arrangieren
arrest *71* festnehmen
arrival *37* Ankunft
arrive *64* ankommen
arrive on the scene *174* erscheinen
art and design *29* Kunst und Design (Fach)
artificial *108* künstlich
as far as **51* so weit
as well **132* auch
as well as *39* ebenso wie, sowohl ... als auch ...
Asian *171* asiatisch
ask for *164* bitten um
ask questions *18* Fragen stellen
ask the way *88* nach dem Weg fragen
asleep *180* schlafend
aspect *150* Aspekt, Seite
aspirin *132* Aspirin, Kopfschmerztablette
assignment *113* Hausaufgabe
association *150; 177* Verband; Assoziation
assure *158* versichern
at all *133* überhaupt
at last *39* endlich
at least *55* wenigstens
at New Year *32* zu Neujahr
at night *71* nachts
at school *46* in der Schule
at the back *88* hinten
at the same time **132* gleichzeitig
at times *89* manchmal

at weekends 9 am Wochenende
at what point 62 an welchem Punkt
at work 20 bei der Arbeit
at your earliest convenience 170 möglichst bald
ate 31 simple past: eat
athletics 85 Leichtathletik
atmosphere 89 Atmosphäre, Stimmung
attach 115 anschließen
attack 179 angreifen
attend 72 versorgen (Verletzte/n)
attention 177 Aufmerksamkeit
attorney *77 Rechtsanwalt, Rechtsanwältin
attract *95 anziehen
attraction 105 Reiz, Attraktion
attractive 35 attraktiv, anziehend
Australia 181 Australien
authority 125 Behörde
avenue *75 Allee, Boulevard
average 173 Durchschnitts-
average: on ~ 104 im Durchschnitt
avocado *51 Avocado
avoid 53 vermeiden
awake 123 wach
award 109 verleihen
awful *59 furchtbar
awkward 54 unbeholfen, ungeschickt

back 87 zurück
back: in the ~ of 45 hinten in
bag 138 Tasche, Tüte
baguette *51 Baguette
baker's 132 Bäckerei
balance 53; 135 Gleichgewicht; Kontostand, Saldo
balanced *53 ausgeglichen
balcony 93 Balkon
ban 119 verbieten
band 85 Band, Gruppe
bank account *134 Bankkonto
bank clerk *134 Bankangestellte/r
Bank Holiday 128 öffentlicher Feiertag
bank manager *134 Bankmanager/in
banker's card *134 Scheckkarte
banking 134 Bankwesen
baseball 76 Baseball
based on 180 basierend auf
basic *53 einfach
Basque 79 Baske/Baskin
bathroom 36 Badezimmer
Bavaria *84 Bayern
Bavarian 79 Bayer/in
beach 30 Strand
beach holiday 35 Strandurlaub
became 63 simple past: become
become 40 werden
bed: in ~ 15 im Bett
bedtime 149 Schlafenszeit
beef 46 Rindfleisch

beefburger 116 Hamburger
began *43 simple past: begin
behalf: on ~ of 171 im Namen von
behave 181 sich verhalten
Belgium 80 Belgien
believe it or not 31 ob Sie es glauben oder nicht
belong to 85 angehören, Mitglied sein in
belt *115 Gürtel
bend 63 Kurve
benefit 185 Vorteil, Nutzen
Best wishes 171 Viele Grüße
bet 79 wetten
bill 116 Rechnung
billion 184 Milliarde
biology 94 Biologie
biro 132 Kuli, Kugelschreiber
biscuit 185 Keks
bit: a ~ *43 ein wenig, etwas
black market 183 Schwarzmarkt
black: in the ~ 135 in den schwarzen Zahlen
blame *60 die Schuld geben
blame: be to ~ 55 schuld sein
blind 186 blind
blow 114 blasen
body language 156 Körpersprache
boil 53 kochen
book 28 bestellen, buchen
book shop *13 Buchhandlung
boot 174 Stiefel
bored 54 gelangweilt
boring 32 langweilig
born 113 geboren
borough 76 Stadtbezirk
borrow *67 sich etwas borgen
boss 162 Chef/in
both ... and 40 sowohl ... als auch
bother *95 stören
bothered: I can't be ~ *143 ich habe einfach keine Lust
bottom 60 Hintern
bought 49 simple past: buy
bouquet *132 (Blumen-)Strauß
boutique 135 Boutique
bowl 117 Schüssel
bracket 18 Klammer
brain 75 Gehirn
brake 69 Bremse
brake 69 bremsen
brave 122 mutig, tapfer
bread roll 140 Brötchen, Semmel
break 113; 159 (los)brechen; überwinden
breakdown 122 (Nerven-)Zusammenbruch
breakfast cereal *51 Frühstücksflocken
breast 172 Brust
bridge *122 Brücke
brief 182 kurz
brilliant 118 großartig, glanzend
bring forward 135 übertragen
bring up 173 aufziehen

brochure *45 Broschüre, Prospekt
broke 113 simple past: break
broken 186 past participle: break
broken home 120 zerrüttete Familienverhältnisse
brought 59 simple past: bring
brown bread *51 Grau-, Mischbrot
building 70 Gebäude
building site *13 Baustelle
built 93 past participle: build
burger 46 Hamburger
burglar *95 Einbrecher/in
bus route 89 Busstrecke
bus service 89 Busverbindung
business 28; 39; 155 Unternehmen; Branche; Anliegen
business studies 22 Betriebswirtschaftslehre (BWL)
business woman 68 Geschäftsfrau
businessman 160 Geschäftsmann
busy 35 belebt
but 77 außer
butter *132 Butter
button *115 Taste, Knopf
by car 93 mit dem Wagen
by the way *13 übrigens
Bye. 20 Tschüs

cab 71 Taxi
cabin attendant 104 Flugbegleiter/in
cable 115 Kabel
caffeine 119 Koffein
calculation 114 Berechnung
calculator 114 Taschenrechner
California 138 Kalifornien
Californian 30 kalifornisch
call *115 Anruf
call 40 nennen
caller 155 Anrufer/in, Besucher/in
calm 104 ruhig
camp 83 zelten, campen
camping holiday 35 Campingurlaub
can 138 Dose
cancer 119 Krebs
candle 181 Kerze
cannabis 183 Haschisch
canteen 84 Kantine
cap 26 Mütze
capital 171; 176 Großbuchstabe; Hauptstadt
captain 85 Kapitän
car 71 (Eisenbahn-)Wagen
car crash 181 Autounfall
car showroom 68 Autosalon
carbohydrates 53 Kohlenhydrate
carbon copy (cc) 170 Durchschrift
card 10 Karte
care 144 Betreuung
care 15 sich kümmern

care for 95 versorgen
career *43 Karriere
careers adviser 61 Berufsberater/in
careers officer 159 Berufsberater/in
careful 71; 96 vorsichtig; sorgfältig
Caribbean 173 Karibik
caring 95 rücksichtsvoll
carpenter 12 Tischler/in
carpet 114 Teppich
carpet beater 114 Teppichklopfer
carry forward 135 übertragen
carry on *143 weitermachen
case 38 Fall
cash 36 einlösen
cash dispenser *134 Geldautomat
cassette 95 Cassette
cat's eye 63 Katzenauge, Rückstrahler
catalogue *43 Katalog
catch 144 einfangen
catch 113 erreichen
category 64 Kategorie, Klasse
caterer 22 Lieferant/in von Fertiggerichten
catering 22 Gastronomie (als Fach)
catering manager 46 Gastronom/in
cause 162 verursachen
cc 98 Kubikzentimeter
centre 6 Mitte, Zentrum
centre of town 37 Stadtzentrum, City
century 63 Jahrhundert
cereal 53 Getreide
certain 151; 182 bestimmt; sicher, gewiß
certainly 75 sicherlich, gewiss
certainty 146 Gewissheit
CFCs 138 FCKWs
chairman 159 Vorsitzender
chairperson 60 Vorsitzende/r
champagne 173 Champagner
chance 85 Gelegenheit, Chance
change 143 (Ver-)Änderung
change 66 umziehen; 69 wechseln
change gear 69 in einen anderen Gang schalten
changeable 125 veränderlich
Channel *34 Ärmelkanal
channel 129 Kanal, Programm
chapter 115 Kapitel
character 104; 180 Original; Charakter, Wesen
charge 99 erheben
chariot 62 Kampfwagen
charity 125 Wohltätigkeitsorganisation
chart 154 Tabelle
chase 72 verfolgen
chat 153 plaudern
cheap 71 billig, günstig
check in 37 (sich) anmelden

chef 22 Chefkoch/köchin
chemical 141 Chemikalie
chemist's 77 Drogerie, Apotheke
cheque book *134 Scheckbuch
chicken 46 Huhn, Hähnchen
childcare 148 Beaufsichtigung von Kindern
childhood 122 Kindheit
choice 47 Auswahl
choose 37 wählen, aussuchen
chose 98 simple past: choose
chosen 105 past participle: choose
Christmas 86 Weihnachten, Weihnachts-
Christmas Day 128 der erste Weihnachtstag
chronological 110 zeitlich
circle 177 Kreis
circulation 171 Zirkulation
city break 83 (kurzer) Städteurlaub
city holiday 35 Städteurlaub
civil war 108 Bürgerkrieg
claim 95; 187 beantragen, beanspruchen; behaupten
class 63 Kategorie
clean 113 putzen
cleaning 94 Saubermachen
cleaning lady 160 Putzfrau
clear 138; 176 klar; durchsichtig
clever 56 begabt
client 105 Kunde, Kundin
climbing club 85 Bergsteiger-/Kletterverein
clip s.th. to s.th. *115 etw. an etw. anklemmen
clockwise 66 im Uhrzeigersinn
closely 177 genau
closing date 164 Einsendeschluss
clothing 125 Kleidung
clue 108 Ahnung
coach 105 Reisebus
coal *143 Kohle
collapse *154 zusammenbrechen
colleague 153 Kollege, Kollegin
collect 140 sammeln
collection 42 Sammlung
college: be at ~ 22 studieren
combination 177 Kombination
combine 178 zusammenfügen
come along 109 erscheinen, auftauchen
come from 7 stammen aus
come off 183 sich entwöhnen von
come on 168 los, komm schon
comedian *125 Komiker/in
comfort 148 Komfort
comfortable 37 bequem
commercial 45 (Fernseh-)Reklame
commercial 170 Handels-
common 100 gewöhnlich
communicate 150 sich verständigen
communication 150 Kommunikation

community 183 Gemeinde
community centre 95 Bürgerzentrum
commute 99 pendeln
company 52 Unternehmen, Firma
company brochure 170 Firmenprospekt
compare 43 vergleichen
comparison 173 Vergleich
compatible (with) 159 passend (zu); (einer Sache) entsprechend
competition 45 Wettbewerb
complain 54 sich beklagen
complete 7 vervollständigen, abschließen
completely 119 völlig
complicated *34 kompliziert
complimentary close 170 Schlussformel
comprehensive 85 Gesamtschule
computer programmer *165 Programmierer/in
computer studies 22 Informatik
computer-based 159 auf Computerbasis
computing 115; 153 Computertechnik; Computerwissenschaft
concentrate 176 sich konzentrieren
concerned about 94 besorgt um
conclude 180 schließen, folgern
conclusion 177 (Schluss-)Folgerung
confident 56 zuversichtlich
congestion 99 Stockungen, Verkehrsstaus
Congratulations! 166 Herzlichen Glückwunsch!
connect 115; 150 einstöpseln, anschließen; verbinden
connected with 95 verbunden mit
connection 104 Anschluss
consideration 61 Erwägung
construction 22; 108 Bau (als Fach); Bauwerk
consumerism 146 Konsumismus
consumerist 129 Verbraucher-
contact 170 Kontakt
contain 108 enthalten
content 53 Gehalt
contribute 183 beitragen
contribution 173 Beitrag
control 146 beherrschen, kontrollieren
control 179 Kontrolle
controlled 180 beherrscht
convenient 37 günstig, praktisch
conversation 21 Gespräch
cooker 86 Herd
cooking 22 Kochen
cool 138 kühlen
cope with 124 fertig werden mit
copy 170 Exemplar
copy 114 fotokopieren

corn 28 Getreide
correct 7 berichtigen
correctly 46 richtig
correspondence 170
  Briefwechsel, Korrespondenz
cosmetics 38 Kosmetika
cost 173 Kosten
cottage 6 kleines Haus
cough 119 Husten
could 62 simple past: can
counsel *124 beraten
counselling 124 Beratung
counsellor *124 Berater/in
count 139 zählen
countryside 30 Landschaft, Land
couple: a ~ of *34 ein paar
course 22 Kurs, Lehrgang
cover 61 behandeln, erfassen
covered 174 zugedeckt
CPU 115 Prozessor
crack 95 (erfolgreich) bekämpfen
crack *95 Crack
crash 123 Unfall
crash helmet *67 Sturzhelm
crash into 69 prallen gegen
craze 184 Fimmel
crazy (about) 15 verrückt (auf)
create 183 (er)schaffen,
  hervorrufen, verursachen
credit 132; 135 Kredit; Haben
credit card 36 Kreditkarte
crime 95 Verbrechen
criminal 176 Verbrecher/in
crisp *51 Chip
critical 127 kritisch
crop 28 Feldfrucht
cross *34 überqueren
crossroads 88 Kreuzung
crowded 31 überfüllt
cup-winning 118 im Pokal
  siegreich
currency 82 Währung
current 164; 170 gegenwärtig;
  aktuell
curriculum vitae 85 Lebenslauf
curve 177 Kurve
customer *13 Kunde, Kundin
cut down 145 fällen
cut off 145 abscheiden
CV 61 Lebenslauf
cycle *115 Rad fahren
Czech 180 Tscheche/Tschechin

dairy food 53 Molkereiprodukt(e)
damage *143 schaden,
  beschädigen
Dane 180 Däne/Dänin
danger 119 Gefahr
dark 176 düster
data handling 148
  Datenverwaltung
date of birth 10 Geburtsdatum
day: a ~ 24 am Tag
day: in those ~s *67 damals
day: the other ~ 54 neulich
day: these ~s *43 heutzutage
deaf 164 taub

deal with 159 lösen
death 118 Tod(esfall)
debit 135 Soll
debt 124 Schulden
decide 37 (sich) entscheiden
decision *43 Entscheidung
defend 62 verteidigen
definitely 101 bestimmt, sicher
definition 100 Definition
degree *60 akademischer Grad
deliberately *60 absichtlich
delicatessen 76
  Feinkost(geschäft)
delicious 83 köstlich, lecker
deliver 129 liefern
demand 162 Forderung
demand: in ~ 39 gefragt
demonstration 84 Vorführung
Denmark 80 Dänemark
dental nurse 95
  Zahnarzthelfer/in
dentist 155 Zahnarzt, Zahnärztin
deodorant 177 Deodorant
department *45 Abteilung
departure gate 77 Flugsteig
depend on 100; 177 sich
  verlassen auf; abhängig sein von
dependent on 120 abhängig von
depending on 164 abhängig von
deposit 143 Pfand
depressed 54 deprimiert
deprived 125 benachteiligt
description 97 Beschreibung
desert 98 Wüste
design 145 entwerfen,
  konstruieren
design *45; *84 Entwurf, Design;
  Konstruktion
design technician *84
  Konstruktionstechniker/in
designer *84; 178
  Konstrukteur/in; Grafiker/in
dessert 47 Nachspeise
destination 99 Fahrtziel,
  Reiseziel
destroy 102 zerstören,
  vernichten
detached house 7
  Einfamilienhaus
detail 93 Einzelheit
detective story *132
  Detektivgeschichte
develop 23 entwickeln
developed country 138
  Industrieland
development 94 Entwicklung
dialogue 13 Dialog
diet 46; 47 Diät, Ernährung;
  Schlankheitskur
diet: be on a ~ 47 eine
  Schlankheitskur machen
dietician 52 Diätberater/in
difference 79 Unterschied
different 16 verschieden
differently 62 anders
difficulty 186 Schwierigkeit
dining room 93 Esszimmer

diploma *124 Diplom
direct 188 direkt
direct (s.o. to somewhere) 92
  (jmdm.) den Weg (zu/nach)
  sagen
direction 62 Richtung
directions 90 Wegbeschreibung
directly 171 direkt
disability 186 Behinderung
disabled *125 behindert
disadvantage 90 Nachteil
disagree 161 nicht einverstanden
  sein
disappear 161 verschwinden
disaster 124 Katastrophe
discount offer 45 Sonderangebot
discover *43 entdecken
discrimination 158
  Diskriminierung
discuss 118 besprechen
disease 53 Krankheit
dish 47 Gericht
dish of the day 47 Tagesgericht
disk 156 Diskette
dislike 153 das, was man nicht
  mag
dislike 151 nicht mögen
dissatisfied 161 unzufrieden
distance 69 Entfernung
district nurse 94
  Gemeindeschwester
divorce 162 sich scheiden lassen
divorced 6 geschieden
do up 69 fest schrauben
do well *45 Erfolg haben
do-it-yourself shop 132
  Baumarkt
do: be to ~ with 154 um …
  gehen
document 114 Dokument
dole: live on the ~ *60
  Arbeitslosengeld bekommen
dose 118 Dosis
double yellow lines 88 absolutes
  Halteverbot
downtown 77 ins Zentrum
dramatically 128 dramatisch
drawing 97 Zeichnung
dream 137 Traum
dream 137 träumen
dress in 174 sich kleiden in
drill 114 Bohrer, Bohrmaschine
drink and drive 66 unter
  Alkoholeinfluss Auto fahren
drinkable 161 trinkbar
drinking water 144 Trinkwasser
drive s.o. crazy 54 jmdn. zur
  Verzweiflung treiben
driving instructor 68
  Fahrlehrer/in
driving licence 67 Führerschein
driving test 66 Fahrprüfung
drop 128 umfallen
drop out 123 sein Studium
  abbrechen
drop-out *122 Aussteiger/in
drove 62 simple past: drive

drug *95 Droge, Rauschgift
drug dealing 71 Drogenhandel
drug-related *124 mit Drogen verbunden
drugstore 77 Drogerie
drunken 128 betrunken
dry out *124 eine Entziehungskur machen
during 71 während
Dutch 78; 180 Holländisch; Holländer (Plural)
dynamite 109 Dynamit

e-mail 156 als elektronische Post senden
early: be ~ (for) 18 (zu) früh kommen
earn 38 verdienen
earphones *115 Kopfhörer
Earth 138 Erde
earthquake 112 Erdbeben
eat out 86 zum Essen gehen
eaten 116 past participle: eat
eccentric 78 exzentrisch
economical 98 wirtschaftlich
economics *29 Volkswirtschaftslehre (VWL)
ecstasy *95 Ecstasy (Droge)
educate *53 erziehen
educated 39 gebildet
educational 85 Ausbildungs-
effect 118 Wirkung, Auswirkung
efficient 79 effizient
effort 166 Mühe, Bemühung
eighties 174 Achtziger
either ... or 116 entweder ... oder
eject *115 auswerfen
elderly 94 älter
electric 114 elektrisch, Elektro-
electrical repair 29 Reparieren von Elektrogeräten
electrician 28 Elektriker/in
electricity 173 Elektrizität, Strom
electronic engineering 164 Elektronik
electronics 168 Elektronik
element 177 Element
elevator 76 Aufzug
else 90; 175 sonst; andere(r, s)
emergency 69 Notfall
emergency service 154 Notdienst
employ 139 einstellen
employee 37 Arbeitnehmer/in
employer 60 Arbeitgeber/in
employment 61 Arbeit, Beschäftigung
enable *115 ermöglichen
enclose 61 beilegen
enclosed 170 (einem Brief) beigelegt
enclosure (enc) 170 Anlage
encourage 129 ermuntern
end *154; 175 beenden; aufhören
end 171 Ende, Schluss
end up (...ing) 78 schließlich ...
end: in the ~ *122 zum Schluss

endless 176 endlos
energy 95 Energie
engaged 154 besetzt
engine 28 Motor
engineer *21 Ingenieur/in, Techniker/in
engineering 22 Ingenieurwesen, Technik (als Fach)
enjoy oneself 65 sich amüsieren
enjoyable 35 angenehm
enormous 106 enorm, gewaltig
enough *51 ausreichend, genug
enquire 154 anfragen
enter 45 teilnehmen an
entertainment 90 Unterhaltung
environment 95 Umwelt
environmental 144 Umwelt-
environmentally 177 Umwelt-, umwelt-
environmentally friendly 143 umweltfreundlich
envy 148 beneiden
equal 39 gleich
equality 186 Gleichberechtigung
especially 45 besonders
estate agent 93 Immobilienmakler/in
estimate 118 schätzen
ethnic 125 ethnisch
European 180 Europäer/in
European Union 80 Europäische Union
even 32 selbst, sogar
even if 98 selbst wenn
even so *53 trotzdem
even though 54 obwohl
event 130 Ereignis
eventually 177 schließlich, endlich
ever 71 jemals
ever since 162 seitdem
everyday 114 alltäglich, Alltags-
exactly *75 exakt, genau
exam 22 Prüfung, Examen
exam: take an ~ *27 eine Prüfung ablegen
examination 186 (Abschluss-) Prüfung
except 98 außer
excited 74 (freudig) aufgeregt
excitement 30 Aufregung
exciting 30 aufregend
exclude 159 ausschließen
excursion 37 Ausflug, Exkursion
Excuse me. 88 Verzeihung.
executive model 68 Modell für Anspruchsvolle
exercise 14 sich bewegen
exercise 184 Übung
exercise: take ~ 15 sich bewegen
existing 180 bestehend
experience 165 Erfahrung
experience 30; 158 erleben; erfahren
experiment 46 Versuch, Experiment
expert 178 Fachmann/frau

explain *60 erklären
exploit *43 ausbeuten
explore *34 erforschen, erkunden
explosion 113 Explosion, Sprengung
explosive 109 Sprengstoff
express 17 ausdrücken
expression 97 Ausdruck
extra 133 zusätzlich, extra
extract 164 Auszug
extreme 172 äußerst, extrem
extremely 174 sehr
eyesight 69 Sehvermögen

face 156 Gesicht
face (s.th.) 99 (einer Sache) ausgesetzt sein
face up to *122 sich abfinden mit
facility 88 Einrichtung
fact 46 Tatsache
factory 60 Fabrik
fail 69 nicht bestehen, durchfallen
faint 94 ohnmächtig werden
fair *53 gerecht
fall in love 126 sich verlieben
fall over 31 hinfallen, umkippen
fall to pieces 172 (in Stücke) zerfallen, zerbrechen
false 7 falsch
familiar 176 vertraut, bekannt
family man 68 Familienvater
family saloon 68 Limousine
family status 10 Familienstand
famous *43 berühmt
fan 114 Ventilator
fantastic 146 fantastisch
far more 31 weit mehr
fare 104; 105 Fahrgast; Fahrpreis
farewell 84 Abschieds-
farm worker 28 Landarbeiter/in
fashion 14 Mode
fashionable 64 modisch, modern
fast food 51 Schnellgerichte
fat 47 Fett
fault: it's your ~ 43 es ist deine/Ihre Schuld
favourite 85 liebste(r, s), Lieblings-
fed up 113 satt
feel 45 sich fühlen
feel about *43 halten von
feeling 17 Gefühl
fell 31 simple past: fall
felt *67 simple past/past participle: feel
female 38 Frau
female 38 weiblich
feminine 177 weiblich
feminism 162 Feminismus
feminist 39 feministisch
fence 145 Zaun
ferry *34 Fähre
fertiliser *144 Dünger
few 38 wenige
few: a ~ 38 ein paar
fiancé 6 Verlobter

fibre 53 Ballaststoffe
field 144 Feld, Acker
fifties 98 Fünfziger
fight 62 kämpfen (mit)
figure 140 Zahl
fill in 45; 135 eintragen; ausfüllen
fill out 71 ausfüllen
film *115 (ver)filmen
final 159 endgültig
finally 63 schließlich
find out 154 ermitteln
find out about 135 sich erkundigen nach
finding 174 Ergebnis
fine 32 in Ordnung
Finland 80 Finnland
Finn 180 Finne/Finnin
fire brigade 154 Feuerwehr
fire officer 26 Feuerwehrmann/frau
fireman 160 Feuerwehrmann
firm 141 Firma
first aid 94 erste Hilfe
firstly 187 zuerst
fit 100 passen (zu)
fitness 146 Fitness, Kondition
fix 140 reparieren
flew *34 simple past: fly
flexible 148 flexibel
flight 36 Flug
flight attendant 13 Flugbegleiter/in
floor 70 Etage
florist's 132 Blumengeschäft
flower *132 Blume
folks *77 Familie
following 36 folgend
fond: be ~ of 19 gern mögen
food mixer 117 Mixer, Mixgerät
food product 52 Nahrungsmittel
food scientist 52 Nahrungswissenschaftler/in
footballer 118 Fußballspieler/in
for ever *53 (für immer und) ewig
for three days 70 seit drei Tagen
forbid 138 verbieten
forbidden 132 verboten
foreign 80 Auslands-, Außen-, ausländisch
forest 176 Wald
forever 184 für immer
forget 70 vergessen
forgotten 108 past participle: forget
form 186 Form, Gestalt
former 183 ehemalig
fortune 109 Vermögen
fought 62 simple past: fight
found *34 simple past: find
foundation 23 Grund-
four-wheel drive 68 Vierradantrieb
frame 170 Rahmen
free time 14 Freizeit
freedom 178 Freiheit

french fries 47 Pommes frites
frequently 16 oft
fresh *51 frisch
fridge 28 Kühlschrank
friendly 177 freundlich
frighten *59 Angst einjagen
frightening 71 furchterregend
fruit tree 144 Obstbaum
frustrated 54 frustriert
frustrating 60 frustrierend
fry 53 braten, frittieren
full-time *124 ganztags
fun 30 Spaß
funeral 181 Beerdigung
further 34 weiter
further education 6 Weiterbildung
furthest 34 am weitesten
future 148 (zu)künftig
future 39 Zukunft

garage 28 Autowerkstatt
gardener 29 Gärtner/in
gas 77; 138 Benzin; Gas
gas station 77 Tankstelle
general 22 allgemein
generation 119 Generation
gentle 94 sanft
gently 96 behutsam, sanft
geography 85 Erdkunde
get around 71 herumkommen
get away with it 58 ungestraft davonkommen
get cross with *67 böse werden über
get in 105 ankommen
get into *29 einsteigen in
get on well with 6 gut auskommen mit
get on with 11 (gut) auskommen mit
get ready (for) 51 Vorbereitungen treffen (für)
get up 27 aufstehen
get used to *53 sich gewöhnen an
gift 45 Geschenk
gimmick 45 Verkaufstrick
give a shampoo 28 (jmdm.) die Haare waschen
give in (to s.o.) 56 (jmdm.) nachgeben
give up 124 aufgeben
give way 66 Vorfahrt einräumen
given 97 past participle: give
glad 32 froh
glamorous 181 glanzvoll
glass 140 Glas
global warming 138 Erderwärmung
glory 176 Herrlichkeit
go ahead 154 anfangen
go for a walk 18 spazieren gehen
go for lunch 112 zu Mittag essen gehen
go jogging 15 joggen
go off 113 losgehen

go on 31; 83 weitergehen; dauern
go online 149 sich ans Internet anschließen
go out with 6 gehen mit
go swimming 18 schwimmen gehen
go window shopping 19 einen Schaufensterbummel machen
go with 61 passen zu
go without 53 verzichten auf
go wrong 31; 98 schief gehen; kaputt gehen
going: be ~ to ... 78 werden
golden 177 golden
golf course 145 Golfplatz
good at 13 geschickt in
Good luck! 20 Viel Glück!
goods 129 Waren
gotten 71 = got (past participle)
government 99 Regierung
grade *77 Note
graduate *60 (Hochschul-) Absolvent/in
graphic design 148 Grafik
graphic designer 29 Grafiker/in
grass 172 Gras
grateful 170 dankbar
great 138 groß
Greece 80 Griechenland
green bean 47 grüne Bohne
greenhouse 145 Gewächshaus
greenhouse gas 138 Treibhausgas
greet 37 begrüßen
grill 53 grillen
grilled 47 gegrillt
grocer's 136 Lebensmittelgeschäft
grow 28; 148 anbauen; wachsen
guarantee 132 garantieren
guess 113 raten
guess: I ~ 71 ich meine
guitar 18 Gitarre
guy 6 Kerl
gym 14 Turnhalle

habit *124; 180 Abhängigkeit; Gewohnheit
hairdressing 28 Friseurhandwerk
hairstyle 28 Frisur
hairstylist 28 Coiffeur/Coiffeuse
half way down 88 auf halbem Weg
hammer *132 Hammer
hand signal 66 Handsignal
hand: on the other ~ 174 andererseits
handlebars 174 Lenkstange
handsome 39 gutaussehend
handwriting *165 Handschrift
handy 89 in der Nähe, praktisch
hang (a)round *77 herumhängen
hang out *77 herumhängen
happen 32 passieren, geschehen
happiness 160 Glück, Zufriedenheit

harass *61* belästigen
hard *22* schwierig
hardworking *164* fleißig
harm: there's no ~ in *55* es kann nichts schaden, wenn man
harmful *141* schädlich
hatchback *68* Hecktürmodell
hate *78* hassen
Have a nice time. *20* Viel Spaß.
have got *14* haben
have to *40* müssen
headmaster *159* Schulleiter, Direktor
headmistress *160* Schulleiterin
headteacher *159* Schulleiter/in
health and safety *60* Arbeitsschutz
health and social care *23* Gesundheits- und Sozialfürsorge (als Fach)
health centre *52* Ärztezentrum
health visitor **155* Sozialarbeiter/in
health-conscious *184* gesundheitsbewusst
heart *108* Herz
heart attack **154* Herzinfarkt, Herzanfall
heating *143* Heizung
heel *188* Absatz
helmet *26* Schutzhelm
helpful *161* hilfreich, hilfsbereit
helpline *154* Telefonseelsorge; Informationsdienst; Notruf
herb *144* (Heil-, Würz-)Kraut
herd **144* Herde
heroin **124* Heroin
hers *38* ihre(r, s)
Hi there. *13* Grüß dich.
hi-fi *86* Hi-Fi-Gerät
hidden *132* versteckt
high school **77* Schule der Sekundarstufe
High Street shop *128* Geschäft in der Innenstadt
high-speed *68* Hochgeschwindigkeits-
highlighted *28* hervorgehoben
Highway Code *69* Straßenverkehrsordnung
hill **102* Hügel,
hire *176* mieten
historic *176* historische(r, s)
history *85* Geschichte
hold the line *154* in der Leitung bleiben
hole *114* Loch
holiday destination *105* Urlaubsziel
holiday: for your ~s *30* in Urlaub
holiday: on ~ *12* auf Urlaub
Holland *180* Holland
home delivery *130* Lieferung ins Haus
home security *95* Sicherheit im Haushalt
home shopping *130* Einkaufen von zu Hause aus

home town *6* Heimatort
homeless **122* obdachlos
homelessness **124* Obdachlosigkeit
honestly **75* ehrlich
hoover *114* Staubsauger
hope **13* hoffen
horrible *86* entsetzlich
horse riding **21* Reiten
horseback: on ~ *99* zu Pferde
horticulture *29* Gartenbau
host *84* Gastgeber-
hot *47* heiß, warm
hotel receptionist *37* Empfangsherr/-dame in einem Hotel
house husband *68* Hausmann
household *138* Haushalts-
housework *160* Hausarbeit
housing *125* Häuser, Wohnungen
How about …? *20* Wie wär's mit …?
How are you doing? *133* Wie geht's?
How do you like …? *20* Wie gefällt dir/Ihnen …?
however *38* doch, jedoch, aber
hubcap *69* Radkappe
huge *136* riesig
human *140* menschlich
humankind *159* Menschheit
Hungarian *180* Ungar/in
hurry up *93* sich beeilen
hurt *66* verletzen
hysterical *119* hysterisch

I'll *78* = I will
ice cream *53* Speiseeis
ideal *86* ideal
identification **134* Ausweispapiere
if *30* falls
if you like **84* wenn Sie so wollen
ignore *96* ignorieren
illegal *118* illegal
illness *120* Krankheit
illustrate *143* illustrieren, veranschaulichen
illustration *150* Illustrierung
image *180* Bild, Vorstellung
imaginative *164* fantasievoll
imagine *77* sich vorstellen
immediately *160* sofort, umgehend
impatient *94* ungeduldig
implication *148* Auswirkung
impolite *161* unhöflich
important *40* wichtig
impossible **102* unmöglich
impress *188* beeindrucken
impressed *170* beeindruckt
impression *165* Eindruck
improve *99* verbessern
inch **67* Inch, Zoll
include *173* einbeziehen
including *173* einschließlich
income *173* Einkommen

incoming *157* ankommend
incompatible *159* nicht passend
incorrect *180* falsch, unrichtig
increase *129* erweitern
increase *183* Zunahme
increasingly *172* zunehmend
incredibly **34* unglaublich
independent *75* unabhängig
independently *104* unabhängig
Indian *116* indisch
individual *180* Individuum
inexpensive *109* preiswert
influence *136* beeinflussen
information system *23* Informationssystem
information technology *23* Informatik (als Fach)
ingredient *117* Zutat
initial *171* Initiale
injured *186* verletzt
injury *186* Verletzung
innovation *108* Neuerung
insert *134* einfügen
inside *88* innen
inside address *170* Innenadresse
inspect *170* sich ansehen
install *115* installieren
instant coffee *108* Pulverkaffee
instantly *172* sofort
instead of *18* anstatt
institution *186* Institution
instruction *102* Anweisung
instrument *170* Instrument
intelligent *39* intelligent
intend *151* beabsichtigen
interest *182* Interesse
interested in *38* interessiert an
interesting **29* interessant
intermediate *23* Mittel-
international **13* international
interrupt *113* unterbrechen
interview *165* ein Vorstellungsgespräch führen mit
interview **13* Vorstellungsgespräch
interviewer *71* Interviewer/in
into the middle *113* in die Mitte
introduce *63* einführen
introduce **21* vorstellen
introduction *84* Einleitung, Einführung
intrude on *182* sich eindrängen in
invent *63* erfinden
invention *108* Erfindung
invite *20* einladen
involve **84; 148* mit sich bringen; einschließen
involved: be ~ in *123* beteiligt sein, verwickelt sein in
Irish: the ~ *79* die Iren
iron *108* Bügeleisen
ironing: do the ~ *112* bügeln
island *103* Insel
it's all about … *144* es ist eine Frage von
It's all gone. *116* Es ist alle.
Italian *78; 180* Italienisch; Italiener/in

Italian 78 italienisch
italics 42 Kursivschrift
Italy 80 Italien

jack 69 Wagenheber
Japan 46 Japan
Japanese 47 japanisch
job application 167 Stellenbewerbung
job interview 42 Vorstellungsgespräch
job market 125 Arbeitsmarkt
join 20; 164 sich anschließen, mitgehen; anfangen bei
journalist 160 Journalist/in
journey 18 Reise, Fahrt
joy 183 Freude
jump off *102 abspringen
junction 63 Kreuzung, Abfahrt
just like 79 genau wie
just now 51 im Moment

keen: be ~ on (someone) 14 scharf auf jmdn. sein, jmdn. sehr gern mögen
keen: be ~ on (something) 15 etw. sehr gern mögen
keep 113 halten; unterhalten
keep fit 147 Fitnesstraining
keep fit 14 fit bleiben, in Form bleiben
keep going 156 aufrechterhalten
keep s.o. away from s.th. 183 jmdn. von etw. fernhalten
keep s.o. happy *43 jmdn. glücklich machen
keep waiting 154 warten lassen
keep ...ing 60 ständig ...
kept 62 simple past: **keep**
key in 129 eingeben
keyboard 115 Tastatur
kind 95 Art
kiss 133 Kuss
knew 50 simple past: **know**
knife wound 71 Schnitt-/Stichwunde
knowledge 23 Wissen, Kenntnis(se)
kph 98 km/h (Kilometer pro Stunde)

lake 30 (Binnen-)See
land 176 Land
land 81 landen
landscape 145 Landschaft
landscape contractor 145 Gartengestalter/in
lane 63 Spur
last 107 dauern
last 188 dauern
late night shopping 130 Einkaufen spät am Abend
latest 96 neueste(r, s)
Latin 180 südländisch
laugh at 54 lachen über, auslachen
laughable 162 lächerlich

launderette 88 Waschsalon
law 118, 128 Gesetz
lawyer *77 Rechtsanwalt, Rechtsanwältin
layout 171 Layout
lazy 15 faul
leaflet 95 Broschüre, Prospekt
leak 28 undichte Stelle, Leck
lean 53 fettarm
learner driver 67 Fahrschüler/in
learnt *82; 186 simple past/past participle: **learn**
leather 174 Leder
leave 106 abfliegen
leave out 61 auslassen
lecture 75 Vorlesung
led 183 simple past: **lead**
left: have ~ 74 noch haben
left: on the ~ 11 auf der linken Seite
leg: pull s.o.'s ~ 62 jmdn. auf den Arm nehmen
legal 119 gesetzlich, legal
legend 182 Legende
leisure activity *82 Freizeitbeschäftigung
leisure centre 88 Freizeitzentrum
less and less 60 immer weniger
Let me see. 88 Lassen Sie mich mal überlegen.
let s.o. do s.th. 57 jmdn. etw. tun lassen (= erlauben)
letter box 45 Briefkasten
letter of application 61 Bewerbungsschreiben
letterhead 170 Briefkopf
lettuce *51 Kopfsalat
level 23 Stufe
liberal 119 liberal
liberty 70 Freiheit
library 88 Bücherei, Bibliothek
lie 142; *165 liegen; lügen
life skill 183 lebenswichtige Fähigkeit
lifestyle 146 Lebensstil
light 66; 122 Ampel; Licht
light 66 Scheinwerfer
like 153 das, was man mag
like it or not 45 ob man will oder nicht
likeable 161 sympathisch
likely 62 wahrscheinlich
line 154; 170 (Telefon-)Leitung; Produktgruppe
line: in ~ with 63 in Übereinstimmung mit
lip 172 Lippe
list 71 auflisten
live up to s.th. 146 etw. gerecht werden
lively 32 lebendig, rege, lebhaft
living room 87 Wohnzimmer
loads of 79 eine ganze Menge
loaf *51 Brotlaib
loan *134 Kredit, Darlehen
local 37 örtlich

local time *105 Ortszeit
lonely 30 einsam
long distance 156 über eine große Entfernung hinweg
long for 156 sich sehnen nach
long-term 118 langfristig
longer: no ~ 41 nicht länger
look 120 aussehen
look after 37; 150 sich kümmern um; betreuen, aufpassen auf
Look after yourself. 44 Pass gut auf dich auf.
look at *75 sich anschauen
look forward to 61 sich freuen auf
look like 14 (jmdm./etw.) ähnlich sehen
look up 45 nachschlagen
look: it ~s like *21 es sieht aus, als ob
looks 39 Aussehen
lose weight 42 abnehmen
lost 124 past participle: **lose**
lot: a whole ~ *77 viel
lots of *34 viele
lottery 102 Lotterie
loud 70 laut
love to *75 liebe Grüße an
love: be in ~ with 74 lieben, verliebt sein in
lovely 86 schön, hübsch, reizend
low 55 elend
low-calorie 47 mit wenig Kalorien
lower 69 herunterlassen
loyal 164 treu
Ltd. 164 ≈ GmbH
luckily *122 glücklicherweise
lunch: have ~ 46 zu Mittag essen
lunchtime 104 Mittagszeit, Mittagspause
Luxembourg 80 Luxemburg
luxury 135 Luxus
luxury item 103 Luxusgut

machine 99; 184 Maschine; Gerät
machine gun 108 Maschinengewehr
machinery 144 Maschinen
mad 144 wahnsinnig
madam 77 gnädige Frau
mail order catalogue 129 Versandhauskatalog
mail shot 45 Postwurfsendung
mailbag 54 Posttasche
mailbox 77 Briefkasten
main 48 Haupt-
main dish *51 Hauptgericht
mainly *45 hauptsächlich
major 108 Haupt-, bedeutend
make a booking 37 eine Reservierung vornehmen
make friends with 188 sich anfreunden mit
make it 31 es schaffen
make s.o. do s.th. 57 jmdn. etw. tun lassen (= veranlassen)

make sure *69* sich vergewissern
make the first move *56* den ersten Schritt tun
make up *80* bilden
make ... better *50* wiedergutmachen
male *38* Mann
male *38* männlich
mall **77* überdachtes Einkaufszentrum
manage *148* zurechtkommen mit, bewältigen
management *42* Management, Führung
managing director *84* Geschäftsführer/in
mankind *159* Menschheit
manufacture *109* herstellen
manufacturer *39* Hersteller/in, Produzent/in
map *80* Landkarte
margarine *117* Margarine
mark *63* markieren
mark *54* Note
market *39* vermarkten
marriage *173* Ehe, Hochzeit
married *10* verheiratet
married: get ~ *147* heiraten
marry *58* heiraten
mask *172* Maske
match (with) *11* zusammenfügen
math **77* Mathe(matik)
maths **29* Mathe(matik)
matter: no ~ ... **122* egal ...
may not be *30* sind zwar nicht
meal *48* Essen, Mahlzeit
mean *32; *43; 71* bedeuten; meinen, sagen wollen; heißen
meaning *81* Bedeutung, Sinn
mechanic *12* Mechaniker/in
mechanical *159* mechanisch
media job **43* Medienarbeit
medicine **132* Medikament
meet *59* kennen lernen
meet: I'd like you to ~ ... *20* ich möchte dich/Sie bekannt machen mit ...
meeting *151* Besprechung, Sitzung
meeting point **102* Treffpunkt
member *93* Mitglied
memo *157* Notiz, Aktennotiz
mention *185* erwähnen, nennen
menu *46* Speisekarte
message **75* Mitteilung, Nachricht
metal *140* Metall
methane *138* Methan
method *129* Methode, Verfahren
micro-light *99* superleicht
microfilm **102* Mikrofilm
microwave *108* Mikrowellenherd
mid- *175* Mittel-
might **95* könnte
milkman *133* Milchmann
millionaire *63* Millionär/in
min. *37* Min.

mind *14* etw. gegen etw. haben
mind: have in ~ *68* denken an
mine *41* meine(r, s)
mini- *132* Mini-
minority *125* Minderheit
mirror *55* Spiegel
miserable *122* unglücklich, elend
miss *31; 88* vermissen; verfehlen
missing *45* fehlend
mission *102* Auftrag
mistake *61* Fehler
misunderstand *156* missverstehen
mix *117* verrühren, mixen
mixing bowl *117* Rührschüssel
mixture *144* Mischung
mobile phone *150* Mobiltelefon, Handy
model *38; 61; 68* Mannequin, Dressman; Muster; Modell
model *38* vorführen
modelling job *38* Auftrag als Mannequin/Dressman
modelling work *39* Arbeit als Mannequin/Dressman
modern *156* modern
monitor *115* Monitor
monument *176* Denkmal, Monument
moon *102* Mond
more and more **43* immer mehr
more like it **77* wahrscheinlicher
more or less *89* mehr oder weniger
morning: in the ~ *18* morgens
mostly *78* hauptsächlich, größtenteils
mother-in-law *10* Schwiegermutter
motor car *64* Auto
motorbike **102* Motorrad
motoring *68* Autofahren
motorist *95* Autofahrer/in
motorway **67* Autobahn
mountain *30* Berg
mouse *115* Maus
move *89* umziehen
movement *39* Bewegung
movie **77* Spielfilm
mph *66* = miles per hour – Meilen pro Stunde
Ms *170* Frau/Fräulein
multi-storey car park *88* Parkhaus
multiple choice *159* mit Auswahlantworten
murder *176* ermorden
murder *71* Mord
murderer *72* Mörder
muscle *14* Muskel
mysterious *188* geheimnisvoll

nail **132* Nagel
name *140* nennen
nanny *78* Kindermädchen
nation *180* Nation
national *22* National-, Staats-

national park *30* Nationalpark
nationality *78* (Menschen einer bestimmten) Staatsangehörigkeit
natural *188* natürlich, echt
nature *183* Natur
near *37* nahe
necessary *66* nötig, notwendig
necessity *135* Notwendigkeit
need *95* Bedürfnis
need *23* brauchen, benötigen
needle *94* Nadel
neither *159* auch nicht
nervous *94* nervös
nervously *187* nervös
Netherlands: The ~ *80* die Niederlande
New Yorker *106* New-Yorker/in
news **75* Neuigkeiten
newsagent *88* Zeitungshändler
nice *31* schön
Nice meeting you. *20* Nett, Sie kennenzulernen.
night life *37* Nachtleben
nightclub *146* Nachtklub
nightmare **67* Alptraum
nineties *174* Neunziger
no. *37* Nr.
nobody *31* niemand
noise *152* Lärm; Geräusch
noisy *37* laut, geräuschvoll, lärmend
normally *27* normalerweise
Northern Ireland *80* Nordirland
not at all **43* überhaupt nicht
not even ... *89* nicht einmal ...
not just *39* nicht nur
not only ... but also *38* nicht nur ..., sondern auch
not too *47* nicht besonders
note *186* Notiz
notes *102* Notizen
notice *166* bemerken
nowadays *39* heutzutage
nowhere *124* nirgends, nirgendwo
nuclear power **143* Atomkraft
nurse *12* Krankenschwester, Krankenpfleger/in
nursery nurse *12* Kindergärtnerin
nut **51; 69* Nuss; Schraubenmutter
nylon *108* Nylon

obsession *184* fixe Idee
obvious *172* offensichtlich, deutlich
obviously *183* offensichtlich
occupational therapist *23* Beschäftigungstherapeut/in
odd one out *86* etwas, das nicht dazugehört
of 16 and over *23* ab 16 Jahren
of course *39* natürlich
of your age *55* deines/Ihres Alters
of your own *7* eigene(r, s)

off *122* aus
off *136* ... Rabatt
off-road vehicle *68* Geländewagen
off: be ~ *20* wegfahren
offer: on ~ *176* im Angebot
office administration *22*
 Büroorganisation
office administrator *164*
 Büroleiter/in
office development *145*
 Bürogelände
office equipment *150*
 Büroartikel, Büroeinrichtung
office politics *148* Büropolitik
office worker *158*
 Büroangestellte/r
old age *119* (hohes) Alter
old-fashioned *129* altmodisch
on and on *78* immer weiter
one way ticket *77* einfache
 Fahrkarte
one-year *22* einjährig
one: the ~ *21* der/die/dasjenige
ones: the ~ *56* diejenigen
onto *186* auf
onto *96* auf (+ Akk.)
open *134* eröffnen
open late *128* spät aufbleiben
opening times *130*
 Öffnungszeiten
opportunity *38* Gelegenheit,
 Chance
opposite *62* entgegengesetzt
opposite *32* Gegenteil
optical *170* optisch
optician *88* Optiker/in
optimistic *122* optimistisch
or so *71* so ungefähr
order *63; 69; 129* Befehl;
 Reihenfolge; Bestellung
order *47* bestellen
order: take ~s *52* die Bestellung
 aufnehmen
ordinary-looking *39*
 durchschnittlich aussehend
organic *141* organisch
organisation *125* Organisation
organise *125* organisieren
ostrich *46* Strauß (Vogel)
others *94* andere
otherwise *125* sonst
ours *39* unsere(r, s)
out of work *11* arbeitslos
outdoor *105* gern im Freien
outdoor pursuit *85* Aktivitäten
 im Freien
outline *124* umreißen, skizzieren
outside *90* außerhalb von
over *146* vorbei
over here *19; 70* herüber; hier,
 hierzulande
over there *21* dort drüben
overalls *26* Overall
overdose *118* Überdosis
overdraft *134*
 Kontoüberziehung
overlook *159* übersehen

overseas aid *125*
 Entwicklungshilfe
overtake *63* überholen
overtime *160* Überstunden
overweight *15* übergewichtig
own *144* besitzen
own: on his ~ *6* alleine

pace *63* Schritt
package *177* Verpackung
packaging *138* Verpackung
packet *131* Päckchen, Packung,
 Schachtel, Tüte
paid *101* conditional: pay
pain: be a ~ *89*
 lästig/ärgerlich/schwierig sein
pair: in ~s *28* paarweise
Pakistani *60* Pakistani
palm tree *176* Palme
paradise *176* Paradies
parcel *156* Paket, Päckchen
parking space *103* Parkplatz,
 Parklücke
part *115* Teil
part-time *13* Teilzeit-
particular *125* besondere(r,s),
 bestimmte(r, s)
particular: in ~ *174* insbesondere
particularly *178* besonders
pass *66; 135* bestehen;
 überreichen
passionate *79* leidenschaftlich
passport *36* Reisepass
password *102* Kennwort
past *38* Vergangenheit
pasta *47* Nudeln
path *145* (Fuß-)Weg
patient *94* geduldig
patient *155* Patient/in
patrol car *71* Streifenwagen
pavement *77* Bürgersteig
pay attention to *113* beachten
pay cheque *134* Lohn-
 /Gehaltsüberweisung
pay in *135* einzahlen
pay out *135* auszahlen
PC *68* ≈ Wachtmeister
peace *93* Frieden, Ruhe
peaceful *37* friedlich
peach *136* Pfirsich
peak *176* Gipfel
penfriend *87* Brieffreund/in
penicillin *132* Penizillin
pension *60* Rente, Pension
per *37* pro, per
per pro (pp) *170* im Auftrag (i.A.)
percentage *128* Prozentsatz
perfect *86* vollkommen, perfekt
performance *81* Veranstaltung
perfume *178* Parfüm
period *180* Zeit(raum)
permanent *144* dauerhaft
personal *178* persönlich
personal tutor *85* Tutor
personality *188* Persönlichkeit
persuade *45* überzeugen,
 überreden

pesticide *144* Pestizid
pet *132* Haustier
petrol *77* Benzin
petrol station *91* Tankstelle
petrol-driven *132* mit
 Benzinmotor
photo booth *88* Fotokabine
photocopier *114* Fotokopierer
photocopy *153* fotokopieren
photograph *16* Foto
photographer *43* Fotograf/in
photography *132* Fotografie
piano *15* Klavier
pick on *54* kritisieren
pick out *113* herausnehmen
pick up *139; *154* aufheben; (mit
 dem Auto) abholen
pickpocket *71* Taschendieb
pie *47* Pastete
pity: That's a ~. *116* Das ist
 schade.
pizza *139* Pizza
place *63* setzen, stellen
place of work *12* Arbeitsstelle
place to live *10* Wohnort
place: in the first ~ *119* von
 vornherein
plain *39* alltäglich, nicht schön
planet *141* Planet
plant *84; *132* Fabrik; Pflanze
plastic *138* Kunststoff
plastic surgery *172* plastische
 Chirurgie
plate *67* Nummernschild
platform *102* Bahnsteig, Gleis
play *70* Theaterstück
player *21* Spieler/in
pleasant *102* angenehm
Pleased to meet you. *13* Es freut
 mich, Sie kennen zu lernen.
plug *115* Stecker
plug in *115* einstöpseln,
 anschließen
plumber *28* Installateur/in,
 Klempner/in
point *163* Punkt
point of view *55* Standpunkt
point: get to the ~ *188* auf den
 Punkt kommen
poisonous *46* giftig
police force *82* Polizei(truppe)
police officer *26* Polizeibeamte/r
policy *183* (praktische) Politik
polite *67* höflich
politician *118* Politiker/in
pollute *141* verschmutzen,
 verunreinigen
pollution *99*
 Umweltverschmutzung
poor *124; *143* arm; schlecht
pop star *160* Schlagersänger/in
popular *40* beliebt, populär
Portuguese *82* Portugiesisch
position *42* Stelle
positive *60* positiv
possibility *122* Möglichkeit
possible *32* möglich, denkbar

possibly 38 möglicherweise
post box 88 Briefkasten
post office 88 Postamt
postbox 77 Briefkasten
postcard 74 Postkarte
poverty *124 Armut
power 177 Macht
practical 22 praktisch, praxisorientiert
practically 71 fast
practice 10 Übung
practise 13 üben
prediction 146 Vorhersage
prefer 86 vorziehen
pregnant 186 schwanger
prepare oneself 187 sich vorbereiten
president 74 Präsident/in
press *115 drücken (auf)
press 146 Presse
pressure 118 Druck
pretty 55 ziemlich
price 32 (Kauf-)Preis
price list 170 Preisliste
price: for the same ~ 136 zum gleichen Preis
print 177 drucken
prison officer 95 Gefängnisaufseher/in
private 145 privat, Privat-
prize 109 Preis
prize-giving 84 Preisverleihung
probable 64 wahrscheinlich
probably 30 wahrscheinlich
problem page 127 Problemseite
problematic 124 problematisch
produce 138 produzieren
product 38 Produkt, Erzeugnis
production 175 Produktion, Herstellung
production-line *84 Fertigungsstraße
profit *144 Profit, Gewinn
programme 176 Sendung
progress: in ~ 108 im Gange
project *84 Projekt
project work 186 Projektarbeit
promise 151 versprechen
promising 120 vielversprechend
properly 69 richtig, korrekt
protect 62 schützen
protein 53 Protein
protest 141 protestieren
provide 95 zur Verfügung stellen
psychiatric 124 psychiatrisch
psychological 124 psychologisch
psychometric test 159 psychometrischer Test
public 182 Öffentlichkeit
public transport 99 öffentliche Verkehrsmittel
public: in ~ 172 in der Öffentlichkeit
publicity campaign *45 Werbekampagne
pull s.o.'s leg 62 jmdn. auf den Arm nehmen

punctuation 171 Zeichensetzung
pupil 46 Schüler/in
purpose *125 Zweck, Absicht
push 158 drängen
put down *51 niederschreiben
put in 114 einsetzen
put s.o. off s.th. *53 jmdm. die Lust an etw. nehmen
put through 154 verbinden

qualification 22 Qualifikation
qualified 46 ausgebildet
quality 94; 136 Eigenschaft; Qualität
quality control *84 Qualitätskontrolle
questionnaire 159 Fragebogen
quiet 35 still, ruhig
quiet 93 Stille
quite 55 völlig
quite a lot 70 ziemlich viel
quiz 108 Quiz

race 158 Rasse
racial discrimination 60 Rassendiskriminierung
racing driver 68 Rennfahrer/in
radio-controlled 84 ferngesteuert
rail service 89 Zugverbindung
railway station 92 Bahnhof
raincoat 26 Regenmantel
rainfall 144 Regen
rainforest 139 Regenwald
raise *125 auftreiben
ran 122 simple past: run
rang 111 simple past: ring
range 170 Sortiment
range (of) 159 Auswahl (an)
ranging from ... to 177 von ... bis
rarely 15 selten
rat 60 Ratte
rate 157 Tarif
rather 80 ziemlich
rather than 51 lieber als, anstatt
reach 102 erreichen
reaction 119 Reaktion
reader 171 Leser/in
reading glasses 170 Lesebrille
Ready? 108 Fertig?
realise 57 erkennen, feststellen
really *27; 31 sehr; unbedingt
Really? 13 Tatsächlich?
reason: for no ~ 118 grundlos
reason: for this ~ 38 aus diesem Grund
reasonable 55 vernünftig
rebuild 125 wieder aufbauen
receive *115 empfangen
recent 173 letzte(r, s), jüngste(r, s)
recently 71 neulich, in letzter Zeit
reception 154 Empfang
receptionist 12 Empfangschef, -dame
recipient 170 Empfänger/in
recognise 16 erkennen

record *115; 118 aufnehmen; aufzeichnen, belegen
rectangle 63 Rechteck
recycle 138 recyceln
recycling 140 Recycling
red: in the ~ 135 in den roten Zahlen
reduce 138 reduzieren
reduction 141 Reduzierung
redundancy 60 Entlassung (wegen Überkapazität)
redundant 143 arbeitslos
redwood 74 Redwood (Baum)
refer to 140; 170 sich beziehen auf; hinweisen auf
referee 85 Referenz
reference (ref) 170 Zeichen
refrigerator 140 Kühlschrank
region 176 Gebiet, Gegend
regret 119 bereuen
relationship 124 Beziehung, Verhältnis
relative 186 Verwandte/r
relax 176 sich entspannen
reliable 98 zuverlässig
relieve 120 lindern
religion 158 Religion, Glaube
remain 104 bleiben
remember 59 denken an
rent 6 mieten
repair 12 reparieren
repeat 118 wiederholen
rephrase 159 anders ausdrücken
replace 13 ersetzen
reply 55 Antwort
reply 55 antworten
report 71 Bericht
representative 170 Vertreter/in
Republic of Ireland 80 Republik Irland
request 155 Bitte
request 154 bitten
required 164 verlangt, gefordert
rescue 72 retten
reservation 36 Reservierung
reserved 180 zurückhaltend
respond to 163 reagieren auf
response 155 Antwort
responsibility 12 Aufgabe
responsible *45 verantwortlich
rest *45 Rest
result 87 Ergebnis; Note
return *36 Rückfahrkarte
return the call 155 zurückrufen
return ticket 77 Rückfahrkarte
reuse 138 wieder verwenden
reverse 69 zurücksetzen, rückwärts fahren
review 8 Wiederholung, Rückblick
revise 22 wiederholen
revision exercise 86 Wiederholungsübung
revolution 128 Revolution
rewind *115 zurückspulen
rewrite 11 umschreiben
rich 104 reich, wohlhabend

ride: take a ~ *71* eine Fahrt unternehmen
right *59* Recht
right now *6* zur Zeit
right-handed *62* rechtshändig
Right. *102* Gut.
right: on the ~ *11* auf der rechten Seite
ring *106* anrufen
rival *174* Rivale, Rivalin
road sign *63* Verkehrszeichen
road: on the ~ *62* unterwegs
rob *176* berauben
rode *62* simple past: ride
rollerblade *31* Inline-Skates fahren
rollerblades *174* Inline-Skates
Roman *63* Römer/in
Roman *62* römisch
romance *149* Romanze, Liebe(sgeschichte)
romantic *30* romantisch
roof *149* Dach
round here *88* hier in der Nähe
round the world flight *173* Flug rund um die Welt
round trip ticket *77* Rückfahrkarte
roundabout *66* Kreisverkehr, Kreisel
rubbish *53* Mist
rude *173* unhöflich
run *28* leiten, führen
run away *122* weglaufen
rush hour *152* Hauptverkehrszeit
Russia *82* Russland
Russian *180* Russe/Russin

salary *135* Gehalt
salesperson *68* Verkäufer/in
salmon *47* Lachs
salon *28* Friseursalon
salutation *170* Anrede
same day delivery *132* Lieferung am selben Tag
same: the ~ *56* gleich
sandy *176* sandig
satisfaction *104* Befriedigung
satisfied *90* zufrieden
satisfy *124* befriedigen
satisfying *125* befriedigend
sauna *157* Sauna
save *51; *122* sparen; retten
save up *98* sparen
saw *145* Säge
say *51* sagen wir ...
Scandinavian *180* skandinavisch
scare *46* Schrecken
scenery *30* Landschaft
schedule *81* Programm
scheme *125* Plan, Programm
school lunch *51* Mittagessen in der Schule
science *85* Naturwissenschaften
scientist *52* (Natur-)Wissenschaftler/in
scooter *143* (Motor-)Roller

score *109* Spielstand
Scotland *30* Schottland
Scottish *79* schottisch
screen *129* Bildschirm
screw *114* Schraube
screwdriver *114* Schraubenzieher
scribe *114* Schreiber
season *118* Saison
seat *105* Sitz
seatbelt *66* Sicherheitsgurt
second *96* Sekunde
secondary school *77* Schule der Sekundarstufe
secondly *188* zweitens
secret *58* Geheimnis
secret agent *102* Geheimagent/in
secretarial *61* Sekretariats-
secretary *12* Sekretär/in
secure *95* sicher, fest
seed *145* Saat
seem *34* scheinen
select *160* auswählen
self-employed *150* selbständig
self: to ~ *135* an selbst
sender *171* Absender
senior *162* leitend/höher
sense of humour *70* Sinn für Humor
sensitive *160* empfindlich
sent *156; 171* simple past/past participle: send
separated *6* getrennt
sergeant *71* ≈ Polizeimeister/in
serious *99* schlimm, schwer, ernst
seriously: take ~ *138* ernst nehmen
serve *12* bedienen; servieren
service *58* Bedienung
set up *111; 115; 156* gründen; aufbauen; installieren
set: be ~ *176* spielen
settled *163* abgemacht
seventies *174* Siebziger
several *75* einige, mehrere
sewing machine *108* Nähmaschine
sex education *95* sexuelle Aufklärung
sex object *39* Sexobjekt
sexism *38* Sexismus
sexist *39* sexistisch
sexual harassment *60* sexuelle Belästigung
sexually *61* sexuell
shall *163* sollen
shame: it was a ~ *75* schade
shampoo and cut *28* waschen und schneiden
shape *172* Form
share *113* teilen
sharp *177* spitz
shelter *122* Unterkunft
shepherd's pie *47* Auflauf aus Hackfleisch und Kartoffelbrei
shock *181* erschüttern

shoot *72* (an)schießen, erschießen
shop *128* einkaufen
shop assistant *12* Verkäufer/in
shopfloor *84* Werkstatt, Produktion(sstätte)
shopping arcade *77* Einkaufspassage
shopping hours *128* Ladenöffnungszeiten
should *54* sollten
shout *180* (laut) rufen, schreien
shower: have a ~ *113* duschen
shown *83* past participle: show
showroom *136* Ausstellungsraum
shut *128* zumachen
shy *54* schüchtern, scheu
sidewalk *77* Bürgersteig
sign *96; 172* (Verkehrs)Zeichen; (An)zeichen
sign *171* unterzeichnen, unterschreiben
signal *69* blinken
signature *170* Unterschrift
silicon chip *108* Siliziumchip
silly *125* töricht, albern
similar *28* ähnlich
simple *37* einfach, schlicht
since *70* seit(dem)
single *36* Einzelzimmer
single *6* ledig
single ticket *77* einfache Fahrkarte
situation *10* Situation, Lage
sixties *174* Sechziger
ski *30* Ski laufen
skier *67* Skiläufer/in
skiing holiday *83* Skiurlaub
skill *23* Fertigkeit, Fähigkeit
skin *172* Haut
skirt *188* Rock
skyline *76* Silhouette, Skyline
sleeping tablet *118* Schlaftablette
slim *185* schlank
slogan *44* Werbespruch, Slogan
slowly *67* langsam
smart *108* intelligent
smoking *53* Rauchen
smooth *44* glatt
snack food *45* Häppchen
snobbish *80* snobistisch, versnobt
snobby *79* snobistisch, versnobt
snowy *176* verschneit
so far *71* bisher
soap *132* Seife
soap powder *132* Seifenpulver
Social Services *155* Sozialamt
socialise *20* sich mit Leuten unterhalten
society *118* Gesellschaft
soft drink *51* alkoholfreies Getränk
soft drug *119* weiche Droge
software *115* Computerprogramm(e)
solar power *142* Sonnenkraft
sold *41* simple past: sell

solution *100* Lösung
solve *99* lösen
someday *77* eines Tages
somewhere *89* irgendwohin
sophisticated *129* hochentwickelt
Sorry! *108* Tut mir leid!
sorry: I'm ~ *20* es tut mir leid
sort *13* Art, Sorte
sort out *158* klären
sort: that ~ of thing *13* derlei
sound *69* Geräusch
sound *29* sich anhören
sound effect *113* Geräuscheffekt
soup *116* Suppe
South Africa *181* Südafrika
southern *6* Süd-
spaceship *102* Raumschiff
Spain *79* Spanien
Spanish *78* Spanisch
Spanish: the ~ *180* die Spanier
spare time *19* Freizeit, freie Zeit
speak: this is … ~ing *37* hier spricht …
speaker *53* Sprecher/in
special *67* besondere(r, s)
specialist *177* Fachmann/Frau
specialist *130* spezial, Fach-
speed freak *67* Raser
speed limit *69* Geschwindigkeitsbegrenzung
spell *154* buchstabieren
spelling *153* Rechtschreibung
spend *31; 39* verbringen; ausgeben
spent *31* simple past: spend
split up *154* sich voneinander trennen
spoil *122* verwöhnen
sponsorship *45* finanzielle Unterstützung
sports car *68* Sportwagen
sports event *45* Sportereignis
sports holiday *30* Sporturlaub
spy *102* Spion/in
squash court *89* Squashplatz
stadium *76* Stadion
stairs *185* Treppe
star *102* Stern
start *69; 81* starten, anlassen; anfangen, beginnen
start: for a ~ *71* zunächst einmal
starter *47* Vorspeise
statement of account *134* Kontoauszug
States: the ~ *75* die Staaten
statistics *180* Statistiken
statue *70* Statue
stay in *19* zu Hause bleiben
stay with it *166* nicht aufgeben
stepfather *6* Stiefvater
stepmother *10* Stiefmutter
stereotype *78* Stereotyp
stereotyped *180* stereotyp
stomach *172* Magen
stone *63* Stein
stop *46; 53* aufhören; verhindern
store *128* Laden, Geschäft

store clerk *77* Verkäufer/in
storm *113* Unwetter, Gewitter
strange *47* fremdartig, seltsam
stranger *178* Fremde/r
street map *93* Stadtplan
street: on the ~s *122* auf der Straße
street: walk the ~s *71* auf die Straße gehen
strength *158* Stärke
stress *61* belasten
stress *60* Stress
stressful *60* stressig
strict *119* streng
strictly *148* streng
strongly *182* heftig
stuck: be ~ *103* festsitzen
studies *25* Studium
studio *176* Studio
study *22; 37; 52; 58* studieren; lernen; lesen; erforschen; betrachten
stupid *54* dumm, blöde
subject *28* (Schul-)Fach
suburb *89* Vorort, Außenbezirk
subway *71* U-Bahn
succeed *118* Erfolg haben
success *183* Erfolg
success rate *183* Erfolgsrate
successful *120* erfolgreich
such *79* solche(r,s)
such as *186* wie zum Beispiel
suddenly *95* plötzlich
suffer *124; *125* leiden unter; leiden
suffer from *165* leiden an
suggest *56* nahelegen
suicide *118* Selbstmord
suit *26* Anzug (für Männer), Kostüm (für Frauen)
suitable *158* geeignet
suited to *94* geeignet für
summit *138* Gipfel
Sunday shopping *128* Einkaufen am Sonntag
suntan *82* Sonnenbräune
supplier *170* Anbieter, Lieferant/in
support *180* unterstützen
suppose: I ~ … *122* eigentlich
sure *36* natürlich
surely *99* sicherlich
surf *149* surfen
surfer *75* Surfer/in
surgery *155* Praxis
surprise *110* überraschen
surprise *180* Überraschung
surprised *153* erstaunt
surprising *180* überraschend
suspect *118* vermuten
suspected *118* mutmaßlich
Swede *180* Schwede/Schwedin
Sweden *80* Schweden
Swedish *78* schwedisch
swimming pool *89* Schwimmbad
switch *115* Schalter, Knopf
synonym *107* Synonym

take *186* (sich Notizen) machen
Take care. *20* Pass gut auf dich auf.
take off *69* entfernen
take over *84* übernehmen
take place *71* stattfinden
talent *146* Talent, Begabung
talk over *158* besprechen
tape *186* (Ton-)Band
target s.th. at s.o. *39* mit etw. auf jmdn. zielen
taste *46* schmecken
taught *67* simple past: teach
tax *99* Steuer
tea bag *132* Teebeutel
teach s.o. s.th. *66* jmdm. etw. beibringen
team *84* Mannschaft, Team
technique *187* Methode
telephone *156* anrufen
tell (from) *55* erkennen (an)
temper: have a hot ~ *180* jähzornig sein
tend to *176* neigen zu
tent *147* Zelt
terraced house *6* Reihenhaus
terrible *32* schrecklich
terrified: be ~ *118* schreckliche Angst haben
test *90; 177* untersuchen; ausprobieren; testen
test drive *96* Probefahrt
test-drive *68* Probe fahren
textbook *186* Lehrbuch
than *30* als
thankful *166* dankbar
that's it *89* das ist alles
the more … the better *139* je mehr …, desto besser
the night before last *71* vorgestern abend
theatre *82* Theater
theirs *41* ihre(r, s)
theme park *176* Freizeitpark
thin *185* dünn
thing: that sort of ~ *13* derlei
things are different *38* die Lage ist anders
things like that *51* derartige Sachen
think of *10* denken an
think of *16* halten von
think straight *119* klar denken
third world *139* Dritte Welt
this morning *70* heute früh
thorough *154* gründlich
though *67* obwohl, doch
thought *51* simple past: think
threat *118* Gefahr
throw away *138* wegwerfen
tied to *148* an … gebunden
tiger *139* Tiger
tight *188* eng
till *88* bis
time off *133* freie Zeit

time: have a great ~ *31* sich großartig amüsieren
time: in recent ~s *108* in den letzten Jahren
time: on ~ *44* pünktlich
times (a week/year) *14* ... mal (in der Woche/im Jahr)
tip *104* Trinkgeld geben
tiring *104* anstrengend
title *146* Titel
tobacco *119* Tabak
tomato *47* Tomate
tone **155* Ton
tool *114* Werkzeug
top speed *98* Höchstgeschwindigkeit
top: on ~ of that **122* obendrein
total *98* Gesamt-
totally *100* völlig
touch *60* anfassen, berühren
tough *183* hart
tour guide *12* Reiseleiter/in
tourist *71* Tourist/in
tourist information *37* Fremdenverkehrsamt
tourist office *37* Fremdenverkehrsbüro
towards *38* gegenüber
town centre *37* Stadtzentrum, City
town: in ~ *10* in der Stadt
toy car **132* Spielzeugauto
toy shop *132* Spielzeugladen
tractor **144* Traktor
trade *70* Handel
trade fair *170* Handelsmesse
trade union *148* Gewerkschaft
traditional *144* traditionell
traditionally *159* traditionell
traffic jam *99* Verkehrsstau
traffic policeman *68* Verkehrspolizist
traffic warden *95* ≈ Verkehrspolizist/in
tragically *181* tragisch
train *29; 158* ausgebildet werden; ausbilden
train: on the ~ *15* im Zug
trainee chef *28* Küchenlehrling
trainer *45* Turnschuh
training course **60* Lehrgang, Ausbildung
translate *106* übersetzen
transport *34* Verkehrsmittel
transport company *126* Transportunternehmen
travel agency *267* Reisebüro
travel agent *27* Reiseverkehrskaufmann/-frau
travel courier **82* Reiseführer/in
travel enquiry *36* Reiseauskunft
travel sick **34* reisekrank
traveller *30* Reisende/r
traveller's cheque *36* Reisescheck
treat **144* behandeln
treat *54* behandeln

treatment *162* Behandlung
tree surgeon *145* Baumdoktor/in
trend *148* Trend
trip *74* Ausflug, Reise
trouble: get into ~ *121* Schwierigkeiten bekommen
truth **59* Wahrheit
try out *146* ausprobieren
tube: on the ~ **77* mit der U-Bahn
tulip *80* Tulpe
tunnel **34* Tunnel
Turk *180* Türke/Türkin
Turkey *83* die Türkei
turn down *143* drosseln (Heizung)
turn on *115* einschalten
turn right/left *66* rechts/links abbiegen
turn s.th. into s.th. *59* etw. in etw. verwandeln
turn: it's your ~ *108* du bist dran
turn: take ~s *135* sich abwechseln
turning **92* Abfahrt, Abzweigung
tutor *186* Tutor
TV repairer *29* Fernsehmonteur/in
TV: on ~ *15* im Fernsehen
two-year *23* zweijährig
type *45* Art
typewriter *153* Schreibmaschine
typing **29* Maschineschreiben
tyre *69* Reifen

UK *79* = United Kingdom
unable *158* unfähig
under ground *90* unter der Erde
underlined *13* unterstrichen
undernourished *184* unterernährt
understand *46* verstehen, begreifen
understanding *23* Verständnis
understood *164* past participle: **understand**
unemployed **60* arbeitslos
unemployment *60* Arbeitslosigkeit
unequal *38* ungleich
unfair **43* unfair, ungerecht
unfit *119; 179* unfähig, ungeeignet; unfit
unfortunately *138* leider
unfriendly *78* unfreundlich
unhealthy *184* ungesund
uniform *26* Uniform
unimportant *161* unwichtig
union *148* Gewerkschaft
United Kingdom *80* Vereinigtes Königreich
unless *188* wenn ... nicht
unlikely *146* unwahrscheinlich
unlucky *123* unglücklich
unpleasant *162* unangenehm
unpopular *162* unbeliebt
unsuccessful *161* erfolglos

unsuitable *158* ungeeignet
up to date *125* auf dem neusten Stand
up-to-date *151* aktuell
upright *105* aufrecht
upset **53* betrübt
urgently **155* dringend
use *106* Gebrauch
use *28* bedienen
used to *108* gewöhnt an
useful *78* nützlich
user *183* Benutzer/in

valley *30* Tal
varied *30* vielfältig
various different **43* verschiedene
vary *171* unterschiedlich sein
vast *176* riesig
vegetarian **51* vegetarisch
vehicle *68* Fahrzeug
vehicle maintenance *28* Fahrzeugwartung
vet *12* Tierarzt, -ärztin
veterinary nurse *158* Tierpfleger/in
victim *179* Opfer
video *86; 184* Videorecorder; Video
video tape **132* Videoband
videophone *156* Fernsehtelefon
view *86* Aussicht, Blick
village *86* Dorf
violence *72* Gewalt
violent *71* gewalttätig
virtual *129* virtuell
visa *147* Visum
visitor *70* Besucher/in
vitamin *53* Vitamin
vocational *22* beruflich, Berufs-
vodka **51* Wodka
voluntary work *167* freiwillige Arbeit

wait: I can't ~ *31* ich kann es kaum erwarten
Waiter! *116* Herr Ober!
Wales *80* Wales
walking holiday *83* Wanderurlaub
wallet *113* Brieftasche
war *183* Krieg
warm *176* warm
warn (about) *63* warnen (vor)
warning *63* Warnung
wash one's hair *113* sich die Haare waschen
wasp *174* Wespe
waste *138* Abfall, Müll
waste *142* verschwenden
watch (the) television *14* fernsehen
water-skiing *85* Wasserski
way: I'm in a bad ~ **122* mir geht es schlecht
weakness *158* Schwäche
weapon *109* Waffe

wedding *157* Hochzeit
weekend: on the ~ *77* am Wochenende
weekly *129* wöchentlich
weightlifting *14* Gewichtheben
Well done! *109* Gut gemacht! Bravo!
well-balanced *51* ausgeglichen
well-being *183* Wohlergehen, Behaglichkeit
well-known *40* sehr bekannt
well-off *122* wohlhabend
well-paid *84* gut bezahlt
Welsh *79* Waliser
wet *34* nass, feucht
What about …? *13* Wie ist es mit …?
What can I get you? *47* Was darf ich Ihnen bringen?
What does … do? *7* Was macht … (beruflich)?
what kind of …? *36* was für ein(e) …?
what sort of …? *29* was für ein(e)
What's it like? *13* Wie ist es?
whatever *143* was auch immer
wheat *144* Weizen
Where is … from? *7* Woher kommt …?
wherever *78* wohin (auch immer)
whether *120* ob
while *37* während
whistle *67* sausen, pfeifen
whole: on the ~ *89* im Großen und Ganzen
wide *159* breit, groß

widely *156* weit
widowed *10* verwitwet
wild *176* wild
Will you excuse me? *20* Entschuldigen Sie, bitte.
willing *95* gewillt, bereitwillig
wind farm *143* Windkraftanlage
window-shopping *76* Schaufensterbummel
wine producer *176* Winzer
winter: in ~ *15* im Winter
wise *123* weise
wish *151* wünschen
with s.o. in mind *186* im Hinblick auf jmdn.
withdraw *135* abheben
within *108* innerhalb von
within *174* innerhalb von
won't *82* = will not
wonder *79; 173* sich fragen; sich Gedanken machen
wood *18* (kleinerer) Wald
woodland *144* Wald(gebiet)
word: in other ~s *79* mit anderen Worten
work *55* klappen
work experience *27* Praktikum
work out *60; 114* gut gehen, klappen; ausrechnen
work the streets *71* Streife fahren/gehen
work with *7* (zusammen)arbeiten mit
worker *84* Arbeiter/in
working practice *148* Arbeitspraxis, -weise
workout *86* Training

workshop *12* Werkstatt
World War II *108* der Zweite Weltkrieg
world-famous *76* weltberühmt
worried *22* besorgt, beunruhigt
worry (about) *15* sich Sorgen machen (um)
worse *34* schlechter
worst *34* am schlechtesten
worth *122* wert
wounded *72* verwundet
write down *21* aufschreiben
writer *100* Schriftsteller/in
writing *87* Schreiben
wrong: don't get me ~ *71* verstehen Sie mich nicht falsch
wrote *113* simple past: **write**

year: a ~ *38* im Jahr
yet *70* schon, bereits
you just got to *71* man muss/Sie müssen einfach
You kidding? *71* Machen Sie Witze?
yours *41* deine(r, s), Ihre(r, s)
Yours faithfully *170* Mit freundlichen Grüßen, Hochachtungsvoll
Yours sincerely *61* Mit freundlichen Grüßen
yourself *40* sich
youth *128* Jugendliche/r
youth culture *118* Jugendkultur

zip fastener *108* Reißverschluss

EIGENNAMEN

Alcatraz ['ælkətræz]
Alps ['ælps]
Athens ['æθɪnz]
Aylesbury ['eɪlzbəri]
Berkeley ['bɜːkli]
Beverley Hills [ˌbevəli 'hɪlz]
Birmingham ['bɜːmɪŋəm]
Brazil [brə'zɪl]
Brighton ['braɪtn]
Bristol ['brɪstl]
Bronx ['brɒŋks]
Brooklyn ['brʊklɪn]
Calais ['kæleɪ]
California [ˌkælə'fɔːniə]
Cape Horn [ˌkeɪp 'hɔːn]
Cape of Good Hope [ˌkeɪp əv gʊd 'həʊp]
Central Park ['sentrəl pɑːk]
Cheltenham ['tʃeltnəm]
Chicago [ʃɪ'kɑːgəʊ]
Chinatown ['tʃaɪnətaʊn]
Connecticut [kə'netɪkət]
Corsica ['kɔːsɪkə]
Disneyland ['dɪznilænd]
Disneyworld [ˌdɪzni 'wɜːld]
East End [ˌiːst 'end]
Edinburgh ['edɪnbərə]
English Channel [ˌɪŋglɪʃ 'tʃænl]
Euston ['juːstən]
Fisherman's Wharf ['fɪʃəmənz wɔːf]
Florida ['flɒrɪdə]
Genoa ['dʒenəʊə]
Glasgow ['glɑːzgəʊ]
Gloucester ['glɒstə]
Golden Gate [ˌgəʊldən 'geɪt]
Grand Canyon [ˌgrænd 'kænjən]
Harlem ['hɑːləm]
Hollywood ['hɒliwʊd]
Isle of Wight [ˌaɪl əv 'waɪt]
Istanbul [ˌɪstæn'bʊl]
Japan [dʒə'pæn]
Japantown [dʒə'pæntaʊn]
Leeds [liːdz]
Loch Ness [lɒx 'nes]
Los Angeles (LA) [lɒs 'ændʒəliːz]
Manhattan [mæn'hætn]
Marseille [mɑː'seɪ]
Monaco ['mɒnəkəʊ]
Naples ['neɪplz]
Newcastle ['njuːkɑːsl]
New York [ˌnjuː 'jɔːk]
Ohio [əʊ'haɪəʊ]
Oxford ['ɒksfəd]
Paris ['pærɪs]
Portugal ['pɔːtʃʊgl]
Queens [kwiːnz]
Rio ['riːəʊ]
Rocky Mountains [ˌrɒki 'maʊntɪnz]
San Francisco [ˌsæn frən'sɪskəʊ]
Scottish Highlands [ˌskɒtɪʃ 'haɪləndz]
Shepherd's Bush [ˌʃepədz 'bʊʃ]
Sierra Nevada [siˌerə nɪ'vɑːdə]
Southampton [saʊθ'hæmptən]
St Moritz [ˌsæn mə'rɪts]
Staten Island [ˌstætən 'aɪlənd]
Statue of Liberty [ˌstætʃuː əv 'lɪbəti]
Strasbourg ['stræsbɜːg]
Sudan [suː'dɑːn]
Tenerife [ˌtenə'riːf]
Times Square ['taɪmz skweə]
Tokyo ['təʊkiəʊ]
Trans-Siberian Railway [ˌtrænz saɪ'bɪəriən]
UK [ˌjuː 'keɪ]
Union Square ['juːniən skweə]
United States [juːˌnaɪtɪd 'steɪts]
Upper East Side [ˌʌpə 'iːst saɪd]
Upper West Side [ˌʌpə 'west saɪd]
Venice ['venɪs]
Victoria [vɪk'tɔːriə]
Victoria Falls [vɪkˌtɔːriə 'fɔːlz]
Vietnam [ˌviːet'næm]
Winchester ['wɪntʃɪstə]
World Trade Centre [ˌwɜːld 'treɪd sentə]
Zimbabwe [zɪm'bɑːbwi]

LISTE DER UNREGELMÄSSIGEN VERBEN

be, was/were, been [biː, wɒz, wɜː, biːn] — sein
beat, beat, beaten [biːt, biːt, ˈbiːtn] — schlagen, besiegen
become, became, become [bɪˈkʌm, bɪˈkeɪm, bɪˈkʌm] — werden
begin, began, begun [bɪˈgɪn, bɪˈgæn, bɪˈgʌn] — anfangen, beginnen
bite, bit, bitten [baɪt, bɪt, ˈbɪtn] — beißen
break, broke, broken [breɪk, brəʊk, ˈbrəʊkən] — brechen, zerbrechen
bring, brought, brought [brɪŋ, brɔːt, brɔːt] — bringen, mitbringen, holen
build, built, built [bɪld, bɪlt, bɪlt] — bauen
burn, burnt/burned, burnt/burned [bɜːn, bɜːnt, bɜːnd] — brennen, verbrennen
buy, bought, bought [baɪ, bɔːt, bɔːt] — kaufen
catch, caught, caught [kætʃ, kɔːt, kɔːt] — fangen
choose, chose, chosen [tʃuːz, tʃəʊz, ˈtʃəʊzn] — wählen, aussuchen
come, came, come [kʌm, keɪm, kʌm] — kommen
cost, cost, cost [kɒst, kɒst, kɒst] — kosten
cut, cut, cut [kʌt, kʌt, kʌt] — schneiden
do, did, done [duː, dɪd, dʌn] — tun, machen
draw, drew, drawn [drɔː, druː, drɔːn] — zeichnen
drink, drank, drunk [drɪŋk, dræŋk, drʌŋk] — trinken
drive, drove, driven [draɪv, drəʊv, ˈdrɪvn] — fahren
eat, ate, eaten [iːt, et, ˈiːtn] — essen
fall, fell, fallen [fɔːl, fel, ˈfɔːlən] — fallen, hinfallen
feed, fed, fed [fiːd, fed, fed] — füttern, ernähren
feel, felt, felt [fiːl, felt, felt] — (sich) fühlen, empfinden
fight, fought, fought [faɪt, fɔːt, fɔːt] — kämpfen
find, found, found [faɪnd, faʊnd, faʊnd] — finden, suchen
fly, flew, flown [flaɪ, fluː, fləʊn] — fliegen
forbid, forbade, forbidden [fəˈbɪd, fəˈbæd fəˈbeɪd, fəˈbɪdn] — verbieten
forget, forgot, forgotten [fəˈget, fəˈgɒt, fəˈgɒtn] — vergessen
get, got, got [get, gɒt, gɒt] — bekommen, erhalten
give, gave, given [gɪv, geɪv, ˈgɪvn] — geben, schenken
go, went, gone [gəʊ, went, gɒn] — gehen, fahren
grow, grew, grown [grəʊ, gruː, grəʊn] — wachsen, züchten
hang, hung, hung [hæŋ, hʌŋ, hʌŋ] — hängen, aufhängen
have, had, had [hæv, hæd, hæd] — haben, nehmen
hear, heard, heard [hɪə, hɜːd, hɜːd] — hören
hide, hid, hidden [haɪd, hɪd, ˈhɪdn] — (sich) verstecken
hit, hit, hit [hɪt, hɪt, hɪt] — schlagen
hold, held, held [həʊld, held, held] — halten, festhalten
hurt, hurt, hurt [hɜːt, hɜːt, hɜːt] — (sich) wehtun, (sich) verletzen
keep, kept, kept [kiːp, kept, kept] — aufbewahren, aufheben
know, knew, known [nəʊ, njuː, nəʊn] — kennen, wissen
lead, led, led [liːd, led, led] — führen
learn, learnt/learned, learnt/learned [lɜːn, lɜːnt, lɜːnd] — lernen
leave, left, left [liːv, left, left] — abfahren, abreisen, weggehen
lend, lent, lent [lend, lent, lent] — leihen, verleihen
let, let, let [let, let, let] — erlauben, zulassen
lie, lay, lain [laɪ, leɪ, leɪn] — liegen
light, lit, lit [laɪt, lɪt] — anzünden, beleuchten, anmachen
lose, lost, lost [luːz, lɒst, lɒst] — verlieren
make, made, made [meɪk, meɪd, meɪd] — machen, zubereiten
mean, meant, meant [miːn, ment, ment] — bedeuten, meinen
meet, met, met [miːt, met, met] — treffen, sich treffen mit
pay, paid, paid [peɪ, peɪd, peɪd] — bezahlen
put, put, put [pʊt, pʊt, pʊt] — setzen, stellen, legen
read, read, read [riːd, red, red] — lesen
ride, rode, ridden [raɪd, rəʊd, ˈrɪdn] — reiten, fahren
ring, rang, rung [rɪŋ, ræŋ, rʌŋ] — klingeln
rise, rose, risen [raɪz, rəʊz, rɪzn] — steigen
run, ran, run [rʌn, ræn, rʌn] — laufen, rennen
say, said, said [seɪ, sed, sed] — sagen

see, saw, seen [siː, sɔː, siːn]	sehen, besuchen
sell, sold, sold [sel, səʊld, səʊld]	verkaufen, führen
send, sent, sent [send, sent, sent]	senden, schicken
set, set, set [set, set, set,]	setzen, stellen
shake, shook, shaken [ʃeɪk, ʃʊk, 'ʃeɪkən]	schütteln
shoot, shot, shot [ʃuːt, ʃɒt, ʃɒt]	(an)schießen, erschießen
show, showed, shown [ʃəʊ, ʃəʊd, ʃəʊn]	zeigen
sing, sang, sung [sɪŋ, sæŋ, sʌŋ]	singen
sink, sank, sunk [sɪŋk, sæŋk, sʌŋk]	sinken
sit, sat, sat [sɪt, sæt, sæt]	sitzen
sleep, slept, slept [sliːp, slept, slept]	schlafen
speak, spoke, spoken [spiːk, spəʊk, 'spəʊkən]	sprechen, reden
speed, sped, sped [spiːd, sped, sped]	zu schnell fahren
spell, spelt/spelled, spelt/spelled [spel, spelt, speld]	buchstabieren
spend, spent, spent [spend, spent, spent]	ausgeben, verbringen
spill, spilt/spilled, spilt/spilled [spɪl, spɪlt, spɪld]	verschütten
stand, stood, stood [stænd, stʊd, stʊd]	stehen
steal, stole, stolen [stiːl, stəʊl, 'stəʊlən]	stehlen
strike, struck, struck [straɪk, strʌk, strʌk]	(an)zünden
swim, swam, swum [swɪm, swæm, swʌm]	schwimmen
take, took, taken [teɪk, tʊk, 'teɪkən]	nehmen, bringen, einnehmen
teach, taught, taught [tiːtʃ, tɔːt, tɔːt]	unterrichten
tell, told, told [tel, təʊld, təʊld]	sagen
think, thought, thought [θɪŋk, θɔːt, θɔːt]	denken, meinen, finden
throw, threw, thrown [θrəʊ, θruː, θrəʊn]	werfen
understand, understood, understood [ˌʌndə'stænd, -'stʊd]	verstehen, begreifen
wake up, woke up, woken up [ˌweɪk 'ʌp, ˌwəʊk 'ʌp, ˌwəʊkən 'ʌp]	aufwachen
wear, wore, worn [weə, wɔː, wɔːn]	tragen
win, won, won [wɪn, wʌn, wʌn]	gewinnen, siegen
write, wrote, written [raɪt, rəʊt, 'rɪtn]	schreiben

GRAMMATISCHE GRUNDBEGRIFFE

adjective ['ædʒɪktɪv]	Adjektiv, Eigenschaftswort
adverb ['ædvɜːb]	Adverb, Umstandswort
adverb of frequency [ˌædvɜːb əv 'friːkwənsi]	Häufigkeitsadverb
adverb of manner [ˌædvɜːb əv 'mænə]	Adverb der Art und Weise
comparative [kəm'pærətɪv]	Steigerungsform des Adjektivs
conditional [kən'dɪʃənl]	Bedingungssatz
demonstrative pronoun [dɪ'mɒnstrətɪv prəʊnaʊn]	Demonstrativpronomen
gerund ['dʒerənd]	Gerundium
indirect speech [ˌɪndərekt 'spiːtʃ]	indirekte Rede
infinitive [ɪn'fɪnətɪv]	Grundform des Verbs
noun [naʊn]	Hauptwort, Substantiv, Nomen
object pronoun ['ɒbdʒɪkt prəʊnaʊn]	Objektform des Pronomens
passive ['pæsɪv]	Passiv
past participle [ˌpɑːst 'pɑːtɪsɪpl]	Partizip Perfekt
past passive [ˌpɑːst 'pæsɪv]	Passiv der Vergangenheit
phrase [freɪz]	Redewendung
plural ['plʊərəl]	Mehrzahl
possessive adjective [pə'zesɪv ædʒɪktɪv]	adjektivisch gebrauchtes Possessivpronomen
possessive pronoun [pə'zesɪv prəʊnaʊn]	Possessivpronomen
prefix ['priːfɪks]	Vorsilbe
present continuous [ˌpreznt kən'tɪnjuəs]	Verlaufsform des Präsens
present passive [ˌpreznt 'pæsɪv]	Passiv der Gegenwart
present perfect [ˌpreznt 'pɜːfɪkt]	Perfekt
present perfect passive [ˌpreznt 'pɜːfɪkt pæsɪv]	Passiv des Perfekts
present simple [ˌpreznt 'sɪmpl]	einfache Gegenwart
principal parts [ˌprɪnsəpl 'pɑːts]	Hauptbestandteile
quantifier ['kwɒntəfaɪə]	Mengenbezeichnung
question tag ['kwestʃən tæg]	Frageanhängsel
reflexive pronoun [rɪ'fleksɪv prəʊnaʊn]	Reflexivpronomen
simple past [ˌsɪmpl 'pɑːst]	einfache Vergangenheit
singular ['sɪŋgjələ]	Einzahl
subject pronoun ['sʌbdʒɪkt prəʊnaʊn]	Subjektform des Pronomens
suffix ['sʌfɪks]	Nachsilbe, Endsilbe
superlative [suː'pɜːlətɪv]	höchste Steigerungsform des Adjektivs
tense [tens]	Zeitform, Tempus

Acknowledgements

Photos:
AKG, London: 35 r; **Bildarchiv Preussischer Kulturbesitz:** 114; **Sylvia Corday:** 142 tl;
Y de Henseler: 143 ct, 145 c & cl, 98; **Abbie Enock/Travel Ink:** 76 c;
Format Photographers: © Ulrike Preuss 53 l; © Jacky Chapman 124 t; Sheila Gray 95 tl;
Getty Images: 6 br, 13 tl, tr, cr, & fr; 14; 15 br; 19 tr; 26 cl; 27 tl, bc, bl, & br; 28 tc; 30 br, tc & l; 31 t & b; 35 l & bc, 38 l, 39 r; 44 tl, tr, bl & br; 52 c & br; 67 l; 70 l & r; 71 r; 76 bl, tr, cr, & br; 94 cr; 117 br; 126 l; 143 b; 145 a; **S & R Greenhill:** 6 tl, 6 tr, 6 c, 15 tr, 19 br, 26 bl, 28 bl, 38 r, 47 tr, 68 bl & br, 93 t, c & l, 94 b & cl, 104 t & tc, 118, 119 tl; 126 r;
Hangland Farm: 46 b; **Image Bank:** 84 r, 110 c; **Sally Jenkins:** 35 tc, 50 c, tr, bl, cfr, cr, br, 62, 64 7, 66 nos. 2, 3, 4, 7, 8 & 9; **Last Resort:** 88 tr; 114 bl, 115 cr, 119 br, 168; **G Metcalfe:** 6 tl, 12 tc, 13 c, 19 tc and l, 26 cr, br & fr; 28 tr & bc, 37 tl, tr, bl and br, 86;
Oxford Scientific Films: 47 br; **Pictor:** 22, 66 no. 6, 104 4, 145 tr, 158, 165 br;
Rex Features: 95 r, 99 t & b, 104 bc, 105 b, c & r, 120; **Sainsbury's:** 46 r, 131 nos. 2, 3, 4, 5, 6, 7 & 8; **Science Photo Library:** 110 k; **Spectrum:** 12 bl, 30 tr; **Jeff Tabberner:** 88 lower 3, 110 a, b, c, d, e, f, g, h, i, j & l, 114 9; 115 3, 117 2, 131 tr, 139, 140 a, b, c, d, e, f, g & h; 145 tl, 148; **Telegraph Colour Library:** 39 l, 50 tl, 52 tr, bl & cr, 54 t & b, 55, 66 br, 76 cl & bl, 78–79, 98 br, 94 r, 117 bl, 122 tl, tr, tc, bc, br & bl, 129 t, 142 bl & br, 143 c, d, & e, 145 b, 147, 149 b & r, 154, 165 b and tr; **Topham:** 6 bc, 12 tl, tr, cr, br, tcl & cbl, 15 tl, 19 l, 26 fl, 27 tr, 30 bc, 43, 52 tl, 53 r, 67 r, 68 tr, bl & br, 89 tr & l, 95 cl, 109, 124 l, 125, 128–9, 142 tr, 143 a, 144 tr & bl; **Travel Library:** 83 tl.

Illustrations:
Paul Chappell; Clive Goodyer; David Lock; John Martin & Artists; Oxford Illustrators and Oxprint Design.

Jacket photographs:
Getty Images: t & br; Telegraph Colour Library: l.

Maps:
Carlos Borrell, Berlin.

Key:
r = right, l = left, t = top, b = bottom, c = centre, f = far.